SIXTH EDITION

CONTENT AREA LITERACY

AN INTEGRATED APPROACH

John E. Readence
University of Nevada, Las Vegas

Thomas W. Bean
University of Nevada, Las Vegas

R. Scott Baldwin
Adams State College

 KENDALL/HUNT PUBLISHING COMPANY

4050 Westmark Drive P.O. Box 1840 Dubuque, Iowa 52004-1840

CONTENTS

7   Literature and Content Literacy   99

8   Vocabulary   116

9   Comprehension: Principles and Integrated Approaches   142

PREFACE

The sixth edition of CONTENT AREA LITERACY: AN INTEGRATED APPROACH presents preservice and inservice teachers with theory and related teaching strategies designed to assist middle and secondary students in reading and learning from their textbooks. In this edition we have attempted to integrate the current state of the art with some ideas of our own. In addition, this text differs from the previous editions in that it includes a CD-ROM Digital Supplement which provides an additional wealth of information showing the power of contemporary technology for content literacy development. One of the most unique features of this book is the ability to have students search, read, analyze, and synthesize a rich collection of digitized articles, activities, and textbook practice selections as they navigate the book and the course.

In this edition, we continue to introduce teaching strategies designed to assist students in reading and learning from textbooks. This edition consists of two parts. Part A of this book includes five chapters that introduce content area literacy. Chapter 1 provides rationale and knowledge base for content area literacy. Chapter 2 explores the world of technology and its relationship to content area literacy. Chapter 3 follows with an examination of the reading process and a discussion of cultural and linguistic variables that influence literacy. Chapter 4 introduces readers to the socio-political nature of textbooks and then focuses on quantitative and qualitative procedures for evaluating and introducing textbooks. Chapter 5 concludes this section of the book with a discussion of both norm-referenced and naturalistic assessment.

Part B consists of 7 chapters of strategies for teaching and learning in the content areas. Chapters 6, 7, and 8 focus on lesson planning, literature, and vocabulary, respectively, while Chapters 9 and 10 both address comprehension. Chapter 11 is about writing in the content areas and Chapter 12 introduces study strategies.

We ask those individuals who have reactions or suggestions regarding the information and strategies presented in this book to write to us in care of Kendall/Hunt Publishing Company. We are interested in your thoughts about content area literacy, our textbook, and our CD-ROM.

JER
TWB
RSB

HOW TO USE THIS BOOK

Through the use of new features of this edition, each chapter is offered as a model for the strategies advocated by this book. We are attempting to practice what we preach by making the entire book a model that reinforces concepts and demonstrates that suggested techniques CAN work. Hopefully, preservice and inservice teachers using this book will then have an example as they construct lesson plans and apply the suggested strategies in their own classrooms.

The page design provides an uninterrupted flow of text. Each chapter has unique features designed to enhance comprehension of the concepts presented. These features are listed here, and necessary directions for using the features are included so that the directions do not have to be repeated throughout the chapters.

 Chapter Openers

Anticipation Guide

Located at the beginning of chapters in Part A, these Guides offer students an opportunity to react to a series of statements before they study each chapter.

Directions: Before reading the chapter, take a moment to read each statement. If you agree with the statement, place a check in the Agree column. If you disagree with a statement, place a check in the Disagree column. Be ready to explain your choices.

Vignette

Located at the beginning of chapters in Part B, this instructional aid enables a student to react to a lesson scenario before reading the chapter.

Directions: Before reading the chapter, read and react to the short vignette. Answer the questions that follow the vignette and be prepared to justify your responses. You may wish to work in pairs or small groups. After you read the chapter, we will ask you to reread the vignette and react again to the questions.

Rationale

These short paragraphs explain the reason for the writing of the chapter.

Learning Objectives

To make learning more efficient, each chapter opens with a list of learning objectives that describe goals that should be accomplished by studying the chapter. These objectives are designed to focus attention on the major issues in the chapter.

Graphic Organizer

The graphic organizer is a visual display of pertinent vocabulary terms and their interrelated concepts designed to provide teachers with an advance structure for new vocabulary and concepts that will be presented in the chapter.

In Text Learning Aids

Activities

Activities are found throughout each chapter and are provided to afford students additional exposure to the new concepts discussed.

CD-ROM Icon

A CD-ROM accompanies this textbook and provides convenient access to supplemental information about content literacy. Throughout the book you will see the following icon CD in the margins. Each CD icon is paired with a reference or citation **highlighted in blue**. The icon tells you that pertinent information is available on the CD, and the highlighted word is the key to finding it. Further instructions for using this exciting new feature are in Appendix A at the back of the text.

End of Chapter

Chapter Summary

Each chapter concludes with a concise summary organized around the opening learning objectives.

Reaction Guides/Vignettes

These activities repeat the Anticipation Guides and Instructional Vignettes from the beginning of the chapter. Their purpose is to confirm or disconfirm your original decisions from the beginning of the chapter.

Directions for Reaction Guides: Reconsider your responses to the statements at the beginning of the chapters in Part A. If the information in the chapter supports your original choice, place a check in the Confirmed column. Then write what the text says in your own words in column A under Why is my choice confirmed?. If the information does not support your choice, place a check in the Disconfirmed Column. Then write what the text says in your own words in column B under Why is my choice not confirmed?.

Directions For Vignettes: Reread the instructional vignette at the beginning of the chapters in Part B. React again to the questions.

Mini Project

These projects allow students to apply their newly learned information from the chapter.

Group Projects

These are exercises which are meant to provide students the opportunity to reinforce concepts introduced in the chapter and to give students the opportunity to go beyond the content of the chapter. They require integration and application of chapter concepts. These discussions allow students not only to demonstrate that they know the facts in the chapters, but that they can utilize those facts to deal with more complex issues.

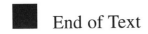 End of Text

Glossary

The glossary serves as a ready reference for italicized vocabulary terms encountered in each chapter.

Recommended Readings

Recommended readings are identified by chapter in the Bibliography, and are given as additional readings to extend and refine the information presented.

References

References are identified by chapter and listed in the Bibliography, thus providing a comprehensive list of references in one section.

Index

An index is provided for quick page reference for important terms from the text.

Appendices

The appendices are provided to give information on how to use the accompanying CD-ROM. Specifically, Appendix A provides installation instructions and a user's guide for the CD-ROM. Appendix B includes directions for using *The Rosetta Stone* ™ language sampler.

LEARNING WITH TEXT AND TECHNOLOGY

O N E

Content Area Literacy: A Rationale

Anticipation Guide

Agree	Disagree	
________	________	1. Every teacher is responsible for literacy.
________	________	2. A content teacher's prime responsibility is to deliver subject matter information.
________	________	3. Literacy instruction should be left to reading teachers.
________	________	4. Providing students with a purpose for reading will improve their reading performances.
________	________	5. Upon leaving elementary school, students should have mastered the skills necessary for content literacy.

Rationale

Office of Civil Rights Enforces Bilingual Education
Illiterate Student Sues Local High School
English Only Referendum Looms
State Mandates Standards-Based Education

Every year our high schools churn out thousands of students who can't read and understand the fine print on a bag of potato chips. Many more depart with reading skills so inadequate that they can't begin to cope with our print-bound, technological culture. And the public impression appears to be that this problem is chronic and getting worse. Daily newspapers and magazines routinely print articles that blast our public schools and lament how much our students don't know in comparison to Japanese students today or the American students of decades past. There is also a growing realization that the United States is a multicultural society in which disenfranchised ethnic and linguistic minorities are demanding the redefinition of American schools (Macedo, 1993). In addition, we are riding an immigration tsunami which will guarantee that in our public schools 1 child in every 4 will be Hispanic by the year 2020 (Gersten & Woodward, 1994). Diverse and complex issues such as social equity, bilingual education, and formulas for funding public schools combine to make universal literacy in the United States one of the great challenges of the 21st century.

This text is based on the conviction that America's literacy dilemmas are ultimately solvable and that each and every teacher can play a role in the resolution. In fact, we believe that programs in which reading is the subject matter are inferior to programs in which each teacher is committed to making students literate with respect to the specific source materials that make up the curriculum (Bean & Readence, 1995).

The present chapter will discuss the educational and social meaning of literacy, the knowledge base of content area literacy, and the rationale for incorporating literacy strategies into content area classrooms. In addition, we will describe some of the standard misconceptions about content area literacy and investigate the common reluctance of subject matter specialists to accept responsibility for teaching any reading strategies.

LEARNING OBJECTIVES

- Define literacy from historical and social perspectives.

- Describe the knowledge base of content area literacy.

- Refute common misconceptions about literacy instruction.

- State the instructional recommendations that are integrated into the literacy strategies recommended in this text.

GRAPHIC ORGANIZER

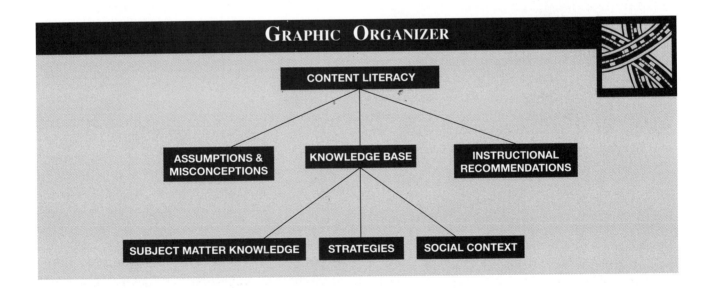

What Is Content Area Literacy?

Literate is derived from the Latin *litterae* (i.e., letters). The standard dictionary definition of literate is to be able to read and write. That seems straightforward except that people aren't simply literate or illiterate: they are literate or illiterate to some degree which is defined by historical and social contexts. Beginning in 1840 the United States Census Bureau began assessing literacy by asking individuals if they could read and write simple messages in any language. People who answered "Yes" were classified as literate. By this definition 20% of the U.S. population considered themselves illiterate in 1870 as opposed to less than 1% in 1979 (Kaestle, 1991). By the standards of one hundred years ago, virtually all Americans are literate today. But literacy is relative to societal demands, and reading and writing skills that would have been sufficient in 1670 or 1870 are clearly inadequate in today's world of credit cards, mass advertising, computers, big business, and income tax forms.

It is widely believed that the ability to read and comprehend the bulk of a daily newspaper is a measure of functional literacy (i.e., how well one needs to read to get by on a day to day basis). This might be good enough to meet the job demands of a lumberjack but probably not the daily reading and writing tasks of a corporate lawyer. In a relative sense we might consider the lumberjack to be literate and the lawyer to be illiterate using the newspaper yardstick as a minimum requirement. Because there is no universal standard for literacy today, we are forced to answer "Literate for what?" in response to the question "Is Frank literate?" In like manner, the issue of literacy in content areas must be contextualized and defined in terms of the reading and writing demands of specific classrooms. For example, students in a 10th grade biology class are literate to the extent that they can learn from and react appropriately to the written materials (textbooks, lab directions, magazines, etc.) used in the class. Hence, *content area literacy* is defined as the level of reading and writing skill necessary to read, comprehend, and react to appropriate instructional materials in a given subject area. The fundamental purpose of this text is to communicate knowledge and strategies that you can use to help your students become more literate in your subject area.

Assumptions and Misconceptions

Although content area literacy instruction has been with us for a number of years, content teachers have been reluctant to accept an instructional emphasis that fuses reading with content. Why? To begin with, there seem to exist a variety of false assumptions about reading instruction in general and students' ability to read upon entering subject matter classrooms. The following are some of these assumptions:

1. Students have learned to read in elementary schools.

2. Students have sufficient prior knowledge to cope effectively with the important information in content textbooks.

3. The processes involved in reading and comprehending efficiently in content textbooks are identical to those utilized in reading from basal readers in elementary school.

4. Content reading means teaching phonics and other skills not directly related to their subject areas.

5. Teachers are information dispensers.

Belief in these assumptions presupposes that students have mastered the processes necessary to enable them to glean essential information from reading, regardless of writing style and content. It also presupposes that students can meaningfully blend new information with prior knowledge and efficiently utilize textbook aids designed to refine and extend important concepts. A close examination of these assumptions reveals how wrong they are.

Reading instruction has been the traditional interest of the elementary school, the assumption being that normal students in normal programs SHOULD enter subject matter classrooms knowing how to read. If reading is defined in terms of elementary tasks, e.g., basic decoding skills, the assumption is reasonable. In contrast, the assumption is pure fantasy if reading is defined in terms of subject matter tasks, e.g., expanded homework and independent reading assignments, required note taking in class, and vastly increased dependence upon textbooks with varied and complex organizational patterns. It does not make sense to assume that students will automatically modify elementary reading skills to suit these subject matter reading demands.

Read the following paragraph from Sartre (1948) and summarize it in your own words from recall.

> We are completely in agreement with him on this point: That symbolization is constitutive of symbolic consciousness will trouble no one who believes in the absolute value of the cartesian cogito. But it must be understood that if symbolization is constitutive of consciousness, it is permissible to perceive that there is an immanent bond of comprehension between the symbolization and the symbol. (p. 65)

Did you have difficulty reading the passage? If you were familiar with existential philosophy and Sartre, you might have breezed right through it. However, if this material was foreign to your own personal experiences, adequate comprehension probably proved elusive. In addition, the burden of many new terms and concepts may have caused the passage to seem obscure.

In order to learn to read this passage with full understanding, you would have to be provided background knowledge in the subject area and introduced to its new vocabulary and concepts. Even then the long, complicated sentences could prove tedious and confusing.

Such are some of the difficulties inherent in reading from textbooks. Rose (1989) has documented these difficulties in his personal account of literacy and illiteracy among today's college-bound populations, describing individuals "straining at the boundaries of their ability, trying to move into the unfamiliar, to approximate a kind of writing they can't yet command" (p. 188). You now have some sensitivity for the demands placed on young students in reading their subject matter materials. Students usually lack experiential background and are unfamiliar with the vocabulary and concepts in social studies, science, or any other content areas. It is presumptuous, and possibly damaging, to expect students to perform well automatically with subject-matter texts.

College students with Arts and Sciences majors are often taught with a mind set to convey a body of information to students rather than provide instruction in reading and learning from text. Unfortunately, for some teachers, this mind set continues once they leave the university. For instance, Hinchman (1985), in a qualitative study of secondary teachers' plans and conceptions of reading, found that teachers consider reading as a means of "covering the course content" (p. 254). Reading was viewed as a way to dispense information, rather than as a means to read and learn with the textbook. Similarly, Armbruster et al. (1991), who analyzed middle school science and social studies lessons in which the textbook was the focus of teaching, found four instances of explicit instruction in how to read and learn with text. Teachers did not teach or even encourage students to practice essential text learning processes. Finally, Goodlad (1984), in a comprehensive study of schooling in America, confirmed the notion that some teachers see their role as that of an information dispenser. He found that:

> . . . about 75% of class time was spent on instruction and that nearly 70% of this was "talk"—usually teacher to student. Teachers out-talked the entire class of students by a ratio of about three to one . . . the bulk of this teacher talk was instructing in the sense of telling. Barely 5% of this instructional time was designed to create students' anticipation of needing to respond . . . when a student was called on to respond, it was to give an informational answer to the teacher's question. The two activities, involving the most students, were being lectured to and working on written assignments. (pp. 229-230)

Thus, many teachers, both preservice and inservice, are not even aware of content literacy and the potential this emphasis would have for aiding students in reading and learning with their textbooks.

Perhaps a final complication to utilizing content literacy in subject-matter classrooms is the well-intended, but detrimental, slogan that "every teacher is a teacher of reading." Tell social studies teachers, for instance, that they are teachers of reading and you may understand how receptive they are to the concept. If apoplexy does not occur, their certain retort will be that they are teachers of social studies, not reading! The reading model content teachers usually witness, emphasizing the previously mentioned skills characteristics, will not encourage them to attend to the reading needs of their classes. Moreover, their resolve that they are subject-matter specialists first is a valid one.

Singer (1979) surveyed the attitudes of subject matter teachers toward teaching reading in the content areas. Where previously such groups of teachers were less than enthusiastic toward the slogan "every teacher is a teacher of reading," Singer found favorable attitudes by such teachers when asked their opinion concerning the statement that "every teacher teaches students to learn with texts." This statement connotes a model of reading instruction that focuses on aiding students in learning with text rather than learning isolated skills.

The authors agree with this reemphasis. Content literacy currently has too many prior associations with learning to read and skills instruction. Under this reemphasis, content teachers are considered catalysts for learning, whose responsibility it is to aid students in reading and learning with text (Searfoss & Maddox, 1992). The focus of content literacy instruction is on reading to learn, not on learning to read.

Let's examine in depth the roles of the teacher, the reader, and the textbook as each relates to success in learning. First, if texts were meant to be read in isolation, there would be little, if any, need for someone called a teacher. Similarly, if texts are so easy to read that a reader needs little or no help to learn the material, a teacher, again, would be superfluous. Yet, as our Sartre quotation illustrated, such is not normally the case with text materials. Texts are usually challenging and present students with a myriad of problems.

Second, it makes sense to describe content reading as a means of improving communication. There is sort of a long-distance communication that materializes between an author of a text and a reader attempting to comprehend it. The reader is, in effect, trying to communicate with authors of texts by constructing meaning from their words and thoughts. Given, then, the goal of the reader and the difficulty of texts, a facilitator is needed to promote this interaction between reader and text. Indeed, this should be the role of the teacher.

If teachers consider themselves to be information dispensers, then there is no need for textbooks. Teachers who make text reading assignments and then go over in class exactly what is in the text not only make class boring but also encourage students to neglect to read their assignments. This type of teacher is certainly not encouraging the development of independent readers who can take their place as useful citizens and lifelong learners in our society. A teacher who focuses only on the content ignores the processes needed by students to comprehend the content in immediate and future reading situations.

The teacher's role is to encourage the thinking processes essential to understanding, i.e., to facilitate learning with text. Teachers, then, can promote this interaction if they conceive of themselves as facilitators of the learning process in that they have inherent advantages over textbooks or any other information dispensing device. Schallert and Kleiman (1979) have cited four skills that teachers can exercise that a text cannot: (1) tailoring the message; (2) activating prior knowledge; (3) focusing attention; and (4) monitoring comprehension.

Teachers can tailor the message by adapting their presentations to the needs, abilities, and experiential backgrounds of their students. They already know what students know and do not know and can interact with them during their presentations. Second, teachers can activate prior knowledge by reminding students of what they know and how it relates to what they are to learn. Third, teachers focus attention by increasing students' interest and motivation to learn new material and by directing them to pay attention to selected pieces of the text. Finally, teachers can monitor comprehension by checking to see if students understand important parts of a text presentation. Clearly, texts cannot accomplish any of these tasks.

Nevertheless, while it is true that textbooks cannot do these things, it is also true that textbooks are not designed to do this. They are designed to give information. Materials don't do the teaching; teachers, by definition, do the teaching and this teaching includes helping students acquire the processes necessary for successful learning.

Knowledge Base of Content Area Literacy

NCATE (National Council for the Accreditation of Teacher Education) is the national organization that gives official approval to colleges that offer teacher education programs. One of NCATE's requirements is that a college must have a knowledge-based rationale for its programs. A *knowledge base* is the professional

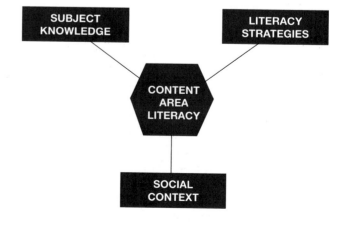

literature on research and best practice in teacher education. In essence, a knowledge base describes what you need to know to be a good teacher; and the knowledge base for content literacy—depicted in the diagram—defines what you must know to help your students learn with, and critique, the textbooks, magazines, and documents in your discipline.

The obvious and traditional component in the knowledge base is the disciplinary expertise you bring to teaching. Your chances of being a successful art, chemistry, or English teacher are enhanced to the extent that you are generally knowledgeable in your subject area. To aid you in this effort various states (e.g., Nevada, California) are establishing frameworks which specify what knowledge your students should know as a result of their learning in the various subject matter areas.

The second component of the knowledge base is the set of literacy strategies and principles which are designed to enhance your ability to assist students in mastering vocabulary, comprehending difficult texts, studying, and evaluating what they read. To this end, the International Reading Association and the National Council of Teachers of English have prepared the *Standards for the English Language Arts* (1996). In this document these two organizations delineate what they believe students should know about language and what they should be able to do with language as a result of what they learn in school. Their aim is to make sure all students have the opportunity to develop the skills in literacy they need to be successful in school and in their future careers in the workplace. The chapters that follow will articulate this part of the knowledge base.

Social context is the third leg of the content literacy knowledge base, and it is as powerful as the following true story suggests:

> In my first year as a ninth grade English teacher, I had one class of 28 boys and no girls. These young men were the reputed dregs of the school: low achievers, truants, and trouble makers—one was sent to youth detention for robbing the blind man at the post office. I will always remember the day I handed out spelling books with a big number 3 on the front. Most of the boys were reading at a primary school level, and I wanted to have them working with materials at their instructional level. I explained to the class that learning to spell wasn't so difficult and that these spelling books would help them earn better grades in school. They said nothing; but when class was over, 28 copies of *Fun With Spelling* went into the wastebasket in the back of the room. I never forgot the lesson.

The teacher in this story may have known a lot about English spelling (leg one of the knowledge base); and he may have had an appropriate instructional strategy in mind (leg two of the knowledge base); but what he completely failed to consider was the social context in which the instruction had to take place. Those ninth grade boys were not about to walk around a tough, urban school advertising to their peers the fact that they were using third grade books. Getting kicked out of school or failing English for the year would no doubt have been preferable to them.

Schools are institutions with rules and agendas that tend to reflect the values of adults and the dominant culture. Within the school are a variety of subcultures with their own beliefs and goals, and they are frequently in conflict with each other. Adults, children, European Americans, Hispanics, African Americans, Haitians, fundamentalist Christians, and many other groups will view the school, its curricula, and your teaching in different ways because these events are filtered through alternative cultural realities (O'Brien & Stewart, 1992). For example, T.S. Eliot thought *Huckleberry Finn* was a masterpiece, and Ernest Hemingway considered it the source of modern American literature. But to many African Americans it is a demeaning novel that reinforces racial stereotypes (Carey-Webb, 1993). Should it be required reading, as it is in 70% of public high schools (Applebee, 1992)? Or should it be banned from the library as it was several years ago in Mark Twain Junior High in Fairfax County, Virginia? There are many points of view and no simple, obvious solutions. However, it should be clear that what you teach and how you teach it must be influenced by the social context in which the instruction takes place.

What Makes This Textbook Integrated?

To begin with, content area literacy is the integration of subject matter knowledge and literacy strategies within a social context, and we have attempted to make the text responsive to this knowledge base. We have also adopted the following set of instructional recommendations which are integrated into the strategies you will encounter throughout the book.

1. *Present content and processes concurrently.* Moore and Readence (1992) described several possible approaches to learning with text. Among those discussed were: a) presenting isolated skills; b) aiming toward content; and, c) presenting content and processes concurrently.

a. *Presenting isolated skills* is typical of a dated elementary model of reading. The method consists of the direct teaching of skills, with no consideration for content. Students use special materials or workbooks not related to the texts students are assigned to learn in their regular classes. For instance, students may be taught how to detect the sequence when their reading assignment requires the interpretation of graphs. Though the teacher may intend that the students will transfer their newly acquired skills, this approach, like most skill-centered remedial programs, fails because students also need to be taught how to transfer skills from one material to another. More importantly, they fail to see any purpose in learning skills divorced from content.

b. *Aiming toward content* focuses on acquiring content versus how to acquire that content. In other words, the teacher sets purposes for reading and during a follow-up discussion checks to see if the purposes were met. However, this method also is unsuccessful because there is no instruction in how to extract the information from the text. Students are told what to do but not how to do it. Thus, students are not provided the means to complete their assigned tasks; telling students what to do is not synonymous with instruction and is not sufficient to improve students' reading abilities.

c. Students learn best and acquire content most successfully when their attention is focused directly on the material to be learned. *Presenting content and processes concurrently* does this by providing direct instruction in the processes necessary to acquire content in addition to pointing out what content is to be acquired. For example, if the content to be learned is organized into a cause-effect format, the teacher would first present a lesson on organizing content according to that format before giving students the actual content in which they would use their knowledge of that process. Thus, text information is stressed alongside the processes needed to attain it. Specifying what should be attained, without specifying how to do it is pointless. Taking process into account as well as content acknowledges that: (1) reading is indispensable to the successful learning of all academic subjects, and (2) content as specified in a text is only one part of the dynamic interaction between reader, text, and teacher in classroom learning situations. As a consequence, the learning of content and the teaching of processes to help learn it become **integrated** within a total lesson framework.

2. *Provide guidance in all aspects of the instructional lesson—before, during, and after reading.* Learning content is not simply reading the assigned pages, answering the end-of-chapter questions, and listening to the teacher present what has already been read. Generally, students need to be prepared to read a text, need guidance in reading for selected ideas, and need reinforcement to retain the material learned.

More specifically, before reading, students need to be aware that using their prior knowledge and having purposes for reading aids the comprehension process. In addition, teachers can explicitly demonstrate to students how to learn with text through *modeling*. In this technique, teachers become a role model by explaining how they comprehended something; i.e., a reporting of the mental operations involved in their comprehension of a particular text. Students can then repeat the process in order to comprehend on their own.

During the reading, students are searching for information to satisfy the purposes set by the teacher and/or themselves. The teacher may use some adjunct material to guide the students' search. After reading, teachers check to see if preset purposes have been attained.

One useful way to give feedback to students is to have a *debriefing* session, which includes self-reports, introspection, and hindsights by students. Debriefing does not cover content alone, but also entails checking out the processes students used to comprehend the text in relation to what was modeled for them. As students become more adept, the demonstration and guidance teachers provide should be faded, or withdrawn, so students can be moved toward independence in their reading and learning. Thus, helping students learn content is **integrated** throughout all phases of the instructional lesson.

3. *Use all language processes to help students learn with text.* The authors believe that all language processes, not just reading, can be utilized as a means to approach learning with text. While reading will undoubtedly remain the major means of dealing with text, other language processes can play key roles in helping students learn content. Indeed, Postman (1979) suggested that all teachers become language educators and consider using all language processes to enhance students' ability to cope successfully with subject matter materials. Recent research on writing (Tierney & Shanahan, 1991) has further pointed out the interconnections between reading and writing and has suggested that reading be viewed as a composing process. In effect, writing, listening, and speaking become additional tools to teach more content.

It is our belief that the receptive language processes of reading and listening should be **integrated** with the expressive processes of writing and speaking to promote thinking and learning with content materials. The integrative aspects of reading and the other language processes are shown above. In

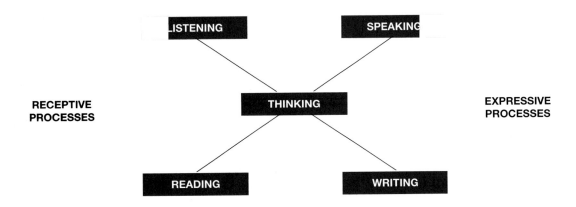

a system such as this, content reading takes on the larger notion of "content communication" or "content literacy" by emphasizing those teaching practices which integrate language processes and thinking as one learns content.

4. *Use small groups to enhance learning.* Wood (1987) has pointed out that while the lecture method is the dominant means of instruction in our classrooms, one of the most effective is small group instruction. Additionally, Johnson, Maruyama, Johnson, Nelson, and Skon (1981) synthesized the literature on cooperative versus competitive instructional efforts. They found that when students were encouraged to work collaboratively with peers, productivity and achievement were enhanced. We realize that the lecture method is prevalent in teaching, yet many of the strategies advocated in this text are best used with, or even require, small group instruction. We recommend such strategies because they promote active learning situations and emphasize peer interaction.

Initial attempts at small group instruction may be chaotic and create management problems; however, this is only part of learning to interact within a group for both the students and the teacher. Once both are accustomed to such instruction, we feel that this method will pave the way for greater output in learning content, both in depth of understanding and in breadth of cognitive and affective experiences. Thus, teachers become cost-efficient when they **integrate** small groups into their teaching; i.e., they enhance the learning environment through good teaching practices which, in turn, create more knowledgeable students.

5. *Use technology to promote learning with text.* There is no doubt that teachers need to be aware of new and emerging technologies as well as how their application in the classroom will promote students' learning of their subject. In particular, instruction with computers seems most promising as an educational innovation. This technology can provide new methods of presenting information, new ways of structuring and organizing instruction, and new ways to motivate students to learn. As schools begin to provide students at all levels with access to new technology, it is incumbent upon teachers to **integrate** the use of technology, especially computers, with text and video sources to enhance students' learning in their classrooms.

To this end, the next chapter of this text will provide an overview of technology and its emerging importance in the content classroom. Additionally, you have been provided a CD-ROM with this text. On this CD-ROM you will find a variety of information. First, it presents subject matter text to allow you to apply the strategies advocated in this book to actual classroom material. Second, it provides additional articles to supplement your learning of the concepts and strategies presented in each chapter. Finally, it provides adjuncts to each chapter to augment and reinforce your learning. It is our hope that this CD-ROM emphasizes our belief in the importance of technology in content area teaching.

 ## Strategy Implementation and Reality Checks

The chapters that follow contain dozens of strategies for improving content area literacy, and we hope that you will have an opportunity to experiment with them in real classrooms. Be patient! Don't expect instant results the first time you use a strategy recommended in this text. First attempts at strategy implementation are problematic, and expertise requires time and patience. Try a strategy several times before you render a final judgement on its utility.

As you begin trying a new method, keep in mind the following model of strategy implementation. Implementing strategies in the classroom entails movement through five developmental stages:

(a) awareness; (b) knowledge; (c) simulation; (d) practice; and e) incorporation. Awareness is necessary before one would seek knowledge about a strategy. In this case, awareness is simply recognizing that content learning and reading texts requires a special knowledge base for efficient processing.

Knowledge occurs when teachers acquire insights about specific strategies that will help students learn with text. Simulation occurs when teachers experiment with specific strategies outside the classroom. They try out strategies on other teachers to obtain preliminary feedback and modify procedures to suit their students' needs. Practice entails the actual use of a strategy with students. This step also entails experimentation and modification. Finally, at the incorporation stage, a strategy becomes an automatic part of a teacher's instructional repertoire and a natural part of teaching.

We should also acknowledge that there are limitations to the strategies we recommend. For one thing, they tend to be idealized practices that may or may not be realistic in terms of the time and effort required to implement them, given the realities of your teaching environment and the diverse nature of students (O'Brien, Stewart, & Moje, 1995). There are urban schools, for example, where students are not allowed to take textbooks out of the school because of the high rate at which the books are sold or destroyed by the students. Environmental constraints of this magnitude will vastly alter what makes sense in the way of strategy instruction. In addition, the success of some of the strategies is predicated on the assumption that students want to learn or that they at least are willing to fake wanting to learn in order to get passing grades. In school cultures in which formal learning and grades are viewed as irrelevant, many literacy strategies probably will not work. On the other hand, it is possible that under teaching conditions that are far from ideal some of the strategies in this book will give you the edge you need to survive and succeed in the profession (Wood, 1992).

Our advocacy of content literacy instruction is based on the belief that it can better equip preservice and inservice teachers with strategies to facilitate students' learning with text. We do not claim that all strategies we recommend will work for all teachers with all students. Rather, we encourage you to discover for yourself which ones work best for you and your students.

To get a better feel for the philosophy behind this text, read the directions and examine the list of practices in the activity that follows. These will be expanded upon in later chapters. For any immediate clarification of terminology used in the list, consult the glossary.

These practices are recommended for enhancing reading and learning in the content areas. If you are an inservice teacher, circle the appropriate number showing how much you do each of these. If you are a preservice teacher, observe a content area teacher to see which practices are used.

1—Almost always	4—Seldom
2—Most of the time	5—Never
3—Sometimes	

Recommended Practices for Teaching in Content Areas

		1	2	3	4	5
1.	The teacher utilizes all language processes to enhance students' learning with text.					
2.	The reading levels of the students are known by the teacher.					
3.	Lessons capitalize on students' cultural backgrounds.					
4.	The teacher has evaluated the text for the presence or absence of characteristics which make a well-organized text.					
5.	Materials for instruction, including the textbook, are chosen to match the reading levels of the students.					
6.	Books and other materials are available for students who read below and above the readability level of the text.					
7.	Textbook aids, such as illustrations, maps, and graphs, are explained or called to the attention of the students.					
8.	Class time is spent discussing how to read the text effectively.					
9.	The teacher presents the special vocabulary and concepts introduced in the text materials assigned for reading in the context of a well-planned lesson.					
10.	Prior knowledge of the text concepts is activated before reading the text.					
11.	Purpose is provided for each reading assignment.					
12.	Assignments are stated clearly and concisely.					
13.	The teacher adapts instruction to suit the ability and language levels of students.					
14.	The teacher asks questions designed to promote thinking at all levels of comprehension.					
15.	The teacher provides some form of study guide, listening guide, or outline to aid in comprehension.					
16.	The course content requires more than reading a single textbook.					
17.	A variety of reference materials and software are made available.					
18.	Students are taught to use appropriate reference materials.					
19.	Students are encouraged to read widely in materials related to the text.					
20.	Small group instruction is used where appropriate.					

SUMMARY

The present chapter was designed to provide a rationale for content area literacy. Literacy has been defined, and assumptions and misconceptions presently surrounding content area literacy have been listed and discussed. Content literacy as an integrated knowledge base has been offered as a viable means by which to emphasize learning with text, and an overview of the textbook has been provided in the form of a list of instructional practices advocated by the authors.

REACTION GUIDE

Confirmed	Disconfirmed	
_____	_____	1. Every teacher is responsible for literacy.
_____	_____	2. A content teacher's prime responsibility is to deliver subject matter information.
_____	_____	3. Literacy instruction should be left to reading teachers.
_____	_____	4. Providing students with a purpose for reading will improve their reading performances.
_____	_____	5. Upon leaving elementary school, students should have mastered the skills necessary for content literacy.

A
Why my choice is confirmed.

B
Why my choice is not confirmed.

1. _____   _____

2. _____   _____

3. _____   _____

4. _____   _____

5. _____   _____

MINI PROJECT

1. Write a sentence or paragraph using the technical vocabulary from your own content field. Exchange this with a class member from a different subject-matter area. Can you understand each other's passage? Why or why not? What might help you increase your understanding?

2. Reflect on your literacy experiences by writing an autobiography of them from your earliest memory of being read to through elementary school, middle school, and high school to the present. Comment on what you read, your feelings associated with reading or being read to, key people who influenced your feelings about reading, and places where you acquired books.

GROUP PROJECTS

■ From a content literacy perspective, justify the teaching of reading in a tenth grade biology class.

■ Describe how the meaning of literacy has changed over the last 100 years.

■ Diagram the content area literacy knowledge base and define the relationships among its components.

TECHNOLOGY AND CONTENT AREA LITERACY

RATIONALE

When the authors of this book were born, automobiles all had manual transmissions, no air conditioning, no cellular phones, and no convenient ATMs to drive up to for fast cash. Passenger planes were propeller driven only. There were also no televisions, automatic dishwashers, digital clocks, or hundreds of other technological conveniences which are now taken for granted in most American homes.

In spite of the many ways that technology has changed our lives, schools of today are in many ways instructionally similar to the schools of hundreds of years ago. Lecture and oral recitation characterize most secondary classrooms, and the blackboard is still the prevailing visual aid. However, we believe that the current revolution in computer technology is about to change the fundamentals of classroom instruction in the very near future. This chapter will tell how and why.

■ Explain why the computer revolution has not yet reached most classrooms, but why it might in the near future.

■ State several appropriate uses of computers in the classroom. Define the terms, *CD-ROM, hypertext,* and *virtual reality.*

■ Cite some of the current and potential misuses of computer technology.

GRAPHIC ORGANIZER

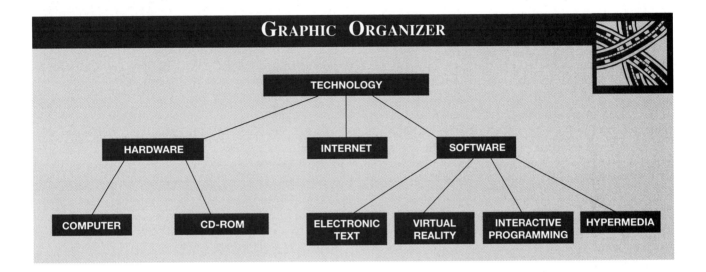

Technology: Imagining Our Future

We are completely in agreement with him on this point: That symbolization is constitutive of symbolic consciousness will trouble no one who believes in the absolute value of the cartesian cogito. But it must be understood that if symbolization is constitutive of consciousness it is permissible to perceive that there is an immanent bond of comprehension between the symbolization and the symbol.

In Chapter 1 we asked you to read the above passage by Sartre. We assumed that unless you were heavily steeped in the tradition of existential philosophy, you would find it very difficult. Now suppose that you are reading this passage on a computer screen. By touching a word with your finger or a mouse, you can bring up its definition. Suppose that you understood the words, but not the context in which they are being used. Imagine being able to highlight a phrase and have its syntax explained to you. Imagine reading this passage and knowing that the term cartesian refers to the work of

French philosopher Rene Descartes (1596–1650), but you don't know anything about him or why the term refers to him. Suppose you could highlight his name and pull up a biography along with a portrait of him. Imagine wanting to know how to pronounce a word like cogito and being able to touch the word on your computer screen and have it spoken to you.

Everything described above is possible using current and affordable computer technology. Technologies such as these are coming into widespread use in classrooms. If properly implemented and used, we believe that they will transform education in many important ways—in particular they will have an impact on areas such as content area literacy.

This chapter introduces you to the use of computers in the classroom. We assume that computer-based education is not only an emerging but an evolving field. Technologies which were seen as being innovative a few years ago are quickly outdated as increasingly powerful and inexpensive software and hardware become available.

For instance, the ENIAC (Electronic Numerical Integrator and Computer), which was the first modern computer, was built in the 1940s. It was created as a result of people realizing that information could be represented by the absence or presence of electrical current (pluses or minuses). The ENIAC, which weighed 30 tons, filled an entire room and took a whole staff of engineers to keep it running, and used vacuum tubes (electrical switches that generated either a positive or a negative current).

Today, computers hundreds of times more powerful than the ENIAC, and small enough to fit easily in our briefcases, are in widespread use. We are convinced that these new machines are of revolutionary importance and have the potential to affect all aspects of our lives, including our work as teachers. This chapter is intended to provide you with an introduction to computers and how they are affecting both how we teach and learn.

We ask you to use your imagination a bit as you read this chapter. Changes are occurring at such a rapid rate in the computing field that it is almost impossible to predict the future. This is particularly true with respect to the storage of information. A byte is the amount of space neccessary to store one character, such as a letter or number. A kilobyte is 1,000 bytes, a megabyte is 1,000 kilobytes, and a gigabyte is 1,000 megabytes. Floppy disks that hold 1.2 megabytes were state of the art only a few years ago but have been largely supplanted by CD-ROMs that hold 650 megabytes. As we write this textbook, DVDs (Digital Video Disks), which hold 6 gigabytes, are being produced. DVDs have enough storage space for 300,000 pages of text or a full length movie. The next step up in storage will be the terabyte, 1,000 gigabytes, which would be enough to hold the entire contents of a small college library—all on a piece of plastic that looks like a five inch audio disk. The CD-ROM accompanying this textbook is an example of how increased storage space and new techologies can support learning.

 ## Computers and Their Introduction into the Classroom

The widespread introduction of computers into elementary and secondary classrooms began in the early 1980s. While we frequently hear people talk about a revolution resulting from new models of computing being introduced into the schools, it is clear that educational computing has not had the impact anticipated by early enthusiasts in the field.

While it cannot be denied that computers, in one form or another, are found in almost every school in America, the question arises as to how they are actually used. You do not, for example, see computers used by most teachers to keep records, or to organize their day-to-day instruction with students. In the average elementary school, you are liable to find a computer or two in the back of a classroom or library resource area—occasionally there will be a specially constructed computer laboratory, where students go for instruction once or twice a week. At the secondary level, you are more likely to find computers in a lab or library resource area. What is important to realize, however, is that computers are rarely integrated into the total curriculum, but instead are most often used on a supplementary basis.

If you look carefully at how computers are typically used in the classroom, you will find them primarily employed as "patient drill-masters that occasionally supplement didactic explanations with a memorable situation" (Bosco, 1989, p. 111). This is far from the best use of computers for instruction. Significantly, there is little or no evidence to suggest that teachers and the schools are likely to adapt and use computers in the most effective or efficient way possible. In the case of computers, the old maxim that "If you build a better mousetrap people will beat a path to your door" does not necessarily hold true. While we are convinced that computers have a revolutionary potential to change how and what we learn, we are also convinced that the schools have an enormous potential to disregard the new technology.

Historically, whether we are talking about computers, film, radio, or television, innovative instructional technologies have consistently met with resistance from teachers and educators at large. This failure of instructional technologies to be integrated into the classroom has been clearly demonstrated by Larry Cuban (1986) in his book *Teachers and Machines: The Classroom Use of Technology Since 1920*. According to Cuban, instructional technology has consistently failed to bring about the revolutionary changes predicted by its advocates. Beginning with an examination of the introduction of motion pictures in the schools nearly a century ago, and continuing with the introduction of new forms of media such as radio and television, Cuban provides a convincing historical demonstration of how new educational technologies meet with only limited use by teachers in the classroom. For example, during the 1950s and 1960s a variety of mechanical teaching machines were introduced to the public schools (Cook, 1962), a decade or more before the invention of microprocessors and digital calculators. At the time there were many educators who believed that teaching machines would change the fundamental character of education—or even replace teachers altogether. But even before microcomputers entered their first classroom, the teaching machines had proven to be little more than a curious fad. Will computers in the classroom suffer the same fate?

The New Teaching Machines

The use of computers in education is a relatively new field. We are still struggling with basic questions such as what types of hardware to use, what are suitable instructional materials for students, and how to train teachers to teach with the machines. Such questions reflect both the uncertainty and excitement of the field.

When properly used, computers encourage experimentation in education. Students can test ideas and discover concepts as they work at a pace that best suits their ability and interest.

Currently available software allows children to take part in adventure games or to design their own programs. Programs such as *Where in the World is Carmen Sandiego?* or *Where in Time is Carmen Sandiego?* allow students to participate in sophisticated simulations in which they manipulate powerful educational databases in order to assemble clues about the whereabouts of a missing detective.

Hypertext systems, which involve large and relatively easily programmed linked visual and text databases, make possible whole new types of curriculum and ways of learning:

> The concept of hypertext is quite simple: Windows on the screen are associated with objects in a database and links are provided between these objects, both graphically (as labelled tokens) and in the database (as pointers). (Conklin, 1987, p. 17)

Schools across the country are beginning to use simple hypertext systems such as the *CD-ROM* (compact disk read-only memory) based *Compton's Illustrated Encyclopedia* or the *Grolier Electronic Encyclopedia*. In the case of the *Grolier Electronic Encyclopedia,* 21 volumes, 33,000 articles, and 9 million words of text are available. By typing in a single search word (Whales, for example), the system will search every reference to the subject in the encyclopedia. An electronic cutting and editing system allows the user to take notes and compile a personalized data bank.

Another example of hypertext or *hypermedia* (hypertext and visual and auditory sources) are the "Smart Books" produced by Scholastic. These electronic books are based around existing traditional print books and are repurposed electronically to take advantage of CD-ROM and hypermedia technologies. In the Smart Book version of *Malcolm X* by Walter Dean Meyers one cannot only read the book, but hear excerpts from speeches by Martin Luther King and Malcolm X, access news footage from the 1960s, meet the author of the book, have access to a timeline of the Civil Rights Movement, and hear biographies of major Civil Rights leaders. In addition, the program can read the book aloud, allow students to have full access to a dictionary, and also let them take notes on what they are reading.

Scholastic's Smart Book edition of *If Your Name Was Changed at Ellis Island* by Ellen Levine lets children hear stories of immigrants' trips through Ellis Island, meet famous Ellis Island immigrants, meet contemporary immigrant children, use maps and graphs, explore the Ellis Island complex, and visit a Japanese internment camp. With Robert D. Ballard's *Exploring the Titanic* children can not only read the book, but observe scientists and shipwreck specialists search for the Titanic, explore it with robot submarines, and learn about its history.

There are many other examples of electronic books and hypermedia systems that can be described. The possibilities of what can be done represent some of the most interesting developments in contemporary education and computing. Yet it should be realized that electronic books and hypermedia are not the only important innovations in educational computing. At the secondary and college level, programs like Wolfram's *Mathematica* provide a means by which to visually present mathematical functions to students thus allowing them to focus on mathematic concepts rather than computational details. Other programs, such as Snowbird Software's *The Electric Chemistry Toolkit,* introduce students to the more difficult aspects of chemistry by means of powerful computer simulations.

Among other interesting innovations in educational computing is *virtual reality.* Virtual reality is, in a certain sense, the ultimate extension of hypermedia. By putting on computer clothing, which includes devices such as eye-phones (a tiny pair of video screens that are mounted in front of each eye that provide stereo vision of a computer-created reality), data gloves (in which sensors lining one's hand communicate movement to a graphics computer), and stereo earphones and positional sensing equipment, one can enter a simulated computer environment (Levy, 1990).

Using a data glove in combination with the eye-phones, for example, you can experience a simulation in which you have entered a baseball stadium. As you hold your hand in front of your face a baseball glove appears. A ball flies toward you. You make the catch. Pulling back your hand, you throw the ball and it moves in the direction you have thrown it. In your mind you have entered a graphic reality, a hypermedia simulation. Traditional laws of physics may or may not apply. Virtual reality technology is available in crude forms with video games. Mattel sells a device called a power glove for under $100 which literally allows you to control the action of a computer game through the movement of your hand. The use of such technologies in education—at all levels—obviously has enormous potential. Imagine for a moment, being able to have high school students actually participate in the dissection of a human body, or in flying a spacecraft.

The use of less sophisticated computer activities for students will undoubtedly continue for the immediate future. Traditional models of computer-assisted instruction involving frame after frame of drill and practice will probably give way to increasingly sophisticated simulations. Providing the learners the opportunity to control their own environment, to use the computer as a tool for creativity which they will program themselves, we hope will become more widespread. We believe that comput-

ers are best used when they become creative tools for learning. As Seymour Papert, the developer of the children's programming language LOGO argued, the computer should not be used to program the child:

> In my vision, the *child programs the computer* and, in doing so, both acquire a sense of mastery over a piece of the most modern and powerful technology and establish an intimate contact with some of the deepest ideas from science, from mathematics, and from the art of intellectual model building. (Papert, 1980, p. 5)

Papert adopts Piaget's belief that the child is capable of building his own intellectual structures; as Piaget maintains, the child learns that to understand is to invent (Piaget, 1976).

FOCUS ON ESL AND BILINGUAL EDUCATION

There are many methods for teaching people how to speak a new language. However, experts agree that the most effective method is immersion (not to be confused with submersion), which places the language learner for an extended period of time in an environment that reflects as closely as possible the natural speech and culture of the new language. Usually this means that all instruction is carried out in the target language (Goldstein & Liu, 1994; Milk, 1990). A program called *Rosetta Stone* is now available on CD-ROMs and uses microcomputers to simulate an immersion format for teaching people of any age to speak a second language. The computer uses a combination of pictures, writing, and speaking—**only in the target language**—as learners move from one level of complexity to another. The CD-ROM accompanying this textbook includes the complete *Rosetta Stone* Language Sampler with lessons in Chinese, Dutch, Spanish, and a number of other languages. Quick Start directions for accessing and using the *Rosetta Stone* program are in Appendix B of this book.

■ The Internet

The *Internet* is a complex set of interlinking computer networks that began in the 1970s as part of a military strategy in the United States to maintain communications in the event of a nuclear war. Today the focus of the Internet is anything but military and nobody owns it. Millions of people around the world are communicating through the Internet by e-mail, and hundreds of thousands of companies and organizations advertise their products and communicate with vast audiences through Web sites.

Recent legislation at the federal level is designed to ensure that all public schools in the United States will have Internet access within the next few years. Given the tremendous amount and variety of instructionally relevant information available on the Net (Ryder & Graves, 1996), it is not difficult to imagine this technology reshaping public education. A complete discussion of the uses, abuses, first amendment issues, and directions for learning how to use the Net are beyond the scope of this book. However, there are many How To books about the Internet (e.g., Heide & Stilborne, 1996) and we urge you to get one if you aren't already e-mailing and surfing the Net.

At various points in the text we will suggest Web sites that have information relevant to the teaching profession. Using the Internet, find one of the following Web sites, identify its name, and briefly describe its purpose.

http://www.ncbe.gwu.edu/

http://www.virtualcopy.com

http://www.educom.com

http://ericir.syr.edu

http://www.comenius.com/

On the Non-neutrality of the Computer

C. A. Bowers in his work, *The Cultural Dimensions of Educational Computing,* questions, in reference to educational computing, whether or not the computer is a neutral technology. According to him:

> . . . the most fundamental question about the new technology has never been seriously raised by either the vocal advocates or the teachers who have attempted to articulate their reservations. The question has to do with whether the technology is neutral; that is, neutral in terms of accurately representing, at the level of the software program, the domains of the real world in which people live. (Bowers, 1988, p. 24)

Bowers argues that computers and their software must be understood as "part of the much more complex symbolic world that makes up our culture" (Bowers, 1980, p. 24). According to him, we need to critically examine how we look at computers. Instead of simply understanding computers in a technical and procedural context, we need to deal with them in a larger cultural context—how they shape our ways of interpreting the world around us. In doing so, we must ask what it is that the computer and hypertext and hypermedia systems select for amplification and for reduction—in other words, what gets emphasized and deemphasized as a result of their use (Bowers, 1980).

Already problems are emerging related to sex equity and the use of computers. Many computer games such as some of those found on the Nintendo system are sexist. If the games are the first introduction many children have to the world of computing, then their common themes of rescuing a maiden or damsel in distress (*Super Mario Brothers 2,* etc.) represent inappropriate messages for boys and girls (Provenzo, 1991). Likewise, the preponderance of games based on violence and aggression is equally inappropriate.

Computer simulations and educational programming must avoid stereotyping at all costs. In light of the discriminatory content of television and other forms of media, it is not likely that computers are going to be less reflective of stereotyping. It is the hope of the authors that we recognize the issue early enough in the development of the field that measures can be taken to prevent such discrimination before it becomes as widespread as it has in other forms of media. While raising issues such as these, we must question whether or not the computer itself has specific assumptions built into its logic and the logic of its programs that prevent it from being a neutral technology.

SUMMARY

Teachers in the content areas need to be aware of not only new and emerging technologies, but how their application and use may be particularly valuable for the subjects they teach. Hypertext and hypermedia systems can provide students with important support materials that can contextualize difficult passages and phrases. In addition, vast sources of supplementary information can be made available should the reader be interested. What are the advantages of such systems? How will they change the process of learning? Will they significantly affect the traditional role of the teacher? These are just a few of the important questions you and teachers like you will need to address in the near future.

Computer instruction, when combined with video and text sources, promises to be an exciting technological and educational innovation. New methods of presenting traditional information, new methods of problem solving, new ways of organizing and structuring large databases, and new ways of providing personalized instruction are just a few of the opportunities available. Schools must provide students at all levels with access to the new technology and make sure they have equal access to resources whatever their socioeconomic background, race, or gender. At the same time, we must make sure that the new technologies do not limit or impede our capacity to be humane and critical interpreters of the world in which we live and work.

REACTION GUIDE

Confirmed   Disconfirmed

_____   _____   1.   Computers in education are probably a fad.

_____   _____   2.   Computers should be used to program children.

_____   _____   3.   Classroom instruction in the near future will be fundamentally different because of the Internet.

_____   _____   4.   The computer is morally neutral.

_____   _____   5.   The first electronic computer was built during the U.S. Civil War.

Continued

A	B
Why my choice is confirmed.	Why my choice is not confirmed.

1. _____   _____

   _____   _____

2. _____   _____

   _____   _____

3. _____   _____

   _____   _____

4. _____   _____

   _____   _____

5. _____   _____

   _____   _____

MINI PROJECT

The CD-ROM *Digital Supplement* includes the complete text of the Jack London novel *The Call of the Wild*. As you read and work your way through the various chapters of *Content Area Literacy: An Integrated Approach,* think of how you might apply the strategies from the text if you were teaching a group of children using *The Call of the Wild.* Use the Adobe Acrobat Reader 3.0 to find the novel on the CD-ROM and practice with Reader 3.0 to find the answers to the following Questions:

1. How many times does the word *savage* appear in the 160-page novel? _____

2. What PDF page does the word *Angry* (with a capital A) first appear? _____

3. Do a proximity search using "Buck" and "club" and describe briefly what is happening in the

   story. _____

4. What word precedes the phrase "urgent and prompting"? _____

5. Use the thesaurus option to find two words in the novel with meanings similar to *danger.*

   _____   _____

■ Up until this point in time the actual impact of computers on classroom instruction has been disappointing. Explain why.

■ Discuss the advantages and disadvantages of a multimedia encyclopedia over a traditional printed encyclopedia.

■ Compare and contrast the ENIAC with modern computers that have multimedia capabilities.

■ Explain how the computer revolution might contribute to the social evils of gender bias, stereotyping, and physical violence.

■ American educators have in large part embraced the notion that the use of computers in the schools is inevitable and even desirable. In many respects the increasingly widespread use of computers in our culture and in our schools parallels the introduction of the automobile at the beginning of this century. Although the automobile made rapid and convenient travel possible, it also engendered highway construction, air pollution, and frequent accidental deaths. Both from a personal and an educational point of view, what might be some of the hidden costs of introducing computers into our schools? Can these problems be avoided, or are they inevitable?

THREE

LANGUAGE, CULTURE, DIVERSITY, AND THE READING PROCESS

ANTICIPATION GUIDE

Agree	Disagree	
_____	_____	1. Knowledge of a student's culture is not important in teaching subject matter.
_____	_____	2. Programs designed for second language learners help them gain subject matter comprehension.
_____	_____	3. Comprehending text material is a creative, constructive process.
_____	_____	4. Reading and writing are unrelated cognitive processes.
_____	_____	5. Whole class discussion discourages wide student participation.

RATIONALE

The uniquely human acts of reading and writing have been cherished by people for centuries because literacy and power are so closely related. In the young adult book, *From slave to abolitionist: The life of William Wells Brown* (Warner, 1993), African American William Wells Brown provides a harsh, realistic account of his flight from 20 years of slavery and the tearing apart of his family. His autobiography, first published in 1847 reveals the powerful role literacy played in his flight to freedom. Through great personal danger and dedication, William Wells Brown learned to read and write, giving him the voice needed to fight slavery and prejudice for 22 years as a lecturer and author. In 1834, on the run to Canada and freedom, he traded candy for lessons in reading at an abolitionist's home in Ohio. He progressed to a stage where he could read complex texts and, ultimately, contribute to the antislavery movement.

Soon I bought an arithmetic book and a grammar and studied them equally hard. Next I bought other, general books and in leisure moments, I read them to improve my skills—and my knowledge. This reading of books whenever possible became my lifelong practice. Wherever I might be, there will always be with me a volume of grammar, mathematics, history, or literature. (p. 92)

While students often view content area textbooks as overwhelming and at times dull, for William Wells Brown they represented a route to learning and a voice in the political struggle for freedom. In the early 1830s, teaching an enslaved African American to read was a crime that would result in severe punishment (Nieto, 1996). Denied literacy as a slave, William Wells Brown knew reading and writing were keys to fighting a system that was brutal and unjust.

Today, many immigrant populations from South America, Asia, and elsewhere continue the struggle to adapt to unfamiliar surroundings in the United States after fleeing conditions of war, poverty, and persecution in their native lands. Schools have experienced an increasing number of non-native speakers of English, and this trend is expected to continue into the 21st century. By the early part of the 21st century, only one of two young people will be European American while one of four will be Hispanic (Au, 1993). Culture and language differences can help or hinder students' progress in content literacy depending on the knowledge and strategies you as the teacher have at your disposal. Latino, Cambodian, Vietnamese, African American, American Indian, Hawaiian, European American, Pacific Islander, and countless other groups can flourish or flounder in our content area classrooms based on what we know about their cultures and how we conduct lessons that capitalize on this knowledge. Do we incorporate multicultural features in our lessons, or are we merely maintaining the mainstream European American traditions of individual competition and assimilation?

In addition to greater numbers of second language learners in classrooms, rural families migrating to urban centers constitute another group for whom literacy in the content areas may present a significant challenge (Purcell-Gates, 1995). In her tutoring of a nonliterate Appalachian family, Victoria Purcell-Gates (1995) tapped young Donny's interest in his Kentucky mountain home with its woods and abundant wildlife. She used his hands-on experiences as a vehicle for creating his own expository books and, ultimately, as a bridge to reading published textbooks. Treating literacy as cultural practice, Purcell-Gates balanced a keen sensitivity to Donny's oral language culture with explicit teaching of new concepts in the literate culture of text.

> When learners are having problems understanding, however, direct explanations and instruction are called for until the learner can begin to participate in the cultural practice more as an insider than an outsider. (p. 98)

In this chapter, we explore the related dimensions of language, culture, *diversity*, and the reading process with an eye toward some activities and strategies that will help you broaden the cultural styles you use in the classroom. Subsequent chapters will expand on specific strategies in the areas of lesson and unit design, young adult literature, vocabulary, comprehension, writing, studying, and other content area literacy approaches.

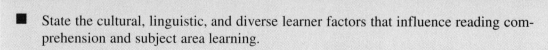

LEARNING OBJECTIVES

- State the cultural, linguistic, and diverse learner factors that influence reading comprehension and subject area learning.

- State the cognitive and text-based factors that influence reading comprehension and subject area learning.

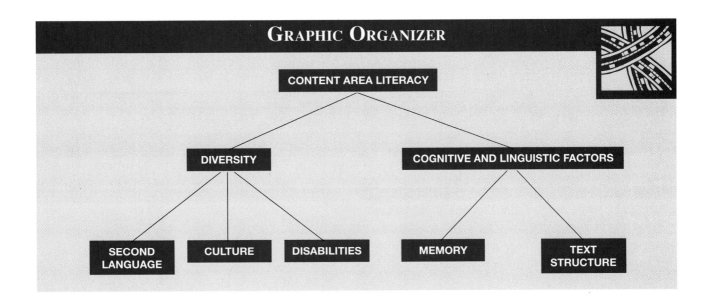

 Language, Culture, and Diversity

A substantial number of immigrants from Europe and South America who are now middle-aged can recall suppressing their native languages when they arrived in American classrooms. Many have now lost this vital link to their past. For example, author Sonia Nieto (1996) recalls her degrading experiences as a young Puerto Rican arrival to America. Her native language was Spanish, and teachers quickly transmitted the message that this language was not valued. She struggled simultaneously to learn content area concepts and English as a second language while the potentially powerful boost her native Spanish might have given her was devalued. Nieto (1996) argues that teachers can capitalize on a student's native language in content area instruction, especially since most contemporary bilingual education programs provide for the use of the native language as a bridge to using the second language.

For example, Grace, a Filipino immigrant employed at a rural flower farm in Hawaii wrote the following query to her employer:

> Claudia,
>   I have a ? Do you know what is a Bombay.
>   Some one order that but I don't know what is it.
>   Thanks,
>   Grace

Grace formatted her query about the Bombay like a letter but using grammatical structures familiar to her. Nevertheless, she got her message across. As it turned out, Claudia did not know what a "Bombay" was either. At this point in her use of English as a second language, Grace would benefit from a small amount of explicit instruction. She would then have a model to use in future queries.

Programs designed for second language learning vary according to the emphasis on immersion in the target language (Nieto, 1996). Generally, programs may be characterized as: (a) immersion bilingual education, (b) English as a second language, (c) transitional bilingual education, (d) developmental bilingual education, and (e) two-way bilingual education. *Immersion bilingual education* is termed submersion by Nieto because it parallels her demoralizing experiences as a native speaker of Spanish expected to abruptly shift into English as the dominant language of instruction. *English as a second language,* or ESL, provides structured lessons in English while the student may choose to maintain facility in the native language. The goal is to learn English through a structured program of lessons. Kasper (1994) paired ESL classes with content course material in psychology. She found that this double exposure to the subject matter enhanced both second language acquisition and content learning. In the ESL classes, students read complementary articles that expanded on ideas in the core text for the psychology course. They completed comprehension exercises and significantly outpaced their peers in non-paired classes on measures of language facility and content knowledge. Kasper's study indicates that ESL students need substantial support to be successful in content area learning. When the support is provided, they do as well as native speakers on final exams and other measures (Kasper, 1994).

Transitional bilingual education consists of content area instruction in the native language while the student engages in ESL instruction with the proviso that the native language will be phased-out in three years. In contrast, *developmental bilingual education* does not have a time limit for phasing-out the native language. Finally, *two-way bilingual education* may be the most attractive because both native English and non-native English speakers learn each other's language while they do the bulk of their content learning in the strong, native language.

This last form of two-way bilingual learning, as well as classrooms where non-native English speakers find their native language is valued and used in content learning, have a number of benefits. Since language and culture are inextricably linked, a teacher who demonstrates respect and enthusiasm for language diversity advances students' self-esteem and identity. A classroom where students feel their native language and culture is valued can help reduce the high dropout rates experienced by non-native speakers. Even more importantly, valuing a student's native language helps students from diverse cultures maintain the often close family relationships with parents, siblings, grandparents, and extended family members. In instances where students are immersed in English and denied the use of their native language, the whole network and culture a student knows is treated as if it is less important than mainstream culture. This assimilation model results in real resentment and detachment from one's family. Many successful middle-aged immigrants abandoned their native identities to survive in America and recall these experiences with a good deal of pain.

Today, there is a renaissance of multicultural literature, poetry, and music. The following poem, written in Hawaiian Islands Dialect or pidgin, treats a universal topic. Hawaiian poet, Leomi L. Bergknut (1997), used the unique linguistic structure, intonation, and deep cultural understanding to show how it feels when you are walking across campus and someone gives you "stink eye."

Stink Eye*

You ever give
Sombody one stink eye?
If, you wen do em
Den you know
Wat I stay writen about.

Da udda day wen
I wuz cruizin to class,
I wen feel
Sombody givin me
Da stink eye.

I know,
Cuz I could
Feel em at
Da back
Of my neck.

And da moe I walk,
Da moe I catch
Dat feelin dat make me wonda—
Who stay givin me
Da stink eye?

So, I turn aroun
And I know wuz you!
So, I give
Da stink eye back to you!
Da stink eye!

And den you
Wen stay laugh at me
And den you tell me
"Wat?
Wat you like?"

Stupidhead!
No give me
Da stink eye
Cuz you just might
Not live to regret it!

Kathy Au (1993) has done a substantial amount of curriculum design work focusing on students who speak Hawaiian Islands Dialect in the Kamehameha Early Education Project. She regards reading and writing in any language as a solid foundation for learning. Thus, she recommends having students answer questions using some of their native language as they move toward proficiency in the target language. Sarah Hudelson's (1994) extensive work with Spanish speaking students led her to the conclusion that a good foundation in the native language provides a framework for subsequent language learning. Furthermore, she argues that there is no single best way to enhance second language learners' second language literacy development. However, there are a number of approaches and strategies you can use in your content area to both value diverse students' existing knowledge and build on this base.

Second Language Strategies in Content Classes

The most important overriding strategy is to consciously make your classroom an inviting place for all

*Reprinted with permission of Leomi L. Bergknut (1997) and *Kanilehua*.

Take a moment to write a short response to the following prompt.

How do you feel about the notion that a second language learner should be immersed in English and not use his or her native language as a foundation for understanding content lessons?

students but especially for students from diverse cultural and linguistic backgrounds. Nieto (1996) recommends using students' native language in bulletin board displays. This could include signs, news articles, and other items related to your particular content area. Au (1993) advocates the use of dialogue journals discussed in the writing chapter later in this text. Dialogue journals involve the teacher and students writing to each other before the start of a class to ask questions, comment on any confusion over a lesson, and generally communicate in a free writing fashion where spelling and grammar worries take a back seat to straightforward communication of a message between two people. Similarly, learning logs where students write their reaction to a specific writing prompt help focus second language learners on the upcoming content topic of a lesson. Students can make predictions, activate prior knowledge, and develop a pre-reading orientation to an assignment through a well structured learning log prompt.

Using labels for items in class that include both English and other languages represented in the classroom will help expand second language students' technical vocabulary in science, math, social studies and other content fields. Clear, concise explanations of required classroom activities, along with peer support, particularly in editing writing, will help second language students immensely. In reality, many of the teaching strategies designed for ESL students also make good sense for all learners (Searfoss, Bean, & Gelfer, 1998).

For additional information on improving second language reading instruction in the content areas, go to William Grabe's (1991) *TESOL Quarterly* article on the CD-ROM.

Culture in Content Areas

Language becomes the surface manifestation of a more subtle and invisible culture (Au, 1993). Au sees culture as a collection of values, beliefs, and standards which influences how students think, feel, and behave in various social settings including classrooms. Nieto (1996) points to a number of potential gaps in main-

stream and divergent cultures that manifest themselves in classrooms. For example, she states that textbooks often emphasize a European American perspective while stereotyping, ignoring, or misrepresenting African-American and Indian contributions. Sociocultural values of various groups may run counter to mainstream classroom values if the teacher fails to be inclusive. For example, American Indian students who value respect, harmony, and cooperation may have a problem in a competition oriented classroom. Other cultures disapprove of spotlighting a single student in front of the whole class (Au, 1993). Including more culturally compatible strategies like cooperative learning groups can help you achieve an inclusive, culturally responsive teaching style that is inviting to many students. Given the range of cultural diversity possible in today's classrooms, you may find some students view your style as too informal. Some students may regard your classroom as completely disconnected from the community. You can avoid this cultural gap through some labor intensive effort to learn about students' cultures and design lessons accordingly. Content lessons should, when possible, connect the classroom to the problems and diverse values represented by your students. Urban, rural, and suburban communities have unique contributions to make to lesson design.

Culture and Lesson Design

The way in which teachers interact with students of diverse cultures may result in students seeing little connection between their native culture and the mainstream classroom value system of individual survival and competition. Au (1993, p. 20) defines *literacy* as: "The ability and the willingness to use reading and writing to construct meaning from printed text, in ways which meet the requirements of a particular social context." The key phrase in this definition is "willingness to use reading and writing." Unless culturally diverse students see some connection between your teaching and their unique sociocultural experiences, they are likely to just go through the motions in completing text reading assignments, project completion, and other classroom activities.

A culturally conscious style of teaching involves creating very direct links between students' community life outside the classroom and the lessons they experience in the classroom (Ladson-Billings, 1995). For example, when students are allowed to bring in their contemporary music as a vehicle for studying conventions of poetry, they are more likely to experience success in reading this genre and, they are more likely to tackle more challenging Shakespearean sonnets. In addition, by using music from their respective cultures including rap, hip-hop, reggae, Hawaiian, and so on, students' see their respective cultural identities honored and respected. When parents of students visit as scholars in residence to describe their work as electricians, carpenters, lifeguards, hotel receptionists, and so on, their presence clearly demonstrates a direct link between the classroom and community. Without that connection, school is seen as distant and unrelated to day-to-day life for too many adolescents (Bean, 1998).

Another important aspect of a culturally conscious pedagogy involves infusing the classroom with a high level of critical thinking. We feel critical thinking is crucial in any content area lesson design, but it is too often absent.

Gloria Ladson-Billings (1995) studied a group of teachers who exemplified culturally conscious curriculum design in an African-American community. Students were encouraged and guided in critiquing the accuracy of information in the textbooks they read. In a recent project with ninth-graders, we engaged students in a critique of the cultural authenticity of Navajo burial traditions described in the excellent young adult novel, *Heartbeat Drumbeat* (Hernandez, 1992). Students in ninth-grade English conducted library searches, searched the internet, and listened to a guest speaker from the local Indian Center describe Navajo burial traditions. Based on this information and their own analyses, they wrote a novel critique (Bean, Valerio, Money Senior, & White, 1997). We functioned as co-learners with these students, exploring and discussing the cultural authenticity of Hernandez's novel.

You can increase students' motivation in your content classroom by using activities and participation structures that value a multicultural stance. For example, in English or social studies, students can interview and videotape each other's biographies based on an interview questionnaire they develop (Nieto, 1996). Similarly, in history or English, students can develop oral histories by interviewing family members. These projects show clearly that classrooms value the community they serve, and students are less likely to drop out of a setting that supports their success.

Additionally, students' names are special and they each have a unique history as well as a wealth of associations. Throughout our history, names have been shaped by the power relationships of the time. For example, the young adult historical novel *Saturnalia* (Fleischman, 1990) set in Boston during the winter of 1681, provides a poignant account of the main character's search for his lost tribal family. As a printer's indentured servant, his Indian name was changed by his master to the English name William. He sneaks out of the print shop at night after his master's family is in bed to search for his twin Narraganset Indian brother in the cold Boston night. "He had known two worlds, had lived two lives, had even been called by two different names: Weetasket, bestowed by his father at birth, and William, the name he'd worn in his second life, chosen by his second father, the printer, Mr. Currie" (p. 34). The book's rising action culminates in Saturnalia, an ancient Roman holiday when masters and servants trade roles.

You can use the importance and cultural interest of students' names to get to know students' unique contributions to your class. The following activity is a good icebreaker.

ACTIVITY

Your name, especially your last name, has an intricate history that offers a window on your unique culture. Pair-up with another student in the content area reading class and ask that student to tell you about his or her name. Do this for both members of the pair and share this information with the whole group.

As a teacher you can devote a section of the bulletin board in your classroom to a name-history profile of your students. For example, in one content area class, a student with the last name in Hawaiian, Kamalani, explained its meaning and significance.

"Kama" means child and "lani" means heavenly. Thus, this student's name meant heavenly child. Another student from Japan had the last name, Ohsuga. Her name denoted a young rice plant with great potential for growth and success. She shared

Pair-up with another class member and use the survey questions that follow to interview this person about his or her ethnic and cultural biography and values (Kinney, 1993). The interview information can be used to introduce class members, assign small groups, and design lessons that build on students' diversity.

1. Where did your ancestors come from? Country, region, city?

2. Why did they come to _____ (our state, country, etc.)?

3. Where does most of your cultural community live?

4. What are the more popular jobs for your community?

5. What are the popular unique terms and gestures used by the community?

6. Do families stay close geographically as they grow up?

7. Do multiple generations live in the same household?

8. Who are the decision makers in the family?

9. How does the decision making process happen?

10. How are elders treated in the family and community?

11. How is respect shown?

12. Do family members have certain cultural names? What are the popular names?

13. Who are married children influenced by the most in their decision making? Prioritize.

_____ Children	_____ Grandparents	_____ Cultural leaders
_____ Parents	_____ Nieces/nephews	_____ Spiritual leaders
_____ Siblings	_____ Neighbors	_____ Other

14. What are some special values and beliefs your culture upholds?

15. Is your community focused more on the individual or the group? Please state examples.

16. What are some ways a teacher can act that are culturally appropriate in your community?

---

the kanji or ideographic symbol for her name which is: 本 This simple activity of pairing, sharing, and discussing class names helps develop a sense of multicultural community in a classroom and it focuses on the single most important element of language, one's name. The goal of activities like name sharing allows learners from different cultures and perspectives to develop some understanding of another student's world view (Bennett, 1995). This movement toward a multicultural appreciation and related competency is vital for understanding text readings in history, science, music, art, English, economics and other content areas. This brief, name sharing activity can be extend-

ed through peer interviewing, video recording of these profiles, and subsequent reading and discussion in a class in social studies or English.

In addition to interviewing and developing student profiles of cultural norms, you can institute other projects in your content area that link the school, classroom, and community. In science, students can connect with the community through projects in tree planting, beautification through playground clean-up at a local elementary school. In math or economics, a class can help an elementary school establish an in-school store for supplies or food.

Hobbies, food, and music offer additional areas where unique language and cultural differences can contribute to learning. For example, the African-American lyrical patterns found in blues and rap can be used to develop songs to study topics ranging from cell structure in biology to the stages of a revolution in history.

Cooperative learning strategies encompassing small group work with students of diverse cultures and abilities offer yet another means of linking students' sociocultural learning styles and your classroom. For example, Hawaiian students enjoy a participation structure called "talk story" where group performance in a free-flowing discussion of current events, family activities, and community concerns is common. Indeed, the flow of information in "high context" cultures is dominated by oral language networks that rely on talk story exchanges to accomplish the day-to-day business of the community (Bennett, 1995; Hall, 1959). In contrast, "low context" cultures like many urban, European-American communities rely heavily on a paper trail to do business. A profusion of memos, position papers, policy statements, and legal documents characterize the flow of information in a low context culture.

In rural Hawaiian communities talk story as a high context form of "coconut wireless" is still quite common. It saves trees and works remarkably well. Talk story as a cooperative teaching strategy is directly related to the Hawaiian cultural values of laulima (cooperation), ohana (family), and lokahi (unity). Hawaiians and many other Pacific Island and Asian cultures revere their "Kapuna" or elders for their ability to teach culturally appropriate actions. Indeed, much of the cultural lore that needs to be shared with younger generations is not written down but must be passed along in chants and stories.

Teachers sensitive to the special values of a culture like the Hawaiians or American Indians design content lessons that place students in small groups to discuss content text readings, react to reading guides, develop projects, and study for exams. Cooperative learning will be discussed in greater detail in subsequent chapters where we demonstrate specific teaching strategies in vocabulary, comprehension, and writing. Cooperative learning has been recommended as a culturally appropriate strategy for students from high context cultures like American Indians, African-American, and Hawaiian. However, cooperative learning groups mirror the problem-solving approaches used in many low context settings in business and community groups across many cultures. Thus, learning to organize participation structures like cooperative learning will enhance your teaching for most of the students in your content area classes.

In addition to students representing diversity in culture and language areas, you can expect to work with students who may have a wide array of disabilities. Fortunately, many of the strategies advocated in content area literacy parallel those advanced in contemporary special education textbooks on mainstreaming (Salend, 1994).

Students with Disabilities

Diversity in the classroom encompasses linguistic, cultural, and learning disability dimensions. Since 1975, public law 94-142 now referred to as the Individuals with Disabilities Act, has helped ensure mainstreaming opportunities in regular classrooms for students with disabilities (Salend, 1994). Indeed, about 70 percent of students with disabilities are able to participate in learning in regular classrooms and resource room settings rather than isolated, institutional settings. Salend (1994) estimates that about 44 percent of these students have learning disabilities. Students with *learning disabilities* generally have a significant discrepancy between their intellectual potential for learning and their achievement scores, as well as processing difficulties with print and production difficulties with writing (Vaughn, Schumm, Klinger, & Saumell, 1995). The intent of mainstreaming students with physical disabilities and learning disabilities in regular classrooms is to provide the least restrictive environment so that students can enjoy participation in a community of learners. In practice, *mainstreaming* means that students with disabilities spend a portion of their day in regular classes with their peers. While primary responsibility for adapting academic and social dimensions of learning rest with you, the teacher, varying levels of support services will be provided for students with special needs (Salend, 1994). Thus, teaching content concepts in classrooms as we move into the 21st century increasingly means serving in a team of professionals to provide for a wide array of learning styles and needs.

One of the most promising aids to a teacher in serving a population of students who have a range of disabilities is technology. For example, increasingly, the familiar overhead transparency projector will be replaced with a video camera version called an ELMO. This device displays text, graphics, and virtually any image placed on its glass top on a video monitor. It is much more versatile than the overhead projector in presenting visual images.

Students with visual disabilities will have an ever growing collection of print-to-speech translators available. For example, the Kurzweil Reading Machine reads aloud printed material placed on its glass deck

(Salend, 1994). A student can pause text, rewind to hear a word, and control volume, pitch, and speech rate. Students with hearing disabilities can use an Optacon which translates images to tactile Braille-like print or synthesized speech. Another device called the Talking Terminal is a database that reads aloud material. A dizzying array of other devices based on closed-caption technology will help increase hearing impaired students' learning and literacy in content areas.

But for most content area teachers, adaptations to the textbook and regular class assignments remain the most promising route to learning for students with disabilities. Unfortunately, the research on teachers' efforts to adapt textbook assignments suggests that this is happening infrequently at best (Vaughn et al., 1995). For example, in an interview study of middle school and secondary students with learning disabilities, students overwhelmingly agreed that *textbook adaptations* such as study guides, graphic organizers, and listening guides would help them better learn content material (Vaughn et al., 1995). However, they indicated that these textbook adaptations were rarely implemented. The researchers argued that if inclusion is to succeed, teachers will need to become skilled at using many of the strategies we advocate in the vocabulary, comprehension, writing, and studying chapters of this book.

Many of the teaching strategies discussed in future chapters emphasize approaches that assist learners with disabilities. For example, cooperative reciprocal teaching groups, brainstorming a topic in pairs, pre-teaching vocabulary, self-questioning, and comprehension monitoring all assist students with a variety of special needs (Salend, 1994).

In order to understand why you need to develop a body of teaching strategies that accommodate a wide range of students, the next section explores some of the cognitive and linguistic factors that influence the reading and learning process. Think about your own experiences in reading text material as you explore this information on literacy in content area learning.

 ## Cognitive and Linguistic Factors in Text Comprehension

A student's prior knowledge based on experience is the vehicle for comprehending new information in a text. This constructivist view of learning argues that knowledge is constructed from experience (Duffy & Jonassen, 1992). A student builds a body of prior knowledge through the accumulation of experiences, and this uniquely personal body of knowledge guides comprehension of subsequent text reading. As an example, read the following sentence and see if you can figure out what it is referring to.

The phoscheck dropped left of the cat.

If you lived in a canyon in Southern California where the early fall Santa Ana winds fan wild fires that regularly destroy homes and forests, the term phoscheck would be very familiar from numerous news reports and personal experience. In firefighting operations, phoscheck, a fire retardant, is dropped from helicopters. The term "cat" refers to a Caterpillar tractor cutting a fire line near where the chemical fire retardant is being dropped.

Prior knowledge, then, is constructed from experience and stored in memory. Understanding how information is organized in memory will help you appreciate individual differences in reading comprehension.

The Organization of Prior Knowledge in Memory

Cognitive structure is a term used to describe the way in which an individual stores experiences and concepts. In such structuring, each individual forms a system of categories based largely on common cultural and experiential patterns. For example, Eskimo culture specifies a rich category system for the quality of snow. In Hawaiian culture that category is virtually nonexistent. Such categories serve to aid an individual in organizing and understanding experiences by promoting an efficient memory search of prior experiences during problem-solving tasks. The diagram on the next page depicts a portion of a possible category system for classifying various kinds of mammals.

A category system such as this functions as a representation of knowledge in memory that can be searched to make sense of the surrounding environment. In general, information located at a high level (e.g., mammals) in our cognitive structure is more easily retrieved than lower level details such as hourglass or bottlenose dolphins (Norman, 1976). For example, although the category dolphin is readily accessible when we see a dolphin or a picture of one, the more than 50 types of dolphins would be much harder to recall. The accessibility of subsets of a category is highly dependent on individual differences with respect to one's past experience, culture, and interests. A student who was raised near the sea and has a strong interest in marine biology may have a readily accessible and highly detailed cognitive structure for the cat-

```
                    ┌─────────────┐
                    │   MAMMALS   │
                    └─────────────┘
         ┌───────┬──────┬────┴─────┬──────────┐
    ┌────────┐ ┌──────┐ ┌──────┐ ┌──────┐ ┌──────────┐
    │ PEOPLE │ │ DOGS │ │ CATS │ │ COWS │ │ DOLPHINS │
    └────────┘ └──────┘ └──────┘ └──────┘ └──────────┘
                                    ┌────────┼──────────┐
                              ┌───────────┐ ┌────────┐ ┌───────────┐
                              │ HOURGLASS │ │ COMMON │ │ BOTTLENOSE│
                              └───────────┘ └────────┘ └───────────┘
```

egory dolphins, while the general population of students possess a much less elaborate network for this category.

As a student moves into the secondary grades, an ever-expanding wealth of prior knowledge is available to cope with the flood of new information introduced in the content areas. While the concept of cognitive structure explains how this prior knowledge is organized in memory, *schema theory,* patterned after Piaget's formulation, provides a more detailed explanation of comprehension (Tierney & Pearson, 1992 a,b, Weaver & Kintsch, 1991). A person's schema or knowledge structure can be regarded as the central guidance system in the comprehension process. An individual searches existing schemata to make sense of incoming information from the text. The degree to which this incoming information is consistent with the expectations generated from existing schemata determines the presence or absence of comprehension.

Concept Learning in Content Areas

Take a moment and consider each of the following statements:

1. All bees sting.
2. If you are bitten by a tarantula in the hills of southern California, you might as well be dead.
3. The earth is flat.

Each of these statements comprise erroneous knowledge structures or schemata that students sometimes stubbornly cling to, despite a teacher's best efforts to convince them otherwise (Bean, Cowan, & Searles, 1990; Chinn, & Brewer, 1993). Indeed, the first two misconceptions may be consistent with your schema for bees and tarantulas. Yet a male bee does not have a stinger—you can hold a male bee in your hand without any fear of injury. And, although tarantulas are poisonous and even deadly in South America, the southern California variety are not deadly. Finally, at the secondary and college levels, students generally

know that the earth is not flat and it does not look like a frisbee.

If we define learning as the accumulation of ever more rich knowledge structures in science, social science, physical education, English, and the arts, how is it that students manage to dispense with misconceptions they may have staunchly held for many years? Recent discussions of concept learning have their roots in Piaget's notions of assimilation and accommodation, but they attempt to capture the slowly evolving nature of knowledge acquisition. For example, Vosniadou and Brewer (1987) argue that while Piaget's broad learning categories of assimilation and accommodation are indeed powerful, we need to examine how students progress from novices to experts within specific subject area domains such as science and social studies. Based on their studies of young children's developing view of the earth as a sphere, they find that Rumelhart and Norman's (1981) three-category view of concept development best explains the slow, cumulative process by which a learner acquires new concepts.

Rumelhart and Norman use the terms accretion, tuning, and restructuring to chart the course of concept learning. *Accretion,* much like assimilation, simply involves the accumulation of facts within existing schemata. Thus, in physics, a student may hold theories resembling those of Aristotle (i.e., the earth is flat), rather than Newton (i.e., the earth is round). Confronted with counterevidence in the form of models, films, teacher explanation, and so on, a student may modify this flat earth schema slightly, concluding that the earth is a flat disk like a frisbee. This gradual change in an erroneous concept is called *tuning.* Finally, given enough instruction and counterevidence, a learner may progress to a radical *restructuring* of erroneous concepts, concluding that the earth is indeed a sphere.

Without adequate teacher guidance, students' stubborn misconceptions may override information presented in a text. Alvermann, Smith, & Readence (1985) found that middle grade students' existing mis-

In your content area (science, art, math, etc.) you learn a number of concepts (e.g., Newton's second law of motion) that defy common sense or conventional wisdom. Identify two such concepts from your content area and write a statement for each that is the commonly held belief by people who have not studied your field. Share these statements with another class member from a different field. Did they agree or disagree with the two statements. Why? What were their reasons?

conceptions in science caused them to ignore incompatible information presented in a text about the sun. Hynd, Qian, Ridgeway, and Pickle (1991) found that even those students who have taken physics courses cling stubbornly to misconceptions about the motion of objects. For example, students' intuitive thinking may cause them to believe that a pebble launched from a slingshot will first move forward and then begin falling. Rather, objects move forward and downward simultaneously in a curved path. This example and others suggest you need to take the time to informally assess students' preconceived notions about topics when you suspect their understanding may be erroneous or only partially adequate.

Despite potential problems with misconceptions, linking new concepts to some familiar, existing concept remains a powerful strategy we can use to advantage in content teaching. Indeed, perhaps the most prominent way in which a learner attempts to cope with new information, such as the structure and function of a cell in science, is through a comparison to some existing knowledge (Bean, Singer, & Cowan, 1985; Halford, 1993; Rumelhart & Norman, 1981). For example, a beginning biology student with little knowledge of a cell's features might benefit from seeing how a cell's parts and functions are analogous to the parts and functions of a factory. The factory analogy acts as a catalyst in forming a new, separate schema for a cell. Teachers routinely resort to verbal analogies when they see students looking perplexed. Sometimes these analogies are successful and at times they fail to connect with students' experiences, especially if students are approaching English as a second language. Furthermore, overly simplistic analogies may reduce students' understanding of complex material (Spiro, Feltovich, Coulson, & Anderson, 1989). Thus, as a content teacher, you need to identify students' existing knowledge and provide experiences in reading, listening, speaking, and writing that help them progress smoothly through tuning and restructuring knowledge. Activities such as the anticipation guide and brainstorming, especially reflective written brainstorming in a dialogue journal, provide us with some sense of students' prior knowledge. We can then anticipate

misconceptions that may arise as students read and take measures to help them modify existing information that may be naive or in error. In later chapters we will introduce specific strategies aimed at exploring students' concept development through reading and writing.

Prior Knowledge of a Topic and Reader Interest

Contemporary models of the reading process present comprehension as a complex interaction of reader knowledge, text variables, reader interest, and the quality of teaching that assists text comprehension (Schraw & Dennison, 1994). Studies indicate that a strong relationship exists between reading interest and comprehension (Guthrie & Greaney, 1991; Schraw & Dennison, 1994; Wigfield & Asher, 1984). Not surprisingly, students comprehend reading material better if it concerns a topic they like to read about (Asher, 1980; Baldwin, Peleg-Bruckner, & McClintock, 1985). For example, Belloni and Jongsma (1978) found that reluctant readers achieved significantly higher comprehension scores on stories dealing with topics of individual preference compared to topics of low interest. Asher, Hymel, and Wigfield (1978) reported similar findings. In a refinement of this first study, Asher (1980) had students respond to a 25-item picture rating scale featuring cars, sports, and other topics of potential high or low interest. Students displayed greater comprehension of passages that most closely corresponded to the picture they assigned a high interest rating.

Baldwin, Peleg-Bruckner, and McClintock (1985) determined that topic interest was not simply a reflection of prior knowledge. Their study showed that topic interest, especially among boys, makes a substantial contribution to students' comprehension even when prior knowledge of a topic is low.

Despite the obvious power of a close match between students' expressed interest and a text that matches those interests, you as the teacher also have a profound impact on interest. As a teacher, you help students establish a purpose and a particular frame of reference or schema for reading text assignments. Indeed,

Schraw and Dennison (1994) found that when students read a five-page text from various teacher-directed perspectives, they rated those reading conditions as most interesting when the texts matched their purpose for reading. The researchers argued that interest in a text may be influenced by the steps taken by the teacher to guide students' interaction with text. Because content area assignments often entail reading expository material which may depart from a student's preferred interests, you need to carefully guide students' understanding of text. Building prior knowledge and generating topic interest through purpose setting activities like anticipation-reaction guides can make a difference. In later chapters we will be introducing some systematic procedures for discovering students' reading preferences. More importantly, we will introduce techniques a content teacher can employ to insure that our students become life-long readers.

Motivation to Learn from Content Texts

When students are confronted with expository textbooks that seem to hold little intrinsic appeal, their motivation for reading and learning may sink to a low ebb. Without adequate teacher guidance and ingenuity, students in content fields such as science and social science may sluggishly go through the motions of learning, dispensing only minimal effort. Recent discussions of motivation suggest that the effort a person is willing to expend on a task is a product of (1) the degree to which the individual expects to perform successfully if they try reasonably hard, and, (2) the degree to which they value the available rewards for success (Good & Brophy, 1997). Thus, if you lecture, assign text reading, and ask students only low level factual questions that encourage memorization and forgetting, students are likely to lapse into a reluctant, sluggish mode of participation. If you want to encourage students to actively link new knowledge to their existing background knowledge, to critically evaluate ideas advanced in your class texts and discussions, and to value their growing concept knowledge, the following general principles are important (Good & Brophy, 1997).

You need to provide a supportive, well-structured classroom environment and assignments that are challenging but not frustrating. Your learning objectives should be those worth pursuing rather than busy work that merely encourages memorizing facts and copying text-based definitions. For example, if you are studying a unit on the Constitution with a focus on the Bill of Rights, you might engage students in a discussion of student rights as a prelude to their text reading.

Slicing the complexity of lengthy tasks into manageable increments that students can accomplish in a

short period of time helps reduce that feeling of helplessness and inertia associated with tasks students perceive to be beyond their capacity. Similarly, teaching students to set their own realistic learning goals may help reduce frustration. These goals may be in the form of reading a small section of a chapter or answering a specific, reasonable portion of the chapter questions. Along with reducing the scope of a task, providing immediate feedback and rewarding success through pleasurable activities, points, or simply praise will go a long way toward helping students' motivation and interest in your content area.

Finally, opportunities for active student responses to text concepts are crucial to enthusiasm for content learning. Projects, experiments, discussions, debates, role playing, and computer simulations all contribute to students' interest in learning content that could otherwise be potentially dull fare. Classroom activities that place students in cooperative learning dyads and triads with their peers, especially if they are engaged in solving problems or grappling with higher order questions, also enhance motivation. In addition, if you provide immediate feedback on how students are succeeding or experiencing difficulty, this too will help them see the value in their efforts. Finally, when students have opportunities to complete finished products, whether they be in the form of essays, reports, models, a play, artwork, or a gourmet meal, they have a vivid and tangible record of their efforts (Good & Brophy, 1997). We can all remember, possibly in some detail, those learning situations in which we produced something of intrinsic value. You need to strive for lessons that capture these principles. In subsequent chapters we will introduce specific strategies designed to involve students actively in content learning. Additionally, we will consider those students for whom content learning is especially challenging because of a persistent cycle of failure. We offer some strategies for coping with the wide-ranging individual differences typical of our content classrooms.

Characteristics of Memory

This section introduces some important concepts concerning human memory. Since a student's prior knowledge is represented in memory, it is essential that you understand how memory aids or disrupts the efficient use of prior knowledge in the comprehension process.

Cognitive psychologists typically differentiate two aspects of memory. These are short-term memory and long-term memory. In reality, these terms represent hypothetical constructs about memory rather than particular locations in the brain. The following diagram illustrates the flow of information as it is processed by our memory system.

INFORMATION → SHORT-TERM MEMORY → LONG-TERM MEMORY

Short-term memory is often called working memory because it holds information on a temporary basis until the information is either processed into long-term memory or erased to accept more incoming information (Brainerd, 1983). Short-term memory contains traces of the most recent information we are attending to at any given moment.

The single most important feature of short-term memory is its limited capacity for storing information. Miller (1956) showed that the short-term storage capacity for individual items of information was seven, plus or minus two. Your struggle to retain a new friend's phone number is a concrete example of Miller's seven, plus or minus two principle in operation. Including the area code, a phone number such as 618-296-9149 exceeds the storage capacity of short-term memory. Fortunately, there is a way to circumvent the seven, plus or minus two, limitation. Miller used the term *chunking* to describe the recoding of information into fewer, more manageable units. Using a chunking strategy, the phone number 618-296-9149 can be held in short-term memory as three, rather than ten, discrete items (i.e., [618] [296] [9149]). However, short-term memory has a second limitation that even chunking cannot overcome.

The second important feature of short-term memory is its fleeting nature. Information such as a new friend's phone number must be constantly rehearsed if it is to remain available in short-term memory for longer than a few seconds. If attention is diverted for even a moment to something else, the limited storage capacity of short-term memory will be overloaded and the phone number erased to accept the new, incoming information. Both the fleeting duration of short-term memory and its limited storage capacity have important implications for the reading process in general and content teaching in particular.

In terms of the reading process in general, if a student plods along in print at a laborious pace attempting to sound-out every unfamiliar word, short-term memory will be overburdened. The result of this word-by-word reading is that students can forget the beginning of a sentence before they get to the end. Students must learn to read text material, including unfamiliar words, in the most efficient way possible to overcome the limits of short-term memory. In a later chapter we will introduce some decoding strategies that encourage fluent reading.

In the content areas, some modes of presenting unfamiliar material may inadvertently impose excessive demands on students' short-term memories. The oral presentation of a large amount of new information in social studies or science may exceed the capacity of students' short-term memories. Problem-solving tasks in mathematics present similar problems. Word problems, which involve the temporary storage of one part of the problem while the student simultaneously processes additional information, place excessive demands on the limited storage capacity of short-term memory (Brainerd, 1983). Finally, the processing limitations of short-term memory suggest that rote memorization of content material is likely to be an ineffective study strategy.

The processing limitations of short-term memory should be kept in mind when a teacher plans or analyzes content teaching and learning tasks. Fortunately, *long-term memory,* or permanent memory, plays an important role in compensating for the limitations of short-term or working memory.

In contrast to short-term memory, long-term memory seems to have an infinite capacity for storing information. Long-term memory is the storage system for all our prior knowledge. It comprises our individually complex schema of the world, shaped by cultural experiences and beliefs. As such, long-term memory is a highly organized system. Indeed, the ease with which we can retrieve information from long-term memory is directly related to how well the information was organized at the time of initial processing from short-term memory.

One of the most powerful ways to encode information in long-term memory is through writing. Increasingly, writing is seen as a learning strategy that teachers should integrate across content areas (Bean, 1994). In Chapter 11 we offer a number of specific writing-to-learn approaches you can weave into your own teaching repertoire to enhance students' comprehension and long-term retention of concepts.

Long-term memory does have one limitation. The rate at which information can be processed into long-term memory is relatively slow (Craik & Lockhart, 1972). However, the ease with which information is processed into long-term memory depends in large measure on how meaningful the information is in terms of the student's prior knowledge. The more meaningful the information, the easier it will be processed.

The chart that follows summarizes the two major aspects of memory treated in this section. Thus, in general, content teachers should acknowledge the importance of prior knowledge and meaningful organization in long-term memory information processing in their teaching. Students will be able to comprehend new information in a content area if you take time to demonstrate how the new information builds upon and extends what they already know about the topic. And, students will be able to retrieve information from long-term memory if you model and encourage mean-

Characteristics	Short-term Memory (Working Memory)	Long-term Memory (Permanent Memory)
Capacity	Limited	Practically Unlimited
Persistence	Very Brief	Practically Unlimited
Retrieval	Immediate	Depends on Organization
Input	Very Fast	Relatively Slow

ingful organization of new information when it is first presented to the class.

Although cognitive factors play a major role in reading comprehension, linguistic factors also influence the reading process. In this section we will describe and demonstrate specific linguistic aspects of written language that interact with cognitive factors to aid or inhibit reading comprehension.

The Language of Text

Authors of stories and even challenging scientific text use predictable organization patterns or *text structures*. For example, stories usually begin with a setting and one or more characters. The reader follows the main character's attempts to solve a problem or achieve a goal. This familiar text structure makes it relatively easy for a reader to make predictions about story events (van Dijk & Kintsch, 1983; Weaver & Kintsch, 1991). Even more difficult expository text in science has an identifiable pattern of organization. For example, biology texts usually inform the reader about properties and functions of a topic such as carbohydrates or enzymes.

A text's pattern of organization is the larger ideational framework that binds together its complex system of paragraphs. This *macrostructure,* which may range from a cause-effect discussion of the Sherman Anti-Trust Act in history to an informational description of photosynthesis in science, is integral to expository text (Meyer & Rice, 1984). Similarly, the relationships that bind together individual sentences in a text into a coherent structure comprise a text's *microstructure.* Microstructure and macrostructure features of text become important as you attempt to gauge how friendly or unfriendly a text is for students. In Chapter 4 we introduce a process for evaluating a text along these dimensions.

Students who are made aware of the overall structure of a particular text can use this knowledge in comprehending, studying, and discussing key concepts. Moreover, a text that provides a discernible organizational pattern places fewer demands on the limitations of short-term memory than poorly structured text (van Dijk & Kintsch, 1983). In Chapter 9 we discuss text structure in detail and introduce comprehension strategies that capitalize on this important linguistic aspect of text.

ACTIVITY

Give yourself as much time as you need to read this selection. Jot down the steps you take to figure it out and write a one sentence summary of the author's main idea.

The six year old was brought in with polydypsia and polyuria. It was anorectic. After the work-up, it was found to have toxic neutropis, a left shift.

_____

_____

In this case, knowing that this is a veterinarian's report about a sick dog won't assuage your lack of familiarity with the vocabulary. Moreover, this is scientific writing, which prevents using the surrounding context as an alternative means of grasping the author's main idea. Here's a translation that may help, but some of the precision inherent in scientific prose is lost in the process.

> A six-year-old dog was brought into the vet. The dog had been drinking a lot of water and urinating frequently. It was not eating. After the lab tests it was found to have an increase in white blood cells caused by an infection. Immature cells are also being pumped out due to infection.

This example illustrates that fluent content area reading is an interactive process. Word and sentence level features of text and text structure patterns of organization combine to make a text friendly or unfriendly. Fortunately, teachers can provide direct instruction in both these linguistic features as an integral part of content instruction. In Part B of this text we introduce strategies designed to help students regard even challenging text as reasonably friendly.

The Language of Students

In addition to those features of texts that make them friendly or unfriendly, our earlier discussion of second language learners suggest that students' language facility plays a powerful role in comprehension. If the texts students must read are very distant from their native language, second language students may have difficulty forming the mental pictures necessary for concept learning to occur (Perez, 1982). For example, the following sentence, adapted from Laird and Jossen (1983, p. 10), illustrates the frustration a second language learner may experience in text material containing vocabulary that is largely unfamiliar.

> "Oh! Dakine mea'ai stay so ono," said Wili Wai Kula.

If readers must translate every word of a text with a dictionary or a laborious search through memory, they will have little attention left for comprehension. Moreover, integration of ideas across words and sentences becomes impossible. Contrast the above example with Laird and Jossen's (1983) original text, *Wili Wai Kula and the Three Mongooses,* a Hawaiian version of the familiar *Goldilocks and the Three Bears.*

> "Oh! The *mea'ai* smells so *ono*," said a hungry Wili Wai Kula. She tasted the rice and sausage

on the biggest plate. It was too hot. Next, she tasted the rice and sausage on the medium-sized plate. It was too cold.

In this instance, some of the vocabulary is unfamiliar. However, your prior knowledge of the original fable, combined with some vocabulary knowledge and context clues should help you comprehend "mea'ai," a Hawaiian word for meal, and "ono," which means good. Krashen and Terrell (1983) recommend that text for second language learners strike a delicate balance between familiar and unfamiliar vocabulary. Visual aids and pre-reading guides that help students see how their prior knowledge is related to concepts in the text help students use semantic cues. Otherwise, there is a real tendency for these students to read in a word-by-word fashion or to decode accurately without really comprehending what they have read. Notice that once you see a bridge between the familiar Goldilocks story and the Hawaiian version you can comprehend the selection despite not knowing all the vocabulary. In content areas, students' background knowledge is not likely to be quite this direct. But you can try to select texts that capitalize on familiar topics while adding new information to students' concept learning.

Visual representation of content area concepts helps second language learners connect the new to the known (Schifini, 1994). For example, if students are studying fish in science, the ancient Japanese art of origami (Miyawaki, 1960) will help them develop a hands-on grasp of fish anatomy through paper-cutting, painting, and labeling key parts. Moreover, this form of hands-on activity usually generates many opportunities for language interaction.

In addition, the guide material discussed in Part B of this text can go a long way toward unlocking text concepts in the target language.

The Reading-Writing Relationship

One of the best ways to help students grasp the complex language and structure of textbooks is through writing. Studies and analyses of the reading-writing connection show the high degree of similarity between these activities. For example, Tierney and Shanahan (1991) comment that reading and writing share many of the same cognitive strategies including: goal setting, knowledge mobilization, perspective-taking, review, self-correction, and self-assessment.

Writing increases students' understanding of text structure because it causes them to think like writers. Writing essays helps long-term retention of information because it requires that readers manipulate and organize ideas with greater attention to detail than simply reading text material (Tierney & Shanahan, 1991). For example, the frequently used writing activity where students are asked to form pairs with one person writing instructions on the steps needed to make a peanut butter sandwich and the other person carrying out these steps exactly as written illustrates the tightrope readers and writers walk as they try to communicate. Instructing your partner to put the peanut butter on the bread may result in the whole jar of peanut butter resting on top of a slice of bread. If you have ever struggled to interpret a friend's directions to a party at a new house, you know intimately the juggling act of the writer and reader. Too much explicit information is tedious—too little leaves the reader to make wild inferential leaps. Hence, the peanut butter sandwich that looks as if it was created by a committee and the lost traveler trying to interpret terse directions to a party. Writing helps students think about text ideas carefully and analytically (Bean, 1994).

Writing can become an important bridge to learning across various content areas including math and science (Tompkins, 1990). More importantly, reading and writing serve to open the communication lines in a classroom. Rather than hiding behind texts, students and teachers can openly confront author biases, conceptual conflict, misconceptions, and comprehension difficulties. The more students come to understand that there is an author behind every text, the more they can engage in critical reading. The author behind the text has a particular viewpoint that influences the message conveyed. When students comment in their journals and essays on the ideas portrayed by an author, they develop a personal investment in both the author's words and their own.

In Chapter 11 we consider a number of teaching strategies that will help you capitalize on the growing interest in the reading-writing relationship.

The Classroom Social Context

Finally, in addition to cognitive and linguistic factors, the social context of a classroom has its own linguistic conventions and features. *Sociolinguistics* is the study of language in a cultural context. A number of studies, stemming from the anthropological tradition of intensive participant observation, provide us with an emerging picture of teacher-student and student-student interaction that belies a simplistic view of content teaching. The goal of intensive observational study is to uncover the social patterns that influence teacher and student success in constructing meaning (Alvermann, O'Brien, & Dillon, 1990; Bloome, 1987; Green & Bloome, 1983).

Classroom interaction patterns are, at least on the surface, usually orchestrated by the teacher and based on an intuitive or conscious theory of learning. Thus, teachers instruct, question, praise, and monitor students' comprehension in observable patterns that reveal their particular view of reading comprehension. This may range from simply assigning text reading, questioning students orally and giving a test, to the more carefully guided approach we are advocating.

In Goodlad's (1984) massive observational study of classrooms across the country, he found student passivity to be the norm. Bloome (1987) speculated that cross-cultural differences between students and teachers may result in some students' unwillingness to risk a public display of their knowledge. This reticence may be misinterpreted by the teacher who might well believe a student lacks knowledge of the topic at hand.

In a study of middle school content classrooms in English, science, and health, Alvermann, O'Brien, and Dillon (1990) found a marked discrepancy between teachers' definitions of lessons that involve discussion and actual observation of these same teachers. When they were interviewed by the researchers, these teachers defined a good discussion as student-centered with the teacher serving as a facilitator or devil's advocate. How-

---

ACTIVITY

John Ogbu (1992) provides powerful anthropological insights into academic problems commonly experienced by minority children. Obgu also proposes a theory that explains why some ethnic minorities have more success in public schools than others. Read Professor Ogbu's article and write a 1-2 page essay explaining how his research and theories do or do not seem to explain patterns of minority achievement that you yourself are familiar with.

ever, when observed teaching actual content lessons these teachers relied almost exclusively on carefully controlled lecture and recitation consisting of teacher question, student response, and teacher evaluation. The demands of content coverage and classroom order won out over their intellectualized definitions of discussion when it came to actual classroom application.

In a classroom that follows our model of content teaching, an observer would expect to see various forms of pre-reading strategies in use (e.g., Anticipation Guides), small group discussion of text concepts using the guides, and post-reading Reaction Guide discussion. Yet even with this guided approach, the classroom remains a social environment with its own hidden curriculum that is shaped by social as well as academic factors (Hamilton, 1983).

For example, in an effort to go beyond such oversimplified measures of content learning as time on task, Bloome (1983) observed four junior high classes for six months. He took field notes of classroom discussions as well as audio and video recordings. He found that students often seemed to be on task when they were actually doing something else. The "something else" ranged from reading a friend's note to daydreaming while simultaneously feigning attention and accurately responding to the teacher's questions through the adroit use of cues from a friend.

Bloome (1987) finds that a typical classroom reading and discussion pattern contains the following dimensions. Students are required only to produce text reproductions that merely reiterate text content. Amidst such low level discussions, they become skilled at procedural display—looking as if they are doing the work and participating while simultaneously carrying on other, more personally interesting and rewarding activities. Thus, a teacher-dominated discussion of text concepts produces an overly passive style of student thinking and participation. Pearson and Fielding (1991) argue that the nature of student-

teacher dialogue should foster instructional conversations, not just teacher-directed recitation. In our view, a classroom content lesson coexists with the larger context of the school and the sociolinguistic context of students' lives. A content lesson competes for students attention amidst other, often more compelling, interests. It is likely to compete successfully if most students have adequate opportunities to participate.

Based on their 18-month observational study of 24 science, social studies, literature, health, and human development classes, Alvermann, Dillon, and O'Brien (1987) make a useful distinction between recitation and discussion. Recitation usually consists of a teacher-directed question and answer sequence to review, drill, or quiz lesson content. In contrast, a discussion features three distinguishing characteristics: (1) the discussants present multiple points of view and may change their perspective on a topic after hearing convincing counterarguments; (2) students must interact with each other and the teacher is largely in the background; and (3) students' verbal utterances must be longer than two or three word phrases typical of recitation.

Teacher-student interaction patterns influence students' comprehension and attitude toward the content being studied (Bloome, 1983). Collaborative, small group discussion using pre- and post-reading strategies such as Anticipation/ Reaction guides are a good alternative to teacher-centered discussion. We are not suggesting that there is anything wrong with whole group lectures and discussions. But we do believe that small, problem-solving groups can afford greater opportunities for student participation if they are focused on an important topic with clear task guidelines.

In Part B of this text we consider comprehension strategies that you may wish to adopt to enhance students' critical reading and discussion. Reflective writing can also form a basis for student-centered sharing and discussion of ideas and issues. These elements of content literacy will be elaborated in subsequent chapters.

SUMMARY

The present chapter introduced you to concepts about language, culture, and diversity. In addition, information on cognitive and linguistic dimensions of content literacy were discussed. Among the cognitive factors, we considered the influence of prior knowledge, interest, and memory on students' comprehension. Linguistic factors included cue systems in print, text structure, and the influence of classroom context.

Confirmed	Disconfirmed
_____	_____
_____	_____
_____	_____
_____	_____
_____	_____

1. Knowledge of a student's culture is not important in teaching subject matter.

2. Programs designed for second language learners help them gain subject matter comprehension.

3. Comprehending text material is a creative, constructive process.

4. Reading and writing are unrelated cognitive processes.

5. Whole class discussion discourages wide student participation.

A	B
Why my choice is confirmed.	Why my choice is not confirmed.

1. _____   _____

_____   _____

2. _____   _____

_____   _____

3. _____   _____

_____   _____

4. _____   _____

_____   _____

5. _____   _____

_____   _____

1. Visit a classroom in your content area and interview the teacher to determine how the issues in the first part of the chapter on culture and diversity are handled. Before the interview, develop a few questions to stimulate discussion that focus on sociocultural and linguistic diversity, as well as mainstreaming. Share your results with another class member in a discussion.

2. List at least one method you currently use, or plan to use, to assist second language learner's comprehension of concepts in your content area.

3. List at least three methods you currently use, or plan to use, to mobilize students' existing knowledge of topics in your particular content area. Compare your compilation with listings produced by other class members.

4. Visit a classroom in your content area. Based upon your observation notes, analyze the interaction pattern that occurs and determine the level of comprehension emphasized.

5. Access the *Rosetta Stone* program from the *Content Area Literacy* CD-ROM (see Appendix B for Quick Start directions) and select Lesson One from a language with which you have had no prior experience–perhaps Vietnamese. Practice the lesson until you have reached a 90% accuracy level. Be prepared to discuss in class your observations about this method of language learning and how it compares with other second language methods you've experienced (e.g., textbook drills and tape driven language labs.)

GROUP PROJECTS

- Discuss the roles of prior knowledge and topic interest in reading comprehension.

- Draw a category system, or schema, for musical instruments. Then summarize the relationships represented in your drawing.

- Define and contrast the various approaches to English as a second language instruction in the content areas.

EVALUATING AND INTRODUCING TEXTBOOKS

Agree   Disagree

_____   _____   1. Censorship is both bad and unnecessary.

_____   _____   2. Government regulations require that 10th grade books be written on a 10th grade reading level.

_____   _____   3. It is safe to assume that high school students know how to use a textbook index.

_____   _____   4. The content of subject area textbooks is politically influenced.

_____   _____   5. The biblical version of creation should be included in biology textbooks that cover evolution.

RATIONALE

What is a textbook? Broadly speaking, a textbook could be any book which is used in formal study. This might include, for example, novels, reference books, or other works of non-fiction which may or may not have been designed exclusively for schools. More commonly, textbooks refer to books written specifically for school use and designed to summarize a body of knowledge or to present the fundamental principles of a discipline. The American history tomes, literature anthologies, and other textbooks to which you have grown accustomed vary tremendously in their quality. Some offer excellent presentations while others are too difficult for their intended audiences or suffer from poor organization. In addition, as we will demonstrate, the personal values of authors and the agendas of special interest groups cause textbooks which cover the same content to differ in terms of how they represent the truth.

Estimates of the amount of classroom time students spend reading or doing exercises from textbooks range from 55% to 95% (Zahorik, 1991). From the primary grades through college, textbooks are a pervasive element of education in the United States. Assuming that the average student spends five hours per school day using textbooks, the number of hours spent with textbooks exceeds 10,000 by the end of high school (5×180

× 12). Clearly, how we select those books and what we ask students to do with them will have an enormous impact on how well students learn, what they learn, what they believe, and how well they think.

In this chapter we will examine issues related to the selection and appropriate use of textbooks, first from social and political perspectives and then from an instructional viewpoint. Finally, we will demonstrate a strategy for introducing students to an unfamiliar text.

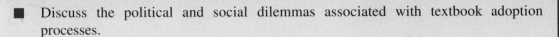

LEARNING OBJECTIVES

■ Discuss the political and social dilemmas associated with textbook adoption processes.

■ State which quantitative and qualitative factors make a text more or less easy to understand.

■ Employ a checklist of quantitative and qualitative factors to evaluate a textbook for use in your classroom.

■ Conduct a textbook preview to acquaint students with the essential learning aids in a text.

GRAPHIC ORGANIZER

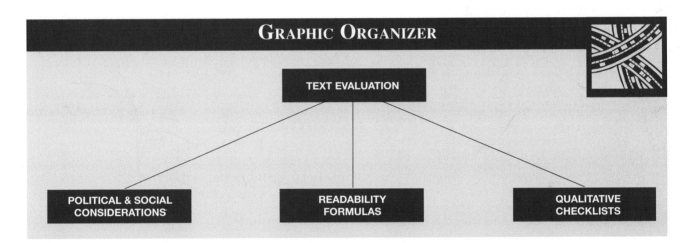

■ Political Characteristics of Textbooks

We customarily associate the word politics with government. However, politics has the broader meaning of any social or cultural arrangement in which people make decisions that have consequences for other people. There are political dimensions to life as diverse as marriage, bridge clubs, and team sports. Public education is no exception.

School systems wrestle with hundreds of political matters every day, and most of them are outside the interest or beyond the control of most classroom teachers. However, there is one political issue which should be of critical concern to every subject area specialist: the selection and interpretation of textbooks. Ultimately, content area teachers must be responsible for the accuracy, truth, and representativeness of the textbooks they use. Which stories and essays should be included

in literature anthologies, for instance? Because it is impossible to include everything in an anthology, something must be excluded. What stays, what goes, and who makes the decision? Should the biblical version of creation be included in biology texts along with theories that espouse evolution? How explicit should health texts be on subjects of human sexuality, AIDS, and abortion? How these issues are resolved fluctuates over time. Textbooks are not almanac-like tomes of facts. Instead, they are books written and published by human beings whose cultural biases can slant, bend, or bury someone else's version of the truth. Consider the following quote from a World War I vintage geography textbook used by one of the author's grandmothers when she was a high school student (Redway & Hinman, 1916):

> The home of the black or "Negro" race is central and southern Africa and some of the Australian islands. The peoples of this race have

coarse woolly or kinky hair, protruding lips, and dark brown or black skin. The black race includes some of the most ignorant people in the world. . . . Most of the yellow race and part of the Malay race have reached some degree of civilization. But some people learn more rapidly than others, and the Caucasian race includes the most enlightened people in the world. (p. 29)

Today we would consider such a racist position unthinkable in a textbook; but such viewpoints were common—even standard—in a country which still did not permit women to vote [The 19th Amendment to the Constitution was ratified in 1920]. Our purpose here is not to condemn the men who wrote your great-grandparents' school books, but rather to make the following point: What we now observe to be obvious and fatal flaws in a 80-year-old textbook were probably accepted as absolute truths by the children who read the book then. Can we afford to place any more faith in the accuracy and moral character of textbooks with a 1998 publication date?

Over the past three decades historical accomplishments of African Americans and other minorities have begun to replace bigotry and neglect in classroom texts, yet many people are not satisfied with the rate of progress. Consider the newspaper article on the left.

When New York finishes rewriting its history book, will history have changed? Will the new version be more consistent with historical reality? The fact that the committee making the recommendation consists of experts in classroom teaching rather than historians suggests that the motivation for rewriting the history books might be political expediency rather than historical accuracy.

Historical truth is slippery. It is possible, for example, to portray American westward expansion in a variety of ways. One account would describe fanatical, materialistic malcontents who out of greed organized a bloody rebellion against lawfully constituted authority and then murdered or expelled those who remained loyal to the legitimate regime. It would be the tale of a people who institutionalized genocide against American Indians and slavery of African peoples by invoking scriptural revelations of their god. *Bury My Heart at Wounded Knee* by Dee Brown is a graphic description of the treatment of American Indians. If you ever get a chance to read the book, it will not be difficult for you to view European Americans as the bad guys.

In the more traditional account of westward expansion, the nation's past is presented as a triumphant celebration of freedom, social progress, human rights, and individual fulfillment. Starting with the flight of a few enterprising and courageous souls from religious persecution, and continuing with a just and glorious revolution against the oppression of a tyrannical monarch, this would be the tale of virtue, both civic and cultural. This version of American history would portray a happy, freedom-loving people, the product of rugged individualism and hard work. It would be the story of manifest destiny with a people resolved to reclaim the wilderness, to civilize the savages, and to spread the principles of democracy across the virgin continent. This view of American history was epitomized in the 1963 movie *How the West Was Won*.

A number of authorities (e.g., Anyon, 1979; Postman, 1970) have suggested that although both versions are extreme, both versions are also true to some degree. Yet one is the approved version that appears in US history textbooks (e.g., Fitzgerald, 1977). The latter, familiar version is taught almost universally in American schools as the truth while the former version seldom finds its way into American history books.

---

* Reprinted with permission of Associated Press.

Censorship

In early Rome there were magistrates known as censors. Their job was to take an accounting of the people and also to look after public morals. From the magistrates' former duty we have acquired the word *census*. From their latter commission we have inherited censor and *censorship*. A censor today is someone who indirectly supervises morality by regulating the films, books, music, or other information to which people may have access. The people who assign ratings of G, PG, PG-13, R, and X to movies are censors. Parents are censors when they will not let their children watch Beavis and Butthead because they believe the show is too crude or too violent. A librarian who decides that a book should not be in the school library is a censor. When publishers decide not to put a story into a literature anthology, they are censors—if they exclude the story because they are afraid of reprisals from the National Rifle Association, the American Civil Liberties Union, animal rights activists, or a fundamentalist Christian organization in California.

American schools have been a focal point in censorship battles, especially over the last 20 years. Across the country there have been periodic textbook burnings, book bannings, and school boycotts (Donelson, 1990). In 1982 *The Adventures of Huckleberry Finn* was banned from classrooms in Mark Twain Junior High School in Fairfax County, Virginia, because the book was "racist" and "anti-American" (*The Miami Herald,* April 17, 1982). In some elementary schools the story of Robin Hood is banned because it teaches children to steal.

Censorship issues involving children and schools are not the same as adult censorship issues. With adults the issue usually is constitutional:

> Congress shall make no law respecting an establishment of religion, or prohibiting the free exercise thereof; or abridging the freedom of speech, or of the press; or the right of the people to assemble, and to petition the Government for a redress of grievances.
>
> *First Amendment to the Constitution*

Presumably, the First Amendment gives adults the right to read whatever they want. However, censorship issues with students are more complex because students, especially young children, are assumed not to have the ability to make sound choices. Someone else makes decisions for them: what movies they may watch, what establishments they may enter, what books they may read, what content they will find in their subject area textbooks. We may feel outraged that books by Judy Blume have been banned from a junior high library— and she has been frequently banned—but few of us would want the same library to carry *Hustler* and *Playgirl* magazines. Either restriction is censorship. When accused of censorship, school officials invariably respond that it is not a matter of censorship but rather a matter of selecting appropriate reading materials for children. They have a point. Censorship in this sense is a fact of life in public education. Books will be chosen for children by someone. The real question revolves around who the someone is that makes the decisions: teachers, administrators, church groups, parents, publishers, or special interest groups in another state (Donelson, 1975)?

ACTIVITY

Directions: Read the Donelson (1975) article on censorship on your CD-ROM. Do you think the issues Donelson discusses are the same as those of today or are they different? Why? Discuss your thoughts with a small group the next time you meet in class.

Textbook Censorship

One of the mightiest—and most hidden—powers in our society rests with those who are in positions to control the meanings of words and the distribution of concepts. Nowhere else in our culture is this power less obvious to the public or more critical to our collective future than in the development of school textbooks.

Textbooks are typically developed as a collaboration between teachers/college professors and an editorial staff within a publishing house such as Scott, Foresman or Allyn and Bacon. As a rule, the lower the grade level the more the final product is the work of professional editors. In contrast, the content of high school and college texts is more likely to reflect the thinking and writing of teachers/professors.

Publishers are businesses that sell books for money. Their primary responsibility is to shareholders and employees and not to the abstractions of accuracy and truth. Compared with the profit motive, all other concerns are secondary. In this respect the publishing business is the same as the oil industry, retail furniture stores, and the hotdog stand at the beach. To make a profit the publishers must meet a market demand. If schools will buy more history books if the covers are made more attractive, the publisher will make more attractive covers. If schools will buy more history books if they are made to contain fewer references to Ulysses S. Grant and more references to Robert E. Lee, then you can bet that Grant will wane as Lee rises.

This is not intended to be an indictment of textbook publishers. Most of them are sincere in their efforts to publish quality books for children, but they are under tremendous pressure from schools and special interest groups to censor social science, literature, and physical science textbooks. For example, if you peruse a secondary literature anthology you will probably find that the anthology has been censored so that some or all of the following are absent from every selection:

- potentially offensive words such as *hell* or *crap*
- references to any drugs—even aspirin
- references to any junk foods like potato chips
- any references—even indirect—to the theory of evolution
- pejorative comments about any minority groups
- any sexist language
- any references to human sexuality
- any discussions of religion
- any stories in which children question the values or moral reasoning of their parents

In looking at the list above, you probably find that some of the censored material would not be objectionable to you. Why do all of these aspects of literature have to be removed? The answer is that the most efficient way for publishers to eliminate potential objections from various censors is to self-censor anything that anyone might find offensive. A fundamental principle of censorship is that censors are sensitive to what is in the text that shouldn't be there. They are seldom worried about what isn't there that should be. Therefore, a special interest group that wants to suppress references to junk foods will not notice that essays about dangerous drugs, information about human sexuality, and pertinent dramas about teenage value systems have bit the dust along with the Twinkies. The result is a carefully homogenized and bland anthology that no longer reflects the adolescent literature it is supposed to represent.

You might imagine that publishers could avoid over-censoring by developing multiple textbooks to suit the needs of individual schools that are more or less progressive, located in different geographic areas, or have different ethnic representations. The problem with this solution is that books are so expensive to develop that the costs of multiple versions is prohibitive. The approximate cost of developing a new literature series, for example, is several million dollars. Another cause of publisher over-censoring is state textbook adoption policies.

Textbook Adoption Policies

When a 10th grade biology textbook is adopted by a school system, the adoption means that high schools within the school system are permitted to order the book for use in grade 10 biology classes. If the textbook has not been adopted, the book cannot be ordered. There are several reasons for having book adoptions. One reason for adoptions is that publishers give significant discounts when textbooks are purchased in large quantities. It is less expensive to buy 10,000 copies from one publisher than to buy 1,000 copies from 10 different publishers. A second reason for system-wide adoptions is that it provides for quality control. A school system will usually have a textbook adoption committee composed of content area specialists, administrators, and in some cases community leaders or parents. Their task is to evaluate textbooks on the market and choose the one which is most suitable for their school system given the variables of price, text difficulty, methodological approach, and general philosophy. In principle, adoptions can take place at the level of the individual teacher, school, school system, or at the level of the state.

There are now 15 states that have state textbook adoption programs, and they include three of the most populous states in the country: California, Florida, and Texas. States have adoptions for the same reasons that school systems do: control of costs and curriculum quality. Procedures vary from state to state and subject area to subject area. Typically, a state will cycle through the various subject areas every five to seven years. Publishers submit textbooks to the appropriate committee, which receives recommendations from individual school systems and special interest groups. The number of books adopted at one time in one subject area varies from 10% to 80% depending upon circumstances. When they buy new textbooks, public schools must then choose from among those on the state adopted list. Once a textbook has been adopted, the tractor trailers roll to book depositories throughout the adoption state. The book depositories are big warehouses that store state adopted books for shipment to nearby schools.

California submits its criteria to publishers years in advance of an adoption decision to let publishers know what the state expects in the way of format and content.

If the state of California says it does not want a literature anthology to contain references to junk food, a publisher can tell its editors and authors to censor any and all references to cheeseburgers and fries or risk having its literature series fail the adoption. Failing to make an adoption in California, for instance, means that the publisher cannot sell the textbook or series to public schools in that state until the next cycle of textbook adoptions.

It is not hard to understand why publishers sweat blood over textbook adoptions. The adoption of a textbook in California or Texas may provide enough revenue to pay for the entire cost of developing the book. This is why publishers will cave in to the demands of state adoption committees, many of which are heavily influenced by special interest groups.

For the last 15 years textbook adoption committees, especially in California and Texas, have been strongly influenced by special interest groups such as Educational Research Analysts in Longview, Texas, and Citizens for Excellence in Education. CEE, a California-based, conservative religious organization with 70,000 members, has been successful in forcing five school districts in California to remove textbooks which CEE claims promote satanism and undermine parental authority (Harrington-Lueker, 1991).

Over the years, special interest groups have caused history textbooks, literature anthologies, science books, and even dictionaries to be modified, removed from classrooms, or stricken from the lists of state approved books. Publishers have become so sensitive to the issues involved that they increasingly censor their own work to avoid the prospect of failing an adoption.

The problem is not the special interest groups themselves. Peaceful political activism is a constitutional right that is guaranteed to all individuals and organizations, including those concerned with the format and content of textbooks and parent empowerment in the education process. The real problem is that the states with the highest levels of coordinated censorship become the common denominator for textbooks across the country. In other words, students in states such as Pennsylvania and Iowa, which do not have state level adoptions, end up using the same textbooks that have been heavily censored to suit the religious, social, or political groups in other states. The truth is that a few people in California exercise considerable control over what students in Pennsylvania are permitted to read.

As you can see, textbooks are not neutral sources of information. They are, in fact, highly politicized. The textbooks you hand to students on the first day of class have been authored by people who have agreed that the publisher is the final authority for what gets written. The textbook has probably been massaged and censored to meet a market demand and to suit the various lobbies that might threaten sales. You cannot afford to assume that a textbook developed for public school consumption is truly representative of any body of knowledge, free of intentional bias, or even factually accurate. Just knowing this makes you a political agent in the instructional process, and the decisions you make about how to use textbooks constitute a political stance of great significance. This is what we suggest:

- Supplement textbooks with trade literature and primary sources of information such as newspapers, professional magazines, unabridged novels, nonfiction single author books, or oral histories. (See Chapter 7 for additional information.)
- Teach your students how—and then encourage them—to use the library. Do not allow the textbook to become the entire curriculum.
- Encourage students to read their textbooks critically. The textbook is not always correct, and there must be room for competing points of view.

Readability

Politics aside, there are a number of other instructional issues related to the selection and appropriate use of textbooks. One of the most important of these involves determining the difficulty level of books.

For the last 60 years educators have had an interest in predicting the approximate difficulty of instructional materials. This is commonly referred to as *readability,* a measure of the extent to which a reader finds a given text comprehensible. Ideally, the level of text material can be matched to the appropriate reading level of students. In reality, though, the selection of a core text has been largely based on teacher intuition. Usually, content area teachers choose text materials based primarily on an analysis of the text content. While the content of a core text is certainly important and should reflect a teacher's instructional objectives, there are additional features of the text that merit careful consideration.

The evaluation of printed material can be a highly refined and systematic process given our current understanding of those features that make textbooks understandable and useful as learning tools. Indeed, some striking features of textbooks do increase or diminish the likelihood of student understanding. Therefore, in order to match the difficulty level of the text to the reading level of students, both quantitative and qualitative factors of text material must be evaluated. *Quantitative factors* include such language variables as word and sentence length. These factors can be counted and measured with a formula to estimate the grade level designation of text difficulty. *Qualitative factors* are more difficult to determine and include such elements as prior knowledge of the reader, organization of the text, student interest, and a myriad of other important considerations.

Quantitative Factors in Readability Measurement

There are a number of different approaches designed to help the content area teacher estimate the difficulty level of text material. Each approach has inherent advantages and limitations. For example, a teacher can simply guess the grade level of a text. Unfortunately, this approach, while attractive in its speed and simplicity, has not proven to be very reliable. In a study of 180 secondary teachers' ability to rank order the difficulty level of text selections representing five content areas, Palmatier and Strader (1977) found that teachers were generally unsuccessful at this task.

A second, more attractive approach to a reliable estimate of text difficulty involves the administration of one or two informal tests based on a portion of the text. These procedures will be described in detail in Chapter 5. In this section we will explore a third approach to predicting the difficulty of text material, the use of readability formulas.

Readability formulas are mathematically derived indices of text difficulty based on an analysis of language variables. Over 30 different readability formulas and graphs have been developed, including specialized formulas for appraising foreign language texts (Klare, 1984). While none of the formulas are absolute measures, they all share some common features that are useful in obtaining a rough estimate of a textbook's readability.

The two most common language variables accounted for in the majority of readability formulas are word and sentence length, and sentence length is thought to be the more reliable of the two (Klare, 1984). In addition to these two variables of word and sentence length, there are extensive compilations of commonly occurring words which can be used to rate the relative difficulty of a text. Words in the text that are not represented on the master list increase the difficulty rating of the text being considered. Formulas based on extensive word lists lend themselves to com-

puter application. Indeed, they can be quite frustrating to compute using manual methods. We will explore a quick classroom method that retains the reliability of more elaborate computerized formulas. (For those interested in a closely related microcomputer formula, see Kretschmer, 1984.)

The Raygor Readability Estimate

The *Raygor Readability Estimate* (Raygor, 1977) is both simple to use and reliable because it eliminates a common source of error found in many readability formulas. While counting sentences in a text sample presents little difficulty, formulas that combine this measure with a syllable count (e.g., the Fry Readability Graph) introduce a moderate potential for error. Two or more evaluators are likely to arrive at divergent answers for the number of syllables in the same text sample. The individual dialects of evaluators and the inherent difficulty in defining exactly what a syllable is, both contribute to unreliable syllable counts among evaluators. A good alternative to a syllable count is determination of the proportion of words with six or more letters in a 100-word text sample. In a study comparing the Fry and Raygor formulas, Baldwin and Kaufman (1979) found that teachers were able to complete text evaluations with greater ease and rapidity using the Raygor Readability Estimate. In addition, the Raygor formula retained the high reliability attributed to the Fry Graph.

Following are the directions and the accompanying graph for the Raygor Readability Estimate. The activity that follows will give you some initial, guided experience with this formula.

1. Count out three 100-word passages at the beginning, middle, and end of a textbook selection. Count proper nouns but not numbers.
2. Count the number of sentences in each 100-word passage, estimating to the nearest tenth for partial sentences.
3. Count the number of words with six or more letters.
4. Average the sentence length and word length measures over the three samples and plot the average on the graph. The grade level nearest the spot marked is the best estimate of the difficulty of the selection.

Keep in mind that passage difficulty will fluctuate within the same text. Therefore, the more 100-word samples you evaluate the more likely you are to arrive at a valid grade level designation.

Directions: In order to gain practice using the Raygor Readability Estimate, use one of the following approaches on "Smoking and Smokeless Tobacco" on the CD-ROM. Keep in mind that this text is intended for a high school health class.

Approach A: Follow the directions for the Raygor using only a single 100-word passage you select from "Smoking and Smokeless Tobacco."

Approach B: Get together with two other class members. Each group member should select a different 100-word passage to evaluate from "Smoking and Smokeless Tobacco." Remember to average the three estimates before plotting them on the graph.

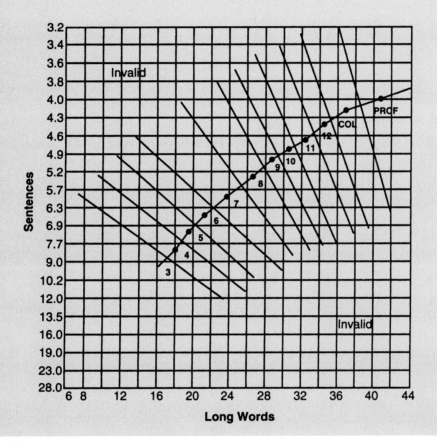

Using the Raygor Readability Estimate will provide readability estimates that are accurate within a range of plus or minus one year. In this way you will have a realistic idea of the difficulty level of the text and can begin to judge how effective it may be with your students.

Qualitative Factors in Text Evaluation

While readability formulas are useful as one component in the analysis of text material for adoption, they do have some inherent limitations that need to be mentioned. Readability formulas provide an estimate of the linguistic features of print that may influence text difficulty. These surface features typically include the average number of polysyllabic words and the average number of sentences taken from three sample passages in a text. Unfortunately, such measures are not applicable to poetry or the symbolic discourse of such disciplines as mathematics and chemistry. Thus, a number of additional factors need to be considered in a comprehensive evaluation of a text.

In a comprehensive discussion of readability, Klare (1984) discussed many of the variables that need to be considered in an analysis of text material. The quality of the writing style needs to be given careful consideration. For example, scrambling the word order of a selection would not materially alter the readability rating. Indeed, the scrambled passage would receive the same rating as a passage with acceptable syntax. Therefore, readability formulas are universally insensitive to writing style.

Some readability formulas imply that short sentences are easier to understand than longer sentences. This is certainly not the case since grammatical structures can aid or disrupt important semantic relations. Pearson (1974–1975) found that grammatical complexity aided middle-grade students' comprehension of sentence level information. In the illustration below, example one would be easier to understand than example two, yet readability formulas that use sentence length as an index of difficulty would rate the second example as the less difficult structure.

1. Marvin slept late because he was lazy.
2. Marvin slept late. He was lazy.

Sentence one is easier to comprehend because the causal relation in the sentence is made explicit by the author's use of the word "because." Conversely, example two disrupts the causal relation, requiring the reader to employ inference in order to establish the implied connection between the two events.

The criticism of short sentences may also be applied to short words. For instance, in the sentence, "The dog the cat bit died," not only is the sentence short but also the words are short. Yet, the sentence will provide some difficulty for students because of the imbedded idea and the unusual grammatical structure. Therefore, the length of words is not necessarily an indicator of easier understanding.

Other text-centered factors, in addition to those already mentioned, also deserve careful consideration in the text evaluation process. The abstract concepts and technical vocabulary an author uses are often complex, particularly in content areas such as science. The explanations of complex concepts, such as the process of photosynthesis, may require longer sentences in order to preserve important meaning relationships. Furthermore, since concept load and technical vocabulary are closely related in the content areas, reducing the use of technical terms would dilute important concepts essential to a discipline. One indication of conceptual difficulty in a text is the degree to which technical terms can be translated to more commonly occurring synonyms. For example, the word "compression" is easily substituted using the more familiar term "squeezed." In contrast, a highly specific technical term like "photosynthesis" will undoubtedly require a good deal of teacher explanation if students are to cope with this concept in their reading.

Although readability formulas have been used to rewrite text material, the practice of mechanically reducing sentence and word length in a selection is not recommended. While the rewritten version may be easier to read on a surface level than the original, important meaning relationships may be disrupted, making the rewritten version more difficult to comprehend. Readability formulas make no distinction between conceptually important information and trivial ideas. Nor do readability formulas differentiate between coherent writing that flows logically from one idea to the next and incoherent, disorganized prose.

Davison and Kantor (1982) compared high school passages that were rewritten to lessen the vocabulary load with the original, presumably more difficult text passages. They found the rewritten versions often disrupted explicit connections among ideas in the original sentences. At the sentence level, a modest amount of incoherence rarely presents much difficulty. However, if this incoherence extends across sentences, the text may present comprehension problems. For example, consider the following brief text.

Reggie wanted to sleep late but John woke him up early for their trip to the north shore. Just as they were ready to leave, Reggie's girl friend June arrived. She wanted to go shopping. THEY took the Toyota.

Now answer the following questions:

1. Who went shopping?
2. Who took the Toyota?

Pronouns are notorious for the potential comprehension problems they can cause when antecedents are unclear. However, readability formulas are not intended to measure these more subtle features of a text.

On the other hand, readability formulas do provide an estimate of vocabulary difficulty. Vocabulary difficulty undeniably influences students' comprehension, even when the writing is coherent (Freebody & Anderson, 1983). Consider the following passage:

Nadine perused the grocery shelves, carefully scrutinizing each jar of peanut butter as if they were rare, prehistoric bones. She systematically ignored the organic products in favor of the more familiar brands. Her ARACHIBUTYROPHOBIA had been getting worse lately. She finally chose a jar of creamy style peanut butter, knowing it would never be opened once she got it home.

If the main idea of this passage is at all obscure it is because of the technical, polysyllabic word arachibutyrophobia. This word may look like it should be fear of spiders, but it actually means "fear of getting peanut butter stuck on the roof of the mouth"! Notice that a single, precise term like arachibutyrophobia is extremely economical for a writer, in this case encompassing 12 short words.

Readers often rely on an author's organizational structure in their attempts to recall important information (Pearson & Fielding, 1991). Moreover, some organizational patterns such as comparison-contrast seem more conducive to long-term recall than less cohesive patterns such as simple listing. Readability formulas are not sophisticated enough to account for the influence of these higher level features of text on students' comprehension. For these reasons, readability formulas must be used in combination with other qualitative considerations in order to develop a comprehensive approach to the evaluation of instructional materials.

Readability formulas like the Raygor can only hint at potential problems in text. As you examine texts in your content area, consider how well the author weaves ideas together within and across sentence and paragraph boundaries. Also examine technical vocabulary that may present potential problems.

Contemporary texts supply an abundance of student aids designed to enhance comprehension. These include visual aids such as photographs, line drawings, graphs, tables, and diagrams. Other aids might include pre- and post-questions or questions interspersed within a chapter. Some authors also use *metadiscourse* (Singer, 1992), or text intrusions in which the author talks directly to the reader about the information in the text, to aid students in comprehending. In addition, a glossary can be valuable in helping students cope with difficult technical vocabulary. Some contemporary texts also include supplemental films, filmstrips, and cassette tapes.

All of these devices can be valuable aids to students' understanding; however, none are substitutes for carefully guided instruction. Indeed, the very nature of content learning and content texts implies knowledge to be acquired in conjunction with a course of study. Thus, teacher-centered factors are likely to influence students' comprehension more than all the text-centered factors combined. Content texts are simply not designed to be read and comprehended in isolation, independent of a carefully guided course of instruction. The degree to which a teacher provides a bridge between what the students currently know about a topic and new conceptual information is undoubtedly the essential ingredient in the teaching and learning process. The amount of instructional guidance you provide before, during, and after reading text assignments will significantly affect students' comprehension of even the least challenging text. For example, Bean, Singer, Cowen, and Searles (1987) have shown that teacher-provided metadiscourse enhanced secondary students' ability to learn basic biology concepts. In the chapters that follow, a number of teaching strategies will be introduced to help you improve students' understanding of text concepts.

Finally, student-centered factors also play a prominent role in content area learning. Two important student-centered factors are the prospective readers' prior knowledge and interest in a course topic. Students generally have a preconceived notion about particular courses and books. Therefore, it is a good practice to have students representing various levels of subject interest and reading achievement directly involved in the text evaluation process. Their opinions and recommendations often provide an alternative perspective which you might find difficult to achieve since your prior knowledge and interest is extensive.

 ## Text Evaluation Guidelines and Checklists

In general, students profit from text that adheres to classical principles of good writing. They can best comprehend authors who use frequent examples and graphic aids while avoiding unnecessary jargon. The following procedure for evaluating text material is designed to combine a quantitative measure of readability with additional qualitative factors, including student-centered information.

A number of different guidelines and related checklists for evaluating text material have been advanced (e.g., Leonard & Penick, 1993; Singer, 1992). While all of these guidelines and checklists are intuitively derived and informal in nature, they comprise the best currently available approach to text evaluation. The 19-item checklist that follows has been adapted from these sources, with some additional factors that are essential to text comprehension.

This text evaluation checklist and decision guide are based on the typical layout of most non-fiction text material. Hence, you may need to adjust the criteria somewhat if you are evaluating fictional material presented in literary anthology or workbook format. The checklist should not be interpreted as a right device for categorically accepting or rejecting text material. Rather, the more ways the textbook meets the given criteria, the better and more useful the book will be for your students. Additionally, the criteria are broad enough to allow for the exclusion of some items that are simply not present in a particular text. For example, item number eight would not be included in an evaluation of the text you are reading right now since pictures are not needed to understand the content. Simply code such items as "not-applicable" (N/A) and continue on. The activity on page 53 is designed to give you some practice in using the text evaluation checklist on the present text.

Text Evaluation Checklist

Directions: Enter the intended grade level of the text. Compute an estimate of text readability using the Raygor Readability Estimate. Complete the 19-item checklist to determine the acceptability of the text for your students.

Title of textbook _____

Author(s) _____

Publisher _____

Copyright date _____

Cost _____

Evaluated by _____

A. Readability

—— 1. Intended grade level of text: _____ . Readability estimate: _____ . Is the computed reading level realistic for the students who will be using the text?

B. Format

—— 2. The book is recently copyrighted and the contents genuinely up-to-date.

—— 3. The text is suitable for achieving the stated course objectives.

—— 4. The text contains a table of contents, an index, and a glossary.

—— 5. The table of contents indicates a logical development of the subject matter.

—— 6. When the text refers to a graph, table, or diagram, that aid is on the same page as the textual reference.

—— 7. Captions under graphs, tables, and diagrams are clearly written.

—— 8. Pictures are in color and are contemporary, not dated by dress unless author's intention is to portray a certain period.

—— 9. Various ethnic groups and male and female characters are depicted authentically in the text.

—— 10. The text suggests out-of-class readings and projects to stimulate additional student interest.

C. Organization

—— 11. The main idea(s) or purpose(s) for reading a chapter are stated at the beginning.

—— 12. Difficult new vocabulary are highlighted, italicized, or underlined.

—— 13. Context clues and synonyms for difficult vocabulary are used in the text.

—— 14. The writing is coherent in that ideas are clearly developed and related to each other, within and across sentence and paragraph boundaries.

—— 15. New concepts are introduced by relating them to previously learned concepts so that the volume of new information doesn't frustrate students.

—— 16. The text refers to practical, real-life situations and multicultural contexts students can relate to and have an interest in.

—— 17. The text includes references to, and quotations from, other sources and authorities to support its statements.

—— 18. The authors include a summary at the end of each chapter.

—— 19. When there are questions and activities at the end of a chapter, they elicit different levels of thinking ranging from text-explicit to experience-based, problem-solving tasks.

Decision _____ **Appropriate** _____ **Marginally Appropriate** _____ **Unacceptable**

Directions: Using the Text Evaluation Checklist, rate the textbook materials from *Personal Fitness: Looking Good, Feeling Good,* and its accompanying chapter, *Stress,* on the CD-ROM as to its acceptability for a high school level classroom.

 ## Introducing the Text

It is unlikely that any single content area text will be the most appropriate for all students in a course. The wide range in students' prior knowledge and subject interests practically insures that your text will be frustrating for some students and too easy for others. Assuming that your particular content area text survives the evaluation checklist and your own informed observations, there is something you can do to help students perceive the text as a familiar learning aid rather than as a threatening obstacle. You can conduct a *preview* of the text to acquaint students with the text they will be using. This simple procedure should be introduced early in the term. It will go a long way toward making students feel they can use the text effectively. Undoubtedly, many of us have had the experience of discovering by sheer chance, often half-way through the term, that our text contained a glossary of difficult vocabulary. The preview is designed to guide students to this and other text aids early in the term.

Conducting a Preview of the Text

The following activity should be conducted as a group task. The teacher reads each item on the preview and indicates its location. The guide will help you conduct a preview of the text in your content area.

Previewing Your Text

Name of subject _____

Title of textbook _____

_____

_____

Author(s) _____

Author(s) qualifications (e.g., job experience, university degrees) _____

_____

Copyright date _____

Has the book been revised (brought up to date)? _____

_____

1. *Prefaces, Forewords,* and *Introductions* contain essentially the same information. These lead-in comments give the author(s) a chance to talk about why the book was written and how it is organized. Often, a suggestion about how to read the book is provided.

   Read the *Preface (Foreword* or *Introduction).* In the space below, use your own words to explain what the *Preface* told you about your text.

   _____

   _____

   _____

   _____

2. The *Table of Contents* provides an early road map of the whole text. It gives a good indication of the learning aids which are provided in the text. Answer the following questions in your own words by referring to the *Table of Contents.*

   (1) Does the organization of topics in the book appear to be logical and easy to follow?

   _____

   _____

   (2) How many total pages are there in your text?

   _____

   (3) How complete do you think the treatment of the subject is in your book (i.e., very complete or only deals with a few aspects of the subject)?

   _____

   _____

   (4) Using the *Table of Contents,* see if your text contains each of the following learning aids. Answer *yes* if you find it, *no* if you don't.

   Glossary _____   Appendix _____   Bibliography _____   Index _____

3. The *Glossary* gives definitions of difficult technical terms used in the text. It is a valuable aid to understanding the vocabulary of a difficult subject. If your text has a *Glossary,* locate at least one difficult word supplied by your teacher and write the definition here.

_____

_____

_____

_____

4. The *Appendix* provides additional information about a topic. An *Appendix* is located in the back of the book and contains information that supports and expands a chapter topic. If your text has an *Appendix* (or *Appendices*), write a list of some of the items you find there.

_____

_____

_____

_____

_____

5. A *Bibliography* gives specific information about authors and books that were consulted during the writing of the text. Some of these books may be recommended as additional reading. The *Bibliography* is usually located at the end of the book (see the *Table of Contents* for its exact location), but it may follow each chapter. Locate the *Bibliography* in your text and write down three books you might want to read in addition to your text.

_____

_____

_____

_____

_____

_____

_____

6. The *Index* provides the fastest means for locating topic information referred to in the text. Locate the *Index* in your book. Study the *Index* and list two or three kinds of information you see there.

_____

_____

_____

7. Many other textual aids, in addition to the *Preface, Table of Contents, Glossary, Appendix, Bibliography,* and *Index,* are included in most texts. See if you can locate each of the following text aids (write *yes* if it's there; *no* if it's not) and indicate in writing how each of these aids might help you understand the subject.

   (1) Questions at the beginning of the chapters

_____

_____

(2) Objectives at the beginning of the chapters

_____

_____

(3) Pictures

_____

_____

(4) Illustrations or diagrams

_____

_____

(5) Graphs

_____

_____

(6) Maps

_____

_____

(7) Words in italics, bold-faced words, large guide words

_____

(8) Pronunciation guide [e.g., paradigm (para dime)]

_____

(9) Footnotes

_____

(10) Headings

_____

(11) Marginal notes

_____

(12) Questions at the ends of chapters

_____

(13) Summaries at the ends of chapters

_____

(14) Practice exercises

_____

(15) Other

_____

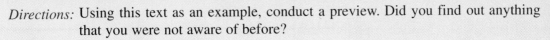

ACTIVITY

Directions: Using this text as an example, conduct a preview. Did you find out anything that you were not aware of before?

In some cases, a teacher may feel it necessary to determine the extent of the students' knowledge about basic textbook elements before conducting a preview.

The following exercise can also reinforce students' understanding of textbook learning aids. It can be used as a model to develop a similar activity in your own content area.

Directions: In column B you will find a brief description of the information contained in a particular textbook learning aid (listed in column A). See if you can match each textbook aid (column A) with its description (column B). Place the letter of the description on the line in front of the textbook aid to which it refers.

A.

1. Index
2. Table of Contents
3. Bibliography
4. Appendix
5. Preface
6. Copyright Date
7. Glossary

B.

A. Author discusses why the book was written and how to read it.
B. The easiest place to locate topic information quickly.
C. Provides additional information about a topic.
D. A road map of how the text is organized.
E. Provides definitions of difficult technical terms.
F. Indicates when the book was published.
G. A listing of what books were consulted in writing the text.

If your text should prove to be unacceptable for some of the students in your content class, there are a number of alternative approaches you can employ. For example, you might consider adopting multiple texts at varying levels of difficulty. Or you can use newspapers, resource speakers, demonstrations, simulations, and discussion groups. Finally, increasing the amount of guidance you provide students before, during, and after reading assignments should go a long way toward making the core text more understandable. Future chapters advance a variety of methods for helping students cope with difficult text material. Such methods range from individualizing assignments for some students to providing additional guidance in vocabulary development and comprehension.

SUMMARY

This chapter has focused on the politics and consequences of censorship and textbook adoption policies. In addition, we have introduced quantitative and qualitative factors that influence students' comprehension of text. The Raygor Readability Estimate was described for classroom use, and the advantages and limitations of readability formulas were enumerated. More importantly, a number of important qualitative factors in text comprehension were described. These included text organization, author's writing style, and students' prior knowledge and interests. An evaluation checklist was presented that encompasses both quantitative and qualitative factors. Finally, the chapter introduced a procedure for introducing students to unfamiliar textbooks.

REACTION GUIDE

Confirmed	Disconfirmed	
_____	_____	1. Censorship is both bad and unnecessary.
_____	_____	2. Government regulations require that 10th grade books be written on a 10th grade reading level.
_____	_____	3. It is safe to assume that high school students know how to use a textbook index.
_____	_____	4. The content of subject area textbooks is politically influenced.
_____	_____	5. The biblical version of creation should be included in biology textbooks that cover evolution.

A Why my choice is confirmed.	B Why my choice is not confirmed.
1. _____ _____	_____ _____
2. _____ _____	_____ _____
3. _____ _____	_____ _____
4. _____ _____	_____ _____
5. _____ _____	_____ _____

MINI PROJECT

1. Apply the Raygor Readability Estimate to a commonly used text in your content area.

2. Complete the text evaluation checklist for the same text you used in mini-project number one. Is the text appropriate for its intended grade level?

■ Why is it inappropriate to use readability formulas to rewrite text passages to have lower readability levels?

■ Identify 10 characteristics of a textbook that might make the book unacceptable or marginally appropriate for use with students.

■ Speculate on the ways in which the truth and accuracy of textbooks in your content area might be compromised by political agendas.

■ By today's standards the Redway and Hinman text is guilty of blatant sexism and racism. Do you believe that the authors and their book should be judged based on current cultural values? Are right and wrong absolute or relative values? Support your position.

■ A group of concerned parents visit you after school to complain about some reading material you have assigned to the students. The parents state that the readings are contradictory to the cultural values of the community, and they have asked you to remove the offensive books from the classroom. Assuming that your principal is unavailable to assist you, what should you say to the parents? Will you remove the books?

ASSESSMENT

Agree	Disagree	
_____	_____	1. Assessment should occur naturally as part of teaching and learning.
_____	_____	2. Adherence to stated course objectives will provide students with effective instruction in content areas.
_____	_____	3. Standardized tests provide teachers enough information concerning students' abilities to begin instruction.
_____	_____	4. The best reading tests to administer to students are those which compare them with other students across the nation.
_____	_____	5. Diagnosis is necessary for effective instruction.

RATIONALE

Instruction is the means by which teachers bridge the gap between what students already know and what they need to know. For instruction to be maximally effective, teachers must possess a knowledge of techniques to assess just what students do know. Assessment information about students' abilities and levels of achievement provides a foundation for selecting appropriate teaching strategies. On the other hand, without assessment information teachers are forced to make hazardous assumptions about what students do and do not know.

This chapter describes the role of assessment in order to promote the instructional match between student and text. Specifically, formal and informal types of assessment will be discussed and placed in proper perspective in the total instructional program. Various types of naturalistic assessment strategies will be described and recommended for use by content teachers. Suggestions will also be offered for assessing prior knowledge.

- Understand the need for assessment in the content classroom.

- Describe the differences between formal and informal testing.

- Utilize various types of naturalistic assessment strategies.

- Use a variety of strategies to assess students' prior knowledge.

GRAPHIC ORGANIZER

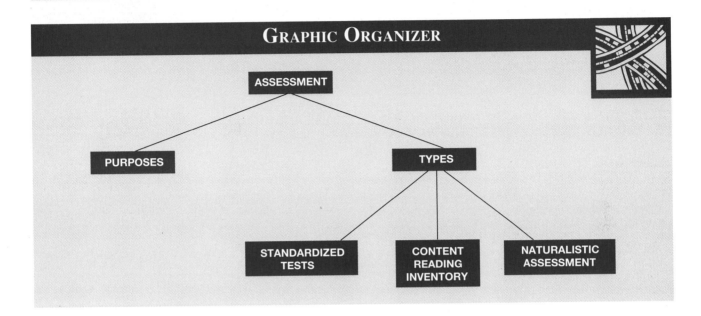

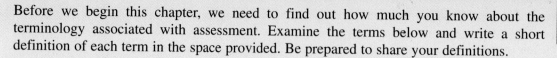

Before we begin this chapter, we need to find out how much you know about the terminology associated with assessment. Examine the terms below and write a short definition of each term in the space provided. Be prepared to share your definitions.

Norms _____

Standard error of measurement _____

Raw score _____

Percentile rank _____

Stanines _____

Standard deviation _____

Norm-referenced test _____

Criterion-referenced test _____

Mean _____

Standardized test _____

Reliability _____

Diagnostic test _____

Validity _____

Standardized scores _____

Purposes for Assessment

The end product of assessment in the content classroom, or any classroom for that matter, is decision-making concerning the kind of instruction to be provided students. Assessment is purposeless if it does not lead to intelligent instructional decisions. Content area teachers should keep this goal clearly in mind as they conduct assessment procedures.

In general, assessment in reading is conducted through the use of various types of tests. As such, tests are administered for two major purposes: (1) program evaluation and (2) student diagnosis. Program evaluation is usually conducted for accountability purposes and formal tests are usually the devices used.

Formal testing instruments, i.e., standardized reading tests, are administered at regular yearly intervals, usually in the fall or spring of the school year. This function is to monitor student progress in reading. With the help of this assessment, school administrators are able to compare the reading levels of their students with those of other students across the nation at the same grade levels. Although such comparisons may help a particular school district justify its need for federal support for its instructional programs, they are virtually useless for instructional decision-making by teachers with regard to the individual needs of students.

Formal testing may also be used to identify weaknesses in the instructional program. If students in school district A as a whole score low relative to the national average on a particular type of test such as vocabulary or comprehension, that district may decide to examine the emphasis placed on that portion of the reading program. Finally, formal testing may serve as a screening device for those students not performing up to reading program expectations. This should indicate to the school district the need for more intensive diagnostic testing to pinpoint areas of skill weakness in individual students. Unfortunately, the results of these tests may be inappropriately used to refer students to special programs without the benefit of further testing.

The second major purpose for reading assessment is student diagnosis. Student diagnosis can provide teachers with the kind of information necessary to make instructional decisions. Informal assessment tools are usually utilized to gather such information (Rakes & Smith, 1992). Specifically, informal tests can be used to diagnose possible reading and learning problems of students. Additionally, such tests can be used to determine the reading levels of students. Knowledge of students' reading and learning problems and reading levels provides a starting point for good teaching. This knowledge eliminates the need to presuppose any learning on the part of the students and provides the essential foundation for instructional decision-making.

Descriptive Terminology of Assessment

Before launching into a discussion of the advantages and disadvantages of particular types of tests, a discussion of some basic distinctions between types of tests is necessary. The distinction between formal and informal tests has already been mentioned. *Formal tests* are often called *standardized,* norm-referenced tests. The major characteristic of these tests is that one can only interpret the quality of a given *standardized score* by comparing it with scores acquired by others. The scores of those "others" are called *norms*. The norms represent a standard against which the performance of others may be compared. Norms are created by administering a test to large groups of students at a variety of grade levels. On the basis of the results of the testing, an average score is calculated for students at each grade level. These averages become the norm, and all students who take the test later are compared with the norming group. For example, let's say the norms established for sixth and seventh grade students, respectively, are 40 and 44 items correct on a particular standardized test. School district A administers this instrument to its seventh grade students resulting in an average of 40 items correct. In comparison to the standard set, it can then be said that school district A's students achieved on a par with sixth graders and that their group performance was below the average for seventh graders.

To examine the notion of standardized scores more closely, examine the figure that follows. This is the normal curve, and all standardized scores are based on it. In this bell-shaped distribution scores are distributed symmetrically about an average score called the *mean*. There are an equal number of scores various distances above the mean as there are in equal distances below the mean. Although the number of scores decrease the farther away from the mean you go, the greatest number of scores (about 68%) occur within one standard deviation of it. The *standard deviation* is a measure of the dispersion, or variability, of a group of scores. It provides a general guide for interpreting an individual's test performance in relation to the mean.

A standardized score is actually a term used to describe any score that may be transformed to other scales. The most common scores used in standardized testing are the raw score, the stanine, and the percentile rank. A *raw score* is simply the total number of correct items on a test. A *stanine* is the score converted to a standard 9-point scale with a mean of five and a standard deviation of two. The stanine is useful when a range of performance needs to be reported rather than a specific point on the normal curve. Finally, the *percentile rank* represents the percent of scores equal to and lower than the score

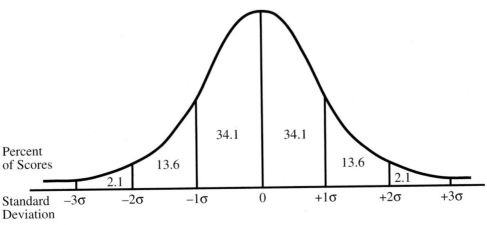

under question. It is the position of a score within the entire group of scores. A percentile rank of 60 means the individual has scored as well as or better than 60% of the people who took the test. The percentile rank does not represent the percentage of correct answers.

Informal assessment tools differ from standardized tests. *Informal tests, or criterion-referenced tests,* do not employ the use of norms as standards for comparison. Rather they employ a relative standard, or *criterion,* which implies adequate achievement for a given task or assignment. The score itself has meaning, even without reference to the performances of others. For instance, if the criterion has been set at 60-percent correct, a student must meet that figure to progress to another level of instruction; otherwise the student might need to work through the unit again and may require some special help to do so. Finally, informal tests are often teacher-made, though some are published. Thus, they can be designed to obtain information specifically related to an individual school's reading program.

A second distinction used in describing tests involves survey and diagnostic tests. A survey test does what its name implies; it surveys global areas of achievement such as vocabulary and comprehension. *Survey tests* are usually standardized tests and therefore are useful for purposes of group comparisons but not for individual instructional guidelines. No specifics with regard to the global areas of the survey are provided. That is, we are unable to determine what the specific areas of weaknesses in vocabulary and comprehension may be. That is what a diagnostic test endeavors to measure. Scores from a *diagnostic test* can indicate strengths and weaknesses in specific skill areas. For example, diagnostic tests provide scores for recognizing main ideas, details, inferences, etc.—the specifics of comprehension. Therefore, it might readily be seen that a standardized, survey-type instrument can be used as a screening device to tell a teacher, for instance, in which global areas a student might be experiencing difficulty. The teacher can then employ diagnostic tests to ascertain which specific areas are causing the difficulty.

Two other distinctions can be made in discussing testing instruments, neither of which requires a lengthy explanation. There are *group* and *individual* tests. As the names imply, tests may be group-administered or individually administered. The other distinction is between silent and oral tests. Again, as the names imply, tests may be silently or orally administered or employ some combination of the two. Usually, standardized tests utilize a format which requires a group, silent administration. At the other end of the continuum are informal tests which are diagnostic in scope and are administered in an individual, oral format. It must be emphasized, though, that many testing instruments fall somewhere in between.

 ## Cautions Concerning Standardized Testing

Standardized tests offer some advantages in a total reading assessment program. Because they are administered in a group setting, they do not take the great amount of time that individual testing requires. Since formal tests are administered silently instead of orally, confusion is also kept to a minimum. Additionally, the scores achieved by students allow school districts to compare the performance levels of their students with other students across the nation. Finally, standardized tests are supposed to be valid and reliable. *Validity* is the degree of accuracy with which a test measures what it is intended to measure. *Reliability* is the degree to which a test gives consistent results when administered repeatedly.

The ease of administration of standardized tests and their use of norms also present some disadvantages. It is essential that content teachers be cognizant of these disadvantages. It is all too easy to obtain students' standardized test scores from their permanent files and make decisions about their abilities based on those scores. Questions content teachers should ask themselves concerning standardized test scores might include the following:

1. What exactly does a score, such as 7.0, on reading mean?

2. What exactly are standardized tests measuring?

3. How accurate a picture do I obtain about the reading ability of students from examining their test scores?

The following discussion of cautions concerning standardized tests will attempt to answer those questions and other questions you may have in mind.

1. Inappropriate Norms. Even though great care is taken by test makers in standardizing a test, the norms established for comparison may be inappropriate for a particular class. The norms may be based on students with whom your students should not be compared. For instance, how could one compare a score of 7.0 achieved by a low socioeconomic group member with norms that may have been calculated from a group of students from a different socioeconomic group? How accurate an indication of achievement could you get out of a student such as this? Certainly, the norming population needs to be considered.

2. *Extraneous Factors.* It must be emphasized that the scores achieved by a student on a formal test are only a measure of that student's performance at that particular point in time. They may not necessarily be indicative of a student's true ability. An individual's performance may vary radically from day to day depending on extraneous factors which can complicate matters. Factors as simple as the amount of sleep students had the night before, to factors as complex as the emotional stability of their homes may interfere with students' daily performance in school as well as their performance in testing situations.

3. *Timed Testing.* Most standardized tests employ a time limitation in their administration procedures. Thus, a premium is placed on speed in completing the test. We are all probably reminded of personal experiences with friends or students who may be categorized as slow, but accurate; i.e., students who lack speed in completing tasks but thoroughly weigh alternatives before responding accurately. The slow but thorough reader may fail to complete the comprehension section of a test and thus get a low score when compared to the established norm. In reality, the student's comprehension could be excellent.

4. *Prior Knowledge.* Since comprehension occurs when students are able to associate the unknown with the known, prior knowledge may be a factor in test performance. In fact, there is a question as to whether standardized instruments actually measure reading comprehension or prior knowledge. Test items which may be answered from prior knowledge without the aid of a reading selection are said to be passage independent. Items which require students to read a selection in order to answer them correctly are termed passage dependent. It may be virtually impossible to eliminate the effect of prior knowledge on test performance. However, depending on the degree to which prior knowledge is a factor in particular test questions, the resulting scores can yield an unfair comparison between individuals.

5. *Comprehension Skills.* Standardized tests of reading comprehension, in many cases, emphasize factual recall of relatively insignificant facts. Is this the type of comprehension utilized in most reading situations? Sternberg (1991) points out that such tests are at great variance in their demands with the demands of reading in most school tasks and in everyday life. Certainly factual recall is important, but it is only one dimension of comprehension.

6. *Interest.* Everyone is aware of the effect of interest in reading. In fact, reading comprehension is better when the topic of a passage interests the reader. On the other hand, lack of interest may militate against the completion of a reading task. If the passages to be read on a standardized test are of little or no interest to students, it is bound to affect the students' ability to answer comprehension questions based on the passage.

7. *Guessing.* Most standardized tests employ a multiple choice format for their questions. They are designed in this manner to facilitate scoring by machines and for convenience (Readence & Moore, 1992). With such a limited format, guessing can unduly raise test scores. If four choices are offered, chances are one in four that a correct guess can be made. In any given test situation, two people with identical reading skills could get different test scores simply because one person happened to guess better that day. In fact, on most standardized tests, it is possible to receive grade-level equivalents, e.g., fourth-grade level, by guessing. Fry (1972) has described these pure-chance scores as orangutan scores.

8. *Test Floors and Ceilings.* When formal tests are standardized through averaging scores of students at a particular grade level, limits are placed on the range of performance at that grade level. Students are not supposed to score below a certain grade-level norm or, for that matter, above a certain norm in their performance. In effect, the use of *test floors* and *ceilings* may affect the validity of test scores. Specifically, the ceiling of the test may underestimate a more competent student's performance, while the floor may overestimate a less competent student's ability. In effect, the ceiling may penalize better readers because tests cannot truly measure their ability while the floor may place a poorer reader at a level where success cannot be achieved. Standardization is designed to predict average performance, not performance at the extremes.

9. *Standard Error of Measurement.* This term indicates the variation in test scores that one might expect if that test were administered repeatedly to an individual student. By adding or subtracting this built-in error to a student's obtained test score, one obtains a range of scores within which the student might actually score. For example, if the standard error of measurement is five months and a student's resulting score is 7.0, the range of scores within which the student might actually have scored is 6.5 to 7.5. Awareness of this factor of built-in error is essential when examining scores on standardized tests.

10. *Fallacy of Grade-Level Reporting.* So what does a score of 7.0 mean? First of all, it is an estimation of performance. Second, it really says little with regard to the students' performance; yet it is commonplace to use such scores when discussing reading ability of students. Just because two students both score 7.0 does not mean they are equivalent in reading ability. There are countless ways in which individuals may perform to attain a score of 7.0, yet each performance may be unique. Grade-level scores

obscure differential performances of individuals with like scores in the same grade, or in different grades. Further analysis of each student's performance is necessary.

Content teachers must keep these cautions in mind when examining standardized test scores or when provided information concerning them by other school personnel. Such scores provide the basis for comparing group performances and for program evaluation. Many of the factors which cause standardized tests to provide inaccurate scores for individuals (e.g., guessing and personal interests) balance out in group situations, thus making results far more accurate for groups than for individuals. However, they do not provide the kind of information necessary for making instructional decisions. The authors recommend the use of the content reading inventory for this purpose.

 The Content Reading Inventory

The *content reading inventory* is designed to obtain information about the ability of students to learn successfully with specific text material. Since the content reading inventory is an informal-group-silent-diagnostic assessment, numerous advantages are inherent in it and far outweigh the disadvantage of the time it takes to prepare the instrument. First, the content reading inventory is quick and easy to administer in a group setting. Second, since it is teacher-made, it is designed to obtain information concerning students' reading and learning skills. Third, the content reading inventory is textbook-based. This makes the diagnostic information relevant since it is taken directly from the major source of instruction in the subject matter area. Fourth, since it is teacher-made and textbook-based, it provides for ease in scoring. Criteria for judging test answers are objective, eliminating subjectivity as a deterrent in effective scoring. Finally, this instrument later may become the basis for teaching. Once the teacher has obtained essential diagnostic information, the test may become an instructional instrument with which the teacher can begin to acquaint students with the author's style and the organization of the textbook.

The content reading inventory consists of three major sections. The first section of the inventory concerns knowledge of, and ability to utilize, the various aids within the textbook or supplemental to it. Specifically, the test covers book parts common to most textbooks such as the table of contents, index, and pictorial aids. The students' ability to use resource aids which supplement the textbook such as the encyclopedia or card catalog are also examined. The premise behind this section of the content reading

inventory is that the ability to effectively utilize the internal and external aids of the text is critical to learning from it.

In the last two sections of this inventory, students are asked to read a short three- to four-page selection from the text. Section two then determines the ability to deal with the technical and specialized vocabulary encountered in the reading. Both vocabulary through recall and in context are examined. Section three examines the ability to comprehend text explicit and implicit information as well as to grasp an author's text structure. A representative content reading inventory, therefore, should contain the following sections:

Section I: Textual Reading/Study Aids
  A. Internal Aids
    1. Table of Contents
    2. Index
    3. Glossary
    4. Chapter Introduction/Summaries
    5. Pictorial Information
    6. Other Pertinent Aids

  B. External Aids
    1. Card Catalog
    2. Reader's Guide
    3. Encyclopedias
    4. Other Pertinent Aids

Section II: Vocabulary Knowledge
  A. Recall
  B. Contextual Meanings

Section III: Comprehension
  A. Text Explicit Information
  B. Text Implicit Information
  C. Text Structure

Content Reading Inventory Guidelines. To construct, administer, and score a content reading inventory, the following guidelines are offered:

1. Plan to construct approximately 20 to 25 questions. It is recommended that 8–10 questions be constructed for section I, 4–6 for section II, and 7–9 for section III.

2. Choose a short 3–4 page selection for students to read.

3. Explain to students the rationale for using the content reading inventory. Administer the inventory in two sections being careful to orally read each question to the students before they begin.

4. Section I is administered first, as the ability to use the various parts of the total text is examined.

5. Sections II and III are administered next. Care is given that appropriate readiness is established for students to read the selection. Questions for these sections are based solely on the short selection, not the entire text.

6. The completed content reading inventory is scored using the following criteria:

% Correct	Text Difficulty
86%–100%	Too easy
64%–85%	Adequate for instruction
63%–	Too difficult

It is cautioned that students who miss a majority of the questions within a particular category might need help in that area.

ACTIVITY

Complete the following example of a content reading inventory. It is designed just as you, as the content teacher, would construct and present a content reading inventory to your students. Your task, just as that of your students would be, is to answer the questions. Section I is based on the total text; sections II and III are based upon Chapter 8.

Content Reading Inventory

Section I: Textual Reading/Study Aids

Directions: Using your textbook or your previous knowledge, answer each of the following questions.

A. Internal Aids

1. On what page does Chapter 4 begin? What is the title of the section of which it is a part?

   _____

2. On what page(s) would you find information regarding the Guided Reading Procedure?

   _____

3. Where would you look in the text to find the definition of "fading"?

   _____

4. Of what use is the section entitled "Rationale" at the beginning of Chapter 8?

   _____

   _____

5. Using the GWP checklist in Chapter 11, what recommendations would you make concerning the

   student's writing? _____

6. Where would you look to find out how this text is organized? _____

B. External Aids

7. What library guide would aid you in locating a book on attitudes and attitude development?

   _____

8. If you were to give an oral report in class about content area literacy and you knew that much of the information you needed would be in current periodicals, what guide would you use to help you

   find the information? _____

9. Name one set of encyclopedias. How are the topics in it arranged?_____

   _____

Directions: Read the sections in your text entitled Words and Vocabularies in Chapter 8. Based upon what you have read, answer the questions in sections II and III.

Section II. Vocabulary Knowledge

10.   Define the concept of "word" as used in this text. _____

_____

11.   Compare and contrast denotations and connotations. Provide an example. _____

_____

12.   Define the italicized word as it is used in this sentence: "A vocabulary is a *corpus* of many thousands of words and their associated meanings." _____

_____

13.   What term refers to the process by which new information is incorporated into existing schemata?

_____

14.   Define the italicized word as used in this sentence: "Technical vocabulary present labels for unfamiliar concepts that must be accommodated by modifying *extant* schemata." _____

_____

Section III: Comprehension

15.   Why do adult language users have little difficulty agreeing whether or not a particular sequence of sounds or symbols is a word? _____

16.   Learning new words (concepts) requires more than a simple explanation by the teacher. Why?

_____

17.   What are the largest vocabularies for literate adults? _____

18.   Describe the differences between the words (concepts), Cold War and crass. _____

_____

19.   Describe the process involved with regard to the schemata of students when the word "secant" is presented them. _____

20.   Explain the role of the school with regard to the development of the expressive and receptive vocabularies of students. _____

21.   How is the section entitled Vocabularies organized? _____

Now that you have completed this content inventory, turn to the end of the chapter for the answers. Classify your performance according to the criteria specified previously for the content reading inventory. The majority of individuals taking this test will find this text adequate for instruction. A few of you may score above or below that level. As can be seen, the content reading inventory can provide the teacher with information concerning the difficulty level of the text as well as specific information concerning students' ability to effectively utilize the textbook. The following checklist is provided as a format for teachers to record the information gathered from the content reading inventory.

Classroom Summary

Subject _____   Title of Text _____

Grade and Section _____   Teacher _____

Student Name	Table of Contents	Index	Glossary	Chapter Introduction/Summary	Pictorial Information	Other Internal Aids	Card Catalog	Reader's Guide	Encyclopedia	Other External Aids	Vocabulary-Recall	Vocabulary-Context	Text Explicit	Text Implicit	Text Structure
1. John Bead	✓		✓	✓	✓		✓		✓			✓	✓		
2. Tom Rean	✓	✓		✓			✓		✓		✓	✓	✓		✓
3. Scott Bee		✓	✓	✓			✓	✓	✓		✓		✓		✓
4.															
5.															
6.															
7.															

If the results of the content reading inventory indicate student deficiencies in certain areas, teachers may want to use the inventory as an instructional tool. Since the questions asked on the inventory are probably similar to those teachers ask in the classroom, they can expect the students' responses to be similar to those they would make in class discussions. Therefore, the content reading inventory provides the framework for teachers to initiate a preview of the text, as described in Chapter 4. The premise behind this strategy is that the teacher will model the use of the various text parts and efficient use of the author's organizational structure. In this way all students can be effectively introduced to their textbook in a systematic manner. The preview also offers students an introduction to proper utilization of the various reading/study aids authors incorporate into textbooks.

Students may also break into small groups and be given the task of arriving at a consensus of opinion as to the correct responses on the content reading inventory. Students having difficulties coping with the various aspects of the textbook will be afforded the opportunity to experience how other students arrived at their responses to the questions. Again teachers should follow these task group discussions with a whole-group discussion insuring an effective introduction to the textbook.

Task groups may also be utilized to provide additional practice in areas of need as indicated by the analysis of the summary information sheet that tabulates the results of the inventory. For instance, if the class as a whole seems to have difficulty processing text implicit information, the teacher can construct a series of questions emphasizing the use of this skill and assign them to the task groups. Through peer interaction and a whole-group discussion/followup, the teacher can provide students experience with some of the processes necessary to enhance learning with text.

The diagnostic use of the textbook enables content teachers to initiate instruction in their classrooms on an informed basis. No assumptions are made about what is already known; therefore, instruction is based upon establishing the background necessary for effective comprehension of new material. Thus, knowledge of the students' ability to successfully cope with their text material is essential.

However, since only a few items are assessed in each area, the content reading inventory is only a beginning—a point of departure—for assessing students' abilities. In essence, the results of this inventory allow teachers to begin the development of student *portfolios,* or systematic collections of students' work in the classroom (Gillespie, Ford, Gillespie, & Leavell, 1996; Moje, Brozo, & Haas, 1994; Tierney, Carter, & Desai, 1991). As teachers observe students interacting with text in their daily reading and writing assignments, they will acquire additional information that will corroborate or refute the initial findings and add to the portfolios.

◼ Naturalistic Assessment

It must be remembered that any test is a measure of a student's performance at that point in time only. Additionally, the administration of a single test or two does not provide sufficient information for drawing firm conclusions about a student's abilities. The teacher still needs to add to information gained from testing and to update student portfolios continually. Certainly, the more information we attain, the more valid an assessment can be of a student's abilities. But, that does not mean administering more content reading inventories. Rather, it requires that teachers be sensitive to the entire instructional situation and the major variables involved in it. This means that the teacher should pay attention to the reader, the text, the task required of the reader, and the processes needed to complete that task. In other words, assessment needs to be carried on naturally as students interact with text and deal with their daily reading and writing assignments. Such assessment is called naturalistic (Moore, 1986) or authentic (Valencia, Hiebert, & Afflerbach, 1994).

Observation

The daily routines of the classroom provide rich sources of diagnostic information, and the thorough teacher makes use of it. What this calls for is simply a conscious effort on the part of teachers to observe and study their students at work in the classroom. *Naturalistic assessment* is based on observing and interacting with students as they respond to the naturally occurring activities of the classroom versus assessing them in more contrived testing situations. In *observation* teachers attempt to make judgments about what they see. They observe students in a variety of circumstances and try to detect patterns of behavior that may signal some difficulty. These sources of information can be tapped regularly, and any findings should be recorded in the form of a checklist, teacher journal, or anecdotal record to their portfolios. This information can then be tied in with that gained from testing.

Observation may be the most reliable and valid means of assessing students' reading and writing abilities. It is highly reliable because teachers avoid a major problem of traditional assessment measure—lack of consistency—by basing any conclusions they make upon many observations over a period of time. And these conclusions are valid because they are based on behavior patterns that have occurred time and time again in real reading and writing situations as a natural part of an instructional lesson. Additionally, teachers can assess not only what has been learned but also how well students apply that learning.

Observations may be unstructured or structured, depending on how detailed teachers wish their information to be. If the observations are to be unstructured, teachers can use *anecdotal records* which are notes used to record students' behaviors as they interact with and discuss text. Because anecdotal records are open-ended in nature, teachers can decide what is important to record given the task, the specific behaviors being observed, and any previous assessment data.

For instance, the instructional strategies described in this text can become rich sources of diagnostic information for teachers if they employ assessment by observation. Readence and Martin (1988) provided one concrete example of this by pointing out that anticipation guides, described in Chapter 10, can be used for assessment by observation if teachers note how much students do, and do not, know about a topic. If desired, teachers can also observe how well students (1) pose their own questions; (2) anticipate what is to come in the text; (3) justify their responses to guide statements; (4) cope with potentially conflicting viewpoints as they attempt to make predictions about a topic; and, (5) recognize and reconcile their prior knowledge inaccuracies when they encounter them in their reading.

If teachers wish their observations to be more structured, they can use some form of a predetermined *observation guide* to document the specific behaviors being observed. The guides can be used to expand the anecdotal records from the unstructured observations. With our anticipation guide example, an observation guide could be constructed in the form of a grid, with the behaviors being observed listed on one side and the students being observed listed on top. Such a guide might look like this:

Observation Guide: Anticipation Guide Date _____	Raul	Tim	Lea	Yoshi	Maria	Flo
Poses questions						
Anticipates text						
Justifies responses						
Copes with conflicting information						
Reconciles prior knowledge						

The marking system used with the guide could be as simple as noting the presence or absence of each behavior with a plus (+) or minus (−). A more sophisticated system might employ the use of an (s) for sometime, indicating that at least some of the time a particular behavior is noted, and an (n) for not observed, meaning that the behavior was not seen during that particular observation time. Grades of A–F could also be used once teachers became acclimated to using observation guides.

Finally, information collected purposefully and observations recorded systematically over time are called *field notes*. Field notes are particularly useful when teachers want to gather information on significant teaching and learning situations. For instance, if a teacher wished to conduct some action research on the viability of a new instructional strategy (e.g., K-W-L) for promoting students' comprehension, then field notes would be an effective means of observing the students using the K-W-L over repeated exposures to it. Field notes would serve as documentation for what you did in implementing K-W-L, how students reacted to its use, and how and why you modified K-W-L over time.

Assessment by observation is not necessarily an easy task, and it does require the ability to distinguish important from unimportant information. Much of this ability comes with experience, but it will come more readily to teachers who make a conscious effort to use their observational powers to study students at work. Informal testing is important, but only through observation can we update this information. Remember, assessment is a day-to-day occurrence.

Interviews, Informal Conversation, Journals, and Open-Ended Surveys

Naturalistic assessment also includes the use of student interviews, informal conversations with students, journals, and open-ended surveys. In fact, a primary source of assessment data should be that information that students give teachers. This would include ongoing records of statements about their own class reading and writing, their interest in various forms of reading and writing both in school and outside of school, and their reactions to various instructional strategies, the text and other resource materials, and assignments.

Student interviews and *informal conversations* are ways to encourage students to talk about both the quantity and quality of what they are learning as well as how they are learning. They give students an opportunity to become involved in the teaching/learning process by sharing their thinking. Students should be given an opportunity to discuss the content, process, and motivation concerning particular learning situations. For instance, using our K-W-L example, students could share their thinking on how effective they thought the strategy was, particularly in relation to other instructional strategies, whether they liked using K-W-L, and what modifications they might like to see with the strategy the next time it was used.

It is best to conduct interviews and hold informal conversations with individuals or small groups of students, if at all possible. In this way the feedback you get will be qualitatively better. However, the constraints of most content classrooms will probably necessitate talking with larger groups of students.

One way to insure individual feedback from students, however, is the use of class journals and open-ended surveys. Having students respond in writing will save large amounts of time and still give students their own voice in the teaching/learning process. Using their journals or a survey provided by you will give you a record of students' thoughts and perceptions about their reading and learning tasks.

Portfolios

Throughout this text we have emphasized that teachers need to experiment with the strategies and practices we have advocated; we have emphasized that you need to try these strategies out and modify them to fit the diverse nature of your classroom. In essence, we have asked you to act as a researcher in your own classroom. We would like to expand upon the notion of teacher as researcher in our discussion of portfolios through an analogy drawn from the field of anthropology.

Anthropologists study people—what they know and what they do. Their research attempts to describe what is going on with certain aspects of our culture. Similarly, teachers study students in their own classroom culture as they try to become literate in English, science, social studies, mathematics, etc. Anthropologists assume the role of a participant observer wherein they participate in the culture they are studying as well as observe it. Likewise, teachers participate in the teaching and learning events of their classroom as well as observe students interacting in these events.

Anthropologists collect data which is as authentic as possible, reflecting the naturally occurring events of the culture rather than aberrations resulting from the data collection process. Their data is naturalistic as it represents their observations of the activities of the culture, documents produced by the culture, and their record of interviews and conversations with the members of the culture. This data collection results in thick descriptions of the culture with accompanying documentation to support any conclusions that might be drawn. Teachers collect data through naturalistic assessment by means of observations, records of those observations, student interviews and informal conversations with students, and collections of students' works over time placed in their portfolios.

Finally, anthropologists triangulate their data; they examine the documentation they collect to gain understanding of the culture being studied and check other sources of data for corroboration of their conclusions. The conclusions they draw through the analysis of their data informs them of how to pursue additional data collection. Similarly, teachers examine the various sources of information collected in students' portfolios; they also triangulate their data to check for emerging patterns of how students are learning in their classroom. They analyze the data in the students' portfolios, draw tentative conclusions about their learning, and make instructional decisions based on those conclusions. Thus, assessment informs instruction as teachers act as researchers in their own classroom.

Portfolios act as the vehicle for this research to occur; they serve as a framework for ongoing assessment and a repository of assessment data. Included in the portfolios are results of the content reading inventory, anecdotal records and observation guides, student journals and open-ended surveys, samples of students' work chosen by teacher and the student, and whatever else might be appropriate for your particular content area (e.g., videotape records, writing samples, group projects, word problems, graphic representations, computer work). Portfolios represent what students have learned and are learning and are a record of their development as they attempt to become literate. Portfolios also represent a collaborative approach to assessment and the means to link assessment to teaching and learning. Both the students and the teacher can analyze students' progress.

For portfolios to be successfully implemented in your classroom, students must first be informed of what their purpose is. They also need to be shown the kinds of documentation that will be included in the portfolio. A model from another class would be most helpful with this task. Finally, their involvement in the process needs to be discussed thoroughly. Students need to understand that the portfolio is theirs, and that it will represent a collaboration between you and the students in their learning and your teaching. With time, portfolios can turn assessment into a collaborative effort toward improving instruction.

 ## Assessing Prior Knowledge

Throughout this book we have stressed the importance of prior knowledge in reading and learning with text. In essence, the more knowledge students bring to the printed page, the more likely they will successfully comprehend the text, particularly if they or the teacher activate the appropriate prior knowledge. Conversely, if students lack, or fail to select, the appropriate prior knowledge, their comprehension may suffer. Therefore, teachers may wish to assess students' knowledge about a topic before they encounter it in a learning situation. In this way, teachers can make decisions about the quality and quantity of prereading instruction they provide students. Certainly, if teachers know that students possess a vast store of prior knowledge about a topic under study, it is less necessary to spend great amounts of time in prereading. On the other hand, if students know little about a topic, it would benefit teachers to spend time activating and building background knowledge.

In later chapters we will suggest a number of prereading vocabulary and comprehension strategies as well as some prewriting strategies that teachers can use to initiate instruction in the content areas. Though instructional in scope, each of those strategies can provide teachers with relevant knowledge about what students know and do not know about a topic. However, we would like to suggest some techniques for assessing prior knowledge that are easy to implement and can provide teachers with the information necessary for effective instructional planning and teaching.

Knowledge Rating

The first technique for assessing prior knowledge that we will describe is the simplest and easiest to use. *Knowledge rating* (Blachowicz, 1991) is a strategy for establishing what students already know about a topic by having them rate how well they know the vocabulary. In planning for the lesson teachers would select the vocabulary words they think would be important to understand the concepts to be learned. In doing so teachers would develop a sheet which lists that vocabulary and ask students to rate themselves concerning how well they know the word. For example, to use an example from a previous chapter, if our topic was Warts and Their Cures, the knowledge rating sheet might look like the following:

Knowledge Rating: Warts and Their Cures			
Directions: Decide how well you know each of the words below by checking your knowledge for each.			
	3	2	1
Word	Can Define/Use It	Heard It	Don't Know
spunkwater			
Pliny the Elder			
caustic painting			
electrocautery			
folk treatments			
polyoma virus			
autosuggestion			
nostrums			

Introduce this technique by telling students that in order to get them to begin thinking about the text material that is to be read, they would start by assessing what they already know about the topic. After handing out the sheet, pronounce the words so decoding is not a problem for students. Then ask them to rate their knowledge of each word by checking the appropriate column for their knowledge level. The first time this strategy is used teachers may need to model for students exactly what is expected. For instance, students might have some idea of folk treatments and rate it a 2; others may even rate it a 3. On the other hand, students probably would not know nostrums and would give it a 1. Students would be asked to complete the sheet. Teachers would then tally how many students knew each word. Students' prior knowledge could be ascertained both collectively as well as individually. In this way teachers will have some information about students' knowledge before making a judgement about the amount of prereading instruction to provide.

Word Association

Word association (Zalaluk, Samuels, & Taylor, 1986) is a technique designed to measure students' knowledge about a topic by determining what they associate with that topic. It is both simple to create and score, and it can be administered to a whole class. The reasoning behind this technique is that topics about which students possess considerable knowledge should elicit numerous associations, while those topics about which they possess little or no knowledge should elicit very few, if any, associations. Students simply write down as many words as they can think of in association with a key word. Thus, what is measured is each student's entering knowledge base. Assessing prior knowledge through word association can be accomplished using the following steps:

1. *Prepare the stimulus topic.* The keyword topic is selected and printed at the left margin of every line on a piece of paper. This will insure that students use the keyword to cue associations, not newly generated words.

2. *Provide instructions.* Students are told that their task is to see how many words they can think of and write down related to a keyword they will be provided. They are told that the words they write may be things, places, events, ideas, or whatever comes to their mind when they see the keyword. If word association is a novel task for them, the teacher should model the activity and provide practice and discussion for the students. Students are assured that they are not expected to fill in all the lines on the paper. Finally, they are told that they will be given only three minutes to complete the activity.

3. *Scoring.* Once students have generated their associations, responses are scored quantitatively, one point for each reasonable association. No points are given for unreasonable or erroneous associations. For instance, if the keyword is Mammals, one point would be given to reptiles because they are another major class of the animal kingdom, but none for flowers. An additional point may be given for a superordinate category a student generates, but no more than one extra point can be given for subordinate ideas, no matter how many subordinate words are produced. The reasoning behind this is that the student has begun to use the generated words rather than the keyword as cues. In our example of mammals, one point would be awarded for the superordinate term, marsupials, but only one more point would be awarded for full cluster of subordinate terms such as kangaroo, wombat, opossum, and bandicoot. The following key may be used to score students' word associations:

0–2 points	low prior knowledge
3–6 points	average prior knowledge
7+ points	high prior knowledge

Let's say that you want to assess prior knowledge about the keyword topic the Solar System. One student wrote the following list of word associations:

Milky Way	Venus	Earth
the sun	Mars	
Big Dipper	Jupiter	
planets	Mercury	

In this case the student would be awarded four points for the words listed. One point would be given for Milky Way since the solar system is part of it. One point would be awarded for the sun as it is part of the solar system; the same would hold true for planets. However, only one point would be given for all the separate planets named because they are each a subset of planets. Finally, no points would be given for the Big Dipper since it is a constellation separate from the solar system. Four points would indicate that this student possesses average prior knowledge about the solar system and a teacher would have to plan to provide a normal amount of prereading instruction for this student before giving a text assignment.

Prediction Guide

A final means of assessing students' prior knowledge of a topic is the prediction guide (Nichols, 1983). The *prediction guide* is a series of fact-based statements given to students before they encounter a text assignment. The students are to indicate whether or not each statement is true or false. For instance, a teacher about to cover the Cold War in American history might provide students with a series of prediction guide statements on the topic. By examining students' responses to each of the guide statements, the teacher can discover not only how much students might know about the Cold War, but also what particular aspects about the topic are known or not known. In this way the teacher will gain valuable information for instructional planning. Below is an example prediction guide for Bats and the text from which the statements are drawn (adapted from Webster, 1984).

Prediction Guide: Bats

Directions: Before you read a text passage on Bats, predict which of the statements that follow are true based on what you already know about them. Place a check (✔) on the line next to every true statement.

_____ 1. Bats are the second largest group of mammals.

_____ 2. Some bats are the size of a bumblebee.

_____ 3. Bats transmit disease.

_____ 4. Bats are about as intelligent as dogs.

Bats

Next to the 3,000-odd kinds of rodents, some 900 species of bats make up the second largest order of mammals in the animal kingdom, both in number of species and, by estimation, of individuals alive at any one time. Bats, the order Chiroptera, meaning winged hand, make up nearly one-fourth of all mammalian species.

They range in size from Kitti's hognosed bat, which is the size of a bumblebee and weighs about as much as a penny, to the large fruit-eating bats called flying foxes because of their foxlike faces and their size—they are almost as big as a small fox cub, weighing two pounds and having a wingspan of up to six feet.

Most bats' gargoylelike noses, used for transmitting high-frequency bursts of sound, and their huge ears, used to pick up the echoes from the waves of sound, have contributed to the human perception of bats as eerie, even supernatural, creatures that are probably vicious, filthy, and likely to attack humans and transmit disease.

Recent studies, however, show that bats are gentle; keep themselves meticulously clean; rarely transmit rabies; have a measure of intelligence that scientists equate with that of dogs; can be easily trained; and, in rare cases with a knowledgeable owner, can even become a pet.

Whether or not each statement is actually true and the number of statements should be used in the guide are not at issue here. What matters is that the statements reflect information the teacher thinks is important and that students will need to know after completing the assignment. In this way teachers will know in what areas to provide prereading instruction.

Before we leave this topic, we would like to caution teachers that prediction guides are characterized as a series of fact-based statements that aid you in assessing students' prior knowledge. Please remember that prediction guides are separate and distinct from anticipation guides, which have opened each chapter of this text thus far and are experience-based statements used to activate students' prior knowledge before they read. You may wish to read the section on anticipation guides in Chapter 10 if this distinction is unclear.

SUMMARY

The present chapter has offered numerous suggestions for content teachers to secure appropriate diagnostic information concerning the reading/learning abilities of students. With this information teachers will be able to plan effective instruction in their content areas according to the needs of their students. Purposes for classroom assessment and differences between formal and informal testing have been described. Cautions concerning standardized tests were discussed as well as the construction and use of the content reading inventory. Naturalistic assessment strategies including observations, interviews and informal conversations, and portfolios were described. Finally, suggestions for assessing students' prior knowledge were enumerated.

REACTION GUIDE

Confirmed	Disconfirmed	
_____	_____	1. Assessment should occur naturally as part of teaching and learning.
_____	_____	2. Adherence to started course objectives will provide students with effective instruction in content areas.
_____	_____	3. Standardized tests provide teachers enough information concerning students' abilities to begin instruction.
_____	_____	4. The best reading tests to administer to students are those which compare them with other students across the nation.
_____	_____	5. Diagnosis is necessary for effective instruction.

A	B
Why my choice is confirmed.	Why my choice is not confirmed.

1. _____   _____
   _____   _____

2. _____   _____
   _____   _____

3. _____   _____
   _____   _____

4. _____   _____
   _____   _____

5. _____   _____
   _____   _____

MINI PROJECT

1. In a small group examine a standardized reading test provided by the teacher. Evaluate each subtest of the instrument for the criteria listed below. Use the following classification system: 1 = Satisfactory; 2 = Unsatisfactory; 3 = Not Clear. Add any other evaluative criteria you deem necessary.

   A. Is the stated purpose of each test reflected in the selection of the test items?

   B. Are the directions standardized and clearly written?

   C. Is the test easy for the teacher and student to follow?

   D. Does the test measure what it purports to measure?

   E. Is adequate time allowed for the completion of each subtest?

2. Using a content text of your choice, design a content reading inventory. Utilize the procedures described earlier in the chapter. Administer the inventory, if possible, to three students to ascertain their ability to cope with the text. Evaluate the effectiveness of the content inventory as a device for gathering diagnostic information about students.

3. Visit a classroom in a content area of your choice and observe what types of naturalistic assessment strategies the teacher uses. Write a summary of what you observed and what suggestions you might have for incorporating other naturalistic strategies in that classroom.

4. Select one of the techniques for assessing prior knowledge and try it on a small group of students or your peers. Evaluate its effectiveness.

GROUP PROJECTS

■ The content reading inventory is a method of finding out how well students can learn from a given textbook or other classroom materials. Critique the specific objectives and procedures for the content reading inventory as it is presented in the text.

■ Enumerate the limitations of standardized, norm-referenced tests and provide a brief discussion of each limitation.

■ Define naturalistic assessment and discuss strategies for using it in content classrooms.

Section I: Textual Reading/Study Aids

A. *Internal Aids*

1. Page 42, Learning with Text and Technology. (Table of Contents)

2. Page 250 (Index).

3. The glossary.

4. It provides an overview of the chapter. (Chapter Introduction)

5. The student needs help with supporting details, sentence length, and spelling. (Pictorial Information)

6. The preface.

B. *External Aids*

7. The card catalog.

8. The reader's guide.

9. Answer open; alphabetically (Encyclopedias)

Section II: Vocabulary Knowledge

10. A word is a pattern of auditory or visual symbols which represent schemata. (Recall)

11. A denotation of a word is its broad meaning, while a connotation of a word is defined by its subtle shades of meaning and its limiting grammatical and semantic conditions. Examples open. (Recall)

12. A corpus is a body, or collection, of recorded utterances used as a basis for the descriptive analysis of a language. (Context)

13. Assimilation is the process by which new information is incorporated into existing schemata. (Recall)

14. Extant means existing. (Context)

Section III: Comprehension

15. Adult language users have a common sensitivity to the concept of a word because they know speakers do not interrupt words with fillers such as "um" or "uh" during speech. (Text Explicit)

16. Learning new words requires more than a simple explanation because they are not just isolated bits of information. Rather, words are defined by the ways and the extent to which they are related to all other words. (Text Explicit)

17. The largest vocabularies for literate adults are the listening and reading vocabularies because the schemata required for recognizing word meanings in context are more fully developed. (Text Explicit)

18. Crass is a general vocabulary term which is not specifically associated with a teaching area. Cold War is a technical vocabulary term uniquely related to social studies. (Text Implicit)

19. Secant is a technical vocabulary term which requires students to accommodate their schemata by modifying them or creating new ones to learn a novel word. (Text Implicit)

20. Children enter school with developed listening and speaking vocabularies. Instruction in the school enables these children to be exposed to more and more new concepts. Eventually, this exposure enables the listening vocabulary to further expand and the reading vocabulary to overtake the expressive vocabularies. (Text Implicit)

21. The Vocabularies section is organized around a pattern of comparison-contrast as the types of vocabularies are enumerated and discussed. (Author Organization)

TEACHING AND LEARNING STRATEGIES

S I X

UNIT AND LESSON PLANNING FOR CONTENT LITERACY

SETTING

Shane Bintliff's ninth-grade United States history class. In a unit on the industrial revolution, Mr. Bintliff, a first year teacher, is introducing the unit with an overview of various machine inventions that were influential in improving productivity and transportation. The class has 27 students representing a wide array of achievement levels. Language and ethnic differences abound in this urban high school of 3000 students located in a large city in the midwest.

THE LESSON

Mr. Bintliff begins the class by placing a small model of a steam engine on the table at the front of the room. He tells students he is going to demonstrate how the steam engine works. "It's the single most important invention of the industrial revolution," he says.

Students' eyes are riveted on the colorful red and black steam engine purchased at a model store in the 1970s. They also notice a can of Sterno canned heat sitting next to the steam engine's boiler. The room is alive with expectation that something exciting will happen with the steam engine.

Mr. Bintliff opens the Sterno can, scoops out a small amount of pink gelatinous Sterno on a putty knife and puts it on a metal tray that slides into the steam engine to fuel the boiler. He reaches into his pocket and discovers he has forgotten to bring any matches to light the Sterno. A student near the back of the room offers his cigarette lighter and the ignited fuel slowly heats the small boiler. After a while the engine comes to life, its flywheel spinning and its whistle filling the room with a sound out of the factories that fueled the industrial revolution.

Mr. Bintliff explains how the steam engine's fuel and boiler produce pressure to drive the flywheel. The wheel spins but it is not connected to any other machinery. He then tells students to get their notebooks out and he launches into a 35 minute lecture at the board on "The Industrial Revolution in Great Britain." Some students take notes and listen carefully. Three students put their heads down and go to sleep. Mr. Bintliff directs questions at students periodically during the lecture. "Steven, who invented the steam engine?" Although the city has experienced the closing of many factories over the past 10 years, Mr. Bintliff concentrates his lecture and questions on factual information from the textbook.

With a few minutes remaining in the class period, Mr. Bintliff passes out a word find puzzle containing terms and names of key figures like James Watt, the inventor of the steam engine. Students return their textbooks to a shelf at the side of the classroom, stuff their notebooks in backpacks, and prepare to bolt toward the door. As they leave, many glance at the small steam engine cooling on the table at the front of the room.

▶ Now that you have had a chance to consider this lesson, write down your thoughts on the following questions:

1. What are the good points about the lesson?

2. What are the weak points about the lesson?

3. What, if anything, would you change about the lesson?

RATIONALE

Unit and Lesson Planning for Content Area Literacy

In Chapter 3 we discussed the importance of social context in content area literacy. When you plan a *unit of instruction* that may span 3–6 weeks of individual lessons, the success of the unit is dependent upon how well you develop connections between the content and your students' prior knowledge and experiences. Thus, having a clear sense of students' language, culture, and interests will be crucial in designing and delivering successful lessons. Reinking, Mealey, and Ridgeway (1993) viewed this conditional knowledge of student characteristics as a first step in deciding what content and teaching strategies might best fit students' experiences. Planning time is needed to consider instructional purposes and goals. In addition, students' prior knowledge, ability, and motivation should be considered at the planning stage. Task analysis of text characteristics such as vocabulary and important concepts should guide lesson planning. Finally, how much time will be available for delivering lessons and what grouping structures might be possible? Even if you do an outstanding job of planning a lesson, it will probably not be flawless the first time through. But planning can alleviate a number of problems related to student boredom, pacing, and evaluation.

As you plan lessons and units following the formats outlined in this chapter, you should keep a journal where you reflect on your teaching (Grimmett, Erickson, MacKinnon, & Riecken, 1990). Your professional development as a teacher hinges on constant reflection and efforts to improve lesson design and delivery. Millies (1992, p. 40) said, "the teacher is a lens through which curriculum is filtered." Similarly, Britzman (1991, p. 8) argued that "learning to teach like teaching itself is always the process of becoming in a time of formation and transformation, of scrutiny into what one is doing, and who one becomes."

In this chapter, we introduce a format for unit and lesson planning with an emphasis on formulating clear goals and objectives, using exciting hooks or anticipatory set activities, and ensuring that a lesson takes advantage of students' experiences and interests. This framework should be helpful as you explore teaching strategies in vocabulary, comprehension, writing, and studying approaches. In essence, this chapter provides the umbrella for all the individual teaching strategies that follow.

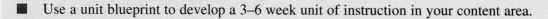

- Use a unit blueprint to develop a 3–6 week unit of instruction in your content area.

- Use a lesson planning framework to write a lesson plan in your content area.

- Write lesson objectives that encompass the four elements of expected performance, product, condition, and criteria.

- Deliver a five-minute lesson to your peers based on a hobby or interest area.

- Deliver a 20-minute microteaching lesson to peers and field experience students in your content area.

GRAPHIC ORGANIZER

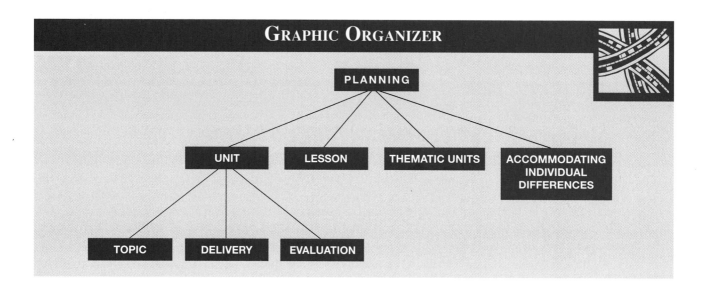

Planning

In the early stages of planning, when you begin to collect materials, draft lessons, and think about what teaching strategies you will use, keep the following points in mind:

1. Present content and processes concurrently. The particular teaching strategies you select for an assignment should grow out of a careful content analysis of the material. What is the purpose of the assignment? What text structure does the author use to portray ideas? This analysis should suggest which vocabulary, comprehension, writing, and studying strategies are likely to be most helpful.

2. Provide guidance in all aspects of the instructional lesson—before, during, and after reading. This requires an awareness that many students need you to explicitly *model* the content reading process at various stages. They need *feedback* on their attempts to comprehend and they need to have instructional guidance removed once they have a grasp of the material.

3. Use all language processes to help students learn the material. Efforts to guide students' understanding of unit and lesson concepts should help them to be effective communicators in speaking, listening, reading, and writing.

4. Use small groups to enhance learning. In order for students to become effective at communicating in a content area, they need ample opportunities to risk expressing their ideas. Small group activities encourage risk-taking and expression.

5. Be patient in new unit and lesson implementation. It takes teachers and students time to become comfortable with new material. Give your new units and lessons enough trial runs with modifications so you can fully judge their effectiveness.

An additional point to keep in mind is the structure of an instructional unit and its related lessons. We conceive of a typical lesson structure as having three phases: prereading, reading, and postreading. In prereading students apply what they know to what they are learning. Teachers can facilitate this process by appraising and, if need be, increasing students' knowledge of the topic under scrutiny before they begin reading text and course assignments. In the reading phase students are encouraged to think deeply about what they are learning. Teachers can guide this process by insuring that students adopt an active, questioning approach to text through reasoning across a full range of levels of understanding. This involves students not only comprehending what the text explicitly states, but also understanding the text in relation to their own prior knowledge and experiences. In postreading, students refine and extend ideas; teachers can involve students in activities that encourage them to synthesize and organize information for long-term retention. Finally, bear in mind that these phases are just useful constructs for talking about teaching, learning, and instructional planning. They are not to be blindly adhered to regardless of the instructional situation. Now that we provided some background, it would be interesting to read how some teachers use the textbook in their instructional lessons. Hinchman (1992) provides such a discussion. The next section will introduce some of the details common to unit and lesson planning.

Developing Units and Lessons

A unit may be as short as a single week of instruction or span three to six weeks (Armstrong & Savage, 1994). In most cases, developing a unit on a topic in your content area will entail using a unit blueprint that contains the following elements (Moore & Quinn, 1994):

1. Topic
2. Goals and Objectives
3. Content Outline
4. Learning Activities
5. Resources and Materials
6. Evaluation Plan

In order to understand the role each of these elements plays in planning, we will follow a secondary natural science teacher at a Kauai, Hawaii, high school as she designs a unit entitled "Ocean Predators: The Shark." The teacher's name is Toni Avila.

Ms. Avila's unit on the topic, "Ocean Predators: The Shark" spans three weeks with a focus on basic shark biology, shark species, and habits of sharks related to attacks reported in the islands. Many of Ms. Avila's students and Ms. Avila are avid watersports enthusiasts. She regularly windsurfs the outer reefs off Poipu beach and many of her students surf, kayak, scuba dive, fish, and swim in the waters on the south and north sides of the island. Thus, in planning her unit, Toni thinks about her students' varied experiences in the nearby Hawaiian waters. She also consults district and state curriculum guideline materials and objectives to include this material in her planning process. And, she goes over all her resource material ranging from texts, tradebooks, videos, Internet web pages, and a set of very large borrowed tiger shark jaws from a marine fisheries friend. In the early planning stages of the unit she has all this material laid out on the living room floor of her apartment. In addition, she is aware of an upcoming exhibit on sharks at the Bishop Museum in Honolulu, about 20 minutes by plane from Kauai.

Ms. Avila also thinks carefully about the range of students in her class. Her students are heterogeneously grouped, spanning a range of achievement levels and needs. As she reviews all this material, the following unit blueprint emerges over the span of a week.

Topic

Ocean Predators: The Shark

Goal and Objectives

Be able to identify biological features of sharks, species, and know what shark habits influence attacks in Hawaiian waters and how to prevent their occurrence.

---

1. The students will be able to identify the biological features of a tiger shark by labeling a shark drawing with its missing features with 100 percent accuracy.

2. The students will be able to distinguish dangerous sharks from harmless species by watching slides of various sharks and checking "dangerous" or "harmless" on a paper listing each slide number. They will also be asked to label the species next to each slide number, and the criteria for success at both tasks is 80 percent accuracy overall.

3. The students will develop shark education materials (posters, videos, pamphlets) to assist the state's effort to reduce shark attacks. These materials will be judged by a panel of science teachers, community members, and State Fisheries biologists using a scale that includes a) accuracy of information on sharks, b) artistic merit, and c) potential impact on beach safety.

Content Outline

Ms. Avila goes to the library and checks out a number of resource books on sharks in addition to the class textbook in order to develop a unit content outline that addresses the planned objectives. She reviews sections of the following materials:

Class text: Mader, S. (1990). _Biology._ Dubuque, IA: William C. Brown.

Additional books from the library:

Howorth, P. C. (1991). _Sharks._ Las Vegas, NV: KC Publications.

Lemonick, M. D. (1997, August 11). Under attack. _Time._

Suzumoto, A. (1991). _Sharks Hawaii._ Honolulu, HI: Bishop Museum Press.

Taylor, L. (1993). _Sharks of Hawaii: Their biology and cultural significance._ Honolulu, HI: University of Hawaii Press.

Because of the unusually large number of fatal shark attacks attributed to tiger sharks, Ms. Avila decides to focus on this shark as a basis for comparing and contrasting information about other sharks. Based on selectively reading and taking notes on these books, Ms. Avila created the following content outline:

I. BIOLOGICAL FEATURES OF A TIGER SHARK
   A. A kind of fish which has:
      1. a vertebral column
      2. median fins
      3. breathes using gills
   B. Two groups of jawed fishes
      1. bony fishes
      2. cartilaginous fishes (sharks)

II. MISCONCEPTIONS ABOUT SHARKS
   A. Misconceptions:
      1. All sharks are the same
      2. Sharks are color blind
      3. Sharks must turn on their backs to bite
      4. They have simple brains
   B. Facts and Characteristics
      1. 350 species and much diversity
      2. Characteristics:
         a) good vision
         b) sensitivity to vibrations
            1. lateral line organs
            2. ampullae of Lorenzini (jelly filled pores of nerve endings on snout and head to sense electrical impulses in hunting)
         c) no gas bladder like fish to control buoyancy—they must swim to avoid sinking
         d) 5 to 7 gill openings
         e) eyelid protection—nictitating membrane
         f) denticles (toothlike) rather than scales like a fish
         g) inflexible fins—tail fin is the driving force
         h) teeth grow continuously
         i) reproduction is internal

III. DANGEROUS VERSUS HARMLESS SHARKS

A. Dangerous sharks (piscivorous feeders)
1. Tiger
2. Great White
3. Hammerhead

B. Harmless sharks (plankton feeders)
1. Basking
2. Megamouth
3. Whale shark

IV. PREVENTING SHARK ATTACKS

A. Sharks hunt using recognized signals of prey:
1. thrashing of a wounded fish
2. smell of blood or other body fluids
3. flailing of appendages of weakened prey

B. Swimmers should:
1. avoid swimming alone
2. wear low contrast clothing
3. avoid wearing shiny jewelry
4. avoid wild splashing and erratic swimming
5. stay close to shore
6. avoid murky rivermouth areas
7. avoid deep channels
8. avoid swimming at night
9. surfers should be alert to sharks—paddle calmly toward shore if one is spotted
10. divers spearing fish should tow their kill on a long line away from their bodies

Ms. Avila has taken a class in content area literacy and she is able to capitalize on a number of teaching strategies. For the opening lesson of this unit she decided to use a comprehension strategy called *Talking Drawings* (McConnell, 1993) to introduce the unit. *Talking Drawings* asks students to draw stick figure drawings that represent what they know about a topic to be studied. These rough sketches become visual prompts for a prereading discussion of the topic in pairs or small groups. Following the text reading, students can revise their talking drawings to include the information they learned and erroneous information can be removed.

The focus of this opening lesson will be on how sharks hunt for food. Ms. Avila's lesson plan follows. It contains all the elements of a good *lesson plan* based on a format outline in Moore and Quinn (1994). Ms. Avila's lesson has eight elements based on Moore and Quinn's (1994) approach to *lesson planning* which may or may not be addressed separately: (a) objectives; (b) set induction; (c) content outline; (d) activities; (e) closure; (f) resources and materials; (g) evaluation; and (h) assignment.

Her objective for this lesson contains the four key elements of any good *objective* (Moore & Quinn, 1994): (a) a clear statement of the performance expected of students; (b) the product that should result from this performance; (c) the conditions for demonstrating the expected performance and product; and (d) the criteria for successful demonstration of the expected performance and product. Thus, for the lesson on how sharks hunt for food, Ms. Avila wrote the following lesson plan and related objective:

Ms. Avila's Lesson

Topic: How Sharks Hunt for Food

Objective: Students will verbally discuss their revised shark drawings in groups of four. Students' revised drawings should have two anatomical features that assist hunting for food.

In this objective, the expected performance is a shark drawing. The expected product is a revised version of the original shark drawing. The condition for demonstrating success at this task is a small group discussion of students' revised shark drawings. The criteria for success is the inclusion of two anatomical features that assist sharks in hunting for food.

Set Induction

1. Using the talking drawings format (McConnell, 1993), Ms. Avila has students draw their impressions of a tiger shark's features. The following drawing was produced by one of her students prior to any reading and study about tiger sharks:

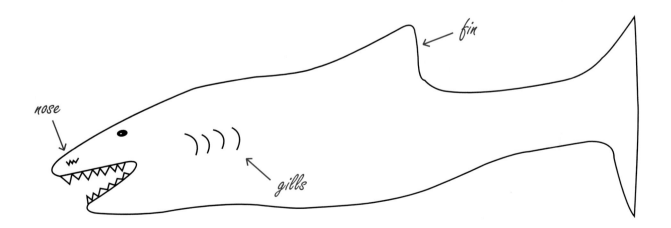

Lesson Content Steps, Outline and Activities

2. Students then shared and discussed their initial drawings in groups of four. A recorder kept track of the information they provided about the shark's features. For example, the group that labeled the drawing here understood a few anatomical features of tiger sharks that might be important for hunting. They included the nose and sense of smell, the gills for breathing, and the dorsal fin for swimming. However, they also felt that sharks might navigate to their prey using sonar.

3. A whole group teacher-guided discussion lead to the development of a shark features drawing on the board with labels for those features mentioned by students at this initial stage of the lesson. The drawing, which resembled a tiger shark more closely than the drawing produced by the group in step 2, had a few additional features useful in hunting including the pectoral fin.

4. Students were then assigned a text passage to read.

5. Following text reading, they revised their initial shark drawings:

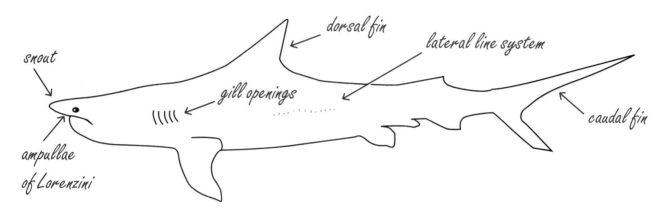

The final phases of a lesson plan structure consist of: (a) lesson closure; (b) evaluation; and (c) assignment. In the case of the shark lesson, students completed the following steps:

6. Small group sharing of the revised drawings with a recorder keeping track of changes and additions to the original drawings. This small group discussion provided the material for the final lesson activity.

Lesson Closure, Evaluation and Assignment

7. A whole class discussion resulted in a composite drawing on the board of the tiger shark and its various anatomical parts that assist hunting. These included the tiger shark's sense of smell and its ability to use its lateral line system or pores along the body to detect vibrations in the water. In addition, highly sensitive pores beneath the shark's snout termed "ampullae of Lorenzini" assist the shark in the final phases of attack by detecting very weak electrical fields emitted by its prey. In short, the tiger shark is a well equipped hunter, even without sonar.

To close the lesson, Ms. Avila advised students to read the section in their book on great white sharks as that topic would be taken up in the next class.

Lesson Resources and Materials

Drawing paper, felt tip pens, overhead transparencies, overhead pens, book on sharks in Hawaii (Suzumoto, A. [1991]. *Sharks Hawaii.* Honolulu, HI: Bishop Museum Press).

Additional learning activities in the overall unit on sharks included shark videos from the local library, a fisheries biologist well known as a shark researcher as a guest speaker, and a field trip to the Bishop Museum where a shark exhibit further countered students' misconceptions about sharks' vision, teeth regeneration, and reproduction. Students also read and critiqued popular novels that involved sharks. They critiqued these based on the accuracy of the scientific information used by the author in describing shark's behavior. In addition, this field trip exposed students to some of the large yet harmless species of sharks including the whale shark and megamouth. Finally, students were asked to develop shark attack prevention brochures for use by the Department of Fisheries in its community education program.

Unit Resources and Materials

Videos, list of potential guest speakers, felt tip pens, overhead transparencies, media supplies for brochure drafts, and trade books:

George, J. C. (1989). *Shark beneath the reef.* New York: Harper/Collins.

McGovern, A. (1978). *Shark lady: True adventures of Euqenie Clark.* New York: Four Winds Press.

Sperry, A. (1963). *Call it courage.* New York: Scholastic.

Evaluation

Text-based quizzes and tests, as well as a panel review of students' brochures using specific criteria in a checklist of features. Thus, both ongoing and final project evaluation will be used to judge students' performance within individual lessons and across the overall unit.

To summarize this section, when you design a conventional unit, it should include the following sections (Moore & Quinn, 1994):

1. Topic
2. Goals and Objectives
3. Content Outline
4. Learning Activities
5. Resources and Materials
6. Evaluation Plan

When you design lessons within this unit structure, a lesson plan should include the following sections (Moore & Quinn, 1994):

1. Topic
2. Objectives
3. Set Induction
4. Content Outline
5. Activities
6. Closure
7. Resources and Materials
8. Evaluation
9. Assignment

The vocabulary, comprehension, writing, and studying strategies introduced later in the book fit within lesson section number 4, Activities. Ms. Avila's use of talking drawings (McConnell, 1993) demonstrates how content area literacy strategies fit within the larger framework of a lesson and unit.

All of these planning elements are important but your delivery of a lesson needs to be flexible enough to allow for students' varying prior knowledge, interest, and achievement. In order to experiment with the process of developing and delivering a lesson, try the following activity.

ACTIVITY

The Five-Minute Lesson

One of the best ways to get accustomed to lesson planning and delivery is to microteach a brief, five-minute lesson focusing on a single, attainable objective. Using the following example as a model, develop and deliver a five-minute lesson based on your favorite hobby. For instance, a student interested in horses devised the following five-minute lesson.

Topic: How to Tie a Quick Release Knot

Objective: Students will be able to verbally state the purpose of the quick release knot in horsemanship with 100 percent accuracy.

Set Induction: "You finish a trail ride with your horse and it's time to remove the saddle to give your horse a bath. You need to tie your horse while you remove the saddle. How would you do this so you can easily untie your horse if he gets spooked?"

Content Outline and Activity: Demonstrate how to tie the quick release knot using a short piece of halter rope and an overhead transparency showing the steps necessary to tie the knot correctly.

Closure and Assessment: Students in small groups of four will have the group leader verbally state the purpose of the quick release knot with 100 percent accuracy.

Resources and Materials: Transparency of the quick release knot steps, short halter rope to demonstrate tying the knot around a chair leg, and book on working with horses, Prince, E. F., & Collier, G. M. (1993). *Basic horsemanship: English and western.* New York: Doubleday.

Continued

The first transparency shows a horse tied correctly with the quick release knot. In an emergency, a sharp tug on the free end will release the horse.

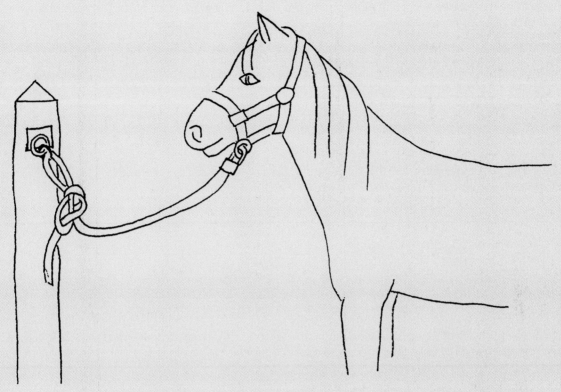

The second transparency in the five-minute lesson shows the four steps needed to tie a quick release knot: (1) Loop the rope through the break away string on the tie down; (2) with the end of the loop, make a bow; (3) tighten the bow to secure the horse; (4) lock the knot by running the loose end through the bow so it will stay secure.

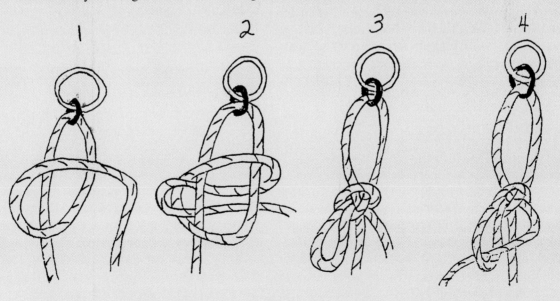

Assignment: Based on this lesson, students would be given short lengths of halter rope to go home and practice the quick release knot for a short performance test at the next class meeting.

Five-minute lessons can cover topics like how to polish shoes correctly, how to slice an onion properly, using a kitchen fire extinguisher, making a child's paper helicopter, tuning a guitar, and any number of other possible topics that lend themselves to a single objective. The process of developing and delivering a five-minute lesson will strengthen your skills in lesson planning and delivery that adheres to clear objectives. Remember, a good objective includes four important elements: (a) a clear statement of the performance expected of students; (b) the product that should result from this performance; (c) the conditions for demonstrating the expected performance and product; and (d) the criteria for successful demonstration of the expected performance and product.

ACTIVITY

In terms of the four critical elements of an objective, critique the following:

Ninth grade world history students will understand how King Charles I handled parliament when he was denied the funds for war.

Based on your analysis of flaws in this lesson objective, rewrite it to reflect the four critical elements of an objective.

_____

_____

_____

The unit and lesson planning framework we have explored so far provides a good beginning point in your planning and use of content area literacy strategies. However, other planning models have been emerging in the last few years that capitalize on core area teacher teams from English, math, science, and social studies engaged in regular lesson and unit planning meetings to develop thematic units that integrate content from diverse subject areas. Another area of increasing importance mentioned in Chapter 3 is total inclusion. How do you plan for a truly diverse, heterogeneous population of students in your classes? We will take up these issues in the next section.

Planning Thematic Units and Lessons

The development and delivery of a *thematic unit* requires a school structure that provides regular planning time for teams of teachers to meet and create curriculum. In addition, a team of core subject area teachers from English, mathematics, science, and social studies typically share the same students. In a secondary school about 130 students are usually served by a core team of teachers. Additionally, teachers from the elective areas of art, music, industrial arts, and physical education may also be involved in planning *integrated, thematic units*. It is only at the point of actually carrying out the unit for the first time that all the bugs can be worked out. This is equally true for lessons and conventional, single subject units.

The following planning steps lead to a potentially powerful thematic unit (McDonald & Czerniak, 1994).

1. Create a binding theme.

For example, one middle school decided to concentrate on eradicating litter on the campus. The core team teachers and elective teachers developed a quarter term thematic unit on "environmental beautification" using their campus as a test case. All 130 seventh and eighth grade students would be involved in the unit across their various core and elective classes.

2. Use concept mapping or outlining to brainstorm and design a preliminary plan for the unit.

3. Decide what concepts will be developed within each content area.

For example, the mathematics, science, and social studies teachers decided to have their students use a campus map and tour the campus to collect specific data on amounts of litter at various key areas of the school. This information was then entered in a computer database and descriptive bar graphs showing areas of substantial litter were plotted. The English teachers assisted students in writing research reports chronicling the location of litter and potential solutions to the problem. Elective teachers in art had students videotape the data collection process and ultimately students developed antilitter posters. In music, they created songs related to litter eradication, and the English classes developed dramatic skits for a whole

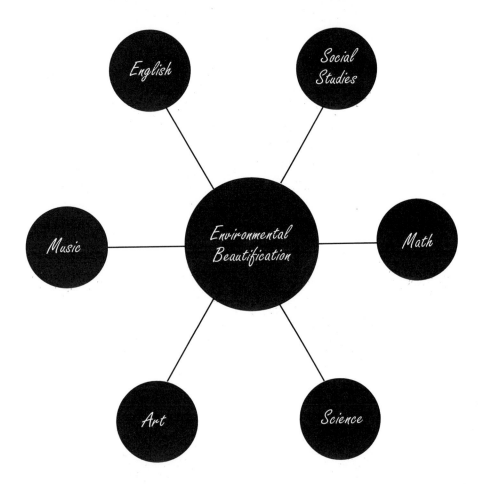

school assembly to recognize the custodial staff and introduce a campus beautification incentive program. New trash cans were placed at key litter sites mapped by students and a weekly drawing awarded prizes for litter control.

This third step of listing key concepts parallels the lesson and unit planning steps you explored earlier in the chapter, but it relies on all team members coordinating their content around the central theme. Many middle and secondary schools are moving toward this model because it results in students seeing connections across diverse content areas and it allows teachers to track student progress and engage in cooperative problem solving when they notice a student falling behind. Elementary teachers can create thematic, integrated units of instruction within their own classrooms.

4. Decide how the concepts in step three are connected across content areas.

Each content area contributes the special skills it has to offer. Thus, the art department capitalized on poster making talents, the math area on data analysis, the social studies area on mapping skills, science on data collection, and English on report writing. The music teacher gave students a chance to put their ideas to song and rap.

5. Develop cooperative activities.

The central, cooperative activity that started this unit was the campus mapping and data collection about litter. This activity necessitated reading materials on environmental beautification and learning a great deal about working in groups with specific assignments for each group member. Some students had to count litter in various locations, others recorded the data, and each team had to share its findings with the other teams mapping campus litter.

6. Resources

A number of websites provide resource materials for lesson planning. For example, the following sites provide instructional activities that link to typical textbook concepts:

National Geographic Online (http://www.nasa.gov/)

NASA (http://www.nasa.gov/)

PBS Online (http://www.pbs.org)

Scholastic Network (http://Scholastic.com)

America Online Education (http://aol.com)

Virtual Museums
(http://www.comlab.ox.ac.uk/archive/other/
museums.html.)

Academy One
(http://nptn.org/cyber.serv/APneP)

Education Guide
(http://www.cs.uidaho.edu/-connie/
interests.html)

Armadillo
(http://www.rice.edu/armadillo/Rice/Resources/
reshome.html)

AskERIC Virtual Library (http://ericir.syr.edu)

Teacher Topics
(http://www.asd.k12.ak.us/Andrews/Teacher-
Topics.html)

Apart from the library, computer, video, presentation software and hardware, Internet, and other resources needed for this thematic unit, students and teachers were able to receive a small grant from the local Rotary club to assist in purchasing trash cans, and developing posters, brochures, and incentive awards.

Finally, in designing integrated, thematic units, try to pick topics that are likely to generate excitement and interest (McDonald & Czerniak, 1994). Students should be involved in the planning stages as well as helping to design projects and grouping structures. If possible, seeking whole school involvement is important because it makes clear to students just how crucial this activity is to the whole school. In the case of the litter eradication example, it was a problem that had gotten steadily worse with everyone assuming someone else, the custodians, teachers, and others were responsible. This was a unit that had an obvious impact on the whole school. Unfortunately, it is rare that our day-to-day curriculum has this kind of obvious impact on students' lives. Carefully planned thematic units can have a tremendous impact but they do take time to create and implement.

One potential problem in unit planning that we have not yet addressed is the wide range of individual differences that students will bring to your classes. You may need to vary lesson assignments in your classes based on students' prior knowledge, interest, reading achievement, language variation, and learning difficulties. In Chapter 3 we reviewed some of the current legislation in the area of inclusion and we discussed second language learners and various approaches. In the section that follows, we explore the nature of individual differences and consequences for planning instruction.

 ## Accommodating Individual Differences in Planning

Teaching requires helping individuals to change. Learning occurs by making whatever adjustments are necessary in the learning situation, accommodating instructional methods to match student abilities, and guiding students as they try to cope with new learning situations. Vaughn, Schumm, Johnson, and Dougherty (1991) found just that in a study which examined 231 middle school and 645 high school students' preferences about accommodating instruction. More specifically, they found that these students favored teachers who adapted their instruction over teachers who did not.

In Chapter 3 you learned about two factors, among many, that affect students' ability to learn from text. These were prior knowledge and language knowledge. The quantity and quality of the prior experiences of individuals and their language sophistication vary greatly. Other individual factors that may affect reading achievement as they interact with each other are: (1) physical development, (2) emotional development, (3) rate of learning, (4) mode of learning, (5) motivation, and (6) practice needed. Because of their interactive nature, it might be difficult to speak of each factor singularly. For instance, physical development may influence one's emotional well-being. The same might be said for rate and mode of learning.

Additionally, the notion of *passive failure,* or learned helplessness (Johnston & Winograd, 1985), is another learning difference to be recognized. Students who exhibit passive failure may be defined as those students who are resigned to fail and believe they do not have the ability to succeed in their learning. When faced with failure, they do not persist; they give up. On the other hand, when these students do succeed, they usually attribute it to factors other than themselves, such as luck, good teaching, or the ease of the task. The important point to be made about these students is that they don't fail because of lack of ability; rather, they do not, and will not, employ the appropriate strategies necessary for effective learning.

One last principle regarding individual differences is that sometimes a factor may vary almost as greatly within an individual as it does among individuals. For instance, a student's interest in school may fluctuate dramatically according to subject area. Changing interests, motivations, and life goals are differences that may differ greatly within an individual, especially over time.

A Definition

Accommodating individual differences means many different things to many different people. Certainly one thing it does not mean is largely undifferentiated, whole-group instruction in which the subject, rather than the student, is the focus of instruction. The problems inherent in such instruction have been recognized for some time. For instance, as far back as 1950, Hunt and Sheldon offered that" High school teachers must also realize that much of their frustration is derived from attempting to teach forty pupils as if all the children were able to perform on the same level" (pp. 352–353). Nonetheless, the lecture method is still predominant in content area teaching.

At the other extreme is complete individualization in which instruction takes place totally on a one-to-one basis. This may be an ideal to which some educators aspire; however, in the face of the rigors of day-to-day classroom experiences with large numbers of students, complete individualization is an unrealistic and counterproductive goal.

The kind of instructional accommodation to individual differences, or *individualization,* the authors recommend represents a compromise between the two extremes cited above. It does not embrace complete individualization, which requires individual preparation or text material for each student, nor does it call for the abandonment of grouping strategies. Rather, it incorporates the gamut of grouping procedures—whole group, small-group, and individual—and utilizes these grouping procedures within the structure of unit and lesson planning (Readence & Dishner, 1992).

Grouping and discussion are recommended because the authors feel that active student involvement in a group situation provides for productivity in learning, for example, through plays, science experiments, or unit reviews (Bean, 1998). Students can learn from one another and provide new insight into learning by modeling their thinking for others (Wood, 1992). Feelings of belonging cannot be disregarded in grouping situations either. Additionally, teachers can move into their most appropriate role, as facilitators of learning, through the use of different group structures.

For example, numerous different types of small groups exist that teachers might employ. Among them are the following:

1. instruction groups—which allow teachers to teach a specific process or issue with more individual contact than is possible in a large group,
2. research groups—which gather information on a problem and report the results to the large group,
3. debate groups—which present a contest of ideas to the large group, and

4. digressive groups—which use brainstorming to generate creative solutions to a problem.

Teachers need to be aware that the idea of making an overnight transformation from total whole-group instruction to the practices for accommodating individual differences is unrealistic. Slow, careful adaptation is crucial to the eventual successful implementation of these practices.

Some Suggestions

In order to realistically consider accommodating students' individual differences, teachers must make modifications in the way they present the textbook within the context of the instructional paradigm. Consequently, you must be willing to make these necessary alterations in order to insure that each student has optimal opportunity to find success in your classroom.

The following are suggested modifications for teachers to consider as they employ the instructional paradigm of prereading, reading, and postreading phases. These include: (1) modifying students' prior knowledge, (2) modifying the way in which the material is presented, (3) considering alternatives to the text material, and (4) modifying the assignment made. These suggestions are the authors' attempts to offer you some practical instructional techniques to help you answer the commonly asked question, "What do I do on Monday?"

Modifications in the Prereading Phase. The degree to which readers utilize their prior experiences in reading and learning with text will greatly influence their understanding of that material. Students' failure to associate new information with previously known information as they attempt to assimilate text material increases the difficulty of their comprehension task. Additionally, as you are well aware, some students simply do not have the necessary prior knowledge about all the topics they will encounter in text material.

Fortunately, as students prepare to read their texts you can intervene to modify their knowledge of a topic as well as their interest in it. You can provide guided instruction to activate, or modify, students' schemata through the use of prereading strategies. Prereading strategies serve to activate appropriate schemata and then modify them as new information is entered, thus allowing comprehension to occur.

Modifications in the Reading Phase. Certainly there is cause to wonder about instruction that presents the same material in the same way to all students. Obviously, in this type of instruction no heed is being paid to the differences in the way students learn or how well individual students deal with the difficulty of the concepts and vocabulary inherent in text. Because of these differences, methods for reducing the difficulty level of the learning material need to be considered. With some students it may be necessary to modify the way the material is presented or even the material itself.

Some students may find the text too difficult to read; others may prefer an alternate means of text presentation. In these situations it would seem to be advantageous to capitalize on students' ability to listen and comprehend the material. Listening can be an effective means for student readers to communicate with text authors. It is the opinion of the authors that active listening strategies are utilized too infrequently and that students could benefit extensively from such strategies.

The teacher may read aloud the selected passage from the text after instructing students to listen for particular concepts or other purposes. Students who are able to read the text with ease may be asked to read it to other students who are having difficulty with the reading. Another alternative is use of the tape recorder. Either the teacher or selected students may tape a portion of the text for those experiencing difficulty. These students may follow along as the text is being read, again with specific instructions about what they should be listening for. If a more structured approach is desired as students are listening to a selected passage, *listening guides* are suggested. The listening guide is a skeletal outline of the important concepts in the passage presented in the order and relationship in which they are set out in the passage. Students are asked to write in the desired information as they listen to the selection. The task of filling in the listening guides gives students additional guidance through the outline structure provided. Activities for reinforcement and extension may follow as planned.

An example of a listening guide follows. If a listening guide was employed with the section of Chapter 8 entitled "Principles of Effective Vocabulary Instruction," it might look like the guide below.

Modifications in the Postreading Phase. In addition to modifying students' prior knowledge, the method, or the presentation of the material, assignments required of students may also be modified. Usually the students' comprehension of text material is checked by having them answer a series of questions either found in the chapter's end or in a study guide constructed by the teacher. However, having the whole group of students deal with exactly the same questions is the antithesis of accommodating divergent student abilities.

Earle and Sanders (1986) have suggested some excellent means by which to individualize certain aspects of content assignments. Pearson and Johnson (1978) have also suggested the use of a technique called slicing in assigning tasks to students. Specifically, slicing refers to simplifying the complexity of these tasks by reexamining those that are required and recasting them to ease the demands placed on students.

Text assignments may be sliced in a variety of ways. Slicing enables teachers to accommodate individual differences by graduating the learning steps involved in completing assignments and by providing structured guidance in doing so. Slicing may be utilized in the following aspects of text assignments: (1) length of passage, (2) scope of information search, and (3) information index.

1. *Length of passage.* Though obviously more of a reading task than a postreading task, length of passage will be discussed here under the umbrella strategy of slicing. Sometimes assigning a chapter at a time for reading represents too sizeable a chunk of text for some students, yet this size assignment is very prevalent. In some cases, poor readers might be overwhelmed by as little as five pages; therefore, it seems appropriate to consider slicing the length of reading task for certain students to accommodate their divergent abilities. Reading assignments should be varied according to the number of concepts assigned to each student. Slicing the length of the passage to even a section or paragraph might be appropriate for certain students to insure their comprehension. Caution is given regarding pictorial aids in text. Authors sometimes use such aids to express what could take large numbers of words. Such aids might be considered a unit of instruc-

Principle	Notes
1. _____	_____
2. _____	_____
3. _____	_____
4. _____	_____

tion for some students, while other students may focus on the running text elaborating upon a particular aid.

2. *Scope of information search.* Content textbooks, by their very nature, are bursting with information. It is unrealistic to consider teaching all concepts presented; therefore, the teacher must conduct some form of content analysis in order to make decisions regarding the relative importance of the concepts. The *scope of information search* is determined by the number of concepts for which students are then held responsible. As concepts increase in number, the more exhaustive the scope of the search becomes. On the other hand, the fewer the concepts to be mastered, the more limited the search. The less proficient the student's reading ability, the more difficult an exhaustive search will be, and the greater the chance of negative effects on motivation and retention of new learning. Therefore, slicing the scope of information search according to students' individual differences is appropriate.

The number of concepts for which students are responsible should be dependent upon their differential abilities and the importance of the concepts in the chapter. The number of concepts can be varied by adding or subtracting from the number of assigned tasks on students' end-of-chapter or study guide questions. For example, more proficient readers may be responsible for 12 concepts while others need only deal with three or four. It is cautioned that no matter how many concepts are assigned to individual students in the class, whole-group discussion should follow the completion of their work so that all students are exposed to the selected information.

Two points should be made concerning the scope of information search. First, limiting the search does not necessitate that only text explicit thinking be involved. It is not the level of thinking that is limited, only the number of concepts. Since all students can think and all students should be involved in higher-level comprehension processes, it is misguided to limit

such thinking in an endeavor to reduce the scope of the information search. Second, there is a difference between varying the scope of the search and varying the length of the passage to be read. The number of concepts assigned may be varied while the length of the passage is held constant. For example, in a 3-page selection certain students may be responsible for one concept per page while others may be held responsible for numerous concepts.

3. *Information index.* Keying students into the location of important concepts or in some way structuring their search for that information is the intent of using an *information index.* The extent to which the index is used depends on students' differential abilities, the importance of the information, and the depth of understanding required.

Two ways are suggested for teachers to slice the demands of the learning task using the information index. The first method is to intersperse questions throughout the text. Students can be directed to lightly mark question numbers at the appropriate places in the text chapter. In this way questions can be dealt with at the time they are encountered during the reading, thus slicing the search for the information. For some teachers this marking of questions may also serve as a preliminary step to their eventual development and use of study guides (Chapter 10).

A second method of providing the information index is to provide an actual informational key to the questions. Questions may be keyed to the page, section, paragraph, and/or sentence where students may find the appropriate answer or the information on which the answer is based. This type of information is frequently provided by content teachers when they use study guides with their students. An example of this type of information index is provided below. In this case the students are keyed to the page and paragraph numbers.

What were the causes of the Revolutionary War? (122:2)

SUMMARY

In this chapter we have outlined approaches to unit and lesson planning. The major parts of a unit plan included: (a) topic; (b) goals and objectives; (c) content outline; (d) learning activities; (e) resources and materials; and (f) evaluation plan. In addition, we considered integrated, thematic unit planning, as well as planning for individual student differences. Example lessons and a unit on sharks were provided to guide your own content area lesson planning. Activities included microteaching and analyzing lessons, rewriting objectives, and critiquing a lesson vignette.

Now go back to the lesson planning vignette at the beginning of the chapter. React again to the lesson as you did before. Compare your answers with those you made before you read the chapter.

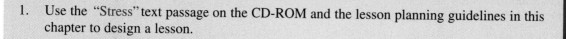

MINI PROJECT

1. Use the "Stress" text passage on the CD-ROM and the lesson planning guidelines in this chapter to design a lesson.

   A. Write two learning objectives for a group of secondary students in a wellness class.

   B. Create a possible set induction activity.

   C. Design a learning activity for the lesson.

   D. Brainstorm additional resources and materials for the lesson.

   E. Brainstorm how you would evaluate students' learning with respect to this material.

2. Meet with colleagues from core and elective content areas to design an integrated, thematic unit.

3. Use the planning modifications such as slicing the task to accommodate student differences for a lesson in your content area.

4. Develop a list of supplementary materials that you might be able to use to augment or to replace a chapter from a textbook in your content area.

GROUP PROJECTS

- Explain why you think integrated thematic units planned by teams of teachers are a) worthwhile, or b) unworkable.

- Think about your experience as a middle and secondary student. In a small group of 4 students, brainstorm and list those characteristics and strategies your best and worst teachers used in lesson planning and delivery.

- The authors describe four different dimensions of slicing activities: length of passage, scope of information, information index, and response mode. Define the general purpose of slicing and evaluate each of these dimensions of slicing activities.

- The authors suggest that content area teachers can modify instructional materials and have students listen to rather than read from textbooks. List some of the authors' specific suggestions and evaluate them in light of current public school realities.

- Illustrate how you as a content area teacher can use specific techniques to combat passive failure in your classroom.

LITERATURE AND CONTENT LITERACY

SETTING

Two eighth grade students, Dale Fallon and Sanae Tokunaga, are leaning over the railing on the second story deck of their suburban South Carolina middle school after a lesson in life science. Their teacher, Mr. Cousteau, introduced a lesson on endangered species by bringing in a large, inflatable child's pool toy in the shape and color of a sea turtle. Its vinyl skin made squeaking sounds as he placed the turtle on the table at the front of the room and said, "Today we're going to learn about the green sea turtle." He then launched into a lecture about types of turtles and their habits. The lecture went on for over 20 minutes. Both Dale and Sanae are conscientious students and they took notes. Many other students slumped in their seats, where they day-dreamed and doodled, looking bored. Mr. Cousteau then assigned some text reading and questions to be answered about endangered species in their textbook.

THE LESSON

Right before the bell rang, Mr. Cousteau told students they were required to find a fiction book to read about turtles for a book report due to him in one week.

We overhear Dale and Sanae's conversation about the turtle lesson as they talk outside Mr. Cousteau's room during recess.

Dale: "How are we supposed to know what books to read about turtles? That guy is so boring!"

Sanae: "Yeah, my brother had Mrs. Read last year for life science at the other middle school and they had a classroom library with a whole bunch of really good novels about endangered species. Maybe I can visit his school and see if I can borrow a book there. The only problem is, my brother Roger is now in high school and Mrs. Read moved to Florida."

Dale: "We can ask Mr. Cousteau for more help but then he'll just get upset and we'll get lousy grades. Let's just go to the library and find a book we can both use for our dumb book report. It's no big deal. I write book reports on books I hate and don't read. Hey, Sanae, I'm sure you've never done that, huh?"

Sanae: "Yeah, right. Sure. All last year in English we had to do these stupid book reports. I just looked for the skinniest books, read the back cover or skimmed the pages and faked my report. Too bad school is such a waste of time."

Dale: "Hey Sanae, have you read this latest Saddle Club book, *Show Horse* (Bryant, 1992)? Too bad we can't read about horses instead of turtles."

Sanae: "You gotta read the Palm Beach Prep book, *Lonely Heart* (Wolfe, 1990). It's so romantic. But I guess we won't have time now. We need to get to the library. You want to meet after school? That way we can pick the same stupid book and get this assignment done. I wonder if Mr. Cousteau has ever read any turtle novels himself? I bet he doesn't have a clue about it. He's just giving us work to do without even thinking about how we feel. You know Nathan in class?"

Dale: "You mean the guy who looks like a computer nerd?"

Sanae: "Yeah, that one. Well, his Dad is a marine scientist who specializes in turtle tagging research. Cousteau didn't even ask him about his Dad's work. I read about it in the newspaper."

Dale: "I bet he gets an A on this assignment."

Sanae: "He gets As on everything. Hey, I gotta go to my social studies class in building Q. See you this afternoon."

▶ Now that you have had a chance to consider this lesson, write down your thoughts on the following questions:

1. What are the good points about the lesson?

2. What are the weak points about the lesson?

3. What, if anything, would you change about the lesson?

RATIONALE

Author Jamaica Kincaid grew up on the tiny island of Antigua, governed by British rule. Her memories of the library where she spent so much time recalled the quiet, reflective power of reading a good book.

> If you saw the old library, situated as it was, in a big, old wooden building painted a shade of yellow that is beautiful to people like me, with its wide veranda, its big, always open windows, its rows and rows of shelves filled with books, its beautiful wooden tables and chairs for sitting and reading, if you could hear the sound of its quietness (for the quiet in this library was a sound in itself), the smell of the sea (which was a stone's throw away), the heat of the sun (no building could protect us from that), the beauty of us sitting there like communicants at an altar, taking in, again and again, the fairy tale of how we met you, your right to do the things you did, how beautiful you were, are, and always will be; if you could see all of that in just one glimpse, you would see why my heart would break at the dung heap that now passes for a library in Antigua. (Kincaid, 1988, pp. 42–43)

By 1974, the library was damaged in an earthquake and left unrepaired for over a decade with the mocking sign "repairs are pending" (Kincaid, 1988, p. 42). In her book *A Small Place*, Jamaica Kincaid vividly charts the tensions between native Antiguans, the colonial British, and the more recent Antiguan independence. In truth, Kincaid's book is a multicultural treatise on the complexities of the aftermath of imperial rule, racism, and pride. But the library provided the chance to explore a vast array of books although they recounted the lives of whites rather than Antigua natives. Nevertheless, as a little girl, Kincaid gravitated toward the lyrical, captivating world of a good book. She said, "I stole many books from this library. I didn't mean to steal the books, really; it's just that once I had read a book I couldn't bear to part with it" (Kincaid, 1988, p. 45).

Unfortunately, many content area teachers assume that librarians and English teachers should be the ones to acquaint students with powerful fiction books beyond the required texts in social studies, science, mathematics, and elective areas. Yet the field of young adult literature is a rich treasure trove of books that can illuminate concepts about endangered species like Mr. Cousteau's turtles (see Will Hobbs' *Changes in Latitudes*, 1988) or the cultural loss of a Narraganset Indian boy cast into indentured servitude in colonial Boston in 1681 (see Paul Fleischman's *Saturnalia*, 1990).

In any content area it is possible to find young adult literature that enriches textbook readings and course concepts. Your task as a content teacher is to become familiar with this rich treasure trove of literature, understand how to survey students' attitudes and interests, and learn about various strategies you can use to link literature and textbook reading. This may sound like a daunting task, but it is really a matter of starting modestly by reading at least one young adult novel keyed to your particular field. Since most of these novels are relatively short, in the range of 125 pages, you may find this process to be every bit as enjoyable as reading the latest adult fiction best seller.

In addition to reading young adult literature keyed to your field of study, you need to become familiar with the increasingly rich array of multicultural literature. Applebee's (1989) national survey of book length works assigned to students in secondary English indicated that no minority authors were in the top 10 list of readings and only one woman author was represented. The literary canon of assigned readings in English has been very resistant to change. In this chapter we will introduce some of the growing collection of multicultural young adult literature that can be used in content area teaching.

LEARNING OBJECTIVES

- Use attitude and interest inventories to survey students' reading attitudes and interests in your content area.

- Select and use trade books linked to units of instruction in your content area.

- Implement a sustained silent reading program.

- Use sources of the trade books to locate and review books you plan to use in your content area.

- Create a plan for further development of your knowledge about trade books you can use in your discipline.

GRAPHIC ORGANIZER

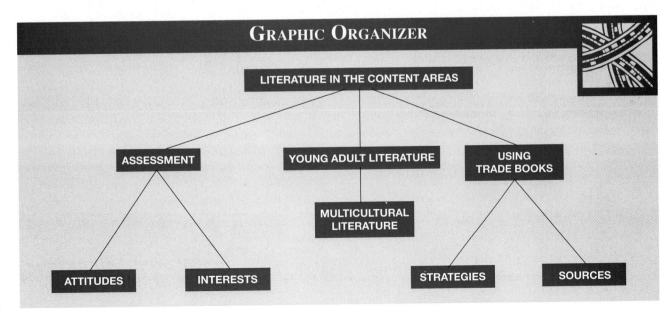

Assessment of Reading Attitudes and Interests

Reading Attitudes

Attitudes may be defined as those feelings that cause a reader to approach or avoid a reading situation. Attitudes toward reading are shaped by a variety of factors. For example, reading attitudes are undoubtedly the result of beliefs "finely tuned by culture" (Cothern & Collins, 1992).

Family and school experiences played a profound role in shaping our own attitudes toward reading. And these factors influence how we, as content teachers infuse or fail to infuse pleasurable reading activities in our own classrooms. Manna and Misheff (1987) asked teachers to write autobiographical papers on their early, middle, and more recent memories of reading. The area of family reading was mentioned as a positive influence by 72 percent of the teachers and libraries were mentioned by 68 percent. Negative factors included reading as a low priority in the home along with school book reports, reading groups, and lecture methods.

In a large-scale survey of 18,185 grade 1 through 6 students' attitudes toward academic and recreational reading, McKenna, Kear, and Ellsworth (1995) noted that reading attitudes declined steadily. By the time students were in 6th grade, they cared little for academic or recreational reading. Unfortunately, declines in voluntary pleasure reading parallel declines in national assessment performance on a variety of reading tasks (Guthrie & Wigfield, 1997). Thus, fostering students engagement in both academic and recreational reading is extremely important for their future success.

Bean (1993) analyzed 45 reading autobiographies produced by preservice content area teachers. When they were asked to consider how they might improve students' attitudes toward reading they reflected on their own former teachers. Fifty-seven percent of these future teachers mentioned the special influence their own English teachers played in encouraging a love of reading. They recalled teachers who organized classroom book clubs and modeled reading of captivating literature, particularly literature keyed to the cultural experiences of Hawaiians, Japanese-Americans, and other Pacific island groups. Teachers from subject fields outside of English were rarely mentioned.

Sixty-nine percent of the preservice teachers Bean surveyed made some claims about how they would handle challenging texts and how they might foster students' love of reading. However, the great majority of these claims were nonspecific. For example, a future science teacher commented, "I am excited about the integration of reading into content classes."

Since attitudes are a critical factor in using trade books in content classrooms to develop a lifelong love of reading, you need to know how to assess students' attitudes toward reading. There are a number of methods for assessing reading attitudes, including personal interviews, autobiographies, and behavior checklists (Alexander & Cobb, 1992). The most common method is the self-report questionnaire. The reading attitude survey on the next page was developed for use with middle and secondary school students (Baldwin, Johnson, & Peer, 1980).

This attitude survey, or others like it (e.g., Alexander & Cobb, 1992), may be used as a pre/posttest for determining the affective impact of programs. It is also possible to look at specific areas of reading attitude. For example, in the BJP Survey:

Items 1, 7, 12 = Attitude toward libraries
Items 4, 6, 16, 19 = Reading self-concept
Other items = General attitude toward reading

It is standard procedure for individual scores to be recorded for purposes of counseling students with bad attitudes. We recommend that this not be done. Students with negative attitudes toward reading are not necessarily unintelligent. As a consequence, if they have any reason to think that they will be singled out and/or questioned because of their negative attitudes, they will take the only intelligent option and lie on the survey. The technical name for this is *response bias,* writing down what one believes the examiner wants rather than what the test taker really believes. A second reason for not generating individual scores is that students whose attitudes toward books and reading are so bad that they need counseling are painfully conspicuous most of the time, and no test is needed to identify them. On the other hand, trying to determine whether or not a program has created a positive change in group attitudes requires some objective measure. Therefore, we recommend that attitude surveys be anonymous and that class, grade, and school averages be used to assess groups rather than individuals. Additionally, once data have been gathered concerning the attitudes of students, attention should be given to promoting reading related to content areas.

Directions: This survey tells how you feel about reading and books. The survey is not a test, and it is anonymous. It will not affect your grades or progress in school, but it will help your school to create better programs. Answer as honestly as you can by checking the term or terms which tell how you feel about each statement.	Strongly Agree	Agree	Disagree	Strongly Disagree
1. Library books are dull.				
2. Reading is a waste of time.				
3. Reading is one of my hobbies.				
4. I believe I am a better reader than most other students in my grade.				
5. Reading is almost always boring.				
6. Sometimes I think kids younger than I am read better than I do.				
7. I enjoy going to the library for books.				
8. I can read as well as most students who are a year older than I am.				
9. I don't have enough time to read books.				
10. I believe that I am a poor reader.				
11. I would like to belong to a book club.				
12. I like to take library books home.				
13. Teachers want me to read too much.				
14. You can't learn much from reading.				
15. Books can help us to understand other people.				
16. I almost always get A's and B's in reading and English.				
17. I like to have time to read in class.				
18. Reading gets boring after about ten minutes.				
19. Sometimes I get bad grades in reading and English.				
20. I like to read before I go to bed.				

Scoring: The positive items are 3, 4, 7, 8, 11, 12, 15, 16, 17, 20. Give four points for a *SA,* three points for an *A,* two points for a *D,* and one point for a *SD.* For the negative items, 1, 2, 5, 6, 9, 10, 13, 14, 18, 19, score four points for a *SD,* three for *D,* two for *A,* and one for *SA.* Scores can range from 20 to 80.

60±80 = Good
40±59 = Fair
20±39 = Poor

Take the BJP attitude survey. How good is your reading attitude? Be honest!

Reading Interests

Students naturally prefer to engage in activities that are likely to boost feelings of competence, autonomy, and relatedness to others (Deci, 1992). In addition, *reading interests* that develop and endure come from feelings of enjoyment and involvement (Schiefele, 1992). In the vignette at the beginning of this chapter, Dale and Sanae expressed disdain for their book report assignment yet they clearly enjoyed chatting about the other fiction they were reading about horses and romance. Indeed, in a case study of four adolescents and their preferred reading outside of school, Vogel and Zancanella (1991) found that each of these individuals had vastly different interests based on their personal biographies. For example, one student,

Martha, was an average student in English but she had an extensive reading interest in baseball. Her description of reading various baseball dramas conveyed "a feeling of engagement and enthusiasm—of critical attention . . ." (Vogel & Zancanella, 1991, p. 55). Another student, Tina was an avid reader of romance series and she related this experience to the assigned reading of Hawthorne's (1850) *Scarlet Letter* in English. An avid reader of the horror genre, Donovan saw reading literature in school as a process of figuring out the interpretation the teacher wanted. All four students valued reading outside of English more than in class reading. Why? The prescriptive literary canon, with rare exceptions like Hawthorne's *Scarlet Letter* for Tina, simply ignored their interests.

ACTIVITY

In a college class with about equal numbers of men and women, have students identify their favorite type of pleasure reading. How are the reading interests of men and women different?

Assessment. The most useful type of interest assessment is one that permits the teacher to match specific interests with specific materials. However, the general interest inventory is the most common type of interest assessment, and an example of one follows.

General Interest Inventory

Directions: The purpose of this inventory is to find out what kinds of things you and your classmates are interested in reading. After every topic there is a blank space. On each space give a grade of A, B, C, D, or F based on how much you would like to read about the topic. An *A* means: It's wonderful; I love it! An *F* means: It's terrible; take the topic away and bury it, quick!

Sports _____	Animals _____
Science Fiction _____	Fantasy _____
Folklore _____	Romance _____
Cars _____	Adventure _____
Humor _____	Mystery _____
War _____	The Arts _____
Supernatural _____	Foreign Lands _____
Science _____	History _____
Poetry _____	Family Life _____
Plays _____	Human Drama _____
Mathematics _____	Health Sciences _____

It is, of course, possible to create interest inventories with varying degrees of specificity; for instance, sports can be subclassified into baseball, basketball, football, tennis, curling, etc. Baseball could be subdivided into fiction stories, nonfiction books about pitching or hitting, and so on. In much the same manner it is possible to create an interest inventory for a specific content area. This type of inventory can provide information about group interests as well as guide outside reading for individuals. The following U.S. history interest inventory is merely one example in an endless chain of possibilities.

U.S. History Interest Inventory

Directions: Everyone in your class is going to be doing some outside reading related to American history. The purpose of this inventory is to help you find books that are actually interesting to *you*. After every topic there is a blank space. On the space next to the topic you would *most* like to read about, put a 1. Place a 2 on the space for your next choice. Place a 3 on the third best choice, and so on until you have evaluated every topic. Do *NOT* use any number more than once.

The Colonial Period (1600–1760)

Biography _____

Human Drama _____

Family Life _____

Freedom and Justice _____

The Revolutionary War Era (1760–1785)

Biography _____

Politics _____

War _____

The Civil War Era (1850–1876)

Slavery _____

Famous Battles _____

Politics _____

Biography _____

Human Drama _____

Western and Frontier Life

Pioneers _____

Native Americans _____

Tales of the Wild West _____

World War II (1939–1945)

Battles in the Pacific _____

Military Planes _____

The War in Europe _____

Atomic Weapons _____

Freedom and Justice _____

Post World War II America

Civil Rights _____

Women's Liberation _____

Vietnam War _____

The Presidency _____

Biographies of African-Americans _____

It should also be pointed out that teachers can modify the above interest inventory to fit the needs of their teaching objectives. For instance, students might rank each general topic area (e.g., The Colonial Period) 1, 2, 3, 4 instead of ranking all topics at once. This may enable teachers to find appropriate material for each general topic area as it is encountered.

 ## Young Adult Literature

A cartoon in "The Neighborhood" series by cartoonist Jerry Van Amerongen (1987) shows a middle-aged couple, Marian and Guy, sitting in a private booth at an upscale restaurant enjoying what should be a romantic, candlelit dinner. However, both Marian and Guy are fully engaged in reading their respective novels, ignoring each other. The caption below the cartoon reads: Marian and Guy have been together a long time.

Developing a lifelong love of reading is the result of many influences. Family, friends, and certainly teachers all play a role in making reading pleasurable or something to be avoided at all costs. The more you become familiar with contemporary young adult literature the more you can create units that integrate this captivating medium.

Surveys of adolescents' reading habits suggest they spend little of their leisure time reading literature (Beach & Marshall, 1991). As a content area teacher, you can change this apathy or avoidance of young adult literature by becoming personally familiar with at least a small portion of the vast array of books that can be linked to your units and lessons. To do so means taking a stance that may not be very familiar. For example, when you think of young adult literature, you may recall reading *A Separate Peace* (Knowles, 1960) or *Catcher in the Rye* (Salinger, 1951). But notice when these books were written. *A Separate Peace* is now almost 40 years old and *Catcher in the Rye,* almost 50 years old. Both depicted the lonely, often traumatic experiences of young adults in private school settings. Both focused on Caucasian students. These relatively early adolescent novels captured the interest of young adults, but they now seem out of touch with the 1990s. If you think of adolescents through the lens of your own adolescent experience and the filter of young adult literature from the 1950s and 1960s, this will limit your horizons. Although we are not saying ignore this older literature, we do strongly advocate getting to know the newer young adult authors who portray multicultural characters, actions, and events that more closely mirror those of our students.

The shift toward greater realism in young adult literature began with S. E. Hinton's (1967) *The Outsiders,* written when she was 16 (Beach & Marshall, 1991). This novel realistically portrayed the passages and transitions adolescents go through as they struggle to find their own identity amidst conflicting peer and family pressures. Young adult literature helps adolescents cope with the dissonance between the ideal and real in daily life by its power to vicariously transport the reader into the lives and times of fictional characters struggling with familiar problems (Beach & Marshall, 1991). In the 1980s and 1990s increasingly complex female and multicultural characters emerged. Hispanic authors like Gary Soto offered a positive, insider's view of life in the barrio. Asian-American literature explored racial discrimination and oppression. The Vietnam war has been widely chronicled in powerful young adult novels like Walter Dean Myers' (1988) *Fallen Angels.* Myers' novel is a poignant account of two young African-American soldiers immersed in the rice paddy skirmishes that robbed their adolescence and forever changed their lives.

Unlike textbooks that present facts to be considered and used in solving problems in science or math, discussing policies in history, or reading the notes of a scale in music, fiction by its nature propels students into high level interpretive thinking (Langer, 1989). Langer conducted a comparative case study analysis of secondary students reading textbooks in science and social studies versus narratives. She found that these students approached the story selections with an open, interpretive stance by using their intuition to figure out what she called "the underside" of the story (Langer, 1989, p. 16). In contrast, Langer found that students read their texts with a more narrow, factual stance. She concluded that stories draw students into high level critical thinking. Earlier work by Rosenblatt (1978) categorized the reader as paramount in the act of reading, actively constructing meaning. But textbooks simply do not allow for the same interpretive stance afforded by a good novel, short story, or biography.

What exactly is *young adult literature*? We like the definition supplied by Nilsen and Donelson (1993, p. 6). They define *young adult literature* as "anything that readers between the approximate ages of twelve and twenty choose to read."

Young adult literature encompasses a wide range of genres including mystery, adventure, science fiction, romance, supernatural, fantasy, sports, humor, and historical fiction (Nilsen & Donelson, 1993). Typical themes revolve around family relationships, rites of passage, alienation, friends and society, death, disabilities, drugs and alcohol, and sexual relationships. A number of powerful novels explore how to define oneself outside the family, coping with the reality that parents are less than perfect, carving out one's own set of moral, ethical, religious, and political principles, developing positive healthy relationships, and projecting possible futures and career choices (Stover & Tway, 1992).

Unfortunately, very few content teachers use or know much about young adult literature (Gerlach, 1992). Rather, they often see all literature as the English teacher's exclusive domain and responsibility. Worse still, many teachers have never read a young adult novel, let alone a contemporary young adult novel.

The purpose of using young adult literature in your content area is to enhance students' content learning. This is a different focus than the English teacher's interest in appreciation and analysis of literature. You can focus on locating those books best keyed to concepts and issues in your course. For example, a history teacher could enrich a unit on slavery with Warner's (1976) diary account, *From Slave to Abolitionist: The Life of William Wells Brown*. This poignant book propels the reader into the day-to-day trials of William Wells Brown, a young slave who eventually escapes his tormentors to become a significant abolitionist writer in the 1850s. His writing far surpasses that of any textbook in its ability to grab the attention of young readers.

Trade books must survive on the open market. These are the books you find at popular bookstores, where there is usually a section on young adult literature. Since there is no perfect list of trade books to be used with every content area, as a teacher you need to explore books keyed to your area and develop a classroom library (Nilsen & Donelson, 1993). Given the labor intensive requirements of creating a classroom library, we suggest you start small by getting to know one or two contemporary young adult novels that relate to one or two topics in your content teaching. Later in this chapter we introduce some of the sources of young adult literature you can explore to locate books related to your units and lessons. We also include an annotated bibliography of trade books keyed to various content areas, but it is important to realize that the list is one we created. You need to develop your own unique collection of novels, magazines, and enjoyable reading material that expands on textbook and class concepts. For example, some authorities on using literature in classrooms recommend creating "book clusters" (Savage, 1994, p. 218). A book cluster is a graphic organizer with the title of a unit like sharks and a listing of trade books that relate to the unit. For example, in our Chapter 6 shark unit, novels such as George's (1989) *Shark Beneath the Reef* were integral parts of the unit planning process. Often, the school librarian can be helpful in suggesting books to use with your proposed unit.

Multicultural Literature

One of the most exciting dimensions of young adult literature is the growing number of multicultural books portraying characters' experiences from a bicultural perspective. Bishop (1993, p. 39) defined *multicultural literature* as "literature by and about people who are members of groups considered to be outside the socio-political mainstream of the United States." Books about African Americans, Asian Americans, Native Americans, Hispanics, Pacific Islanders, and the disabled, fit within this category. The best of this body of literature affords an opportunity for students to see themselves in the books they read, provided the multicultural literature selected portrays characters in a culturally authentic fashion.

Books such as Gary Soto's (1992) *Pacific Crossing* meet this criterion. Soto was born in Fresno, grew up in the barrio, labored as a migrant worker, and is now a Professor at the University of California, Berkeley. In this novel, two 14-year-old boys from a San Francisco barrio journey to Japan to stay with a farming family outside Tokyo where they develop their martial arts and learn about their host family's world far from the familiar barrio. The novel weaves together a rich cultural fabric that embraces Mexican, American, and Japanese features. Soto's book would be a good choice in a world history or geography class in social studies.

Multicultural literature is typically outside the accepted canon of traditional required reading that includes *The Scarlet Letter,* Shakespeare's writing, and so on. Middle school teacher Heriberto Godina (1996) recounted his struggles to establish a multicultural literature strand at his middle school. He was able, through the use of his own funds and a desire to move beyond one-shot multicultural food days, to engage students in his English classes in the reading and discussion of Rudolfo Anaya's (1972) *Bless me Ultima*. "Students began to see reflections of themselves in text, and this provided them with a familiar path for thinking critically and scaffolded their writing" (p. 546). Godina makes a persuasive argument for integrating classical, widely accepted canonical literature, and multicultural literature.

In a very powerful classroom project in Corpus Christi, Texas, aimed at integrating multicultural literature and community talents, Brozo, Valerio, and Salazar (1996) also used *Bless me Ultima* as a basis for exploring cross-cultural approaches to healing. By using take home learning packets that involved making herbal tea, they were able to bring parents into the novel reading and discussion. This community connection made the novel's setting in south Texas come alive for students and families.

As Godina (1996) and Brozo, Valerio, and Salazar (1996) found, when students see themselves reflected in their reading, they view the content classroom as a place of direct relevance to their lives. Reading at the secondary level, as it has so often been described in literacy autobiographies, is no longer work or a task to complete. Rather, reading has powerful, personal meaning for adolescents' identity development.

Nieto (1996) argues that to effectively use multicultural literature in the classroom teachers must become multicultural themselves. The best of multicultural literature confronts racism, bias, and oppression head on. Thus, social issues are a good starting point for selecting multicultural literature (Au, 1993). Students from diverse cultures gain pride in their ethnic origins when they see a character overcome obstacles to succeed. They gain a complex view of American and world societies and issues of social justice (Au, 1993).

What constitutes good multicultural literature? A number of writers have wrestled with this issue. You should try to select books that sensitively and accurately depict characters (Leung, 1993). For example, in Asian-Pacific young adult literature, authors should go beyond stereotypes, avoid historical distortions or omissions, avoid the "super minority" view, and reflect the changing status of women (Aoki, 1993, p. 122). Additionally, young adult literature should shun tokenism where characters from divergent cultures are mere window dressing in a story (Stover & Tway, 1992). These novels should give the reader an honest, accurate portrayal of the human condition experienced by students from various cultures. For example, Linda Crew's (1989) *Children of the River* follows a young girl named Sundara as she escapes her war torn home in Cambodia in 1975 to journey to Oregon. She encounters the subtle prejudice of the 1990s in the local high school where she falls in love with the school's football star. She grapples with her parents' beliefs and the bicultural upheaval experienced by so many students in our secondary schools. Levstik (1993) suggested that this type of historical fiction helps personalize history for students and it helps them see the cause and effect structure of history. In contrast, textbooks present a profusion of objectively documented facts that lose the flavor of the human experience. The best young adult literature is historically accurate, but the human drama rather than places and dates is at the forefront (Levstik, 1993).

Once you have browsed sources of young adult and multicultural young adult literature, found some that relate to topics in your discipline, and taken the time to read a few books, how can you make these books an integral part of your classroom teaching? In the section that follows we offer a few ideas for using literature across the various content fields.

Using Trade Books

Trade books offer one of the best ways to delve into other cultures or to see how other people cope with the problems inherent in being a young adult. Most importantly, young adult literature has been instrumental in improving at risk students' self-concepts and achievement (Miller, 1993). A good novel can illuminate otherwise dull facts in history, science, mathematics, and the elective fields of art, music, physical education, health, agriculture, industrial arts, and a variety of other curricular areas. You really can't afford not to tap this rich resource in your content teaching (Baldwin & Leavell, 1992). The chance to influence students' lifelong love of reading as well as the potential to improve their concept understanding and critical reading in your subject is too important a task to leave exclusively to the adopted textbook. And, the evidence in support of trade books in improving content learning is substantial and growing. For example, students in sixth grade learning about China through a literature-based approach significantly outpaced a group of their peers engaged in textbook study of China on an 88-item concept acquisition test (Guzzetti, Kowalinski, & McGowan, 1992).

Nonfiction trade books can be used to explore text-based topics and as a means to engage students in synthesizing ideas from diverse sources (Palmer & Stewart, 1997). The librarian is key to locating a good collection of nonfiction trade books to support any unit you are working on. In addition, local district resources and the internet offer resources students can learn to explore independently. for example, in a recent literature response project, 9th grade students in English visited the Las Vegas Indian Center and consulted the internet to learn more about Navajo burial practices. They then used this information to critique and write about the authenticity of Navajo burial traditions described in a novel they were reading and discussing (Bean, Valerio, Money Senior, & White, 1997).

Nonfiction trade books and internet resources are often informative, visually attractive, lively, and up-to-date. Although students may be unaccustomed to reading across multiple sources, taking notes, and synthesizing information, they are unlikely to learn these crucial skills without practice. Indeed, as they move into college and work, these will prove to be essential skills for success. Palmer and Stewart (1997) emphasize the need for teacher guidance in how to read, retrieve, and restructure information in nonfiction trade books and other sources.

Reading Aloud to Students

We recommend starting modestly by identifying a unit where you can include a young adult trade book novel of about 125 pages. In selecting a novel to read aloud, look for books that have rich, lyrical language. For example, in a unit on slavery, Mary Lyons' (1992) *Letters from a Slave Girl: The Story of Harriet Jacobs*, takes place in 1861 and vividly recounts Harriet's 7 years of confinement in a relative's storeroom before gaining her freedom. The autobiographical letters that formed the basis for this story accurately portray the dialect of the time. At 158 pages, *Letters from a Slave Girl: The Story of Harriet Jacobs* is an ideal read aloud book.

Read the novel once and then skim through it to identify prediction points and places where you can stop reading at the end of a class period. Allow about 10 minutes at the end of a period to read from the novel and build on concepts introduced in the text and other class activities. With some young adult literature, videos can be located to further illuminate events of the time in compelling human terms. We recommend practicing your read aloud with a cassette recorder to ensure you are likely to capture students' attention. In addition, using prediction questions like "What do you predict will happen to Harriet? Will she gain her freedom?" Or, experience-based questions like "What would you do if you were Harriet?" involve students in the story plot and upcoming events. With some novels you can omit passages that you feel do not move the story forward.

Sustained Silent Reading

Bard College literature professor and writer, Chinua Achebe, is a Nigerian Ibo villager and now, one of the most influential African intellectuals of the 20th century (Winkler, 1994). The headmaster of his secondary school in Nigeria had a rule that after class, three days-per-week, students closed their textbooks and read novels, poetry, or anything for pleasure. Achebe attributed his love for literature to this period of his life. However, he did not see himself or other Africans portrayed in the stories he read, so he set out to become a writer. His first novel, *Things Fall Apart* (1958), has been translated into over 50 languages.

Sustained Silent Reading (McCracken, 1971) is a systematic program that establishes regular reading times for students. Its fundamental objective is to provide students with an opportunity to practice their reading skills using pleasurable content related materials. SSR has a positive impact on student's attitudes toward reading and their long-term interest in reading for pleasure (Aranha, 1985; Guthrie & Greaney, 1991).

There are two separate phases in SSR: (a) instructional readiness, and (b) the reading activity itself. The books can be selected to match a content unit like the slavery example in the read aloud section discussed previously, or books may be self-selected by students if you have a well stocked classroom library or helpful librarian.

Instructional Readiness. Discuss SSR with students. Let them know how the activity will be carried out and why they are doing it. Emphasize that SSR is supposed to be a pleasurable activity. Tell them that they will not be graded or asked comprehension questions over what they read.

Since the stated purpose of SSR is to provide pleasurable practice in reading, the students should be informed that certain types of materials are inappropriate. Textbooks, magazines, comics, and newspapers *should not* be used. Textbooks are seldom selected for pleasure reading, and comics, magazines, and newspapers lend themselves to picture looking rather than reading. If you plan to use SSR to further expand students' understanding of events in history, science, or mathematics units, then you will need a well stocked collection of young adult novels students can select. Your guidance in this area will be crucial as students often have no idea what books match their interests within a content area like science or history. An interest inventory and your own familiarity with literature related to your field will be important preparatory steps before launching into SSR.

The Reading Activity. Once you have completed this *instructional readiness* stage, you can engage students in the Sustained Silent Reading using the following guidelines.

1. *Everyone must read,* and this includes the teacher. SSR is not a ministudy period for students, and it is not a break or prep period for teachers. Doing homework, getting coffee, grading papers, and other extraneous activities are put aside to allow time for pleasure reading. It is essential that the teacher model SSR by reading right along with students.

2. *SSR should be uninterrupted.* Let students know that they are not to sharpen pencils, gossip, or ask questions like "Ms.____, what's this word mean?" In addition, colleagues should know that they are not to disturb a class during SSR. It may be worthwhile to hang a sign on the door: "SSR IN PROGRESS, DO NOT DISTURB!"

3. *The SSR period should* be set at the beginning of the year to ensure the activity is accomplished. SSR has

a settling effect on a class. Ideally, SSR should occur on a regular scheduled basis. We strongly encourage SSR as often as it is realistically possible in your classroom.

4. *The time limits* for SSR will need to vary according to the age and general maturity of the class. We recommend beginning with five minutes and then gradually increasing the time as students adjust to the routine and develop a capacity to attend to reading for more than brief periods of time. Be careful not to increase the time too quickly, perhaps a minute every week or two. Each teacher should judge the amount of time to be allocated to SSR based upon student abilities and curricular demands.

The benefits that can be gained from reading pleasurable content-related material will enrich your instruction, particularly if students are reading material related to the topic under discussion. It is suggested that coupling the findings of the interest inventory previously administered with the time to read those materials during SSR in your classroom will be most beneficial and rewarding for future learning of subject matter material.

5. *Time SSR with care.* We suggest using a kitchen timer placed on your desk and facing away from the students so they won't stare at it. For the same reason, wall clocks make bad timing devices as some students become clock watchers. Avoid using your wristwatch since that encourages students to ask you about time remaining. Simply tell them that the kitchen timer will always indicate when SSR is over for the day.

6. *Avoid doing SSR immediately prior to tests* since it will be difficult—maybe even painful—for students to concentrate knowing that a quiz or test is imminent. On test days, shift SSR to some later part of the class period.

7. *Problem students* can be handled in the following manner. You may have some students whose aversion to reading is so profound that they will refuse, initially, to participate in SSR. The very idea of reading for fun will be totally foreign to some students. Do not badger or pressure them. You can force people to do something, but you can't make them like it. Let problem students "sleep" just as long as they don't bother the group. As these students see others enjoying SSR, they should come to find reading preferable to inactivity.

Let the class know that intentional disruption will result in termination of SSR for the day. If a student does something that causes half the class to stop reading, simply say: I'm sorry, but our SSR is over for today. Put your books away and begin _____. Move right along to the next scheduled activity without acknowledging the culprits or their actions. Because SSR is inherently pleasurable, peer pressure should serve to reduce individual disruptions.

Literature Response Journals and Other Response Strategies

Both reading aloud to students and SSR lend themselves to some follow-up dialogue about the book or books being read. Indeed, students generally want to discuss powerful literature, and this is a good opportunity to build on content learning. *Literature response journals* ask students to reflect on their reading and share these reflections with the teacher, peers, or parents for further written dialogue (Fuhler, 1994). You can give students a few minutes after SSR or reading aloud to write in their journals about how they might handle the situation the main character is in or what they predict will happen next. We recommend collecting journals and responding to them for extra student points. You can collect a few journals each time or collect all of them depending on the schedule you establish with students.

In addition to journal writing about trade book selections, you can organize a panel discussion or debate that asks students to take a position the main character in a novel might advocate or oppose (Beach & Marshall, 1991). For example, in *Saturnalia* (Fleischman, 1990) William, the main character, has a chance to flee Boston with his Narraganset Indian uncle. Students can debate the plusses and minuses of William's ultimate decision in a society that took indentured servitude for granted.

Using overlapping Venn diagrams, you can compare and contrast cultural mores in multicultural literature. For example, in Crew's (1989) *Children of the River,* Sundara, a Cambodian teenager, struggles with her relatives old ways and the contrasting brashness of her Oregon classmates. A Venn diagram consisting of two overlapping circles can be used to discuss those cultural norms that are distinct to Cambodian and European-American cultures and those norms that seem to overlap.

Art, role playing, music, and drama offer additional ways of responding to literature. For example, Miller (1993) had a group of at-risk adolescent females read four novels that exemplified strong women characters. Based on their reading of Walker's (1983) widely known novel, *The Color Purple,* these students created drawings of the main character, Celie, at the beginning of the book and, again, as a stronger person at the end of the book. Or, a strategy like Talking Drawings (McConnell, 1993), introduced in Chapter 6, can be used to create before and after reading drawings about a novel or its characters.

Students engaged in reading multicultural literature like Soto's (1992) *Pacific Crossing* which takes place in Atami, Japan, a small farming village three hours outside Tokyo, can write to school-based pen pals in Japan (Stover & Tway, 1992). Or, as a contemporary alternative to writing, they can make a video with one student interviewing another or a panel of students about the book just read.

Book Clubs

Book clubs in content classrooms offer yet another way to engage students in reading and sharing their interpretations of fiction and non-fiction trade books. Book clubs involve small groups of three to five students gathering to discuss a common reading (McMahon & Raphael, 1997). This sharing helps clarify areas of confusion in reading a novel or other selection, and it offers a good forum for collectively creating interpretations, critiques, and ownership of ideas.

Book clubs can be used in content fields like social studies to expand students' learning (Highfield & Folkert, 1997). For example, studying World War II through novels that view events from a Japanese perspective helps students evaluate textbook accounts critically (Highfield & Folkert, 1997). In addition, guided reading across multiple sources helps students learn how to synthesize information.

In a recent book club discussion in one of our classes, students enrolled in a content area literacy course read David Klass's award winning novel, *California Blue* (Klass, 1994). John, a high school student and the main character finds a special butterfly while jogging in the woods in a logging area of Northern California. It turns out the butterfly is endangered and the livelihood of the town is about to be threatened because of John's discovery. About half way through the novel, John longs to tell his Dad about his discovery but realizes there is great risk involved as his family also earns their living through logging. He feels very alone and decides to keep his discovery to himself, ultimately sharing it with his biology teacher and others he decides to trust. In order to prepare for book club discussion of this and other key episodes in the novel, students kept reading logs. Open-ended prompt questions helped students jog their thinking and writing about these episodes. For example, in this episode, students were asked to write and talk about how they would handle the situation where John wants to tell his Dad about his discovery the next day at breakfast. This prompt question generated a wide array of responses and personal stories about family styles. Some students said they would be secretive because of severe consequences in their families and others indicated they would take the risk of being restricted or worse to stand for their beliefs. This particular novel is ideal for exploring a range of science and social science issues,

particularly issues of citizenship and decision-making (Bean, Kile, & Readence, 1996).

When you decide to implement book clubs in your classroom, take some time to learn more about other teachers' experiences with this exciting addition to a content classroom. In the recommended reading section for this chapter, we offer some good selections to help you get started.

Readers Theater

Readers theater involves a presentation of material that is read aloud in an expressive and dramatic fashion by two or more readers (Young & Vardell, 1993). Readers theater offers students a chance to practice oral reading, group presentation, and a chance to review concepts so they can effectively deliver a performance. To engage students in readers theater you need to: (a) select passages from a novel that move the story forward; (b) reproduce these sections; (c) delete non-critical lines; (d) divide the parts for each student to deliver; (e) label reader parts with students' names; and (f) model the process of reading aloud in a dramatic fashion.

Library Power

Good school libraries contain thousands of fascinating novels, biographies, periodicals, and reference works, all waiting to be discovered. The unfortunate thing is that many students never discover the pleasures and satisfactions of the library. You as a content teacher can introduce students to the wealth of the school library. The following guidelines suggest some of the ways you can do this.

Meet the Librarian and the Library. It makes sense that before you can guide students in the uses of the library, you need to familiarize yourself with its organization and resources. Find out what periodicals, reference works, videos, and other media are available for your subject area. Most librarians are anxious to help faculty members identify, catalogue, and order materials.

Library Orientation. The school librarian or media specialist is an expert in location skills necessary for finding information. Take advantage of those skills by setting up library orientations for groups of students. Even in senior high school, many students will not know how to use the computerized databases to locate books and materials. Some students will not be able to find a work of fiction. The librarian can provide this basic information as well as answer questions about library hours and special rules.

A Case in Point. Imagine that you are a high school American history teacher. You want your students to read beyond the class textbook, and you want them to enjoy their outside reading as much as possible. In order to meet this objective you do the following things:

1. You create a list of broad topics from American history, for example, Freedom and Justice.

2. With the help of the librarian, you catalogue the titles in the school library that fit each topic. (Obviously, the difficulty of the task is determined by the size of the library, the number of topics you want books for, and the number of books you require for each topic.)

3. Create an interest inventory which reflects the original topics, in this case the U.S. History Interest Inventory cited previously.

4. Administer the inventory to students and then recommend specific titles to individual students on the basis of expressed interest.

The following seven selected titles reflect the freedom and justice topic on the U.S. History Interest Inventory.

Fleischman, P. (1990). *Saturnalia.* New York: HarperCollins.

Houston, J. W., & Houston, J. D. (1973). *Farewell to Manzanar.* New York: Bantam.

Myers, W. D. (1988). *Fallen angels.* New York: Scholastic.

Tan, A. (1991). *The Kitchen God's Wife.* New York: Ballantine.

Taylor, M. D. (1976). *Roll of thunder, hear my cry.* New York: Trumpet Club.

Voight, C. (1991). *The Vandemark mummy.* New York: Fawcett.

Warner, L. S. (1976). *From slave to abolitionist: The life of William Wells Brown.* New York: Dial.

As we recommended earlier in this chapter, perhaps the best way to begin using trade book novels in your content area is to locate and read one or two young adult novels a year, starting small and building your collection slowly. That way, you will truly have ownership of the books you read aloud to students and recommend they read. Your book discussions will be more informed, and you will be modeling your own interest in young adult literature. Where can you locate trade books to use in your content area? And, what are some good books in the divergent content areas of sci-

ence, mathematics, music, social studies, and other content areas? In the section that follows we provide a listing of useful sources as you search for books in your own unit and lesson planning. We also indicate a few books that we have found to be useful in expanding students' knowledge in science, history, mathematics, social studies, and other areas.

Sources of Trade Books

As a content area teacher in science, social studies, mathematics, English, music, physical education, agriculture, art, and other areas, you may be interested in locating contemporary young adult literature and other trade books. The librarian, book reviews in journals, teacher conventions, mall bookstores, specialty children's book stores, and publishers' catalogs are some of the possible sources. Keep in mind that there is no substitute for browsing your local bookstore, reading the first few pages of a young adult novel you think might key into your content area, and spending some time reading it. The process of finding just the right book to read aloud, include in SSR, and integrate with a unit in your field is labor intensive. Viewing the development of your own bibliography of trade books for your content area over the span of three to five years is a reasonable goal. Any of the following sources can help you get started.

Young Adult Choices. Each year, the November issue of the *Journal of Adolescent & Adult Literacy* (International Reading Association) publishes an annotated list of recommended books that a team of young adults selected.

In 1996, the International Reading Association published an annotated compilation of young adults' choices from the years 1993–1995, *More teens' favorite books: Young adults' choices 1993–1995.* Newark, DE: International Reading Association. (ISBN 0-87207-149-9).

The *English Journal,* National Council Teachers of English also features young adult literature reviews. It is published eight times per year.

Annotated Bibliographies and Book Reviews. Most annotated bibliographies are organized by content area or theme, making them easy to locate books within the topic area you need. These bibliographies are a good starting point, but ultimately, you need to create your own unique bibliography.

ALAN Review. Assembly on Literature for Adolescents, National Council of Teachers of English. Published three times each year.

Books for you: A reading list for senior high school students. National Council of Teachers of English. See the latest edition.

A *Book Browser* CD is available from the International Reading Association, 800 Barksdale Rd., Newark, DE 19714. It permits rapid searches for books.

Dreyer, S. (latest edition). *The bookfinder: A guide to children's literature about the needs and problems of youth aged 2–15.* Circle Pines, MN: American Guidance Service.

Reed, A. J. S. (1988). *Comics to classics: A parent's guide to books for teens and preteens.* Newark, DE: International Reading Association. (ISBN 0-87207-798-5).

Stoll, D. R. (1997). *Magazines for kids and teens* (2nd ed.). Newark, DE: International Reading Association. (ISBN 0-87207-243-6).

Conventions and Catalogs. Most professional association annual and regional conventions feature a large exhibit hall filled with publishers' displays of books and materials. This is a great place to browse, collect catalogs, and get your name on publishers' mailing lists so you can stay in touch with new books. For example, the annual California Reading Association convention each November features an extensive array of publishers' exhibits with a focus on California's literature initiative. Specialty bookstores like The White Rabbit in La Jolla, California, display their books and feature a quarterly newsletter with annotations and book ordering information. Other book suppliers like Shen's Books and Supplies in Arcadia, California, have a special emphasis on multicultural books, particularly Asian novels and non-fiction. They offer the Kaleidoscope book club with an emphasis on multicultural literature. Publishers like Scholastic in New York have extensive, annotated catalogs and classroom book club order forms.

Finally, your local teacher materials and supplies store and the school and public libraries are good places to browse. Local business and philanthropic clubs are usually interested in raising funds to support literacy activities in classrooms. This is an often overlooked source of support. Purchasing a classroom set of books like Hobbs' (1988) *Changes in Latitudes* for a unit on endangered species in science may seem prohibitive. But with the help of a small grant from a local philanthropic organization, you can at least get started.

Creating Your Own Bibliography. Book lists, catalogs, and journal recommendations of books are convenient but no substitute for browsing, locating a book you think might key into a unit you teach, and reading it. The following briefly annotated list of books includes some of the content areas where trade books can be used to illuminate textbook concepts. Many books are also appropriate for art, music, mathematics, agriculture, industrial arts, foreign language, drama, health, guidance, and physical education. This bibliography is merely a brief listing to get you started on developing your own collection of books and materials.

English

Christenbury, L. (1995). *Books for you: An annotated book list for senior high students.* Urbana, IL: National Council of Teachers of English.

Loughery, J. (1993). *First sightings: Contemporary stories of American youth.* New York: Persea. (ISBN 0-89255-187-9). This anthology contains 20 stories selected from a variety of award winning authors.

Mazer, A. (1993). *American street: A multicultural anthology of stories.* New York: Persea. (ISBN 0-89255-191-7). Includes short stories from Native American author, Duane Big Eagle, and The No Guitar Blues by Gary Soto. A wide range of cultures and times are represented in this anthology.

Geography

Choi, S. N. (1991). *Year of impossible good-byes.* New York: Dell. (ISBN 0-440-40759-1). Chronicles the occupation of Korea in 1945 and its impact on one family.

Myers, W. D. (1988). *Fallen angels.* New York: Scholastic. (ISBN 0-59040943-3). The Vietnam War in 1968 through the eyes of a 17-year-old African-American soldier from New York.

Yep, L. (1975). *Dragonwings.* New York: HarperCollins. (ISBN 0-06440085-9). Chronicles a child's journey from China to America. Moon Shadow joined his father who worked in a San Francisco laundry when he was only 8 years old.

History

Fleischman, P. (1990). *Saturnalia.* New York: HarperCollins. (ISBN 006-447089-X). William is a Narraganset Indian in colonial Boston where he must serve as an indentured servant to a printer. It is 1681 and the servants await Saturnalia, a 24 hour respite when servants and masters trade places.

Taylor, M. D. (1976). *Roll of thunder, hear my cry.* New York: Trumpet Club. (ISBN 0-440-84387-1). The Logan family in Mississippi in the 1930s struggle with discrimination, racism, and oppression.

Uchida, Y. (1983). *The best bad thing.* New York: Macmillan. (ISBN 0689-71069-0). Rinko, a Japanese-American living in California in the 1930s, experiences prejudice.

Yep, L. (1993). *Dragons's gate.* New York: HarperCollins. This novel chronicles the Chinese workers' experiences while building the transcontinental railroad in brutal physical and psychological conditions.

Music

Landis, J. D. (1989). *The band never dances.* New York: HarperCollins. The main character is a female drummer who rides the wave of success into the world of rock arenas while simultaneously struggling with her brother's suicide.

Physical Education

Lipsyte, R. (1993). *The chief.* New York: HarperCollins. In this ongoing series, Lipsyte presents an insider's view of the gritty world of boxing.

Myers, W. D. (1996). *Slam!* New York: Scholastic. "Slam" Harris's superb basketball playing offers a way out of New York's inner city, but his grades haunt his dreams.

Cannon, A. E. (1990). *The shadow brothers.* New York: Bantam. Recounts the problems Marcus and his Navajo foster brother Henry experience in high school track and through Henry's growing interest in his Navajo culture that propels him away from his foster family.

Science

George, J. C. (1989). *Shark beneath the reef.* New York: HarperCollins. (ISBN 0-06-440308-4). Fourteen-year-old Tomas Torres wants to become a marine biologist and struggles with staying or dropping out of school.

Hobbs, W. (1988). *Changes in latitudes.* New York: Avon. (ISBN 0-38071 61 9-4). A family vacation in Mexico leads to Teddy's interest in turtles and efforts to protect their welfare as endangered species.

Klass, D. (1994). *California blue.* New York: Scholastic. John, the main character discovers the double-edged sword of trying to protect an endangered butterfly in a small logging community.

Social Studies: Cultural and Ethnic Identity

Hamilton, V. (1993). *Plain city.* New York: Scholastic. Buhlaire Sims slowly forms a positive sense of the good dimensions of her life imparted by her African-American mother and long-departed half-Causcasian dad.

Hernandez, I. B. (1992). *Heartbeat drumbeat.* Houston, TX: Arte Publico Press. This novel chronicles Morgana Cruz's search for her identity based on her mother's Navajo traditions and her father's Mexican culture.

Lee, M. (1992). *Finding my voice.* Boston, MA: Houghton Mifflin. A Korean-American high school student, Ellen Sung, struggles with violent racism and its impact on her identity in a small Minnesota town.

Velasquez, G. (1994). *Juanita fights the school board.* Houston, TX: Pinata Press. Juanita is expelled from high school after a fight and faces stereotyping and self-doubt as the novel progresses.

Wartski, M. (1995). *Candle in the wind.* New York: Ballantine. Terri Mizuno struggles with racism in a small Massachusetts town.

As a content teacher, having a well developed knowledge of students' reading attitudes and interests, as well as a working knowledge of young adult literature you can tie to your units, will make learning in your classroom a rich experience.

SUMMARY

In this chapter we have discussed the significance and assessment of reading attitudes and interests in the content classroom. Reading aloud to students, sustained silent reading, literature response journals, readers theater, book clubs, and library power were presented as strategies for integrating trade books with young adult literature and textbook concepts inn the content areas. In addition, the importance of becoming familiar with contemporary young adult literature, modeling its use, and developing your own bibliography of sources was emphasized throughout the chapter.

Now go back to the literature and content literacy vignette at the beginning of the chapter. React again to the lesson as you did before. Compare your answers with those you made before you read the chapter.

MINI PROJECT

1. Write a reading autobiography chronicling your reading interests and books read from the time you can first remember being read to until the present.

2. Administer the BJP attitude survey presented in this chapter to a group of middle or secondary students. Summarize the results.

3. Create a reading interest inventory for your content area.

4. Read one young adult novel related to your content area and share it with another person in your field. Use the novel in a read aloud or SSR fashion within a unit of instruction in your content area.

5. Develop a bibliography of young adult literature for use in your content area.

GROUP PROJECTS

- Explain how you would select and use young adult trade book literature in your content area.

- Explain why it is important to supplement texts with young adult trade books.

- Compare and contrast two young adult multicultural novels using a Venn diagram.

VOCABULARY

VIGNETTE

SETTING

Matha Matix's seventh grade math class, a diverse group of students in a multicultural setting. In her unit on "Geometry," Ms. Matix is teaching a lesson on "Angles."

THE LESSON

Ms. Matix begins class by listing the following words on the board: *straight, right, obtuse, acute, vertical, corresponding, adjacent, complementary,* and *supplementary.* She then goes back to each word, pronounces it, provides a definition, and gives a pictorial example. Some students are seen to be writing in their notes. She emphasizes to the class that they will be using the words throughout the lesson on angles. Later, as the bell rings, Ms. Matix gives a homework assignment and tells students they will review the vocabulary words the next day as they go over the assignment.

▶ Bearing in mind that much of this lesson concerns vocabulary, jot down your thoughts on the following questions:

1. What are the good points about the lesson?

2. What are the weak points about the lesson?

3. What, if anything, would you change about the lesson?

RATIONALE

Sometimes a mob might "grift" all day without "turning them over," but this is unlikely except in the case of a "jug mob" which takes a limited number of "pokes." Any pick-pocket who has on his person more than one wallet is something of a hazard both to himself and to the mob, for each wallet can count as a separate offense if he should be caught. Therefore, it is safer to have cash only. "Class mobs" usually count the money each time they "skin the pokes," one stall commonly is responsible for all of it, and an accounting in full is made at the end of the day. (Maurer, 1955, p. 194)

All groups of people, whether they be pickpockets, bridge players, or educators, share special idioms and technical terminology which characterize the group. "Insiders" use this vocabulary freely and through it gain access to the collective knowledge of the group. Likewise, "outsiders" are identified as such and are restricted in their social and intellectual intercourse with the group due, in part, to their ignorance of its specialized vocabulary.

The task of the content teacher is to help students become insiders, whose minds move with facility in the fields of science, English, social studies, or mathematics. To a large extent, this is accomplished by teaching them the technical terminology of each discipline. The following example, in which one student is explaining a math problem to another student, suggests the gravity of vocabulary acquisition in content areas.

> "I don't remember what you call it, but it's like if you have three numbers—5, 9, and 6—and you want to multiply them. It doesn't matter what order you do it in. You always get the same answer, 270."

This student apparently understands the concept of the commutative principle, the process of combining elements in such a manner that the order of multiplication is unimportant. Unfortunately, not knowing the word for this concept limits the student's capacity to utilize it. For instance, one might expect the student's reading or listening comprehension to be seriously impaired given the following textbook statement, ". . . The commutative principle applies to the preceding series of algebraic equations."

In all content areas, new concepts are sequentially introduced and defined in terms of concepts presented earlier. As students progress through texts, reading comprehension can diminish to the point of extinction if students have failed to master the words that symbolize important concepts, even when they have mastered the concepts themselves! In addition, research clearly indicates that teaching vocabulary can have a powerful and positive impact on reading comprehension (Beck & McKeown, 1991). For this reason, considerable attention to vocabulary is fundamental to the purposes of every classroom teacher.

LEARNING OBJECTIVES

- Discuss the pros and cons of various decoding strategies.

- Understand the general principles of vocabulary instruction.

- Justify direct vocabulary instruction as an essential component in your own content area.

- Implement a variety of instructional strategies for introducing and reinforcing new vocabulary.

GRAPHIC ORGANIZER

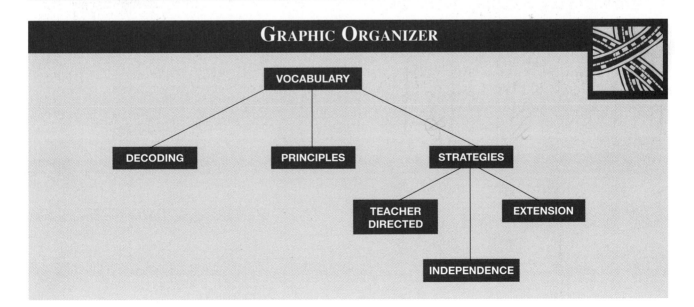

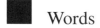 Words

For a variety of technical reasons, the concept of "word" is extremely difficult to define as a unit of language. Curiously, adult language users have little difficulty agreeing whether or not a particular sequence of sounds or symbols is a word. This common sensitivity to the concept of word is a result of defining words as prefabricated units which speakers know are not to be interrupted with linguistic fillers such as "um" or "uh" during speech. For instance, it would be quite natural for a speaker to say "The-work-man-um-will-finish-um-Saturday," but not to say, "The-work-um-man-will-fin-um-ish Saturday."

Words may also be described in terms of semantic relationships; and, since the focus of this chapter is on the meanings of words rather than the sounds of words, the following definition is offered:

> A *word* is a pattern of auditory or visual symbols which represent schemata (concepts).

The most important characteristic of this definition is the inclusion of *schemata,* because it suggests that word meanings—for individual persons—are in an endless state of flux. The concepts which words represent are constantly being modified by daily experiences during which: (1) new information is fitted into existing schemata, or (2) radically new or discordant information is accommodated through the modification of schemata. For instance, most people have internalized the concept of cat, but do they know all breeds by name? Could they correctly identify the habitats and mating customs of each? Could they name a type of cat which does not have retractable claws? If not, then there is a clear potential for the modification of their cat schema.

The point is that the question of knowing the meaning of a word is not subject to a simple yes or no. There is always a need for qualification because a word is known or unknown, strange or unfamiliar, to some degree which is determined by the richness of its known associations.

Learning a new word (concept) requires more than a simple explanation because individual words are not simple isolated bits of information. Words are defined by the ways and the extent to which they are related to all other words. For instance, it would be possible to define the concept, anchor, as a device used on a boat or ship to keep the vessel stationary. However, such a definition does little to build an anchor schema that will allow a student to comprehend and use the word at will. A more effective strategy, one that builds a richer schema, might entail the following: (1) demonstrating the variation in sizes and shapes of anchors; (2) letting students touch or try to lift an anchor; (3) explaining how sailors get an anchor in and out of the water; (4) describing how an anchor keeps a ship from drifting; and (5) explaining why it is a good idea to keep boats from drifting.

On a more abstract level, knowing a word requires understanding its connotations as well as its denotations, sometimes referred to as contextual versus definitional knowledge. The *denotation* of a word is its broad meaning; in this sense, old/aged, end/finale, and surface/superficial are synonymous pairs of words. A word's *connotations* are its subtle shades of meaning and the specific contextual conditions in which it can occur. Connotations are meanings that differentiate among words which would otherwise be considered synonyms. Connotatively, old and aged are not synonyms because they cannot be used in the same contexts. For example, you can talk about "an old rock" but not "an aged rock" because aged connotes "living" as in "an aged woman." In this sense, there are probably few, if any, exact synonyms in English.

The following four sentences were written by students in a ninth grade English class. The sentences were constructed as part of an assignment in which the students were to write sentences and then make word substitutions based on an inspection of the classroom thesaurus. The italic words are those selected from the thesaurus.

1. The dirty old man went to church to ask God for *immunity.*

2. The car had a *putrefaction.*

3. It was clear from her actions that Susan was a fine *madam.*

4. It pays to be a *chivalrous* driver.

Aside from the amusing pictures which some of these sentences paint, what precisely is wrong with them? Denotatively, the words selected from the thesaurus are quite reasonable since pairs like immunity/forgiveness and breakdown/putrefaction are synonymous, or at least closely related in meaning. However, the members of each pair have different connotations that make them unacceptable substitutes in most contexts. For instance, putrefaction connotes a breakdown of a biological nature, and it is anomalous to use the word in reference to something made of such things as steel and rubber.

What we are suggesting is that the acquisition of new word meanings is sufficiently complex that vocabulary instruction should not be consigned to a mindless list of strange words followed by one-line definitions. If it is, the lack of examples and supporting contexts will doom students' understanding of new words to be both superficial and tentative.

 Vocabularies

A *vocabulary* is a corpus of many thousands of words and their associated meanings. An individual's vocabulary may be analyzed in several ways. For instance, every person has a *receptive* vocabulary and an *expressive* vocabulary. The former refers to words that can be read and comprehended in print or heard and understood in spoken context. The latter refers to lexical items which a person can use properly when speaking or writing. In a sense, people have four vocabularies: listening, reading, speaking, and writing, and these categories are not mutually inclusive. Children usually begin school with respectable listening and speaking vocabularies but considerably less reading and writing vocabulary. On the other hand, the listening and reading vocabularies of literate adults—and secondary students—far outstrip their speaking and writing vocabularies. This is true because the schemata necessary to place words in proper contexts must be more fully developed than those required for recognizing word meanings when context has already been provided.

Finally, vocabularies may be classified as *technical* or *general*. Technical vocabulary refers to words such as "denouement," "secant," "Bull Market," "secede," etc., which are uniquely or usually related to individual academic disciplines. General vocabulary refers to words that are not specifically associated with any one teaching area, e.g., "germane," "astute," and "ubiquitous."

A second distinction between technical and general vocabulary involves assimilation and accommodation, concepts introduced in Chapter 3. Assimilation is a process in which new information is incorporated into existing schemata. Accommodation occurs when old schemata are modified or new schemata are created so that information can be assimilated.

For the most part the acquisition of general vocabulary may be described as an assimilation process, whereas the learning of technical vocabulary more often requires some accommodation. By the time students are intellectually prepared to learn words such as germane or astute, they already possess the concepts which those words symbolize, i.e., significant/relevant and alert/perceptive. Consequently, germane and astute are new, perhaps more efficient, labels for previously acquired concepts. Learning them does not demand a radical modification of existing schemata. In contrast, technical vocabulary present labels for unfamiliar concepts that must be accommodated by modifying extant schemata.

Content area teachers are primarily concerned with transmitting novel information and helping students develop new concepts, e.g., Bull Market or secant. For this reason, the focus of the present chapter will be on the teaching of technical vocabulary and a general strategy for independently decoding unfamiliar words.

 Decoding Unfamiliar Vocabulary

Decoding is a process whereby a coded message is converted back into thought. For example, a chef reads a waiter's written message about your order and decodes it, that is, comprehends how you want your steak prepared.

The process is similar in content area textbook communication. Authors put down their thoughts in a written form that their readers then decode. When the decoding process breaks down, comprehension suffers. In our opinion the major stumbling block to efficient decoding of text is students' inability to cope with words and concepts that are unfamiliar to them. There are three basic strategies for unlocking the meanings of unfamiliar words in text: morphemic analysis, context clues, and external references.

Morphemic Analysis

When students encounter long words in print, it is valuable to break such words into more manageable parts. It is well known that a word part may have a meaning of its own. Such a word part is called a morpheme. A *morpheme* is the smallest unit of language which has an associated meaning; i.e., it possesses a definite meaning and cannot be subdivided into smaller units which have meaning. There are two types of morphemes, free and bound. A *free morpheme* can function alone as a word, e.g., "some" or "thing." *Bound morphemes* are those meaningful language units that occur only as attachments to words or other morphemes, e.g., "tele-," "-er," or "-cide." In essence, they are prefixes, suffixes, or roots. Just as a word may be a symbol that represents a schema in our knowledge structure, so may a word part or morpheme. Additionally, two or more morphemes may combine to give a combination of ideas, thus modifying a schema. For instance, "black" and "berry," two separate morphemes, may be combined to form a new or modified schema conveying a combination of meanings. Thus, *morphemic analysis* is a process by which readers can determine the meaning of an unfamiliar word by analyzing its component parts.

Attention to word parts to reveal the meanings of unfamiliar words is a process that goes on all the time. For instance, if a reader encounters a word such as "patricide" in a contextual setting, the reader is likely to focus on the morphemes of the word, "par-tri-" and "-cide" to determine its meaning, particularly if the context is anomalous, or provides no clear interpretation. Such an anomalous context would be:

Robert has committed patricide.

Of course, the reader cannot perform such an analysis if the reader does not have prior knowledge of the two morphemes in patricide. Yet because morphemic analysis focuses on meaning, it provides a more sensible approach to analyzing unfamiliar words than does phonics. Additionally, approximately 80 percent of the words listed in an English dictionary contain words which are composed of Latin or Greek morphemes. Consequently, a knowledge of these roots and affixes can be valuable in analyzing and then remembering the meanings of unfamiliar polysyllabic words (White, Power, & White, 1989).

ACTIVITY

Use your knowledge of morphemes to analyze the following unfamiliar polysyllabic word. Try to derive the meaning of it.

PNEUMONOULTRAMICROSCOPICSILICOVOLCANOCONIOSIS

Were you able to arrive at a definition without consulting a dictionary or did you panic because the word appears ominous? What you have encountered is one of the longest words in the English language, yet one that readily lends itself to morphemic analysis. Perhaps the following context will help you come up with the definition:

Because of his proximity to Mount St. Helens, he contracted pneumonoultramicroscopicsilicovolcanoconiosis.

Using the context clues present in the sentence, in combination with your knowledge of morphemes, probably gave you the definition. The following morphemes are present in the word:

Pneumono—related to the lungs

Ultra—transcending; super

Micro—small

Scopic—related to a viewing instrument

Silico—the mineral, silicon

Volcano—eruption in the earth from which molten rock, steam, and dust issue

Coni (konis)—dust

Osis—referring to a diseased condition

Thus, pneumonoultramicroscopicsilicovolcanoconiosis is a disease of the lungs caused by habitual inhalation of very fine silicon dust particles.

The authors are certainly not arguing that content teachers should have their students master lists of affixes and roots. This procedure is restrictive in that students memorize without meaningful context. Inserting information into long-term memory is best accomplished by making the information interesting and relevant—descriptors that hardly apply to lengthy lists of strange-looking morphemes.

In summary, what we are suggesting is that knowledge of morphemes has the potential for transfer to unfamiliar words that possess the same morphemes.

Students should be taught to apply their knowledge of word parts to unfamiliar words they encounter. In this way they are encouraged to discover their own generalizations by intelligent inference or informed guessing. For instance, in the word you were asked to analyze in this section, you may not have extracted the morpheme, "pneumon" and attached meaning to it directly. Rather, you may have associated the morpheme with the word "pneumonia" to arrive at a meaning for it. It is this type of learning process that the authors advocate.

Context Clues

All human experience is context dependent. Indeed, human behavior can hardly be interpreted without context. As an example, consider the question, "Is it OK for me to take my clothes off?" The answer obviously depends upon the context—at a nudist colony, yes; in church, no! Context is, therefore, a necessary and natural part of human functioning. Such is also the case in reading. For instance, if given the sentence, "Jo Ann loves her new red _____," you would be able to supply a word in the blank even though no graphophonic information is present. Additionally, many investigators in reading education have also stressed the importance of readers' use of context in interpreting and verifying the meaning of words and sentences to be comprehended. Jenkins, Matlock, & Slocum (1989) suggest that the appropriate use of context leads to more effective processing, and overall accuracy in deriving the meaning of unfamiliar words. It is in combination with readers' experiential background that the analysis of context provides meaning to the semantic subtleties of print.

To assess the value of context clues in decoding new vocabulary, we need to examine how context can supply meaning. There are three main types of *context clues:*

A. Definition: The word is defined, usually in the same sentence. For example:

   1. *Uxoricide,* which means to murder one's wife, is the ultimate form of marital abuse.

B. Description: The word is described by the context in such a way that the reader can take a good guess at its meaning. For example:

   2. Their *vociferous* chatter made me wish I had ear plugs.

C. Contrast: The word is compared with some other word or concept, often an opposite. For example:

   3. Mike was *loquacious* while Susan said very little.

Most textbooks rely on context clues when introducing new concepts. Generally, these new words are *italicized,* underlined, or written in **bold print** to call attention to the fact that a new word is being introduced. Typically, the context clue is some form of definition.

It is fairly obvious that context clues work in the sentences above, and students are capable of using such clues when they are presented. The real issue is whether or not sentences such as those in (B) and (C) above occur with sufficient frequency to make context clues a valid strategy for decoding unfamiliar words. Recent research based on the naturally occurring prose of novels, magazines, and textbooks strongly suggests that context clues are not nearly as useful for decoding unfamiliar words as has traditionally been assumed (Schatz & Baldwin, 1986).

Moreover, context clues only seem to work well in the decoding process when the word in question is redundant with the passage and, therefore, unimportant to the overall meaning of the passage. Since the major purpose of a decoding strategy is to promote comprehension during reading, we feel that context clues are less valuable than external references as an independent decoding strategy.

External References

An *external reference* is a source of information that falls outside the passage in which the unfamiliar word occurs. In this sense phonics, context clues, and morphemic analysis are internal sources of information, while textbook aids, dictionaries, encyclopedias, etc., are external.

Textbook aids are elements included in the text to help students with new vocabulary. When students come to an unfamiliar word, context clues and morphemic analysis usually will not be enough to decode its meaning. In most cases, references outside the passage must be used to find the meaning of the unknown words. The three most important references are the glossary, index, and dictionary.

A *glossary* is an alphabetized list of the technical words used in a textbook. With each word is the definition of the word as it is used in the book. For instance, the glossary in this textbook begins on page 225. Not all textbooks have glossaries, but those that do usually place the glossary at the back of the book. Sometimes authors put the glossary at the beginning or end of each chapter in the text.

When a textbook does not contain a glossary, the index is another good reference for finding word meanings. An *index* is an alphabetized list of important terms and topics included in the text. It is always located at the back of the text. Turn to page 249 and look at the index for this textbook. The index lists the page numbers in the text where information can be found on each topic. Frequently, the word for which a student is hunting will be defined in context on one of those pages. This is particularly true of technical vocabulary.

Dictionary. When students need to find the meaning of a nontechnical word, they should use a dictionary. The standard word dictionary is undoubtedly the most commonly used of all reference tools. Unfortunately, it is also probably one of the most misunderstood and misused. Because the dictionary is used so widely, teachers have a tendency to assume that students know how to use a dictionary. This is a dangerous assumption. For example, one of the authors once asked a ninth grader in his English class to look up the word, embroil. After a few minutes he returned to the student's desk only to find her moving her finger laboriously from entry to entry on page four of the *As*. The student did not know that words in a dictionary are arranged alphabetically! This remarkable incident led the author to discover that half the class did not know what guide words were, and that over half did not know how to use the pronunciation key or choose from among the multiple definitions of a word.

If you want your students to use the dictionary, particularly as a means to verify the meanings of unfamiliar words in print, it might be well worth your time to diagnose their familiarity with this important book. The following guide words and entry indicate the most common and important features of dictionaries.

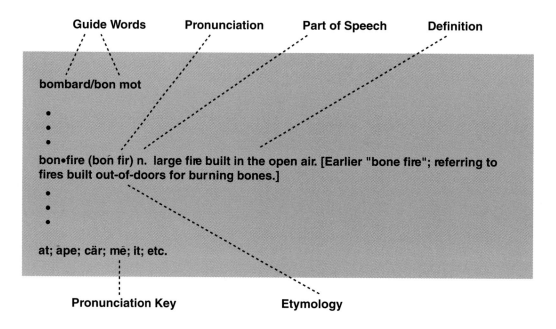

Dictionary skills can be assessed informally by asking students to seek out and explain the various features of specific entries in the dictionary. This can easily be conducted as a group activity in which students must find an answer and then explain how they arrived at it. For example:

> "Turn to page 253 of your dictionary and figure out how to pronounce the word '___' (e.g., daguerreotype is written on the blackboard). Raise your hand when you have the answer, but be prepared to explain to the rest of the class how you got it."

Once you have ascertained which dictionary features students need to practice, discuss them and then provide practice in identifying and interpreting those features. It is, of course, possible to create exercises for students. However, a simpler and more enjoyable activity entails having students compete with each other or with the clock to see how fast they can identify parts of speech, specific guide words, etymologies, and so on.

ACTIVITY

Directions: Create an activity for giving middle or secondary students practice in using one or more features of the dictionary.

 ## A General Decoding Strategy for Textbooks

When students encounter an unfamiliar word as they are reading, they should first finish reading the sentence. If they determine the word is crucial for comprehension, we recommend that they rely heavily on external references, following these steps:

1. First decide whether the word is technical or general. When in doubt, assume the word is technical.

2. If the word is technical:

   a. Try the glossary first.

   b. Then try the index.

   c. Then try the dictionary.

3. If the word is general:

   a. Try the dictionary first.

   b. Then try the glossary.

   c. Then try the index.

4. After you have found a meaning for the word, check the meaning in the context of the sentence to make sure that the definition fits. This is particularly important when you use a dictionary. Context is critical as a verification procedure.

This strategy is recommended as a way for students to deal systematically and independently with unfamiliar words in print. The strategy concentrates on meaning since that is the task of students when they are reading textbook assignments. The strategy also avoids the pitfalls of haphazard or misleading guessing associated with context clues and morphemic analysis. Those who are knowledgeable in a subject area do not need to guess at the meanings of important words; those who are less knowledgeable should not (Memory, 1992).

 ## ■ Principles for Effective Vocabulary Instruction

If there is one thing which contributes most heavily to the burdens of learning technical vocabulary, it is the simple lack of direct instruction. Teachers frequently assume that students will automatically assimilate new words just because they are introduced in textbook assignments. This is a mistake. While incidental learning of word meanings may occur with narrative, story-type material, even across cultures (Shu, Anderson, & Zhang, 1995), this will, more than likely, not occur with textbook material. Consequently, almost any kind of direct instruction is better than none at all (Konopak & Mealey, 1992). The following principles should be considered in conjunction with the specific teaching strategies presented later in the chapter as well as the information presented about lesson and unit planning in Chapter 6.

Be An Enthusiastic Model of Vocabulary Use

Reach out to your students and make them believe that you believe vocabulary development is something more than a dead paragraph from your teacher's syllabus. Let them see you using a dictionary once in awhile, and make an effort to use words you expect the students to learn. In addition to exemplifying new terms in appropriate verbal contexts, you will be demonstrating that they have some practical value. Nothing will facilitate the acquisition of vocabulary more than the enthusiasm which you convey to students.

Make Vocabulary Meaningful

Vocabulary instruction should have a long-term impact upon individual powers of communication and concept development. A vocabulary program that encourages students to squeeze the definitions for 20 words into a temporary memory store so that they can pass Friday's quiz is a waste of time. New words and their meanings must be stored in long-term memory if they are to add to the students' powers of perception and articulation. As we pointed out in Chapter 3, placing information in long-term memory is difficult unless the information is meaningful in terms of prior knowledge. Consequently, new words should be: (1) defined in multiple contexts; (2) drawn from reading or other experiences immediately pertinent to the student; and (3) defined in terms and with examples that clearly fall within the boundaries of the students' prior knowledge. In general, the greater the quantity of meaningful associations that teachers can tie to new words, the greater the likelihood that the students will remember and use them (Cunningham, 1992a,b).

Reinforce Vocabulary

Give students an opportunity to use their new words as they read, write, speak, and listen. There is no substitute for meaningful practice. Research shows that drill, practice, and multiple exposures to a new word in various contexts will improve word knowledge and comprehension (Beck & McKeown, 1991).

Be Eclectic

There are as many good ways to teach vocabulary as there are creative teachers, and probably no single one is best. However, any method can become boring if it is overused. A successful vocabulary program will employ a variety of methods. Moreover, research indicates that a balanced program emphasizing both contextual and definitional strategies works best (Beck & McKeown, 1991).

Teaching new vocabulary prior to reading assignments is a direct application of the *readiness principle*. Readiness refers to the mental state in which an individual is prepared to derive maximum meaning from a learning situation, with a minimum of frustration. Preteaching content area vocabulary is a readiness aid that gives students direction and purpose for reading.

Introducing vocabulary facilitates reading comprehension by reducing the number of unfamiliar words in textbook reading assignments. If new terms are introduced in a meaningful and interesting manner, this will reinforce vocabulary, generate enthusiasm for the reading task, and provide background information that will help students relate what they know to the content of the text. The following strategies for introducing vocabulary are adaptable to reading assignments in most content areas.

Troubleshoot reading assignments for the students by identifying important words that are likely to engender confusion as they read. Then introduce those words before they begin their reading assignments. By introducing difficult terminology, the teacher will facilitate the retention of pivotal vocabulary, provide students with critical prior knowledge of the content they are being asked to assimilate, and improve reading comprehension by reducing the number of alien words in the text.

In most subject areas, reading assignments introduce so many unfamiliar words that it is impossible to teach all of them. Use the following criteria to select the words that seem most critical:

1. Restrict your selections to words that are critical to comprehending the selection.

2. Choose words that define key concepts.

3. Choose terms that you might include on a test.

4. Choose words that have a new technical meaning in addition to a general, familiar meaning, e.g., "complementary" angles as opposed to "complimentary" actions in social situations.

5. Ignore terms that will be of little or no use once a student has passed the test.

6. Don't spend time reinforcing the meanings of words just because they appear in italics. Words should also meet the criteria in 1–4 above.

Teacher-Directed Strategies

In addition to pre-teaching strategies, it is also good teaching to reinforce new vocabulary after reading. Reinforcing new vocabulary allows students to review the words that you introduced before reading and that they encountered during reading. In essence, reinforcement makes the words more meaningful to students. The following teacher-directed strategies for introducing and reinforcing vocabulary are adaptable to reading assignments in most content areas and should be modified as necessary to fit the idiosyncratic nature of individual classrooms. This concurs with the findings of Vaughn, Schumm, Niarhos, and Daugherty (1993) who found that middle and secondary students preferred teachers who made adaptations in their presentations.

Contextual Redefinition

The authors recommend a strategy described by Tierney, Readence, and Dishner (1995) for its simplicity and ease for content teachers. To illustrate contextual redefinition, define each of the following words using only your own prior knowledge.

1. Carapace _____

2. Nonsectarian _____

3. Insipid _____

Were you able to write a definition without going to a dictionary? If not, read the following sentences and see if they help you with the definition of the words. After you write a definition, check the dictionary for your definition.

1. Without its *carapace,* the turtle would be subject to certain death from its enemies or the elements.

2. Although he was a believer in God, he had a *nonsectarian* attitude toward religion.

3. His teaching lacked spirit. He had presented his lesson in a dull manner, failing to challenge or stimulate the students. The teacher knew he had made an *insipid* presentation.

Did the sentences help you with the meaning of the unknown words? If they did, you were utilizing the surrounding context as clues to the meaning of the words. *Contextual redefinition* is a strategy that introduces new vocabulary in rich contexts that help to define words and facilitate memory by giving the words meaningful associations. The process is composed of the following five steps:

1. **Select Unfamiliar Words.** Identify those words that may present trouble to your students and that may be central to understanding the important concepts they will encounter in their reading. Select only a few words to be presented at one time to prevent the lesson from becoming tedious.

2. **Write a Sentence.** An appropriate context for each word should be written with clues to its meaning. The categories of clues discussed earlier should be utilized in the writing of

these sentences. In the sample sentences provided, carapace could be identified by previous experience, nonsectarian by comparison and contrast, and insipid by description or mood. If such a context already exists in the text material the students are about to read, it is appropriate to use that in lieu of creating a new context for it.

3. **Present the Words in Isolation.** Using the chalkboard or a transparency, ask students to provide you with a meaning for the unfamiliar word. Some guesses may be off-base or even humorous, but students should be asked to come to a consensus about the best meaning.

4. **Present the Words in a Sentence.** Using the sentence you developed previously, now present the word in context. Again, ask the students to provide a meaning for the unfamiliar word. It is important that students who volunteer definitions defend their guess by providing the rationale for it. In this way poor readers will be able to experience the thinking processes of other students and how they arrive at meaning. In essence, students can act as models for each other.

5. **Dictionary Verification.** A volunteer or volunteers can look up the word in the dictionary to verify the guesses offered by the class. This step also provides students and the teacher an opportunity to examine any morphemes present in the word and how they might help in its verification.

The students will gain several benefits from this strategy. First, they will realize that trying to identify an unfamiliar word by simply focusing on the word as an isolated element is frustrating, that it makes for haphazard guessing, and that it probably is not very accurate. They will be prompted to develop more reliable methods for determining meaning. Second, students will become actively involved in a more profitable process of discovering new words rather than in the rote memorization of them. Finally, the dictionary is cast in its most appropriate role—that of a tool used to verify the meanings of unfamiliar words by selecting the definition that is syntactically and semantically acceptable in a particular context.

Graphic Organizer

A *graphic organizer* is a visual aid which defines hierarchical relationships among concepts. It lends itself particularly well to the teaching of technical vocabulary (Dunston, 1992; Moore & Readence, 1984).

The graphic organizer may be used in a variety of ways. It may be used as an introductory strategy, as exemplified by the organizers at the beginning of each chapter in this text. Such usage is designed to provide relational guides to the prose that follows them. Graphic organizers may also be used as a post-reading technique to reinforce and summarize. Additionally, the graphic organizer is one strategy that can be used in the same lesson to enhance both readiness and recall of material. In all cases, the graphic organizer can be an excellent mechanism for defining related concepts. The following steps are recommended for generating graphic organizers.

1. **Concept Identification.** An analysis of the content is undertaken to identify all new terms and concepts that will be introduced in the reading assignment. Since there will often be a large number of these terms and concepts, it will save time simply to mark them in your own text. The following list was derived from one chapter in a science text dealing with matter and how it is structured.

Structure of matter	Natural elements
Elements	Compounds
Metals	Nonmetals
Nucleus	Atoms
Mixtures	Physical combination
Natural elements	Orbits
Particles	Electrons
Protons	Neutrons
Electron shell	Energy levels
Molecule	Electrolysis
Inert gases	
Positive electrical charge	
Negative electrical charge	
Atomic theory of matter	
Law of definite or constant proportions	
Chemical combinations	

2. **Concept Selection.** In order to prevent the organizer from being overly complex, it is critical to prune the initial list until it consists only of superordinate concepts, i.e., those that are most important or most essential to the integrity of the reading selection. The organizer is supposed to supplement the reading assignment, not replace it. Once the list has been reduced, subclassify the remaining terms in an informal outline.

Structure of matter
    Chemical combinations
        Compounds
        Molecules
        Elements

Natural elements
   Metals
   Nonmetals
Physical combinations
   Mixtures
      Compounds
      Elements

3. **Diagram Construction.** Arrange the terms in a tree diagram which reflects the structure established in Step 2.

4. **Initial Evaluation.** Once you have created the organizer, step back and evaluate it. Does the organizer accurately convey the concepts you wish to teach? If not, massage the diagram until you are satisfied. One of the advantages of the graphic organizer is that it helps teachers to organize and clarify their own purposes. In addition to accuracy, consider the complexity of the diagram. Students can be overwhelmed if the visual display is too complicated. Under such conditions it may be desirable to present the organizer piece-by-piece.

5. **Organizer Presentation.** The physical presentation of the organizer is unimportant. Handouts, a permanent poster, overhead transparency, or chalkboard may be used as the teacher's resources dictate. The time required for the presentation will vary depending upon the complexity of the organizer and the extent to which the concepts in question are unfamiliar to students. Begin the presentation with a general explanation of the purpose of the organizer and an explanation of how a tree diagram works. Talk students through the organizer, explaining each term, encouraging student questions and discussion, and indicating the ways in which terms are related to each other. In so doing you will be developing vocabulary, improving reading comprehension, and enriching schemata in ways which will make subject matter more meaningful to students.

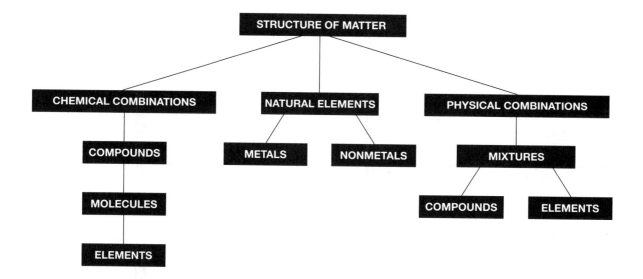

Directions: Using the following words, create a graphic organizer. Be prepared to justify your arrangement.

Vertebrate	Mammal	Invertebrate
Snake	Grasshopper	Reptile
Cockroach	Crustacean	Aardvark
Animal	Whale	Insect
Lobster	Shrimp	Crocodile

Word Origins (Etymologies)

Introductory strategies for vocabulary will be successful to the extent that they are interesting and build meaningful schemata. Etymologies offer a colorful means of helping students remember word meanings. This is especially true for social studies and English where large numbers of relevant words have interesting etymologies.

The *etymology* of a word is its history, where it originated, and how it came to be a part of the language. Language is not a static feature of human behavior, all languages are in a constant state of change. Grammar mutates from one form to another; lexical items become popular and then fall into disuse, e.g., groovy, and the meanings of words change, too. Every word that is now a part of the English language has a past, a present, and a future. Many word histories are quite interesting and can add flavor to an otherwise banal vocabulary lesson.

The etymological portion of a dictionary entry follows the pronunciation guide and part of speech and is enclosed in bold face brackets, although some dictionaries don't include any etymological information at all. The following example is the more colorful portion of the etymology for the word chauvinism taken from *Webster's New Collegiate Dictionary.*

[F "chauvinisme," fr. Nicolas "Chauvin"
fl 1815 F soldier of excessive patriotism and
devotion to Napoleon]

The *F* is an abbreviation for "French," *fr.* stands for "from," and *fl* is an abbreviation of a Latin word which means "flourished about." In addition to its interesting origin, chauvinism provides an example of how word meanings change over time. Originally, chauvinism referred to excessive patriotism or loyalty to a cause or creed. However, in recent years the meaning of the word has narrowed so that it refers primarily to men who are so loyal to their sex that they have condescending or disparaging attitudes toward women, i.e., "male chauvinist pig."

Other sources of word histories are books that provide more complete story lines. The following etymology of the word "berserk" is quoted from *Thereby Hangs a Tale: Stories of Curious Word Origins* (Funk, 1950).

In Norse mythology there was a famous furious fighter who scorned the use of heavy mail, entering battle without armor. His only protection was the skin of a bear fastened over one shoulder. From this he became known as "berserk," or "bear shirt." It was said of him that he could assume the form of a wild beast, and that neither iron nor fire could harm him, for he fought with the fury of a beast of the forest and his foes were unable to touch him. Each of his twelve sons, in turn, also carried the name "berserk," and each was as furious a fighter as the father. From these Norse heroes, it came to be that any person so inflamed with the fury of fighting as to be equally dangerous to friend and foe, as was that legendary family when engaged in battle, was called "berserk" or "berserker." (p. 48)

We submit that few students could forget the word berserk if it were introduced in conjunction with the story of Bear Shirt! This is a clear example of how rich and meaningful associations can facilitate the learning of new words.

With advanced students it may be useful to have them check the etymologies of words in a dictionary. However, the numerous abbreviations, references to classical languages, and clipped versions of the histories may rob interest from otherwise interesting stories. For this reason, dictionary etymologies may be more useful as sources of information that teachers may incidentally insert into vocabulary presentations.

Not all words have flashy histories, and we are not recommending that the etymology of every new word be explored with students. Nevertheless, tossing one or two into a lesson is an excellent means of building interest and promoting recall. Collections of word histories are standard volumes in most secondary school libraries and can be found in the card catalogue under the headings *English Language* or *Etymologies.*

Directions: The following words, listed by content area, have interesting word origins. Select one of the lists and use an unabridged dictionary, an etymological dictionary, or a book on interesting word origins to determine their histories. Describe how you might work one or more of these words into a lesson in your own content area.

Science	Social Studies	English
alkali	assassin	anecdote
barnacle	ballot	dumbbell
cobalt	boycott	enthrall
crayfish	filibuster	fib
hurricane	indenture	gossip
larva	lynch	quixotic
nicotine	senate	sarcasm
parasite	sinecure	tragedy

_____

_____

_____

_____

_____

_____

_____

_____

_____

_____

_____

_____

_____

_____

_____

_____

_____

_____

Semantic Mapping

A *semantic map* (Heimlich & Pittelman, 1986) is a diagram that groups related concepts; it combines this grouping activity with the structure the graphic organizer provides. Semantic maps may be used as pre- or post-reading exercises that reinforce new vocabulary and help students relate their prior knowledge to new experiences and concepts. You and your students can construct a semantic map using the following steps:

1. Select an important word or topic from the lecture or reading assignment. This example is based on *Disastrous Volcanoes* (Berger, 1981). The word in this case will be "volcano."

2. Write the word (volcano) on the chalkboard or overhead projector.

3. Assign students to write down as many related words as they can think of from their own experiences or from their reading of the text. In this case we will assume that students have read the text.

Vesuvius	Vulcanian	Pompeii
Mount St. Helens	cataclysm	lava
ash	earthquake	ring-of-fire
vent	conduit	volcanic bombs
gas	blocks	tsunami
explosions	plug	Krakatoa
pressure	hell	terrifying
plate tectonics	magma	shield volcano

4. Organize the words into a diagram as in this semantic map.

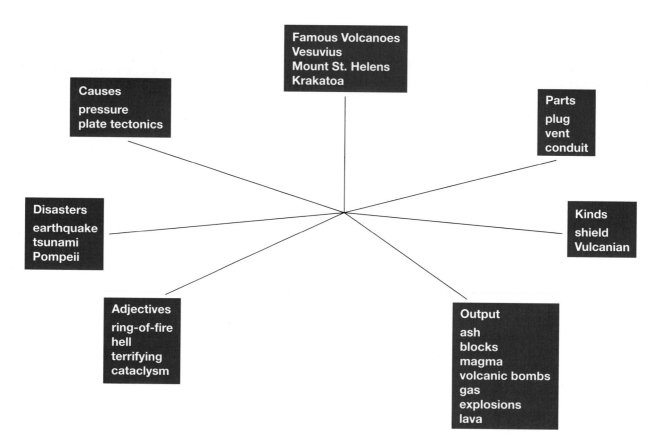

5. Students share words while you write them on the board. As new categories emerge, give the map new arms or add categories of your own. The diagram itself can be as simple or as complex as you desire.

6. Have students give names to the various categories or break categories into subcategories.

    Famous Volcanoes

    Parts of Volcanoes

    Adjectives That Describe Volcanoes

    Causes of Volcanoes

    Volcanic Output

    Related Disasters

    Kinds of Volcanoes

7. Perhaps the most important step in this activity is the discussion and questioning activities that accompany the diagram. For example:

    a. Why are volcanoes considered disastrous?

    b. Which do you think was the all-time most disastrous volcano?

c. Why is "ring-of-fire" a good name?

d. In what ways are Mauna Loa and Vesuvius different? How are they the same?

e. Tell what it would have been like to be on the island of Krakatoa in 1883.

f. "Mark, imagine that you are Krakatoa. Susan, imagine that you are Mount St. Helens. Now, each of you try to convince the other that you are the world's greatest volcano."

ACTIVITY

Directions: Imagine that you have just finished teaching a series of units on human physiology, e.g., parts of the body. Describe how you would conduct an appropriate semantic mapping lesson with your class. Be sure to include the following:

1. 20–30 terms likely to be elicited from students;

2. Probable groups and labels for those terms.

Feature Analysis

Feature analysis (Pittelman, Heimlich, Berglund, & French, 1991) is a procedure that can help students make fine discriminations among concepts. With respect to general vocabulary the procedure works well for teaching word connotations. With respect to technical vocabulary, feature analysis can summarize distinctive ways in which related concepts are similar and different. We recommend the following steps:

1. **Category Selection.** The category should be one which consists of two or more items that are similar. Such categories could be things like kinds of animals, elements, foods, famous historical characters, or words that have the same denotation but different connotations.

2. **List Category Terms.** Place the terms along the left hand side of the blackboard or over-

head transparency. Try not to use a large number of items the first time you use the procedure. In this case we will illustrate some of the similarities and differences among the planets in our solar system.

Mercury	Saturn
Venus	Uranus
Earth	Neptune
Mars	Pluto
Jupiter	

3. **List Features.** Place the features that will be used to describe the terms (planets) across the top of the blackboard. Students may select the features or you may do it yourself. If you ask the students to provide the features, be prepared to give them plenty of hints and directions.

Category: Planets

	Hot	Cold	Big	Small	Rings	Life	Moons
Mercury							
Venus							
Earth							
Mars							
Jupiter							
Saturn							
Uranus							
Neptune							
Pluto							

4. **Complete Feature Chart.** Students should be guided through the matrix as they indicate whether or not each category item possesses a given feature. This can be done individually, in a group, or category item by item. A plus (+) shows that the category item has a feature. A minus (–) indicates that the category item does not have the feature. Every category item must have a plus or a minus for every feature; there should be no blank spots. Students will sometimes argue over a feature. This is good as long as the debate is well organized. In general, a plus sign indicates that a category item usually or mostly has the feature. The presence of two minuses can indicate a third category. For example, if a planet is neither large nor small, then it is probably medium sized.

5. **Explore The Matrix.** The final step is to have the students make observations about the category items. Give students an opportunity to make generalizations on their own. However, questions and hints may be necessary. For example, here are some questions that can be answered based on the information in the feature matrix. The questions are ordered from simple to complex:

a. Which planets are the hottest?

b. Which planets have rings?

c. In what way is Neptune different from Pluto?

d. What makes Earth unique among the planets?

e. Which planet is most like Earth? Why?

Category: Planets

	Hot	*Cold*	*Big*	*Small*	*Rings*	*Life*	*Moons*
Mercury	+	–	–	+	–	–	–
Venus	+	–	–	–	–	–	–
Earth	–	–	–	–	–	+	+
Mars	–	–	–	+	–	–	+
Jupiter	–	+	+	–	+	–	+
Saturn	–	+	+	–	+	–	+
Uranus	–	+	+	–	+	–	+
Neptune	–	+	+	–	+	–	+
Pluto	–	+	–	+	–	–	+

An enterprising student might argue that Mercury, because it has no atmosphere and doesn't rotate in its orbit around the sun, is half cold and half hot, in which case Mercury should be marked + hot and + cold. This sort of reasoning should be welcomed, along with divergent comments, changes in categories, and other student interactions. When conducted in a thoughtful and flexible manner, feature analysis is a good way to build schemata and reinforce vocabulary.

Clues and Questions

This procedure is designed to help students review technical vocabulary. What makes *Clues and Ques-* *tions* interesting is the fact that students provide the questions as well as the answers.

The teacher begins by collecting content area vocabulary that students should review. Each is typed on a notecard and placed in a shoebox or card file. Students randomly select several of these cards. Their task is to write questions whose answers are the words on each card.

The teacher encourages the students to use the textbook index to find where their vocabulary words are introduced and used. In addition, the teacher provides examples of different kinds of questions and clues, e.g., definition, analogy, comparison-contrast, context (see example below). As students finish writing questions, the teacher checks them for clarity and accuracy and then has the student print them on the vocabulary card directly below the word.

Molecule

1. _____ is to compound as atom is to element.

2. What is the smallest unit of a compound which retains all the characteristics of that compound?

3. Two hydrogen atoms and one oxygen atom make one _____ of water.

When the vocabulary cards have been completed, the class is subdivided into small groups with each group having a portion of the vocabulary cards. One student shows a card to the others in the group but does not look at the card. Each of the other students asks a question or supplies a clue until the word is identified. The activity proceeds in round robin fashion until the cards have been exhausted, at which point exchange cards and the clue sessions begin anew.

As a vocabulary builder, the clues and questions procedure has a number of strengths. First, allowing students to create their own questions for a game gives them a novel purpose for using the text. Second, students will benefit from trying to write clear and meaningful questions. And third, participating in the vocabulary review itself will enlarge and reinforce students' technical vocabularies.

 Strategies for Vocabulary Independence

It is essential that students develop strategies that will continue to serve them when they do not have teachers to guide them whenever they encounter a new vocabulary word. In other words, students need to have their own repertoire of strategies to help them learn new words independently. In this section we describe four strategies that are relatively easy for students to learn and use across various content areas. However, as with any learning strategy, students will need to be shown how to apply them when reading and learning with text.

A Verbal and Visual Word Association Strategy

Students can use this strategy on their own to learn and retain both general and technical vocabulary. Research by Eeds and Cockrum (1985) showed that students using this strategy to study vocabulary in a literary selection outperformed students using more traditional methods such as looking up a word in the dictionary and writing its definition. Moreover, the *verbal and visual word association strategy* we describe here was especially effective for low achieving students. In our own work we have also found that this strategy can be learned and used effectively, with adaptations by second language learners in content area classes.

Suppose you are reading along in a novel and you encounter the following passage:

> "Joan had recently taken up jogging. She used to live life in the fast lane—staying out all night dancing and partying till dawn. Now that she was middle-aged, Joan strived for a more *salubrious* lifestyle."

The word salubrious is a general vocabulary term not well known by most people. Let's assume you need to learn and remember this word. The following steps of the verbal and visual word association strategy will help you associate the word salubrious with personal experiences.

1. Draw a square with four boxes in it, as in the example that follows.

Salubrious	Surfing
Promoting Health	Smoking

Write the word salubrious in the top left hand square and its definition in the bottom left hand square. Salubrious, as you may have guessed by now, means healthful. Hence, Joan's jogging suggests she is now leading a salubrious lifestyle.

2. Now in the top right hand square you need to write a personal association for the word salubrious—something you do in your own life that is salubrious. For example, surfing is a healthful activity so you might put that in the upper right hand square.

3. In the bottom right hand square you need to include a word that describes something you do or something you experience that is not salubrious. Thus, smoking, an unhealthful habit, might go here. This verbal association for the word salubrious can then be used to

study and retain a personally meaningful conception of the word. In speaking and writing activities, the word salubrious is one you might feel comfortable using.

A student in social studies trying to learn the word "diplomatic" formed the following verbal association:

Diplomatic	**Franklin D. Roosevelt**
Skilled in International Relations	**Adolf Hitler**

His association for someone who is diplomatic was Franklin D. Roosevelt, a successful American diplomat of World War II. This student's non-example, also from World War II—someone who is clearly not a diplomatic person—was Adolf Hitler.

We have found that second language students benefit from a modification of the original verbal association strategy. By including a visual association with the verbal symbol and omitting the non-example, second language students can quickly grasp and learn unfamiliar general and technical vocabulary using this strategy. For example, the word "nocturnal" can be associated with the drawing of a half moon and stars against a black background. Then, in the lower right hand corner, this student's personal association, owl, is written to reinforce the idea of a creature that hunts at night. Thus, concept development was enhanced with this strategy modification by providing additional reinforcement rather than the constructive non-example.

Nocturnal	
Active at Night	**Owl**

The visual and verbal association strategy can be introduced to students easily and, given some guided practice, it should quickly become part of their repertoire of independent strategies for learning new vocabulary. It works best for nouns and descriptive adjectives. Highly technical terms such as photosyn-

thesis require the more elaborate conceptual networks that may be formed using a graphic organizer, semantic mapping, or the vocabulary self-collection strategy that follows.

Vocabulary Self-Collection Strategy (VSS)

Given the enormous numbers of new words that students encounter in reading assignments, it is not surprising that most students have a difficult time deciding which unfamiliar words to learn. *The vocabulary self-collection strategy* (Haggard, 1992) is a vocabulary acquisition technique that is designed to teach students how to select the most important vocabulary from reading assignments. VSS should first be introduced as a post-reading group activity, following guidelines adapted from Haggard:

1. Student teams identify a word or term important for learning content information. The teacher identifies one word or term.

2. Teacher writes the words on the chalkboard as teams give definitions from context.

3. Class members add any information they can to each definition.

4. Teacher and students consult external references, e.g., glossary, index, and dictionary, for definitions that are incomplete or unclear.

5. Students and teacher discuss and then narrow the list to a predetermined number of words for a final class list.

6. Students record the class list with agreed-upon definitions in notebooks, vocabulary journals, or on notecards.

7. Class list words are used in extension activities and class tests.

Word Map

Once students are proficient at categorizing technical vocabulary through the semantic mapping strategy, they can learn to use word maps to develop ownership of important terminology. Word maps provide students with a procedure for independently studying content area vocabulary (Schwartz, 1988; Tierney, Readence, & Dishner, 1995). *A word map* is a visual representation of a definition, displaying three categories of semantic knowledge: (a) the general class or category to which the concept belongs; (b) the primary properties of the concept and how these properties distinguish it from other members of the class; and (c) examples of the concept.

The accompanying example below demonstrates a student's effort to develop a word map in science class for the word, reptile. The following steps help make students independent users of word maps:

1. Discuss the word map with students emphasizing its value as a study technique.

2. Walk through the incomplete word map, modeling the process with familiar words like "skateboard," "ice cream," "computer," and "sandwich." You can start by simply having students brainstorm associations for these words as you would in semantic mapping, and then align the associations with category labels.

3. Give students independent guided practice with technical words in a rich sentence context. Then progress to words in less rich contexts that require students to consult other sources of information such as a dictionary, glossary, or encyclopedia.

Finally, once students have constructed a word map, you may want to add the requirement that they then create a sentence using the word to see if they have, in fact, internalized its meaning and truly own the word in writing and speaking. For example, the student studying "reptile" wrote: "Snakes are a reptile most people fear." This sentence demonstrates that the student knows specific examples of reptiles.

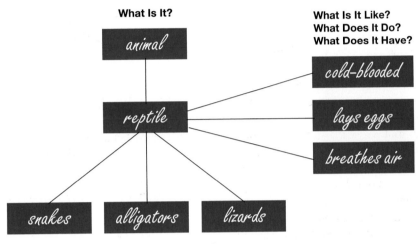

What Is It?

animal

What Is It Like?
What Does It Do?
What Does It Have?

cold-blooded

reptile

lays eggs

breathes air

snakes   alligators   lizards

What Are Some Examples?

TOAST

A final strategy to be discussed to help students achieve vocabulary independence is *TOAST,* an acronym which corresponds to the steps in the procedure—*t*est, *o*rganize, *a*nchor, *s*ay, and *t*est. TOAST was developed by Dana and Rodriguez (1992) to provide students with a system for independently studying vocabulary so they could learn at their own rate and focus on the words which seem the most difficult. For many students TOAST represents a viable alternative to what they themselves use as a means of studying words, which is probably unsystematic at best. Additionally, the strategy is a good rehearsal activity for second language learners. TOAST is comprised of the following steps:

1. **Test.** Students would first pretest themselves on new vocabulary introduced to them in class; by doing so, they could determine which

words were already known to them, which ones they were somewhat familiar with, and which would require additional study time. Students can make vocabulary cards with the word to be learned on one side and the definition and a sentence with that word on the other side. An alternative would be to use a piece of paper folded so a column of words to be learned is on one side and the identifying information is on the larger side of the paper and folded underneath. Students would examine each word and attempt to guess the definition and provide a sentence; guesses could be verified by checking the other side of the card or paper. The pretest could be oral, silent, or written. It also may be done with a partner if time and circumstances allow.

2. **Organize.** Students should organize their words into some framework that will enhance their ability to learn the new vocabulary. They might arrange them into semantically-related groups or place them into categories according to structural similarities. They might also arrange them according to degree of familiarity or unfamiliarity. Some type of organization is important as it will help students mnemonically and facilitate their learning of the words.

3. **Anchor.** Some type of strategy is necessary for students to commit the words to long-term memory. This might entail, but not be limited to: (a) working with a partner to teach and test each other, or even compete with one another; (b) using a tape recorder to tape, listen, and recite definitions and sentences; (c) using timed trials to figure out improvement over a series of trials in writing or reciting the words and their definitions; (d) trying to find another word which would act as a mnemonic link to the target word; or (e) examining the morphemes present in each word.

4. **Say.** This step constitutes the review stage of the procedure. To avoid forgetting newly learned words, they must be periodically rehearsed and reviewed. It is suggested that the first review session occur 5–10 minutes after learning the words; other review sessions can occur later the same day, a week later, and just before the test. Vocabulary that has been forgotten should be relearned using the anchoring strategies from the previous step.

5. **Test.** Students should conduct a posttest after each review to check how well they have learned the words. This test may be conducted in the same way as the pretest.

Extension Activities

Extension activities are pencil and paper exercises designed to reinforce and expand the schemata of newly acquired content area vocabulary. These activities allow students to explore word relationships and, in general, to manipulate and practice new terminology in a variety of ways. Recall and memorization are certainly a part of extension activities; however, these activities should also force students to think about the terms they are learning. The following extension activities are merely examples of exercises that teachers can use to enhance the acquisition of vocabulary in their own content area classrooms.

Analogies

Word analogies are useful thinking exercises. They require students to draw inferences, and they are an attractive method of exposing subtle word associations. In addition, analogies lend themselves to creative and divergent thinking. A word of caution—analogies can be extremely difficult, especially for students who have never worked with them. Be prepared to provide students with simple analogies which can be used as models for verbalizing relationships. For instance,

> *Night* is to *day* as *big* is to _____
> Large, black, little, simple
> *Verbalization:* Night is the opposite of day, so big must be the opposite of something.
> What is the opposite of big? Little.

Analogies are easier to complete if answers are provided; however, that leaves only one correct answer for each analogy. If no answers are provided, the analogies are more difficult but they allow for divergent answers and interesting discussion. The decision should be based on the capabilities of the class.

Directions: The following analogies are about science vocabulary that we have just studied. Pick the answer you feel makes the most sense.

1. *Gas* is to *liquid* as *liquid* is to _____
2. *Proton* is to *positive* as *electron* is to _____
3. *Atom* is to *element* as _____ is to *compound*
4. *Physical* is to *mixture* as _____ is to *compound*
5. *Hg* is to *mercury* as _____ is to *silver*

Solid	Atomic	Water	Energy	Molecule	Negative
K	S	Chemical	Ag	Salt	

Matching Definitions to Scrambled Words

This exercise provides straightforward reinforcement for meanings of basic vocabulary. Scrambling the spellings adds an extra challenge and makes the activity more interesting.

Directions: Below are two lists. The numbered list on the left is composed of some basic math terms that we have studied. (Notice that the spellings are mixed-up.) The lettered list on the right is composed of definitions for the math terms. Place the letter of each definition on the line next to the appropriate math term.

1. rcleci _____
2. ip _____
3. ets _____
4. toinp _____
5. recpiorclas _____
6. nogatnep _____
7. hcord _____
8. irccumfreence _____
9. daiemtre _____
10. miepr _____

A. A number that has only two whole number factors
B. A line segment with endpoints on a circle
C. A closed curved figure on which every point is an equal distance from a fixed point within the curve
D. 3.14159265
E. Two of these are necessary to determine a line
F. A polygon that has five sides
G. A collection of mathematical elements that have something in common
H. A chord running through the center of a circle
I. Two fractions whose product is 1
J. The perimeter of a circle

Puzzles

Word puzzles are activities that almost all students will respond to positively. Consequently, they make good motivational devices for vocabulary review. Hidden word puzzles are easy to make. Simply prepare the answers in any array; and then type in random letters to complete the rectangle. Triple-space between letters in each row and double-space between rows. A word of caution—always give clues that define the hidden words in some way. If the clues are eliminated, the hidden word puzzle simply becomes an exercise in word recognition rather than an extension activity for vocabulary development.

Initial Array

```
            G   R   A   N   T
                    L                           S
                B   O   O   T   H               T
                    C                           U
S   H   E   R   M   A   N   S   P           A   D
T                   I           I           R
A               V   L           C       A   T
N               A           E   K   W
T           D               E
O                       S   T
N
```

Hidden Word Puzzle: Social Studies Civil War Personalities

Directions: What follows is a hidden word puzzle involving famous personalities of the Civil War era. Listed below are brief descriptions of these people. As you figure them out, circle their last names. These names may appear diagonally, horizontally, or vertically; and they may be printed from top to bottom or from bottom to top. Answers may be found in your text on the page indicated in parentheses.

1. Lee surrendered to him at Appomattox Courthouse. (246)

2. President of U.S. during the war. (221)

3. President of the Confederacy. (234)

4. He made a famous charge at Gettysburg. (240)

5. The Union's Secretary of State. (232)

6. He burned Atlanta on his march to the sea. (242)

7. Commanded the army of Virginia. (236)

8. A famous Confederate cavalry officer. (235)

9. Secretary of War for the Union. (232)

10. He assassinated the President. (249)

R	A	M	G	R	A	N	T	A	D	O	D	Q
E	B	E	T	O	T	L	W	M	O	S	S	C
A	F	O	B	B	O	O	T	H	M	Q	T	N
P	H	I	U	E	N	C	J	E	O	B	U	X
S	H	E	R	M	A	N	S	P	S	V	A	D
T	M	U	N	O	T	I	B	I	B	L	R	C
A	J	D	S	B	V	L	C	C	Y	A	T	G
N	U	Z	I	A	O	O	E	K	W	H	P	M
T	O	X	D	M	R	V	I	E	N	F	W	T
O	N	L	E	C	A	E	S	T	R	O	P	E
N	E	W	T	O	N	S	F	I	G	L	S	P

Crossword Puzzles

Crossword puzzles are somewhat more difficult to make because of the need to plan crossovers and draw the boxes. The following steps will simplify the procedure:

1. Select vocabulary and plan crossovers.

2. Place the answers, triple-spacing between letters in rows and double-spacing between letters in columns.

3. Type in the answers, triple-spacing between letters in rows and double-spacing between letters in columns.

4. Take the paper out of the typewriter.

5. Using a ruler, draw boxes around the words.

6. Draw in numbers by hand or type them in the upper left corner of appropriate boxes.

7. If you overextend lines for boxes, just cover them with correction fluid.

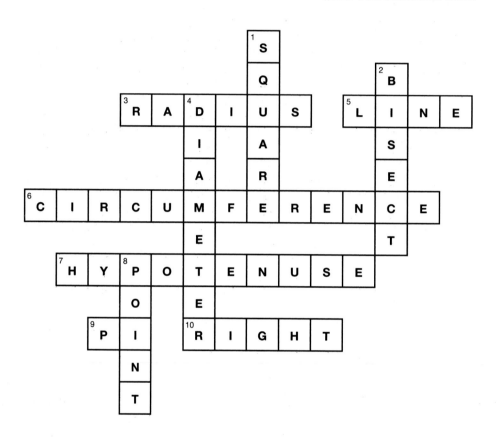

Across:

3. A line running from the center of a circle to the curve
5. An infinite number of points
6. The distance around a circle
7. The longest side of a right triangle
9. 3.14
10. A triangle with two sides perpendicular to each other

Down:

1. A figure with four equal sides and four right angles
2. To divide into two equal parts
4. Twice the radius of a circle
8. Two of these are enough to determine a line

SUMMARY

In this chapter we have attempted to provide a rationale for the direct teaching of vocabulary in content area classes. The advantages and disadvantages of various decoding strategies have been discussed. General principles have been introduced with emphasis on the need to develop both receptive and expressive vocabularies. The primary focus of the chapter has been on pre- and post-reading strategies for introducing, reinforcing, and extending the meaning of content area terminology.

Now go back to the vocabulary vignette at the beginning of the chapter. React again to the lesson as you did before. Compare your answer with those you made before you read the chapter.

MINI PROJECT

Using the text chapter on the **CD-ROM** entitled "The Use and Misuse of Alcohol," do one or all of the following:

1. Choose a teacher-directed vocabulary strategy from Chapter Eight and design an activity appropriate for use in a high school health class.

2. Select a strategy for vocabulary independence and demonstrate how you would use it with students.

3. Develop an extension activity to foster creative and divergent thinking about the key vocabulary related to alcohol.

GROUP PROJECTS

■ Define *word* and include as many of the following terms as possible in your definition: linguistic fillers, schema, concept, denotation, connotation, morpheme.

■ Give concrete examples of how a content area teacher can make vocabulary instruction effective by making vocabulary meaningful and by being instructionally eclectic.

■ Construct a novel graphic organizer (not one from the text) and explain the relationship it depicts.

NINE

COMPREHENSION:
PRINCIPLES AND INTEGRATED APPROACHES

VIGNETTE

SETTING

Jake Spear's ninth-grade literature class. Mr. Spear is in his first teaching job in a multicultural high school. As the class nears an end, he is about to introduce the next novel the students will read, *Les Miserables* by Victor Hugo.

THE LESSON

Mr. Spear:	"Today we are about to begin reading our next class novel, *Les Miserables* by Victor Hugo. Does anyone know anything about it?"
Eunsook:	"I think it's a play that my parents went to see."
Mr. Spear:	"Yes. Anything else?"
Students:	Some shuffling of papers and yawning is seen to occur.
Mr. Spear:	"Okay. This play is set in France in the 18th century. What do you know about that time?"
Manuel:	"Wasn't France involved in a revolution?"
Mr. Spear:	"Yes, what else?"
Students:	Many heads are bowed and some students seem to be occupied with other things.
Mr. Spear:	"Well, I believe we're in for a treat in reading this novel. It is one of my all time favorite works of literature, and I'm sure after reading it you'll think the same!"
Students:	Two students are passing notes to one another. Others are seen staring off into space.
Mr. Spear:	"I want you to read the first 20 pages of the novel for tomorrow. In reading these pages, I'd like you to think about the answers to some questions I'm going to pass out about your reading. Any questions?" He begins to pass out the questions.
Billy:	"When did you say we had to read the pages by?" The bell rings.

▶ Keeping in mind what you already know about the comprehension process, jot down your thoughts on the following questions:

1. What are the good points about the lesson?

2. What are the weak points about the lesson?

3. What, if anything, would you change about the lesson?

RATIONALE

Comprehension of challenging ideas in a content area is rarely easy for students. No collection of textbook aids can substitute for the careful guidance you can provide. In order to accomplish this in your particular content area, you must have a working knowledge of some basic notions about the comprehension process (Wittrock, 1985) and an array of strategies at your disposal.

In the next two chapters we will explore the comprehension process. Specifically, in Chapter 10 we will examine various strategies to facilitate the comprehension process before, during, and after reading. The aim of this chapter is to explore some principles of comprehension and how they are linked to the instructional lesson. Then, we will describe various strategies and how they are integrated across the lesson.

LEARNING OBJECTIVES

■ Be able to explain the principles of guiding comprehension in a content area.

■ Be able to apply specific integrated strategies in your content area which provide guidance before, during, and after reading.

GRAPHIC ORGANIZER

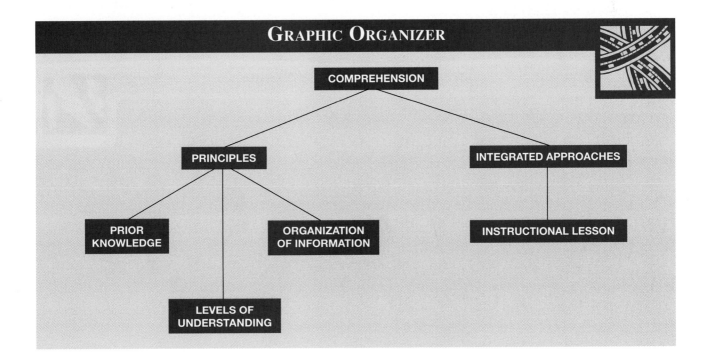

143

Principles of Comprehension

Acomprehensive content area lesson displays an awareness of three psychological principles in the comprehension process. These principles include: (1) the importance of students' prior knowledge in the acquisition of new information; (2) the level of understanding to be achieved in the lesson; and (3) the organization of information to aid long-term retention. Let's examine each of these principles and their respective instructional stages in more detail.

Prior Knowledge

The first principle of comprehending unfamiliar content area material is embodied by students' applying what they already know to what they are learning. We have emphasized this point from the very beginning of this text and reinforced it further in our discussion of the reading process in Chapter 3. Stahl, Hare, Sinatra, and Gregory (1991) have pointed out the importance of prior knowledge for both the quality and quantity of what is comprehended. Fortunately, teachers can exert some degree of control over this aspect of comprehension. Through guided instruction, we can activate, appraise and, if need be, increase students' knowledge of a topic before they begin learning with the text. Teachers can accomplish this task by using a variety of prereading strategies. In a study addressing the role of prereading strategies in activating prior knowledge to promote the comprehension of both expository and narrative text, Dole, Valencia, Greer, and Wardrop (1991) found that both teacher-directed and interactive prereading strategies were better than no prereading

instruction at all. Thus, the principle of prior knowledge corresponds generally to what occurs in the pre-reading stage of the instructional lesson.

Levels of Understanding

The second principle of comprehension emphasizes the fact that content material frequently demands in-depth study beyond the factual, literal level for adequate understanding and application in future lessons. Thus, students must be encouraged to think deeply about what they are learning as it is a key factor in the retention of information. A content teacher can guide this process during the reading stage by insuring that students adopt an active, questioning approach to the text, based on their prior knowledge and experiences. In order to construct lessons that guide students in the assimilation of factual text concepts with their own experiences, it is helpful to have a procedure for characterizing different levels of understanding. Those levels are text explicit, text implicit, and experience-based; and students should be given every opportunity to reason across this full range of understanding.

We have chosen to adopt a view of comprehension consisting of three categories: 1) text explicit, 2) text implicit, and 3) experience-based. The categories have been modified from those suggested by Pearson and Johnson (1978) and, in our opinion, offer the best description of the processes involved in comprehending text at various levels of understanding. As such, this simple framework captures the essence of comprehension—the interaction of prior experience with printed information. In order to gain a more concrete understanding of the three categories, try the following activity.

ACTIVITY

Read the paragraph below and answer the questions that follow.

Failing to remember things is a problem that plagues most of us. We forget to perform routine tasks like stopping at a grocery store on the way home or picking up the dry cleaning. Worse still, we may forget important information such as a new student's name. Fortunately, there are some reasonable solutions to our forgetfulness. (Bean, Haehl, & Bishop, 1983, p. 29)

Q: 1. What is a problem that plagues most of us?
A:

Q: 2. What specific group or audience is the paragraph addressing?
A:

Q: 3. What are your solutions to the problem posed in the paragraph?
A:

In answering question one from the previous activity, What is a problem that plagues most of us?, your response "forgetfulness" was taken directly from the text. In fact, you were able to point to the answer in the paragraph because it was literally stated by the author. Such comprehension is called *text explicit*.

In question two, What specific group or audience is the paragraph addressing?, you had to engage in a different type of comprehension from question one. Your response did not come explicitly from the text; rather, it had to be inferred from a hint in the passage. The phrase "new *student's* name" implies that teachers are the audience being addressed. When you must infer from the text to derive an answer to a question, you are engaging in *text implicit* comprehension.

Finally, answering question three, What are your solutions to the problem posed in the paragraph?, requires still another form of comprehension. Your response this time was drawn from your previous experience. You had to search your schema for strategies you might use to remember a new student's name. In doing so, you may have responded in a number of different ways including bizarre associations, where the student sits, and so on. Your inference, was not derived from the text, but from your existing schema or knowledge structure. This is called *experience-based* comprehension. This type of thinking is at the heart of curiosity, invention, and problem-solving. It is also one of the most neglected forms of questioning in many classrooms (Armbruster et al., 1991; Bean, Sorter, Singer, & Frazee, 1986; Durkin, 1978–1979; Goodlad, 1983).

A recent study of teacher questioning in science and social studies classrooms conducted by Armbruster and her colleagues is particularly depressing as her results echo those of Durkin's study completed nearly a decade and a half earlier that showed teachers assigned and assessed but did not guide students' comprehension (Armbruster et al., 1991). Using detailed observational transcripts of lessons, these researchers, like Durkin, found no instances of explicit instruction in how to read and learn from textbooks. Teachers created lower order questions and delivered them to students at the amazing average rate of 1.3 questions-per-minute. Lower level text explicit questions outnumbered higher order inferential questions 2 to 1. Clearly, we need to seriously alter the nature and content of our classroom questions if we are truly interested in getting students to think about challenging concepts.

Explicating Levels of Comprehension. Let's examine each of the three levels of comprehension in depth. Following Pearson and Johnson's (1978) recommendation, we will be examining question and answer relationships, rather than classifying questions in isolation. *Text explicit comprehension* involves getting the facts of a passage, as stated by the author. The question asked is based directly on the text, and the answer is explicitly cued by the language of the text. Raphael (1984), in an effort to use language familiar to students, uses the phrase, right there on the page, to describe text explicit comprehension. Answers are literally found on the page and readers can actually point to the answer. In essence, you are reading the lines. Text explicit comprehension requires you to tell what the author said, and there is usually only one answer. Therefore, answers to such questions have no middle ground—they are either right or wrong.

Text implicit and experience-based comprehension, on the other hand, require you to think about your answers—they are not explicitly stated by the author and answers may vary depending on each respondent's experiential background. In fact, the less the text is involved and the more experiential background comes into play, the larger the number of possible answers.

Text implicit comprehension involves answering a question derived directly from the language of the text, but also requires the reader to derive an answer when no obvious clues to it are visible in the passage. You are asked to infer what the author meant. Thus, the relationship between the question and the answer is implicit; it necessarily requires some logic to get from the question to the answer. Raphael (1984) calls this "think and search." As such, questions that require paraphrases of text information result in text implicit comprehension. In essence, you take the facts presented by the author and add knowledge from your experiential background to derive a reasonable implicit relationship. In other words, you are asked to read between the lines.

Finally, *experience-based comprehension* results when a question is asked and the plausible answer is derived almost exclusively from previous knowledge. Thus, the answer cannot be derived directly from the text. In Raphael's (1984) words, you are "on your own." Students draw inferences from previous knowledge; hence, they are involved in reading beyond the lines.

Summarized on the following page are the distinctions between the three levels of comprehension:

LEVELS OF COMPREHENSION

Level	Information Source			# of Possible Answers	Alternate Definition
	Question	Inference	Answer		
Text Explicit	Text	No	Text	One	Reading the Lines
Text Implicit	Text	Yes	Text	One Plus	Reading Between the Lines
Experience-Based	Text	Yes	Reader	Many	Reading Beyond the Lines

Implications Concerning Questions. Questions are one of the most prominent forms of comprehension instruction used. Questions are used to activate students' memory processes of text, focus their attention on significant aspects of text material, and aid them in synthesizing seemingly different parts of text into a coherent whole. It may be fairly safe to say that those teachers who are good questioners promote the process of comprehension (Cunningham, 1992). However, there are certain considerations you should be aware of when you attempt to use questions effectively.

First, and foremost, it takes time and thought to compose good questions. Good questions do not flow like water from a fountain. You need to examine carefully the material you have covered in order to ascertain the best kinds of questions to ask. You possess a wealth of information concerning your subject matter area; students do not. Asking questions that come from your knowledge base, rather than from the text, will do nothing more than confuse and befuddle your students.

Second, in asking good questions, be sure not to ask too many text explicit questions. Answers to such questions, though they form the basis for questions at higher levels of comprehension, require little or no thought, do not challenge the student, and do not enhance your role as a facilitator of learning.

Third, asking questions at higher levels of comprehension requires that you give students the freedom to respond. Without this, you may inhibit divergent reponses.

Fourth, be aware that sometimes you may not get the type of comprehension you expect. For example, consider the following sentences: Tom rode through the park at a slow gait, thinking about the day's activities. As Tom daydreamed, she searched the afternoon shadows for a few blades of grass. Your intended text explicit question to students might be: What kind of animal is Tom riding? Although most students are likely to respond with "horse," a few may say "mare." Thus, at times you may be pleasantly surprised at divergent, high-level responses to a seemingly straightforward question. The student has just processed your question differently to draw the above mentioned inference. The point is that you should be prepared for divergent responses to your expectations.

Fifth, the levels of comprehension model has implications for textbook questions, also. Take care to avoid relying entirely on questions provided by text authors. Such questions are written by experts in their field, and as good as these authors may be, they can't possibly understand your students' special needs. Only you, their teacher, can tailor questions that will involve your particular students in comprehension at varying levels. Questions so intended by text authors may not accomplish that task.

Sixth, students can be taught to generate their own questions. If you truly want your students to become active, critical readers of text, you need to become familiar with strategies designed to help them develop a questioning approach to reading (Gillespie, 1990). Helping students adopt this inquisitive stance can boost students' interest in pursuing a topic that may otherwise seem distant from their own personal lives.

Last, though questions are a major means to teach students, the value of statements should not be neglected (Bean, 1985; Blanton, Wood, & Moorman, 1990). They have suggested using statements as a prelude to using questions. This involves using statements at first that will help students to recognize information before they are required to produce it through the use of questions. Such statements will simulate comprehension at higher levels of thinking and familiarize students with that process. Once familiarity has been achieved, questions again become an appropriate and valuable way to help students comprehend text material. In the next chapter we will discuss the Anticipation-Reaction Guide, a strategy which exemplifies the value of statements as a means of enhancing students' comprehension.

Organization of Information

The third principle of understanding, organizing for long-term retention of information, is the most often neglected aspect of comprehension instruction. In the post-reading phase, ideas are refined and extended. Additionally, this final instructional stage relates directly to how well new information will be understood in a subsequent lesson. The post-reading stage of a lesson must involve activities that encourage students to synthesize and organize information.

Specifically, organization of information, relates to the ability to perceive an author's *text structure* or organizational pattern. When you alert students to the structure of an author's thoughts, you provide students with a powerful strategy for organizing information in a memorable fashion. Moreover, as you develop strategies to guide students' comprehension, your analysis of a text passage should reveal the author's pattern of organization. With adequate guidance, students can eventually become adept at detecting an author's structure independently.

The following activity will give you an idea of your well-developed, largely unconscious use of patterns in your own reading.

ACTIVITY

Read the following sentences. Place them in the proper order of occurrence.

He was well thought of by his peers.

John volunteered for extracurricular activities.

His principal gave him an excellent recommendation for the university doctoral program.

He never missed school unless he was very ill.

John was a conscientious teacher.

Recognizing the structure of prose is a great aid for students in comprehending and recalling text material. Students who can perceive the structure that binds the ideas in text will understand and remember ideas much better than if they are viewed only as separate entities (Armbruster, Anderson, & Ostertag, 1989; McGee & Richgels, 1992; Pearson & Fielding, 1991). In the above example, your recognition of the *cause-effect* pattern should have enabled you to organize the text in its proper sequence. Because John was such a good teacher and did fine things for his school, his principal was only happy to fulfill his desire. Additionally, with your knowledge of the apparent organizational pattern, you, more than likely, started the sequence with "John was a conscientious teacher," because the other attributes concerning his abilities logically follow that topic sentence. This same knowledge allowed you to place this sentence last: His principal gave him an excellent recommendation for the university doctoral program. In essence, your knowledge about the world and the organization of text allowed you to make logical predictions about the

arrangement and sequence of the above sentences. It is this same knowledge that students use, or should be taught to use, with their context textbooks.

Helping your students perceive an author's text structure gives them a valuable independent strategy they can use to comprehend text efficiently. For example, Meyer, Brandt, and Bluth (1980) found that ninth grade students' ability to identify and use an author's text structure accurately predicted passage recall scores. Additionally, Taylor and Samuels (1983) found that intermediate grade students possessing an intuitive awareness of text structure patterns recalled significantly more important passage information than students unaware of these structures. They cautioned that only a small percentage of students acquire this ability without direct modeling and guided instruction by a teacher. Teaching students to think like authors makes them more aware of text structure patterns which provide a framework for remembering important content. For example, Armbruster et al. (1989) taught middle grade students to make a visual representation of history text pattern and then attempt to recall these items. History texts often feature a problem-solution text pattern. Placing this pattern in a visual frame assists students in writing a summary of the major ideas and supporting details highlighted in the passage. Thus, a frame guide in history would include three items: (a) a sentence explaining what the problem is; (b) a second sentence telling what action has been taken to solve the problem; and (c) a third sentence explaining what happened as a result of this action. Students can then develop coherent summaries using information in each section of the frame. Your efforts to help students use text structure in comprehension and recall will reap benefits in their reading and writing.

Text structure serves a dual purpose in print: 1) to help writers communicate their thoughts; and 2) to help readers comprehend what authors are attempting to communicate. Since reading is an interaction between the thoughts and language of both writers and readers, text structure serves as a convenient vehicle to facilitate this communication. Meyer and Freedle (1984) have emphasized the importance of the text (the writer's) organization in comprehending connected discourse. Other researchers, such as Rumelhart (1975), have emphasized the importance of text structure that readers impose on text.

While both of these emphases are valid, it makes sense to consider a third position, one to which the authors adhere. Tierney, Soter, O'Flahavan, & McGinley (1989) have described the obvious connection in communication between authors and readers. It certainly cannot be denied that authors attempt to communicate their thoughts to readers through structural patterns in text. These patterns are real and they are visible on the printed page. On the other hand, one also cannot deny that readers attempt to use their logic in thought and reasoning to understand the printed page. The continuous process that readers employ in imposing their own organizational structure to communicate with authors, though not visible, is also very real, as previously discussed in this text. Meaning construction entails active interchange between writers and readers.

Explicating Text Structure. Knowledge of text structure helps to guide students' comprehension of text. While there are many types of patterns of organization in written materials, Niles and Memory (1977) recommend the following as most prominent:

1. *Cause/Effect:* This pattern links reasons with results. It is characterized by an interaction between at least two ideas or events, one taking an action and another resulting from that action.

Example: Because it snowed so heavily, the city traffic came to a standstill.

2. *Comparison/Contrast:* Comparison/contrast patterns of organization demonstrate apparent likenesses and differences between two or more things.

Example: While a lion and a giraffe are both mammals and bear live young, the lion is a carnivore and the giraffe is a herbivore.

3. *Time Order:* Time order is exemplified by a sequential relationship between ideas or events considered in presence of the passage of time.

Example: In December Scott took a job with a new company. Things went so well with the new job that he soon became a supervisor. Now, because of continued successes, he is vice-president of the firm.

4. *Problem/Solution:* Similar to the cause/effect pattern, this pattern is exemplified by an interaction between at least two factors, one citing a problem and another providing a potential answer to that problem.

Example: Certain plants need an environment with a constant, moderate temperature and high humidity or they will die. Consequently, a greenhouse is ideal for those plants.

To further help students in recognizing such patterns, Vacca (1973) provided a useful list of key words or phrases that signal, or cue, a particular text type. Such *signal words* provide mind sets that enhance the perception of text structure and learning from text. Following is a list of suggested signal words:

1. **Cause/Effect:** because, since, therefore, consequently, as a result, this led to, so that, nevertheless, accordingly, if . . . then.

2. **Comparison/Contrast:** however, but, as well as, on the other hand, not only . . . but also, either . . . or, while, although, unless, similarly, yet.

3. **Time Order:** on (date), not long after, now, as, before, after, when. (Vacca, 1973, p. 78)

It should be noted that cue words signaling the problem/solution pattern will be similar to those signaling the cause/effect pattern.

Teaching students to be on the lookout for signal words assists their awareness of an author's text structure and improves their recall. For example, Meyer,

Brandt, and Bluth (1980) found that text in which signal words were underlined facilitated ninth graders' recall of important ideas. More recently, Gordon (1990) studied middle grade students' use of text structure features in their reading and writing. She found that students were blissfully unaware of text structure clues at the start of her study. However, following careful instruction through examples, think aloud modeling, and visual tree diagrams of text structure features, many of these students began to use text structure cues such as signal words in their reading and writing. In the section that follows we outline an instructional procedure for developing your students' ability to use text structure to their advantage.

Suggestions for Helping Students Perceive Text Structure. Perhaps the key factor in teaching students to actively use the organizational structure of text is you, the content teacher. It is erroneous to assume students will recognize and utilize organizational patterns. Direct teaching in the recognition of patterns is essential, and all patterns should be pointed out continually to students. The time you spend in stimulating the perception of organizational patterns will take little away from your instructional time and will facilitate comprehension. Below is a suggested sequence for teaching students to perceive patterns of text organization.

1. **Modeling.** You should demonstrate the use of text structure first before expecting students to utilize it. Passages drawn from their reading should be used to illustrate your demonstration because they are most relevant to the students. Showing students a particular organizational pattern and pointing out why it is a certain type and how that pattern type is organized is essential. Any signal words that clue the reader to the organization of the material should also be pointed out and discussed.

2. **Recognition.** Next, you should walk students through a particular passage type by asking judicious questions that focus their attention on the text structure. For students experiencing difficulty, you may wish to read the material to them first rather than having them read it. In this way your students can concentrate entirely on perceiving the pattern. You may also wish to start with sentences only and then move to paragraphs and longer passages. Essential to this recognition step is students' verbalization of the how and why of the text structure.

3. **Production.** Producing a communication is a logical extension of receiving one. Writing, therefore, becomes a valuable means to reinforce text structure. From time to time all content teachers require students to write. Requiring logical organization in students' own writing can become a vital extension of perceiving text organization. As part of a writing assignment, you should ask students to frame a logical response by utilizing a particular pattern of organization and the signal words associated with it. Skeletal outlines or a graphic organizer may also be provided to facilitate production of an organized writing sample. We demonstrate how to teach structure awareness through writing in Chapter 11.

 Integrated Approaches

In Chapter 1 we introduced the notion that helping students learn content needs to be integrated throughout all stages of the instructional lesson, i.e., students generally need to be prepared to read a text during prereading, need guidance in searching for selected ideas during reading, and need reinforcement to retain the material learned during postreading. In this chapter we explored further critical principles of comprehension and their related instructional stages. While there are strategies which may only focus on certain aspects of the instructional lesson (see Chapter 10 for a discussion of these strategies), we would like to describe here a series of four strategies which should be viewed as more comprehensive in nature. Rather than focusing on one aspect of an instructional lesson, these strategies are integrated across all stages of the lesson—prereading, reading, and postreading—and provide a more holistic view of the comprehension process and integrated lesson planning.

K-W-L

Ogle (1992) created a 3-step integrated strategy designed to encourage active reading of expository text. The *K-W-L* strategy consists of a prereading stage aimed at activating prior knowledge, a reading stage where students seek answers to predetermined questions, and a postreading stage where they can distill what was learned through the reading. K-W-L relies on three categories of information: (a) K - What we *k*now (before a reading); (b) W - What we *w*ant to find out (during reading); and (c) L - What we *learned* (as a result of text reading). In addition, you should assist students in anticipating the organizational structure or likely categories of information a text author will introduce. In the example that follows, the topic of killer bees might present their recent invasion of the southern United States as a problem to be solved. Thus, the category section would include the labels problem and solution.

To prepare a K-W-L lesson, create a framework like the one that follows on the board or overhead and ensure that each student has a copy of this framework.

K-W-L LESSON FRAMEWORK

K- What we know   W - What we want to find out   L - What we learned

Categories of information
1.
2.
3.

Step One. Engage students in a brainstorming session on the topic they are about to read in the text. Next, elicit possible categories the author might use to organize this information on killer bees. The lesson framework on the following page displays students' comments concerning the killer bees selection they were about to read.

Step Two. To help students develop a clear purpose for reading a selection, they should create questions the text might answer. The framework on the following page shows some of the questions students generated for the killer bee text.

Step Three. Finally, students need to record the information they have learned in the framework. In addition, you may wish to have students develop a visual representation such as a graphic organizer or map, or they can write a short summary statement. Students can then share this information in small discussion groups.

Integrated strategies like K-W-L can form a solid foundation for extended research and writing projects. Sippola (1995) suggested that K-W-L might be extended to K-W-L-*S* by having students explore a fourth category of information: What they *still* need to learn. For example, is it really impossible to rid the United States of killer bees? Perhaps additional reading and research with other texts might provide an alternative viewpoint. Thus, K-W-L can lead into more detailed exploration of a topic or theme spanning a full unit which may take weeks to complete.

Other modifications might be considered for students in diverse classrooms. Small groups might be used to generate the information in steps one and two rather than a large group forum. Students might first work in a small group to record what they know and then report it to the large group. The same can be done for information they might seek. This should enable more students to participate and make the learning environment more collaborative and less threatening. In step three a small group might be a better conduit to get students to record/summarize what they found out. Teachers might also modify the strategy by incorporating more modeling and direction until students are comfortable with it. For particularly difficult topics or topics where little prior knowledge exists, the use of a shorter text or a video might be considered. These could serve as an advance organizer to give the students some familiarity with the topic before they actually have to read the assigned text. Similarly, a video could serve to augment, or even substitute for, the text.

Inquiry Chart

Inquiry Charts, or I-Charts, were developed by Hoffman (1992) to nurture critical reading in content classrooms by having students examine multiple sources of information for points of consistency and inconsistency. Based upon the work of Ogle with K-W-L, students use a data chart to record what they know about a topic, what they want to know about it, and what they found from their readings. The chart allows the students to gather the information they get from multiple sources and organize it for summarization, comparison, and evaluation. The I-Chart strategy consists of the following steps.

1. **Planning.** In planning, teachers must decide what: (a) topic is to be explored, (b) questions will drive the inquiry process, and (c) sources will be used for data collection. For example, let's say the topic is the Civil War, and the teacher decides the questions to be explored are: (a) What were the causes of the Civil

K – What we know	W – What we want to find out	L – What we learned
1. They can kill people	1. Why are they called "killer bees"?	1. They are more aggressive than the common honey bee
2. They kill other bees	2. Where are they found?	2. The southern U.S. (Texas)
3. Their sting is worse than honey bees	3. Where are they from?	3. Africa originally. They were brought to Brazil by accident in 1956
	4. How dangerous are they?	4. Very aggressive, but their sting is no more dangerous than other bees. However, they can interfere with the pollination of many fruits and vegetables by the common honey bee, raising the cost of these items.
	5. How can we get rid of them?	5. Scientists claim it is impossible.

Categories of information
1. Problem of killer bees
2. Solution to this problem

War? (b) What were the immediate effects of the war for each side? (c) What were the long-term consequences of the war? and (d) What would the United States be like today if the South had won the war? The teacher might decide that besides the class text, the classroom set of encyclopedias and other textbooks and tradebooks from the school library would serve as resources. Once planning is completed, the I-Chart should be constructed with this information displayed on it and might look like the following:

I-CHART: THE CIVIL WAR
Guiding Questions

TOPIC *Civil War*	1. *What were the causes of the Civil War?*	2. *What were the immediate effects of the war for each side?*	3. *What were the long-term consequences of the war?*	4. *What would the U.S. be like today if the South had won the war?*	Interesting Facts and Figures	New Questions
WHAT WE KNOW						
1. *Class text*						
2. *Encyclo-pedias*						
3. *Library trade book*						
SUMMARY						

SOURCES

2. **Interacting.** In this step students work with the teacher to explore their prior knowledge, share interesting facts and new questions, and read and record. First, students respond to each guiding question along the lines of what they already know. This information is recorded on the I-Chart in the "What We Know" row under the appropriate question. This information is recorded whether or not it is accurate or contradictory. Next, any interesting facts the students come up with and any new questions they think of, unrelated to the guiding questions, should also be recorded in the appropriate space on the I-Chart. Finally, students are asked to go to the additional source material to answer the guiding questions. The amount of time this will take depends on the number of available sources as well as the number of questions. Following the discussion of each source the teacher records the appropriate information for each question on the I-Chart. In this case the information should be as accurate as possible; any new questions or interesting information from the reading should be recorded as well. It is important to understand that the eventual size of the I-Chart will be dictated by the scope of the topic and search required.

3. **Interacting and Evaluating.** In this step the I-Chart is completed, and the findings are evaluated and shared. First, the students are asked to generate summary statements for each of the guiding questions and the interesting facts column. Thus, students are asked to synthesize the information previously recorded, taking into account both converging and conflicting information. Summary statements are recorded on the bottom row of the I-Chart. Next, students compare the information gained from their readings with their prior knowledge and reconcile any misconceptions. Now, students are ready to deal with the new, unanswered questions that arose during their data collection. These questions become the basis for additional research, either individu-

ally or in small groups. Finally, students report back to the whole class their findings regarding the unanswered questions.

Once students become familiar with the strategy, teachers can fade their responsibility; students may begin to select their own topics, generate their own guiding questions, and decide what to record on the I-Chart. Eventually, the strategy could be used with small groups or even for individual inquiry (Randall, 1996). Once students become proficient in synthesizing information into summaries, they may become the basis for students to expand them into paragraphs and, later, complete written reports. Finally, the I-Chart seems to be an ideal tool for exploring multicultural issues in the classroom.

Listen-Read-Discuss

Manzo & Casale (1985) developed the integrated strategy of *Listen-Read-Discuss* to ensure that students genuinely grasp content information. Because students receive multiple exposure to concepts through listening, reading, and discussion, they are more likely to learn and retain information you feel is worthy of this intensive process. There are three steps to a listen-read-discuss lesson.

Step One. The first part of the lesson entails presenting a well structured lecture on the material students are about to read in the text. Students need to have a good grasp of the content you are presenting if they are to participate actively in a listen-read-discuss lesson. Therefore, consider providing a clear lecture guide, perhaps in the form of a graphic organizer, that will serve to cue students to the text's structure. For example, the following graphic organizer might be used to assist high school students' comprehension of a lecture on Japan's rise to a world power. Reading in their text would follow about a 15-minute lecture on the topic. Notice that the graphic organizer displays the cause-effect structure of the text. Items one and three would be provided by the teacher on the graphic organizer lecture guide passed out to students. Those items in italics would be filled in by students as the lecture progresses with clear cues from the teacher signaling each important point.

```
                    ┌─────────────────────────────────┐
                    │  JAPAN BECAME A WORLD POWER     │
                    └─────────────────────────────────┘
                     /                              \
        ┌────────────┐                          ┌────────────┐
        │   CAUSES   │                          │  EFFECTS   │
        └────────────┘                          └────────────┘
```

1. In 1603 Tokugawa clan rules	1. *Unified Japan*
2. *Warriors went into debt—forced peasants to pay high rents*	2. *Peasant uprisings*
3. In 1853 Perry opens Japan to American trade	3. *Large scale foreign influence in Japan*
4. *Japanese adopted some Western ways*	4. *Antiforeign demonstrations*
5. *Japan is the first industrialized country in Asia*	5. *Achieve power at international levels*
6. *In 1889 Japan creates a limited constitution*	6. *The emperor remains supreme ruler*

Once the lecture is completed and students have filled in their graphic organizer lecture guides, the teacher is ready to progress to step two, the reading portion of a listen-read-discuss lesson.

Step Two. The teacher directs students to read the text pages on which the lecture was based. Their purpose for reading should be to compare their understanding of the lecture with the information presented in the text. In addition, they can identify vocabulary and concepts that need clarification and pinpoint any inconsistencies between the text and the teacher's lecture. They are then ready to discuss the information on Japan's rise to international power.

Step Three. The discussion step can begin with small groups and progress to a summary discussion as a whole class. Three major questions should guide students' discussion of the lecture and text reading: (a) What did you understand best from what you heard and read? (b) What did you understand least from what you heard and read? and (c) What questions or thoughts did the topic raise in your mind? This last question is one that is often glossed over in our desire to cover the content. Yet it goes to the heart of students' personal interest in a topic. For example, Japan's influence on our economy has grown considerably over the years. It would be important to raise and consider contemporary issues like this, which have their roots in the mid 1800s.

Guided Reading Procedure

The *Guided Reading Procedure* (GRP) (Manzo, 1975) is an integrated lesson plan designed to help students understand and remember key information from their text. The GRP highlights the comprehension processes of collaborative brainstorming, rereading a selection to correct inconsistencies and fill-in incomplete information, and organizing information for long-term retention and retrieval. In short, the GRP provides a good model of the essential processes for independent growth in comprehension. Manzo proposed the following steps in a well-integrated GRP lesson:

Step One. Have students read a text selection in class according to the following scenario:

a. Set a specific overall purpose for the assignment, e.g., in a health education unit on mystifying maladies, a section on "warts" might suggest the following purpose: Determine whether or not there is an effective cure for warts.

b. Set a second more general purpose: Be prepared to recall as many supporting details as you can without looking back at the text selection.

It is recommended that the approximate length of a reading assignment for the GRP should be 500 words (seven minutes) for junior high students and 2,000 words (10 minutes) for senior high students. This may be adjusted according to students' differential abilities, interests, and attention span.

Step Two. After the initial text reading is completed, have students recall everything they remember and record this information on the board. You may want to have a volunteer or two help you write down the class's ideas, since brainstorming activity tends to produce a barrage of ideas. For example, ideas students acquired from the warts selection might look like the following:

come and go	spunkwater
unpredictable	Pliny the Elder
no cures	caustic painting
electrocautery	folk treatments
medical treatments	polyoma virus
autosuggestion	

Step Three. As students become aware of information not recalled or of inconsistencies requiring correction, have them go back and review the selection to fill in missing information. Include these additions and modifications with the other information on the board.

Step Four. Now have students organize the random, verbatim information recorded on the board into categories, or main ideas and subordinate details. This can be accomplished by voting on the importance of each idea with the teacher playing the role of a devil's advocate by arguing for the inclusion of minor details. The end result may be an outline or a graphic organizer. For example, the warts topic might result in the following graphic organizer:

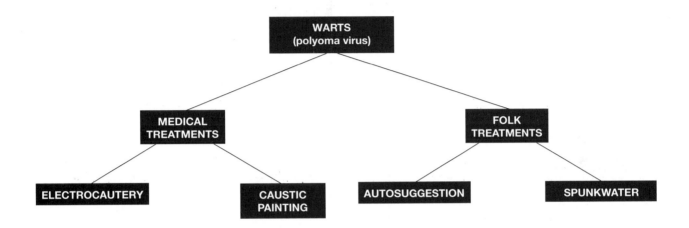

Step Five. Now give students a short-term memory/comprehension quiz on the GRP selection. About 5–10 true-false, short answer, or multiple-choice questions that elicit thinking at the three levels of understanding (i.e., text explicit, text implicit, and experience-based) should be adequate. Have students keep a graph of the quiz results for reinforcement.

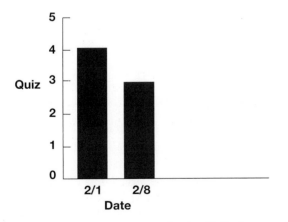

Step Six. This is a key step in the GRP. One week later give students a delayed-recall pop quiz on this same selection. Again, have students graph their delayed results. Chances are, some forgetting will have occurred. However, on subsequent GRP sessions, students will have a mind-set to organize and synthesize information for long-term retention.

In a study designed to field-test the GRP in a content classroom (Bean & Pardi, 1979) an additional pre-reading step was included in the strategy. Before reading a text selection in cultural geography, students conducted a five-minute survey of chapter headings, pictures, and tables and graphs. This survey step became the basis for a pre-reading brain-storming session that helped establish a cooperative, rather than teacher-dominated, purpose for reading. This modification, in conjunction with Manzo's six-step guided reading procedure, helped students retain the important concepts from the cultural geography lesson. You may find that supplementing the GRP with a five-minute survey makes the whole procedure a bit less threatening, particularly for students of diverse classrooms. The survey step activates students' existing knowledge of the GRP topic and gives you a preliminary indication of their readiness to cope with it.

Another modification you may want to make to the GRP involves the short- and long-term quizzes. Since this strategy is designed to guide students' reading of text, as well as to provide a model of the comprehension process, there is no reason why the quizzes cannot be two- (or more) person team efforts. You can still institute a point system for scoring and graphing the GRP quizzes, and the team approach makes the whole activity more exciting.

Needless to say, the GRP, as well as the K-W-L, I-Chart, and Listen-Read-Discuss strategies, will require a good block of time to complete. They should be reserved for topics you feel are important enough to warrant the extra time. Because of the integrated nature of these strategies, students receive multiple exposures to concepts. This may be especially useful for those students who often need extra time to learn content material, particularly given the diverse learners of today's classrooms.

SUMMARY

In this chapter we have expanded on three important principles of comprehension introduced in Chapter 3: prior knowledge, levels of understanding, and organization of information with text structure. We tied these principles to the development of the integrated three-stage lesson structure of prereading, reading, and postreading. Finally, we described four comprehensive strategies—K-W-L, I-Chart, Listen-Read-Discuss, and GRP—which provide the framework for a more holistic view of the comprehension process and integrated lesson planning.

Now go back to the comprehension vignette at the beginning of this chapter. React again to the lesson as you did before. Compare your responses with those you made before you read the chapter.

MINI PROJECT

Using the CD-ROM excerpt "Ears and Hearing," do one or both of the following:

1. Develop three questions at each of the three levels of understanding, and identify the predominant text structure present.

2. Develop a lesson based on K-W-L, the I-Chart, Listen-Read-Discuss, or the GRP. Try out the lesson with a small group of students or your peers. Evaluate the success of the strategy upon completion.

GROUP PROJECTS

■ Identify the text structure of the following passage and draw a graphic organizer that illustrates the structure.

■ The comet came too close to the earth and was caught in the earth's gravity field. As it entered the atmosphere it broke into millions of glowing fragments. An eight pound meteorite from the doomed comet landed on Jan's new car and smashed the windshield. This turned out to be an expensive problem for poor Jan because she had allowed her car insurance to lapse.

■ Describe the nature and purpose of integrated approaches to teaching comprehension.

■ Compare and contrast three levels of students' understanding.

COMPREHENSION:
GUIDING CONTENT LITERACY

SETTING

Lydian Flat's high school band class. In the previous class, Mr. Flat began a lesson on scale theory. In this class he plans to expand on this foundational information by exploring the seven modes of the major scale.

THE LESSON

Mr. Flat begins class by reviewing concepts about scale theory introduced in the previous class lesson. He does this by asking students to respond to questions he throws out to the whole class at the beginning of the period. In the scene that follows, T = the teacher, Mr. Flat, and S = the students.

T: "Can anyone tell me what a scale is?"

S: Some students attempt to assemble their instruments, honking on saxes and clarinets while others raise their hands to answer. Mr. Flat calls on Phil, a guitarist, who answers with a textbook definition:

S: "A scale is a series of tones organized according to a specific arrangement of intervals. An interval is the distance between any two tones or pitches. The smallest interval is the half step which on my guitar is the difference in pitch between two notes one fret apart on the same string."

T: "Okay, Phil, nice answer. Now let's try a tough one. What's a pentatonic scale?"

S: Phil snickers. Clearly this is an easy question for him but the other students become even more intent on fussing with their instruments, resulting in a growing cacaphony.

T: "Alright, alright. Phil, tell us what a pentatonic scale is?"

S: Phil doesn't answer. Instead he cradles his guitar and plays a slow A minor blues riff built on a minor pentatonic scale.

T: "Yes, that's a minor pentatonic scale but its a little ahead of where we are in this unit on scales. We need to consider and play the major scales and learn their key signatures first. And today we'll also be looking at the seven modes of the major scale: the dorian mode in jazz and rock, the phrygian mode which you may recognize from flamenco music, the lydian mode from jazz, the mixolydian mode used in a lot of folk music, the aeolian mode and the locrian mode used in jazz. But before we go any farther, let's start by playing a C major scale together."

S: Students launch into scale practice under Mr. Flat's guidance.

T: Near the end of the class, Mr. Flat hands out a worksheet that lists the major keys and their relative minor keys (e.g., C major and A minor). He informs students that there will be a quiz over this material next week on Wednesday.

S: Before the bell rings, students take apart and clean their instruments, frantically tossing the worksheet into folders and backpacks.

▶ Keeping in mind that this lesson is concerned with understanding scale theory and applying this theory in playing band instruments, jot down your thoughts on the following questions:

1. What are the good points about the lesson?

2. What are the weak points about the lesson?

3. What, if anything, would you change about the lesson?

RATIONALE

The integrated approaches to comprehension introduced in Chapter 9 all have advocated providing guidance to students before, during, and after reading. Additionally, to reinforce the integrated notion that this text recommends, these strategies also advocate the use of all language processes and small groups, whenever possible.

To continue in that vein the current chapter will describe various strategies that can be predominantly classified as prereading, reading, or postreading in scope. While we realize that a holistic view of the comprehension process encompasses all stages of the instructional lesson and that each stage is not necessarily a separate entity, e.g., the postreading stage of one lesson may serve as the prereading stage of the next lesson, the strategies will be divided to facilitate our discussion of each of them. The intent of all of these strategies, however, is similar: to increase students' interaction with the ideas presented in texts so they will acquire and retain important content information. Therefore, the aim of this chapter is to introduce and demonstrate an array of comprehension strategies that will augment those already described in the previous chapter.

LEARNING OBJECTIVES

■ Be familiar with a wide array of prereading, reading, and postreading strategies for guiding students' comprehension of content area concepts.

■ Be able to apply specific teaching strategies in your content area in order to guide students' understanding of your course content.

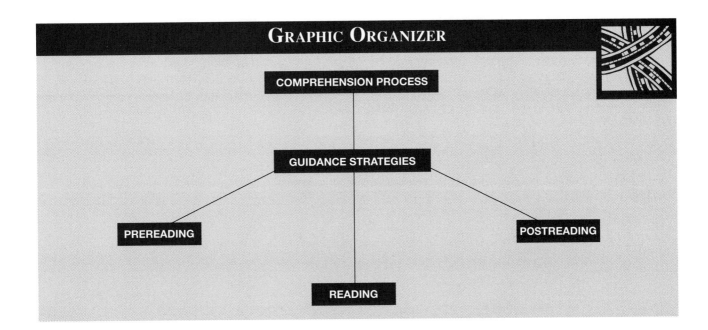

Prereading Strategies

Anticipation Guides

Throughout this text we have been using a number of prereading strategies to introduce each chapter. One of them, the *anticipation guide,* introduces each chapter in Part A and is an attractive way to activate your thoughts and opinions about a topic. As you are well aware by now, many of the guide statements are loaded in the sense that we want to challenge commonly held beliefs about content area literacy. Indeed, one of the major features of an anticipation guide is that it brings misconceptions about a topic to the surface (Head & Readence, 1992). Then we can begin to modify these misconceptions through a well-formulated instructional sequence.

Since anticipation guide statements operate at the experience-based level of understanding, they elicit a response based on one's current belief system. Therefore, at the prereading stage a student may adamantly defend a response to a guide statement with little fear of failure. As the learning sequence progresses into the reading and postreading stages, a mismatch between the students' preconceptions about a topic and the information being introduced should result in a subsequent modification of their initial knowledge base.

An additional feature of the anticipation guide is the way in which it functions as an informal, diagnostic tool. A teacher can appraise prior knowledge at the prereading stage and evaluate the acquisition of content based on postreading responses to the guide statements. Since anticipation guides encourage a personal, experience-based response, they serve as ideal springboards for large and small group discussion. Furthermore, they seem to work equally well with print and non-print media including films, lectures, and field-trips.

Anticipation guides lend themselves to application in diverse subject areas such as science, art, physical education, and history. The following steps apply to the construction of an anticipation guide in any content area.

Step One. Identify the major concepts and supporting details in a text selection, lecture, or film (see Chapter 6).

Step Two. Identify students' experiences and beliefs that will be challenged and, in some cases, supported by the material.

Step Three. Create statements reflecting your students' prereading beliefs concerning a course topic that may challenge and modify those beliefs. Include some statements that are consistent with both your students' experiential background and the concepts presented in the material or lesson. Three to five statements are usually adequate.

Step Four. Arrange the statements on a sheet of paper, overhead transparency, or the chalkboard. Have students respond positively or negatively to each statement on an individual basis. Have them record their justification for each response in writing, so they will have a reference point for discussion.

Step Five. Engage students in a prereading discussion highlighting their current justification for responding positively or negatively to each statement.

With a little practice you will discover that anticipation guides serve to clarify your content objectives and to motivate students to approach a learning task in an active fashion. Used in conjunction with a film, they can reduce the kind of haphazard, passive processing of film concepts that often characterizes the use of media in a classroom. The following physical education Anticipation Guide was developed to accompany a fitness film (Rayl, 1984).

Anticipation Guide: Stretching

Directions: Before watching the fitness film, put a (+) by those statements with which you agree and a (–) by those with which you disagree. Jot down some notes that will help you defend your point of view in a class discussion.

Anticipation

_____ 1. Most doctors prescribe stretching for relief of tension and stress.

_____ 2. A gymnast and a football player should stretch about the same length of time.

_____ 3. Stretching is neglected because it is painful and boring.

_____ 4. Stretching with the aid of a partner can bring about greater flexibility.

In a social studies class, Anticipation Guides help students to appraise ideas critically in a text (Ericson, Hubler, Bean, Smith, & McKenzie, 1987). For example, the following guide was designed to accompany junior high students' reading of a United States history chapter on the Constitution. One student's prereading ideas are included.

Anticipation Guide: The Constitution

Directions: Before reading pages 186 to 193, read each statement and place a (yes) by those statements with which you agree and a (no) by those statements with which you disagree under the section labeled Anticipation. Write your reasons for agreeing or disagreeing so you can be part of a class discussion.

Anticipation

yes 1. Writers of the Constitution were everyday working class people.

Because they had to work for a living and they were not royalty.

no 2. The President, like a king, has complete power to rule the country.

Because he can be kicked out of office by the process of impeachment.

no 3. A Ford mechanic cannot become President.

Because it doesn't matter as long as he is the right age and is elected.

no 4. People who are rich and people who are poor have equal protection under the law.

Because the rich people have more influence over the law because they can bribe the law.

yes 5. Students should have the right to decide what classes they take.

After the 10th grade they should be able to, because by that time they will know what they want from life and they would take courses to prepare for their career.

Even factual texts in United States history can serve as rich sources for critical thinking when they are supplemented with an Anticipation Guide like this one. Students begin to see some link between their lives and the often distant concepts in a text. Moreover, they must adopt a critical stance toward a topic, weighing their preconceptions against the author's ideas. Indeed, philosophers regard the development and evaluation of arguments as the essence of critical thinking (Facione, 1984).

As you work with anticipation guides, you may find it helpful to include an "I'm not sure" response column to accommodate those students who, at the pre-reading stage, are really not ready to commit to a yes or no response (Merkley, 1997). This reduces guessing and provides some insight into a student's background knowledge about the topic.

Anticipation Guides are best used in small group or cooperative learning pairs. Students can then discuss their perceptions of the topic, which helps them see that these statements are not a test. At first, you may need to make it clear to students that these statements are designed to jog their thinking, not to serve as another true-false test of Trivial Pursuit facts to be memorized. In our experience, students at various levels enjoy reacting to well constructed guide statements to narrative and expository material as well as lectures and films.

Text Previews

Text previews are another prereading strategy you can use to introduce students to complex narratives or expository texts (Bean, 1992a, Grave, Cooke, & LaBerge, 1983). A text preview is a teacher-devised introductory passage that provides a detailed framework for comprehending a reading selection. Text previews consist of three sections: (1) an interest-building section; (2) a synopsis of the selection; and (3) a review of characters in a story or important points in an expository selection, along with definitions of key words and questions to guide students' reading.

McCormick (1989) explored the use of text previews with middle grade students in social studies. Compared to a traditional lesson in which students read the text silently without the aid of a text preview, the students who received the text preview lesson outpaced their peers. McCormick found that both less skilled readers and more advanced students gained from the text preview. She recommended that text previews be combined with other learning from text teaching strategies to increase students' comprehension of difficult concepts.

The first text preview we will examine was developed to accompany a well known short story often introduced in junior high. The story, *The Lady or the Tiger*, was written by Frank R. Stockton in 1884. Although its plot is fairly simple, the story contains many archaic words students are likely to find troublesome. The story describes a semi-barbaric princess who falls in love with a commoner. Her father, the king, discovers this and has the commoner placed in an arena before the people of the village where he is confronted with two doors. Behind one door is a beautiful woman, behind the other, a tiger. Tension in the story hinges on whether or not the princess, who knows which door is safe, will save her lover or have him killed out of jealousy. Indeed, the final outcome is never revealed and the reader must infer the princess's decision.

The text preview that follows is one we have used successfully with junior high English classes to introduce and discuss *The Lady or the Tiger* (Ericson, Hubler, Bean, Smith, & McKenzie, 1987).

Text previews like this one draw on readers' background knowledge and increase their interest in reading a selection. We have found that junior high students enthusiastically participate in the prereading discussion stage of a text preview, and the exercise makes them feel they have some power over complex material before they begin reading. One study of below average readers in junior high who were introduced to text previews showed that these prereading aids contributed significantly to students' comprehension of difficult short stories (Graves et al., 1983).

The following steps should guide your development of text previews.

Step One. Create an interest-building section consisting of several statements and questions that connect the major topics and issues with experiences familiar to students. Think about real life, day-to-day events that are analogous to the critical target concepts in a text.

Step Two. Write a synopsis that may, in the case of a story, describe setting, characters, provide definitions of important vocabulary, and include several questions for guiding students' reading. In the case of expository text, we have found that it is effective to use focusing questions in this section, ones that move students from text explicit to higher level implicit and experience-based thinking.

Step Three. Introduce the text preview to students by having them read the first interest-building section, followed by a discussion. Use this same approach for the synopsis and last section. Much like an anticipation guide, a prereading discussion will give you a chance to determine students' background knowledge as they approach a challenging selection.

Since it takes a great deal of effort to develop and introduce text previews, we recommend that you cre-

Text Preview: The Lady or the Tiger*

Build Interest

Many adults read fairy tales to their children. Did any adult ever read fairy tales to you? Which ones do you remember?

Many fairy tales have a princess who falls in love. The young man she falls in love with must often prove himself worthy to her father, the king. Perhaps he must slay a dragon or survive other dangerous experiences. In some fairy tales, the young man even saves the princess from some horrible beast.

Stories like this are not only for children, however. Stories for teenagers and adults may have many similarities with fairy tales. For example, there are many stories in which modern day parents disapprove of the boy their daughter loves, but they change their minds about him when he does something wonderful, and everything ends happily. Can you think of examples from television or the movies which are modern day fairy tales?

Sometimes in a story or television program something happens that you don't expect. Maybe there is a sad ending instead of a happy ending, or the thief turns out to be a king in disguise. Another unexpected ending might involve having the ugly woman turn out to be a beautiful fashion model working undercover for the police. Can you think of other examples?

Synopsis

In "The Lady or the Tiger," a king has an unusual way of deciding if a man accused of a crime is guilty or innocent. The accused man is forced to walk into an arena and must open one of two doors. Behind one door is a ferocious tiger who immediately tears the man to pieces as punishment for being guilty. Behind the other door is a beautiful woman who immediately marries him as a reward for his innocence. All the people of the kingdom are required to attend this trial.

Review of characters, vocabulary, and guiding questions

Now it happens that a common man falls in love with the king's daughter. She loves him in return. But the king finds out about their love and the young man's fate is to be decided in the arena. The princess knows which door hides the tiger and will be able to give her lover a signal.

But she is very jealous of the beautiful young woman behind the other door.

What signal does she give her lover? You will have to read to find out.

Before you read the story, we want to tell you again the three most important people in it. They are the king, the princess, and the young man.

There are also some words we would like to define:

The king is "semibarbaric" and "authoritarian." "Semibarbaric" means that he is only half civilized. The other half of the king enjoys bloody shows in the arena. "Authoritarian" means that he demands that everything be done his way.

The princess is "fervent" and "imperious." "Fervent" means that she openly shows her feelings. "Imperious" means that she demands her own way, just as her father does.

As you read, be thinking of these questions:

(1) What signal does the princess give her lover?
(2) What does the young man find behind the door he opens?
(3) Why did the princess choose that door?
(4) If you were writing this story, how would you have ended it?

---

*Based on "The Lady or the Tiger," by Frank R. Stockton and reprinted with permission of Bonnie Ericson and the International Reading Association.

ate them only for particularly challenging selections. In addition, you may find that having students write text previews for students in other classes is another powerful way to use this strategy.

When you develop a text preview for an expository selection in science or social studies, the interest-building section is critical. Unfortunately, textbooks rarely include the sort of author intrusions found in diet books and other tradebooks sold in most bookstores. Author intrusions generally offer familiar analogies, use personal pronouns, and seek to guide the reader's pursuit of meaning. Your text previews fill this gap by speaking directly to students.

The following text preview was developed and used in a junior high United States history class where students were reading a chapter on the Politics of Protest. During the late 1800s farmers protested unfair business practices that overcharged them for the transportation of their goods. The plight of farmers in the 1800s can be related to the desire of any group for fair treatment. We tried to make this connection in our text preview. The last part of the preview asks seven study guide questions designed to help students grapple with these issues in a contemporary context. One student's responses to these questions are featured.

Text Preview: The Politics of Protest

Suppose that you like to ride a skateboard around your neighborhood. Then, one day, older people in the neighborhood band together and say that there can be no more skateboarding where you live. If you are caught skateboarding, they will take away your board and charge you a $50 fine. How do you feel about this situation? What would you do about it?

The chapter you are about to read shows how groups of people such as small business people, workers, and farmers in the 1890s protested what they felt were unfair practices by big business. Like the people that banned skateboarding, big business had a lot of power in the 1890s. Big business could make life miserable for the little guy. For example, the farmers felt they were paying too much interest on equipment loans from big business banks. Farmers banded together to protest this unfair treatment. They looked for help from the federal government, especially Congress. As you read pages 537 to 539, see if you can answer the following questions:

Right There on the Page

1. How did farmers solve their problems with big business? (p. 538, paragraph 2 & 3)

   Patrons of Husbandry talked about political "junk."

2. What good did the Interstate Commerce Act of 1887 do? (p. 539, paragraph 1)

   It helped lower the rates of railroads.

3. What was the purpose of the Sherman Antitrust Act? (p. 539, paragraph 3)

   To break-up large groups or combinations of big businesses that had become trusts.

Think and Search

4. Why didn't the Sherman Antitrust Act work the way it was supposed to in 1890?

   Because the wording was not very clear. And, the people who were supposed to make it work didn't believe in it.

On Your Own

5. Do you think the Sherman Antitrust Act is working today?

   Yes, they still try to break up large groups.

6. If you were a small farmer in Idaho, do you think your business would be doing well today?

   No, because farms are now owned mostly by big groups. I couldn't keep up with them.

7. Do you think big business monopolies are as much of a problem today as they were in 1890? Why? Why not?

   Yes, but now we break some of them up—like we did with A.T.&T.

This text preview and its guide questions helped students' comprehension of a potentially dull and distant topic—the farmers efforts to gain fair treatment in the late 1800s. Having students work on the guide questions in cooperative learning pairs also helps those students who may be unaccustomed to grappling with experience-based, on-your-own issues. Text previews can be created for particularly problematic text reading assignments in science and other content areas. They help students approach text reading with a schema for a topic based on prior knowledge.

ACTIVITY

Using Edgar Allan Poe's short story on the CD-ROM entitled "The Telltale Heart," develop a text preview to introduce high school students to the story.

ReQuest

This unusual representation of the word request is actually a blend of reciprocal and questioning. The *ReQuest* strategy was developed by Manzo (1969) to help students adopt an active, questioning approach to text reading. Students are guided in this process by the teacher, who models the question-asking procedure and attempts to elicit higher-level, text implicit and experience-based questions.

In the ReQuest activity, both the teacher and students silently read specified portions of the text together and then take turns asking each other questions. Students ask the first series of questions. This order gives the teacher an opportunity to appraise the level of their analysis. If the students merely produce text explicit questions (e.g., What color was the main character's hair?), then the teacher attempts to model higher-order questions on that same section of the text after students have fully exhausted their array of questions. The teacher models higher-order questions such as: What is the significance of the main character's iron-gray hair? (text implicit); How would you feel if you were in the main character's predicament? (experience-based); What do you think is going to happen next? (prediction based on text implicit and experience-based factors). Moreover, when students produce similar questions during their interrogative turn, the teacher should praise their efforts with such phrases as: That's a good question! It really makes me think!

Now that you have a general notion of what ReQuest is all about, we want to outline the preparatory steps for a ReQuest session and illustrate the procedure with a story we devised. The following preparatory steps are essential for a successful ReQuest session:

Step One. Analyze the text selection for major concepts and sections portraying these concepts. For example, a story can usually be divided into the following units: setting and characters; an event that introduces conflict; attempts to resolve the conflict or achieve a goal; resolution of the conflict; and finally, a reaction on the part of the protagonist.

Step Two. Determine prediction points in the story or text selection that allow the reader to form expectations about upcoming events. These prediction points can be labeled in your copy of the material as P_1, P_2, P_3, etc.

> *Example:* She treaded water, trying to remain calm as the full moon illuminated the last features of her once majestic sloop, now sinking into oblivion. The tropical air was warm and the Pacific deceptively gentle, yet she knew, danger was lurking in the depths that surrounded her.

P_1————

> Sharks are particularly bold at night. . . .

Step Three. Explain the general ReQuest procedure to your students.

Example:

Teacher: We'll each read a portion of the text silently. I will close my book and you can ask me all the questions you can think of referring to your book as needed.

Teacher: Let's read the first paragraph. . . .

Step Four. When you reach the final prediction point in the story or text selection, have students generate all the predictions they can think of for the final outcome of the selection. List the predictions verbatim on the board and have students vote on the ones they feel are most plausible. This step is particularly exciting with story selections that have a surprise twist at the end.

The following story and ReQuest scenario illustrates one approach to the use of this procedure in an English class.

The Round Swing

The round swing stood in a little clearing behind the Robinson's cabin. It was nothing more than a tall pine tree with all its branches cut off and a long rope hanging from the top to within about three feet of the ground. A piece of cloth was tied to the end of the rope. The tree was set back about ten feet from the edge of a steep ravine, carpeted with pines at the bottom.

P_1 ————

I looked down, far down into the valley below. And the same nervous sickness that overcame me on the thirty-foot diving tower at summer camp bounced into my stomach. But I had to go on the round swing. There wasn't anyone else to refuse with me. I was alone.

P_2 ————

"I'll go first!" Terry said.

"Okay, I'll hold the rope while you get in," Mike Robinson offered.

Terry put his feet through the cloth seat and tested it with his weight.

"I'm no fat man like Mark Rogers. It won't give," he said.

And then he was running hard around the half-circle plateau. Seated and airborne. Yelling his lungs out in nervous excitement. A human puppet soaring over the valley. Stumbling back onto the other side of the plateau and he was off again. Till the rope had coiled itself tightly around the tree and Terry crashed into it panting.

"Wow! It's great, Mike! Hey, you gotta try it, Kev! It's so hairy!" "Go ahead, Mike. After all, it's your swing," I said.

"Okay. I'll just go around a few times, then you can try it."

He took off, hooting his way over the ravine like Terry. The third time around he skidded back onto the ledge.

"C'mon, Kev! You can try it now!" Terry said.

P_3 ————

"No, I don't know. I'm not that hot on trying it," I said.

"What? You aren't afraid, are you?"

"No, I just don't care about it that much," I answered.

A car crunched over the dirt road, winding its way into the Robinson's front yard. Mike pulled himself out of the swing.

"Hey, that's probably my parents. Let's go inside. Don't say anything about the swing."

"That's okay. We have to go home now anyway. We'll just go through your backyard and work our way down to the river," Terry said.

"Do you know where the trail is?"

"Yeh, Mike. See you later."

"Too bad you didn't get to try the round swing, Kev," Mike said.

"Yeh, some other time," I answered.

Terry looked disgusted but didn't say anything all the way down the trail. When we reached the river I let myself flow along with it.

Three prediction points have been established for guiding students' collaborative discussion and comprehension of this story. The teacher and students would read the first paragraph (i.e., P_1) silently, then the students would ask the teacher questions based on just that section. It has been the authors' experience that even fairly sophisticated students will begin ReQuest by asking rather low-level, text explicit questions. The following hypothetical scenario is representative of a typical ReQuest session:

Student(s): What was the round swing? (text explicit)
Teacher: A rope tied to a pine tree. . . .

Notice that this form of text explicit question has a tendency to stifle further discussion. Also note that the teacher did not provide any positive comment on the quality of the question. At this point in the scenario, let us assume that students have exhausted their array of questions on this paragraph and it is now the teacher's turn.

Teacher: What do you think is going to happen in this story? (prediction via text implicit and experience-based information)
Student A: Someone's going to fall out of the round swing.

Student B: We're going to find out how it feels to ride the round swing.

Student C: It's too early to tell.

Teacher: Okay, let's read the next paragraph and see what happens!

As you can see, in contrast to text explicit questions, the teacher's question, comprising a blend of implicit and experience-based elements, asked students to predict the next event in the story. This type of question generates discussion and provides a good model for students to emulate when it is their turn. In addition, it is impossible to produce a wrong answer on a prediction question. For the sake of illustration, let us assume that some of the students in this example have grasped the concept of asking higher-order questions as we move into the second paragraph (i.e., P_2).

Teacher: Okay, you can ask me any questions you can think of from the first two paragraphs.

Student D: What is below the round swing?

Teacher: A valley.

Student E: What would you do if you were the speaker in the story? (experience-based)

Teacher: Ah, that's a good question—I'll have to think about that a minute. . . . If it looked sturdy enough I might try the round swing. I think I would test out the cloth seat first!

Student F: Where do you think this story takes place? (text implicit)

Teacher: That's interesting to think about. Maybe in the high Sierras somewhere in California? It doesn't really say, so it could be in the hills of Georgia. . . . Probably not in Iowa!"

It should be readily apparent at this point that ReQuest is an attractive method for guiding students' comprehension of a story or text selection. At the final prediction point (i.e., P_3), the teacher would elicit all possible predictions pertaining to the outcome of the story. These would be listed on the board and their probability would be rank-ordered by way of a class vote. Students should be advised that the author's chosen ending is not necessarily preferable to the endings they have generated.

As you can see, ReQuest functions as an effective prereading strategy or, if extended as in the preceding example, it may be useful to guide the entire reading of a selection. Thus, ReQuest overlaps with the reading stage of a well-integrated content lesson.

Comprehension guidance and strategy instruction is especially important for second language learners in your classroom. For example, in a study of low literacy Latina/o students in middle school, Jimenez (1997) found that strategies such as self-questioning and inferencing could be introduced through multicultural literature that captured students' interest. Thus, rather than placing students in text material that may be so frustrating that they reject any attempt to also introduce strategies, you may want to teach self-questioning and other cognitive strategies using more friendly, multicultural literature for second language learners.

Directed Reading-Thinking Activity

Although ReQuest is an ideal means of guiding students toward asking their own questions of well-structured story material, the *Directed Reading-Thinking Activity* (DRTA) works well with expository texts, especially in social studies (Stauffer, 1969). The DRTA is a self-questioning process that encourages students to predict oncoming information in expository text and set purposes for reading that are personally interesting. Questions not answered by a text may call for supplemental reading, class discussion, consultation with an expert source, or further exploration of a topic.

The following steps should guide a DRTA lesson.

Step One. Before reading the text in detail, have students survey a chapter topic by considering the title, headings, illustrations, and diagrams. This survey will form the basis for prereading questions. Longer chapters can be broken-up into smaller increments, if necessary, or students in small groups can each survey a section of the chapter and share their questions.

Step Two. Have students write questions called to mind in the chapter survey. If you have students keep a journal, they can enter the questions there.

Step Three. As a class, discuss various student-generated questions, emphasizing the value of personal purpose setting.

Step Four. Have students read the text to consider answers to their questions. They can then discuss their answers in small groups or as a class.

Step Five. Have students in small groups develop questions that the text does *not* answer about the topic. Through discussion, help them identify sources such as people and other texts able to supply answers to their questions. Provide time and credit for tracking down these answers.

The following DRTA was conducted in a multicultural junior high geography class. Students were reading a section of the text describing peasant life in China leading up to the peasant revolt. They had to consider two sub-headings: (a) Peasants in China, and (b) The Road to Revolt. Here are some of the representative questions and answers they generated for steps one through four.

DRTA: China

Peasants in China

1. What kinds of jobs do peasants work on?

    Farming.

2. Where do most peasants live?

    In the country.

3. Do they have enough food to eat and sell?

    Yes. But they have just a little to sell. To survive, peasants could rent or sell their land. They could sell their children.

The Road to Revolt

4. Why did the rulers dislike peasants?

    Because they thought of them as servants.

5. How did the rulers make life harder for the peasants?

    Peasants did not have enough land to support their rapidly growing population.

Students generated a wide array of interesting questions not answered by the text.

Student Questions Not Answered By the Text

1. What is life like out in China now?
2. Do teenagers go to school, come home, sometimes cook dinner, and do homework?
3. Do the Chinese listen to the same music we do?
4. Do their homes and houses look like ours?
5. Are the parents very strict to their children? Because we get away with a lot of things!
6. What do they do when they have free time?

In this instance, a visitor to the class had spent the previous summer traveling throughout mainland China visiting schools. She was able to provide answers to students' questions. When immediate answers to student-generated questions are not available, it is important to identify available resources that will shed light on the questions and allot adequate time and rewards for sharing this information with the class at a later date. In our experience, authors would do well to pay attention to the experience-based questions students ask in a DRTA lesson. Perhaps our textbooks could be more responsive to the active interest students display in topics that sometimes seem very distant from their lives. In any case, the DRTA increases students' interest in reading for purposes they set.

 ## Reading Strategies

Sitting down with a textbook in the solitude of your own personal study corner is a lonely activity, devoid of the language interaction afforded by the classroom. You may well wonder what possible strategies exist to help students cope with this inherently solitary task.

Indeed, many text assignments are of the "sink-or-swim" variety. "Go home and read Chapter 13 in your text" is an all too familiar edict for many students. Unfortunately, textbooks are rarely amenable to such independent reading assignments. Texts are instructional tools that require a good deal of guidance if students are to gain anything from them. In the section that follows we will describe some approaches that assist students in coping with their individual text reading assignments.

Study Guides

The term *study guide* has been used loosely for years to describe almost any form of supplementary material that accompanies a text. Often, study guides are nothing more than a series of text explicit questions supplied by an author at the end of a text chapter. We subscribe to a very different view of the process involved in the development of a good, content area study guide. The mini-study guide that follows contains the basic ingredients necessary to extend students' thinking beyond a mere parroting of text explicit concepts.

Mini-Study Guide

Directions: Use the information in Chapter 9 to answer the following questions. Compare your answers to those of a colleague.

   *1.   What is the second principle of comprehension advanced in the introduction to Chapter 9? (page 144, paragraph 1)

   **2.   Why is it important for students to be able to produce a text structure in their own writing?

   ***3.   Of the comprehension strategies introduced in Chapter 9, which one(s) do you prefer for use in your content area? Why?

      *   Text explicit
     **   Text implicit
   ***   Experience-based

Notice that a study guide of this form asks students to react to text concepts at multiple levels of understanding. For example, the first question, which is text explicit, includes a detailed reference to assist students in locating the answer. For some students, this detailed form of guidance may be necessary. Indeed, some students may only be able to answer this form of question, particularly in the early stages of the course. In contrast to question one, question three asks the reader to build a bridge of text concepts and individual teaching needs. Both questions two and three offer the potential for discussion and expanded thinking. Although this study guide example has been presented after the fact, in practice study guides typically accompany a text assignment and the reader completes the guide while reading. For example, Armstrong, Patberg, and Dewitz (1988) compared hierarchical guides that progressed sequentially from text explicit to more difficult experiential level questions with nonhierarchical guides that intermixed questions from the various levels. In classes of 11th grade English, they found that study guide students' comprehension of Steinbeck's *The Grapes of Wrath* was significantly better than that of students in a no guide condition, regardless of whether students had hierarchical or nonhierarchical guides. Most importantly, students were able to transfer the comprehension process modeled by the study guides to subsequent short story reading assignments. Thus, the guide provides a pathway to the major concepts in a content area and counters a more traditional, sink-or-swim reading assignment. A good study guide should mirror the thinking process by which a reader extracts information from text (Wood, Lapp, & Flood, 1992). As such, a teacher-devised study guide should:

1. Focus students' attention on major concepts at three levels of understanding (i.e., text explicit, text implicit, experience-based).

2. Foster student reaction to the text material at each student's own, individual level of understanding.

3. Direct students' thinking processes in extracting information from text material.

4. Serve as a basis for follow-up discussion in small groups to collaborate on the explication of text concepts and extend individual comprehension.

One might expect that students would regard study guides as an additional burden along with the text reading assignment. In a study designed to explore secondary students' opinions of study guides,

Laffey and Steele (1979) found that study guides were well received. The majority of students evaluating study guides felt they understood text concepts better as a result of completing and discussing guide material.

The development of a study guide involves a process of content analysis similar to the construction of an anticipation guide. Indeed, developing these two comprehension aids simultaneously with a text chapter is a good idea. The following steps should be followed:

Step One. Determine the major concepts and important details in a text chapter or reading selection.

Step Two. Develop questions that reflect these major concepts and details at multiple levels of understanding. Use vocabulary terms students can understand and, in the first few guides you develop, provide page and paragraph indicators to demonstrate the process of locating and extracting information.

Step Three. Assign the study guide as an adjunct to independent text reading. Then, have students discuss and defend responses in small groups.

Since not all students will be able to answer the whole study guide, the discussion step gives everyone exposure to the complete array of information. This study group step is an integral part of the application of study guide material and is essential to its success as an aid to comprehension. Generally, about 10 questions per study guide should be adequate for a text chapter. The guide should look attractive in that adequate space is allowed for student answers, and information does not appear to be crowded on the page.

The following study guide was used to guide high school students' discussion in United States history. Text explicit questions are labeled right there on the page, text implicit questions, search and think, and experience-based questions, on your own. Raphael (1986) found that using these phrases helps students focus on the source of information needed for answering questions. This study guide was developed to accompany reading, The Confederation and the Constitution. Students read the text and answered the study guide questions. Then, they engaged in small group discussions of their answers and a large group follow-up discussion focusing on the on your own items. One student's answers are included.

Study Guide: The Confederation and the Constitution
 Right There On the Page

1. What political changes occurred in the 13 colonies as a result of the American Revolution? (pp. 119–120)

   Colonial self-rule, the recognition of minorities, new constitution, an increase in voting, and the legislature was more responsive to people.

2. What social changes took place in the 13 colonies as a result of the American Revolution? (pp. 120–121)

   The separation of church and state, department of Loyalists, uprooted the Anglican Church, loosening of morals, weakening of slavery, and the development of the feminist movement.

3. What economic changes happened in the 13 colonies as a result of the American Revolution? (p. 122)

   Inventive influences, the loss of commerce because of England, high inflation, great amounts of land available, freedom of trade, a distaste for government.

4. Can you identify some political, social, and economic *disadvantages* that resulted from the American Revolution?

> *We did not have many great strong leaders that we had before. We really did not have much control. We were on our own so we needed to spend money to manufacture goods and find people to buy them.*

5. Why wasn't slavery abolished in the 1770s?

> *Political fighting over slavery was avoided to preserve national unity. Too many people needed workers to make money and get their lives going again.*

6. Why do you think the authors see the American Revolution as "accelerated evolution" rather than "outright revolution?"

> *Because the Revolution was unknown to many people living in small, isolated villages. And, it wasn't as radical as other revolutions. It made future changes possible.*

On Your Own

7. Would you want to travel through time back to the 1770s during the drafting of the Constitution? If so, why? If not, why not?

> *Yes, so I could maybe put things in or take things out that may help the United States.*

8. If you decide to travel back in time to visit the drafting of the constitution you would be taking with you the powerful knowledge of the future! What advice could you give the writers of the Constitution?

> *Be clearer in what is written. Today, interpretations of the constitution are all different.*

Study guides are particularly important in the early part of a course as students are getting a grasp of an author's writing style and dominant text structures. We have used study guides effectively in the early grades and at the academic level. Study guide questions can form an effective model for student-generated questions. Indeed, study guides help model fluent, efficient text reading. Textbooks are not designed to be read word-for-word. Rather, they should be read selectively with an eye toward important ideas. The following activity is designed to give you further practice with the process of constructing a study guide for a content area text.

Options Guides

An *options guide* is another form of study guide that, unlike the focused guidance provided in a traditional study guide, offers possibilities and predictions to be evaluated in subsequent reading (Bean, Sorter, Singer, & Frazee, 1986). It asks students to function in an active, decision-making role. Unlike a study guide, which is designed to accompany a reading assignment, an options guide is discussed prior to text reading. It then serves as a guide during reading. Options guides are ideal for reading assignments in social studies texts, where students often adopt a passive role, mindlessly turning pages or trying to memorize facts.

Directions: The following three study guide questions pertain to the present section of Chapter 10. See if you can generate three additional study guide questions on this same material.

***1. Based on your own academic experience, can you think of any courses you have taken where you would have appreciated study guides with the text? Which ones? Why?

*2. What is the second step in constructing a study guide?

**3. How does the study guide foster the psychological principle of in-depth processing of text material?

*4.

**5.

***6.

The following steps are used to develop and introduce the options guide.

Step One. Carefully analyze a text reading assignment for major concepts and key sub-headings that foreshadow upcoming events. You want to identify (1) key historical figures and the specific impact they had on other groups of people; and (2) the economy, the arts, religion, and other sociocultural aspects of life.

Step Two. Since up to the time you introduce the options guide students' previous text reading is all they have to go on in discussing the guide, you should construct a brief background statement that will remind students of the material they have read and studied up to this point.

Step Three. Develop one or two central questions that ask students to consider various options open to specific groups of people within the particular historical context the text is presenting.

Step Four. When students have completed a text reading assignment up to the sub-heading or section of text upon which your options guide is based, have them convene in small groups for about 10 to 15 minutes to discuss and complete the before reading section of the options guide. Then, when they finish reading the assignment, they should check their listed options against actual events in the text and complete the guide's after reading section. Engage students in a follow-up small group discussion to clarify any sections of the guide that need further explanation.

The options guide that follows is designed to precede a text reading assignment in world history on the Emergence of Japan. Students have read the portion of the chapter on the developing samurai warrior-class. The first sub-heading of the new reading comprises the major heading for the guide. Subsequent sub-headings were used to list various groups affected by shogun society. Representative group answers before and after reading are listed.

Options Guide: The Kamakura Shogunate (1192–1333) Began

  Background:

  In 1156, civil war broke out between two large landowning families. Each family had a band of loyal warriors called samurai. In 1192, one samurai, named Minamoto Yoritomo, became the supreme general of all Japan. The emperor named him the shogun.

  During this period of military rule, what *options* for political influence do you think were available to the following groups?

  1. Nobles?

      1.1 Before Reading: *They will be even more powerful with the strength of their loyal samurai warriors.*

1.2 After Reading: *The emperor's power was less but the local "daimyos" (nobles) became supreme rulers of their lands. They fought with other daimyos. There was no effective central government in Japan during this time. Later, in the Toku-gawa Era (1603–1868) central government was strong.*

2. Artists?

   2.1 Before Reading:

   In this military era, we feel there will be no time for the arts. Artists will be forced to fight or flee. It will be a very backward time.

   2.2 After Reading:

   It seems strange but the arts did flourish. Poetic "No" plays were created, landscape painting was prized, flower arranging, tea ceremonies, and artistic gardens were important in Japanese homes.

3. Farmers?

   3.1 Before Reading:

   With all the fighting, there will be no time for farming. Agriculture will suffer.

   3.2 After Reading:

   Farmers thrived since the daimyos ruled to maintain peace within their own communities. But gradually, cities grew and merchants became important. The landing of the Portuguese in 1543 made the people aware of European trade possibilities.

4. The Samurai?

   4.1 Before Reading:

   They are soldiers, so, like all soldiers, they will have little power. They must follow orders.

   4.2 After Reading:

   Samurai knights were very loyal to their shogun generals. They felt a total moral obligation to do well in battle. If they did not, they would commit suicide or "harakiri." As we suspected, they didn't have much power. The shoguns held the power.

5. If the Chinese try to invade Japan, how will they do?

   5.1 Before Reading:

   Since they are an older, more powerful people, they will win.

Kubla Khan invaded Japan but his Mongol warriors were swept into a big typhoon. The Japanese called this the Kamikaze or "divine wind." As we said before reading, without this typhoon, China's Mongol warriors might have defeated the samurai.

As you can see, in some instances students generated options that were borne out in the text. In other cases, their predictions proved far afield of what actually occurred. Options guides make potentially dull text reading assignments considerably more interesting. The guides' success hinges in large measure on the small group discussions that precede and follow their use as a reading guide. Consider using options guides for selected topics in social studies as a student-centered alternative to traditional study guides.

A study which introduced students to the use of graphic organizers as an independent study strategy and combined their use with regular options guides, found that to read tenth grade world history students became adept at seeing relationships among disparate revolutions in England, France, and Russia (Bean et al., 1986). Indeed, they were able to make significantly better predictions about the stages of the Cuban revolution before reading about it than students who used traditional outlining to study their text and followed text reading with large group lecture and discussion.

You might consider using a fluid strategy, utilizing more teacher-directed study guides in the early part of a course and shifting to greater use of options guides, DRTA, and other student-directed strategies. A progression from careful guidance to increasing student responsibility helps students develop the independent reading strategies necessary for reading at advanced levels. You may want to begin with fairly detailed options guides, like the one on Japan, and slowly fade to skeletal options guides that place the responsibility on students to speculate about the impact of an event on sociocultural aspects of the economy, arts, agriculture, and so on. In our experience, your efforts to develop guide material will be richly rewarded in increased levels of student understanding and participation.

Analogical Guides

Another form of study guide has been developed for application in science classes. The *analogical guide* is aimed at getting students to study new science concepts they are attempting to learn by thinking about the underlying properties of more familiar concepts and comparing these to new, unfamiliar concepts (Bean, Searles, Singer, & Cowan, 1990; Bean, Singer, & Cowan, 1985).

We use analogies spontaneously in our everyday speech and thinking. For example, if we plan a field trip to a marine biology laboratory and the trip is successful, we may say the job went like clockwork. If our field trip plans failed, we may say they collapsed like a house of cards.

It is not unusual for scientists to use analogies to explain complex processes or theories. For example, scientists use the analogy of a giant pinwheel or disk to understand the nature of the Milky Way. Texts in biology sometimes feature analogies, but students often do not know how they can use these analogies to comprehend and recall concepts. The analogical guide is designed to make students aware of using analogies to understand concepts. In order to get a feel for just how useful analogies are, try the activity that follows.

These cell structure-function relationships comprise just a small part of a basic chapter on the cell. This material constitutes an important foundation for subsequent chapters that explore more complex aspects of the cell, such as cell division. Most biology texts contain a chart of cell parts and functions for students to study. Many students simply memorize this chart without really understanding how the different cell parts function. In your case, we gave you a small number of cell parts to match to their functions. How did you do? Our guess is that you successfully matched nucleus and cell membrane, but (unless your field is science) you flubbed the other four items. Here are the correct answers: 1-e; 2-c; 3-b; 4-a; 5-d; 6-f. Now, consider students who have access to an analogical study guide that a teacher introduces and explains. Do you think your comprehension of these six cell structure-function relations would have been better with such a guide?

Your last science class may have been quite some time ago, or you may be a science teacher. In any case, we would like you to try the following activity. See if you can correctly match the six cell structure parts on the left with their related functions on the right. Simply write the letter of the correct function on the line to the left of the cell part. Good luck.

Structure		Function	
1. _____ mitochondria		a.	controls heredity
2. _____ cell membrane		b.	storage
3. _____ vacuoles		c.	boundary
4. _____ nucleus		d.	intracellular transport
5. _____ endoplasmic reticulum		e.	cellular respiration
6. _____ ribosomes		f.	protein synthesis

Analogical Guide: Cell Structure and Function

Directions: You will be studying the parts of a cell and their functions. In some ways a cell resembles a factory, because, like a factory, a cell uses raw materials to manufacture a product. You will find that comparing the different parts of the cell to the parts of a factory will help you remember the functions of the various cell parts. For example, in the guide, the cell walls are compared to factory walls because both provide support and protection.

Structure	Function	Analogy (Like A)
cell wall	support and protection	factory walls
cell membrane	boundary, gatekeeper	security guards
cytoplasm	site of metabolism	the work area
chloroplasts	photosynthesis	snack bar
endoplasmic reticulum	intracellular transport	conveyor belts
golgi bodies	storage, secretion	packaging, storing, and
lysosomes	intracellular digestion	shipping
mitochondria	cellular respiration	clean-up crew
nucleus	controls heredity	energy generation plant
ribosomes	protein synthesis	boss's office and copy
vacuoles	storage	machine
		assembly line
		warehouses

The overall factory analogy provides a coherent structure for the whole guide. In a study of this guide's contribution to students' comprehension in high school biology, we found that students who were achieving low grades significantly outpaced peers in a control group when the guide was introduced as a means of studying the text (Bean et al., 1985). The control group simply used the cell structure-function chart provided in the text without any analogies. Constructing an analogical guide involves three important steps.

Step One. Analyze the reading task facing students by identifying those concepts you want them to acquire (e.g., a basic understanding of cell structure and function relationships).

Step Two. This is the most difficult and crucial step—creating appropriate analogies that will connect with students' diverse experiences. A good analogy is one that contains underlying properties similar to the target concept, but it is usually dissimilar at the surface level. For example, comparing the cell membrane to a security guard provides a familiar analogy sharing underlying properties of entry and exit control, even though there are no surface level similarities.

Step Three. You need to go over the analogical guide with students, explaining how they can use the analogies on the right side of the guide to comprehend and recall the function of a particular cell structure. Some students may wish to generate their own analogies, so you can gradually transfer responsibility for this process to students.

Whenever we see a glazed look on students' faces during a classroom explanation, we spontaneously search for an appropriate analogy to provide a vivid image of the concept we are introducing. Analogical guides make this process explicit for students by showing them how they can effectively use analogies to link new information with prior knowledge. We recommend that you use analogical guides when appropriate for complex topics in science. Although such guides take some time to create, they help alleviate the sink-or-swim experience many students have as they try to fathom science texts. Their feelings are much the same as you experienced trying to complete the cell structure function matching activity. Unguided reading of a complex text simply produces frustration and hostility rather than comprehension and a feeling of power over the material.

In the section that follows we explore the last stage of a content reading, listening, or viewing assignment, the postreading stage.

 ## Postreading Strategies

Despite the intuitive and proven value of review for long-term retention of content area concepts, this activity remains the most often neglected component of a lesson structure. In her year long investigation of comprehension instruction, Durkin (1978–79) found that important concepts were glossed-over far too rapidly in an effort to cover the book and get on to new material. Over a decade after that research, Armbruster and her colleagues (1991) confirmed that little has changed in the degree to which content teachers guide students' reading of difficult textbooks. In observations of over 387 minutes of instruction in social studies and science classrooms, these researchers found no explicit comprehension instruction. Sink or swim teaching prevailed.

The review stage of a lesson is typically viewed as an independent activity that students perform on their own time. While the phrase, Now it's time to review the concepts we explored last week, may engender a chorus of yawns, review activities do not have to be a devastating bore. It is true, however, when they consist of nothing more than a teacher-centered lecture recounting previously learned concepts, the outcome is likely to be counterproductive. In fact, classroom observations suggest that small group, collaborative discussions are rare, occupying less than 20 percent of classroom time (Wood, 1987). Oddly enough, when we as adults confront some thorny problem, we often collaborate with others in ad hoc groups or more formal committee structures to tackle and solve the problem. Overemphasizing independent review fails to provide experiences that will help students respond to real world challenges in a cooperative fashion.

In contrast to those who see review sessions as teacher-centered activities, we perceive the review process to be a natural outgrowth of the prereading and reading activities in a well-integrated lesson. Activities that acknowledge and, in some cases, refine students' prior knowledge of a topic also can be applied at the postreading stage. For example, the reaction guide you had been filling out at the close of each chapter in Part A is essentially a review activity. The graphic organizer and the study guide also lend themselves to the review process. Indeed, we regard review as more than a solitary pondering of text concepts. Review activities should involve active manipulation and collaborative discussion of information. By definition, *cooperative learning* involves "an equal partnership in which paired students study together with the mutual goal of mastering academic information" (Larson & Dansereau, 1986, p. 516). Indeed, Wood (1987) pointed out that studies of cooperative learning groups suggest that such teams contribute to significant gains in achievement, self esteem, and sociocultural understanding. Additionally, she listed a number of advantages in using such groups in a class:

1. Students are more motivated to learn when they are cooperating rather than competing individually with their peers.

2. Students display a more positive attitude toward both the class and the instructor when there are opportunities for this less teacher-centered form of learning.

3. Students in the role of the tutor and the tutee both benefit. They have to know the material in order to effectively teach it to another student.

4. Students' self esteem is enhanced by helping one another learn content material.

5. Students display more positive perceptions of the intentions of other students. This is especially crucial in multilingual, multicultural classrooms. By working together in coopera-

tive groups, students perceive their peers more positively than when they are isolated from each other. There is a decrease in prejudice and stereotyping.

6. There is a decrease in competitive goal structures. Students come to view other students' ideas as important to their individual learning.

7. Students become less dependent on the teacher as the only source of reliable information. They begin to take charge of problem solving in a cooperative fashion. (pp. 11–12)

We would expect that, given the compelling advantages of using small groups to review content material, teachers would place more emphasis on this mode of instruction. However, Conley's (1987) analysis of small group learning in content classrooms found that, understandably, many teachers are reluctant to break out of the more controlled teacher-centered role. Further, Alvermann, O'Brien, and Dillon (1990), who observed 24 content teachers from English, health, science, and other fields in order to determine the match between teachers' idealized comments about what constitutes a good discussion and what actually happens when these same teachers attempt to use discussion in their classrooms, found a marked disparity between teachers' idealized views of discussion touting active student participation and the lecture and recitation nature of their actual classroom discussions. Teachers worried about releasing classroom control and departing from the rapid fire pace of content coverage.

Using small groups entails a different style of classroom management that is, unquestionably, more of an art than orchestrating instruction from the front of the room and acting as an authority figure. Since we recommend using small groups to discuss material in the various guides introduced in this chapter, and particularly at the postreading review stage of a lesson, what are some of the features that seem to insure small groups work effectively?

Discussion Groups

General Guidelines. It is important to first consider the role you plan to play in guiding small group review. Alvermann, Dillon, & O'Brien (1987) described four possible teacher roles and commented on their characteristic limitations.

The first role they call "the instructor." The teacher retains the normal fountain of truth position and serves to clarify any confusion or difficulties that arise in the small groups. The disadvantage of adopting this role is that it may limit students' sense of their own responsibility for maintaining discussion and resolving problems.

A second possible role is that of "participant." The teacher becomes part of a small group discussion. Although this sounds attractive, you may inadvertently inhibit students from participating. After all, in your normal role you are perceived as the content expert.

A third, and more appropriate role, is that of a "consultant." In this way you are free to rove about the room, responding to request for help from various groups. It is important to restrain yourself from over-assisting a group. Rather, encourage students to exhaust all their efforts in resolving problems or clarifying information before you offer to step in.

A fourth, and most difficult role, is that of a "neutral observer" of small group discussion. In this case, you remain silent, offering neither opinion, clarification, or conflict resolution. Although this may be an ideal role to adopt, it requires a slow, methodical release of responsibility to students that may span many weeks. Indeed, Conley (1987) cautioned that it may take a full semester before students are comfortable and skilled at working in small groups.

An important and often overlooked facet of using small groups effectively is the furniture and layout of your room. If students are in desks arranged by rows, they can easily work in pairs, side-by-side. Or, if you have circular tables, these can be ideal for groups of four to five students. In general, as group size increases, the level of individual participation decreases (Alvermann et al., 1987).

Small groups should be composed of four to five student members of mixed-ability with a clear learning goal (Stevens, Madden, Slavin, & Farnish, 1987). This may range from a discussion of study guide questions or reaction guide statements to debating an issue. Stevens et al. (1987) recommended that students' learning be assessed individually, with the small group receiving recognition for the success of its members. This can be accomplished by adding up individual's scores to arrive at team scores for various assessments.

Conley (1987) also recommended developing clearly defined student roles within a group. One student may be chair for the week, guiding discussion of study guide questions. The group may need a recorder and a gatekeeper to maintain the flow of discussion. These roles can be exchanged periodically. In his analysis of small group learning in content classrooms, Conley found that low ability and high ability students both make important contributions to learning. When a small group is discussing a study guide, low ability students often function as excellent fact-finders, while high ability students may see connections from text-based ideas to more global issues. Both types of students offer opportunities for creative debate, and they learn effectively from each other.

There is general agreement that it is very important to compose groups that include mixed-ability students, so they can balance each others' strengths and weaknesses.

Although these general guidelines for your role in guiding small group learning and review are based on recent synthesis of research in the area of cooperative learning, you must decide how to best use small groups in your own classroom. The next section offers some specific guidelines for developing and managing small groups effectively.

Specific Guidelines. A good way to demonstrate clearly how you want a small group to function is to model this process. Using guide material as a focal point for the discussion, compose a small group at the front of the room and act in the role of a group chair to demonstrate the process for about 10 minutes. Conley (1987) recommended keeping early efforts fairly simple and focused. Remember that students are often unaccustomed to working in this cooperative fashion.

If a group is going off course, straying far afield of the task, how should you respond? Unfortunately, this is not a simple issue. Conley (1987) used the terms heavy and light group monitoring to characterize this dilemma. As we pointed out earlier, if you adopt the role of the authoritarian instructor and monitor too heavily, you may interfere with the development of independent student problem-solving. On the other hand, total chaos in your classroom is equally undesirable. Fortunately, there are some solutions to this problem.

In conjunction with a study of content area guide material, Vacca (1977) found that small study groups functioned productively when the teacher set the stage for the review. To prepare students, the teacher would first explain the goals and advantages of collaborating in the study process via interdependent groups. The key idea here hinges on the phrase, interdependent groups. That is, the success of the group in solving a problem is evaluated collectively, but it also depends on the contribution of the individual members. To achieve such interdependence, stress the following:

1. Explain the desired discussion behaviors that students should strive for (e.g., encouraging each other to respond; valuing each others' ideas; allowing an adequate amount of time for a group member to explain a point without dominating the discussion); and,

2. Explain the reward system by which you would rate group performance.

Reward systems utilized with discussion groups will vary according to the maturity and ability of the students involved. The reward system instituted by Vacca in his study is designed to foster an active small group review session. Each group receives one of four colored disks representing the teacher's estimate of the group's performance according to the desired discussion behaviors. Each disk is worth points comprising part of the students' grades (e.g., red = 0; yellow = 1; green = 2; blue = 3). The group members, in consultation with the teacher, arrive at a group score after each session. This overall group score is also assigned to each member in the group. The scores can be tallied on a chart for the class if students are to be randomly reassigned to groups periodically. This step is probably unnecessary, since the key aspect of this strategy is the tangible evidence of success small groups have with the colored disks during the discussion.

Reaction Guides

A *reaction guide* provides a good prelude to a more intensive review when it serves as a focal point for small group discussion. When you complete a text selection and then reassess your prereading responses to an anticipation guide, you are using a reaction guide to examine your beliefs about a topic. More than likely you alter at least some of your prereading beliefs and can defend this change by referencing explicit statements in the text.

A reaction guide is easy to construct since it is essentially another form of the anticipation guide, and the text analysis steps are the same for both comprehension strategies. You can simply add a second column to an anticipation guide for a postreading reaction to the same statements. While the mechanics of the guide are simple, they should not be used as individual worksheets to be completed in silence. Rather, two or three of the most important statements should be considered and discussed by small groups. For example, we might have used the following statement for Chapter 3:

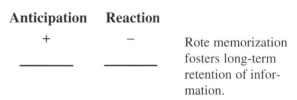

Anticipation   Reaction

| + | − | Rote memorization fosters long-term retention of information. |

Notice that although many students might have agreed (+) with this statement at the prereading stage, upon considering the psychological importance of deep processing and organization for retention, they would tend to disagree (−) at the postreading stage. More importantly, they would be able to defend this shift by referring to relevant portions of the text that lend support to the respective roles of deep processing and hierarchical organization in the memorial process.

Duffelmeyer and Baum (1992) have suggested an adaptation of the Reaction Guide which promotes students' critical reading and thinking skills as well as requires them to actively confront their potential misconceptions. This adaptation is modeled for you with the Anticipation and Reaction Guides used in Part A of this text. In the beginning of each chapter of Part A we asked you to agree or disagree with each guide statement and then to be ready to explain your choices. At the end of each chapter of Part A we asked you to reconsider your responses to the guide statements. If the information you found in the chapter supported your original choice, we asked you to check the Confirmed column and then write the supporting evidence from the text in your own words in the column marked Why my choice is confirmed. If the information did not support your original choice, you were asked to check the Disconfirmed column and then write what the text says in your own words in the column marked Why my choice is not confirmed. The addition of the writing task to the Reaction Guide facilitates additional interaction with the text as students are asked to justify their claims of agreement or confront their misconceptions.

Phony Document Strategy

This critical reading strategy was initially developed for history classes (Vanderhoof, Miller, Clegg, & Patterson, 1992), but we have found it to be applicable in other fields such as English and science. The *phony document strategy* is based on a teacher-authored letter that purports to be historical and authentic, commenting on a key aspect of a novel, historical event, or scientific experiment. While it reads as a perfectly plausible account, it is usually embedded with errors that students must ferret out through critical reading. Indeed, the central purpose of this strategy is to engage students in a close reading of the primary source material referred to in the phony document you have written. At the outset, you let them believe in the possible authenticity of this document. However, they must, in the end, refute its authenticity and point out the untruths and flaws embedded in it. The following steps and example best illustrate our use of the phony document strategy.

Step One. Create a phony, but plausibly written document such as a letter, critique, news article, and so on. Letters and book excerpts or introductions seem to work best.

Step Two. Ask students to read and judge the accuracy of the document and its value as something the school or district might want to purchase for wide distribution to students. They must engage in a close reading, cross-checking information (e.g., dates, assertions, places, and so on) with other sources.

Step Three. Conduct small group and whole class discussions on the document's accuracy and value.

The following phony letter from a literary scholar illustrates the use of this strategy in an American literature class with high school juniors. Students finished reading Arthur Miller's famous play *The Crucible* (1976). This and other activities in the class prepared the students to write from the perspective of a particular character in the play and extend their thinking about key episodes and events. Students read and critiqued the following phony document:

Student Task for P. J. Pennerd's *The Crucible Revisited*

P. J. Pennerd is the Senior Scholar in Humanities at Boston University and the Danforth Foundation Endowed Chair in Literary Criticism. He is an internationally known expert on Arthur Miller's *The Crucible*. His work is widely quoted by other literary scholars. Our nearby university library recently purchased the complete collection of Professor Pennerd's works for student use and analysis. Copies are currently worth thousands of dollars, and our school district and English Department are interested in purchasing this collection for our English curriculum. Your opinion is important in deciding the value of these documents. Please read and comment on this introductory material.

Introduction

The Salem, Massachusetts, witch trials of 1700 resulted in the execution of 50 Salem witches and far surpassed the number of accused witches put to death in Europe during this period. The Salem girls included Abigail Willams, Ann Putnam, Jr., Mary Warren, and others.

Arthur Miller crafted his popular play around these events by creating characters who best exemplify the play's title, *The Crucible*, defined as a severe test or hard trial, or a container for melting and calcinating ores.

The separation of church and state in Salem made Judge Danforth an objective judge for the trials. Innocent until proven guilty were his watchwords and code of conduct. The community, too, abided by this code of conduct. This is best illustrated by Abigail's willingness to cooperate in the trial's proceedings.

Judge Danforth was not worried about being hemmed in by the law. He was most concerned with seeking justice for the community.

In the pages that follow, I will show how Judge Danforth served as the most dynamic and central character of the play, riveting our attention and earning our compassion and sensitivity.

P. J. Pennerd
January 1983

There are a number of flaws in this document and even if you have not read *The Crucible* recently, your knowledge of history will reveal some of the erroneous assertions made by the phony P. J. Pennerd!

For example, at the most basic level, the date of events is wrong. The Salem witch trials occurred in 1692, and 20 accused witches were put to death, not 50. The second paragraph is okay, but in paragraph three, the presumption of innocence until proven guilty is contrary to the beliefs of this Puritan theocracy. There was no separation of church and state in legal decisions of the time. In paragraph four, Judge Danforth was so blinded by his allegiance to the law that he was unable to discern the truth. Unlike claims in the final paragraph, he is unyielding and definitely not dynamic in the way Proctor and Elizabeth are portrayed by Arthur Miller in the play.

Thus, students had to engage in a close reading of the play and challenge any erroneous information in this lofty document. They ultimately recommended not purchasing this material for wide student use.

As you try out the phony document strategy, be careful to make it look plausible. Of course you can only use this strategy occasionally as students will suspect something is up in subsequent, authoritative documents you circulate in class.

Polar Opposites

When students have a concrete series of Reaction Guide statements to support or refute, they are more likely to engage in group discussion. *Polar Opposites* is a strategy that also provides a concrete basis for postreading discussion (Bean & Bishop, 1992).

A Polar Opposites guide consists of descriptive adjectives such as happy versus sad that are supported or challenged by events in the text. Three steps are involved in developing a Polar Opposites guide and using it with students.

Step One. Develop four or five polar opposite statements and their accompanying adjectives. Place five blanks between the adjectives. For example:

Cairo's third city is . . .

new ____ ____ ____ ____ ____ old

Step Two. After students have read a selection or listened to a film, have them place a check mark (✔) closest to the adjective that they feel best describes the events or character. They can also score events and characters using a five-point scale.

Step Three. Have students defend their rating in small group discussion or a writing activity by referring to specific examples or events in the selection.

The following example from world geography (Kleeman, 1983) should help you develop your own Polar Opposites guide. The passage is from the text, *New Exploring a Changing World* (Schwartz & O'Connor, 1975, pp. 364–365).

On the roofs of Cairo there is a third city—a town of modern roof dwellers. Tens of thousands of people live on Cairo's rooftops. In the days when you could fly a small plane over Cairo, you could clearly see its two levels of life. One is on the ground and one is in the air. . . . I have seen on a roof opposite the Continental Hotel, someone cooking under a bamboo shelter, village women washing clothes, naked children, a goat or two, and a mangy dog. These rooftop slums are mostly servants' quarters but in the old city, they are the result of overcrowding.

Cairo's third city is . . .

new	____	____	____	____	____ old
spacious	____	____	____	____	____ crowded
healthful	____	____	____	____	____ unsanitary
safe	____	____	____	____	____ hazardous
rich	____	____	____	____	____ poor
friendly	____	____	____	____	____ hostile
	5	4	3	2	1

In this particular guide, Cairo can be viewed either positively, with a rating of 30 (i.e., 5 points × 6 adjectives), negatively with a rating of 6 (i.e., 1 point per item), or somewhere between these polar opposites. Indeed, some of the adjectives entail careful, critical reading to infer a response. For example, the last pair of adjectives, friendly versus hostile, usually engenders heated discussion. If you are a member of Cairo's rooftop culture, then it is undoubtedly friendly, or at least somewhat friendly. However, for the outsider unaccustomed to this overcrowded lifestyle, Cairo's rooftops may well be hostile. Thus, students can critically evaluate the author's perspective. If it seems to be overly ethnocentric, outside sources may be considered to confirm or deny information in the text. In this way, Polar Opposites can be used to guide students into independent projects involving library and database research.

Polar Opposites provides even the most reticent students with a basis for participating in discussion and writing activities. In order to defend or refute a particular rating, students must return to the text for support. Thus, it encourages critical reading in much the same way as the Reaction Guide.

Graphic Organizers

Although the graphic organizer was suggested as a prereading vocabulary strategy, it is an equally good review guide. Graphic organizers are easy to construct. Teachers find them to be useful across a broad range of content areas (Bean, 1997). In the early stages of a unit, items from the graphic organizer developed by the teacher can be written on notecards. Students working in small groups can attempt to reconstruct the author's conceptual organization or pattern by arranging the notecards in a logical diagram. This review activity can be conducted as a game, if desired, with points awarded for reconstructing successive portions of the unit organizer.

But students need not merely reconstruct information exactly as the teacher's schema portrayed it. Instead they can use the top-level skeletal structure of the teacher's organizer and add on information they have acquired in text reading. Barron (1979) emphasized that such student-constructed post-reading organizers seem to contribute more to comprehension than a teacher-devised organizer. The following activity illustrates the use of a skeletal graphic organizer as a review guide.

ACTIVITY

Directions: Before we go on, think about the comprehension strategies you have acquired so far in Chapter 10 for each of the three stages of an integrated lesson (i.e., prereading, reading, postreading). In the organizer that follows, one strategy has been listed in each stage. Without looking back at the chapter, see if you can supply at least two additional strategies per stage.

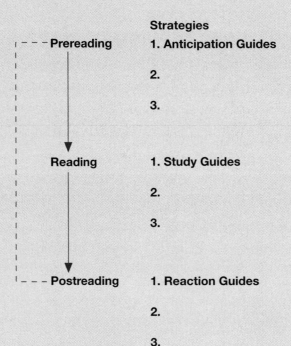

Strategies

- - - **Prereading**   1. Anticipation Guides

                         2.

                         3.

Reading   1. Study Guides

                         2.

                         3.

- - - **Postreading**   1. Reaction Guides

                         2.

                         3.

Contemporary content-based ESL programs usually integrate the dual goals of having sudents work on their second language while simultaneously learning content in history, science, mathematics, and English (Short, 1994). Without careful teacher guidance using comprehension strategies, secondary students asked to both learn a new language and to comprehend difficult content in that language will soon flounder. In a large scale project aimed at testing the value of combining American history content and second language acquisition, Short found that visual strategies like the graphic organizer, flow charts, and Venn diagrams were particularly helpful to second language learners. In addition, modeling proved to be essential for students to make the best use of these strategies.

Multiple Text Inquiry Discussion

The use of single texts in many content classrooms is giving way to the use of multiple texts. In addition, definitions of text are being revised to include a broad range of material. Texts can be a book, chapter, story, novel, poem, essay, biography, internet printout, and so on. But texts can also encompass videos, music, photos, a dramatic play, pantomime, and a dizzying array of other ways to communicate (Hartman & Allison, 1996). If students are going to become skilled at managing the incredible diversity of information sources at our fingertips today, they need opportunities to explore this process in the content areas. A multiple text inquiry discussion is designed to do just that, that is, inquiry-based discussions become richer when students read and attempt to synthesize a diverse collection of material on a topic.

Hartman and Allison (1996) offer the following guidelines for creating an inquiry-based classroom: (a) assemble multiple texts on a topic (ranging from 5 to 20 sources); (b) develop questions that focus discussion on making connections across multiple sources; (c) expect the discussion to extend across many days and, possibly, weeks; and (d) have students record exploratory ideas that emerge in their discussions. Topics should be broad and provocative enough to develop conceptual knowledge that is applicable to other problem-solving lessons students are likely to encounter (Hartman & Allison, 1996).

For example, students in a junior level advanced placement American literature class might explore societal mores and gender roles through reading and discussion of Arthur Miller's play *The Crucible* (1976), the film based on the play, a subsequent reading of *The Scarlet Letter* (Hawthorne, 1986) and its related video, and Amy Tan's (1991) *The Kitchen God's Wife*. Student discussions should focus on comparing and contrasting elements in the drama, novels, and videos. Their goal would be to build rich conceptual, historical, and literary understanding of what it meant to be a woman and a citizen within the social contexts of these works. Many of the strategies introduced in this chapter can be used to take notes from multiple texts (e.g., graphic organizers), to link ideas that are similar or different across texts (e.g., Venn diagrams), and to extend students' thinking and discussion (e.g., higher level questioning).

Topics in science on ecological issues lend themselves to the selection of multiple texts, interviews with experts, internet searches and conversations with other students in far-away communities. For example, the topic of water quality and population growth is one that permeates news articles throughout the country. Working with the school librarian, local community sources, internet searches, and so on, you and your students can assemble a collection of sources for multiple text inquiry discussions.

In order to guide students' small group discussion of multiple texts, you need adequate space to lay out all the materials. Large round tables lend themselves to this process far better than individual desks, but desks pulled together in a circle can suffice. Hartman and Allison recommend sequencing discussion probe questions to move from those that connect information within a single text to questions that connect information across two or more texts. Finally, they suggest prompt questions that connect ideas outside the text to information in the text by tapping students' background knowledge. For example, a single text question probe for an initial discussion of *The Crucible* would be: How were female servants like Abigail Williams treated by their employers in 1692? A question probe designed to integrate discussion of multiple texts would be: How are Proctor's, Hester's, and Winnie Louie's situations alike or different in *The Crucible, The Scarlet Letter,* and *The Kitchen God's Wife?* Finally, a question designed to connect ideas from outside the texts: How have women's roles changed since the times depicted in these three novels?

Butcher paper or some means of small group recording of discussion ideas will be crucial to keep a continuous record of conceptual growth (Hartman & Allison, 1996). Journals and learning logs can be used if space is a problem, or you find yourself teaching in classrooms other than your own. Culminating projects ranging from papers, plays, musical compositions, art and so on should be a natural outgrowth of days or, in some cases, weeks devoted to exploring a multiple text topic. Evaluation of students' projects can be accomplished through a 4-point rubric focusing on the quality of their work. For example, a 4-point project would display unusual creativity, care in presentation, and evidence of integration of ideas across various texts. In contrast, a 1-point project would appear to be thrown together at the last minute with little evidence of connections across texts read and discussed in small groups. Hartman and Allison (1996) provide examples of other topic areas for multiple text inquiry discussion that you will find helpful.

As students become accustomed to your use of a variety of strategies in prereading, reading, or postreading, you may find that a blend of two strategies makes sense. For example, you might introduce the topic of irrational and rational numbers in a math class with a few anticipation guide statements and accompany the reading and problem solving part of the lesson with a study guide that moves students through successively more involved problems. Indeed, vocabulary strategies from Chapter 8 can be combined with the comprehension strategies in Chapter 9 and this chapter or those in Chapter 11 on writing in the content areas. In short, don't be afraid to experiment with the strategies offered in this and other chapters. Modify them to fit your own teaching style and student needs. Field-testing the strategies will, more than likely, improve them. Certainly, you are in the best position to evaluate the success of these strategies in the classroom.

SUMMARY

In this chapter a number of specific teaching strategies were introduced and illustrated based on a view of guiding students' understanding of content material at the prereading, reading, and postreading stages of integrated lesson planning. At the prereading stage Anticipation Guides, Text Previews, ReQuest, and the Directed Reading-Thinking Activity were discussed. Study Guides, Options Guides, and Analogical Guides were introduced as valuable adjuncts to the core text during the reading stage of an instructional lesson. Finally, comprehension strategies for postreading included Discussion Groups, Reaction Guides, the Phony Document Strategy, Polar Opposites, Graphic Organizers, and Multiple Text Inquiry Discussion. It was suggested that these strategies might be used in combination with one another or with various strategies from other chapters in planning for a more holistic view of the comprehension process.

Now go back to the comprehension vignette at the beginning of this chapter. React again to the lesson as you did before. Compare your responses with those you made before you read the chapter.

MINI PROJECT

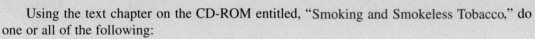

Using the text chapter on the CD-ROM entitled, "Smoking and Smokeless Tobacco," do one or all of the following:

1. Pick one of the prereading strategies advanced in this chapter. Develop this strategy and try it out with a small group of students or your peers. Evaluate the strategy in terms of its value as a means of preparing students for a content assignment.

2. Develop a study guide, option guide, or analogical guide on smoking. Try out your guide with a small group of students or your peers. Use the follow-up discussion phase recommended in this chapter for guide material. Evaluate your guide as an independent learning aid.

3. Develop and try out one of the postreading strategies described in this chapter. Use the strategy with a small group of students or your peers. Evaluate its effectiveness in reinforcing concepts about smoking.

4. Develop an integrated mini-unit on smoking containing one strategy from each of the three stages of instruction described in this chapter. This mini-project is a synthesis of projects one through three.

GROUP PROJECTS

- Select one prereading strategy described in the text and discuss why, how, and when you would use it with students.

- Discuss how graphic organizers can be used as an effective comprehension strategy.

- Identify the type of study guide that you believe will work most efficiently for your content area. Justify your selection by contrasting it with another type of study guide.

WRITING

SETTING

Alpha Polonium's high school physics class. Students have been reading in their physics text about various forms of energy including gravitational force and radiant energy. Toward the end of this class, Ms. Polonium assigns a major research paper on alternative energy due in two weeks.

THE LESSON

Ms. Polonium tells students they are to write a research paper on alternative energy sources such as solar energy or hydroelectric power. She mentions that the paper should be no more than 5 pages long with at least 3 sources besides the textbook they use in class. The paper is due in two weeks, she says.

Students look distraught. Ms. Polonium tries to quell their anxiety in a brief question and answer session just before the bell rings.

T: "Are there any questions?"

S: "Ms. Polonium, we only just started on the unit on alternative energy and the book is hard. How do we find the other three sources?"

T: "You could check the library for books, magazines and other material that discusses solar cars, hydro-electric dams, windmills, and so on."

S: "But how will we know if our paper is what you want? How will we know if we are reading things that are good descriptions of alternative energy? Personally, I feel lost."

The bell rings and students enter the hallway, still conversing about the alternative energy writing assignment and expressing their anxieties about writing in science.

A week and a half later, we look in on one of the students, Kelvin Newton, at home as he struggles with the assigned paper. He's writing about hydroelectric power, trying to organize the paper around advantages and disadvantages of this gravitational energy source. Kelvin completes a first draft and decides it's good enough since only Ms. Polonium will be reading it and she already knows about hydro power. He flips on the television and relaxes, secure in the knowledge that his paper can be put into a nice folder tomorrow night and turned in on time.

The weekend after the papers were due, we look in on Ms. Polonium, spending her Sunday evening bent over students' alternative energy papers with a red pen, correcting spelling and grammatical errors amidst marginal comments on their many misconceptions about alternative energy. Where did they get these ideas, she wonders?

That following Monday, students got their papers back, riddled with marks and Ms. Polonium's remarks about paper content. Students console themselves with the knowledge that writing in this class counts for only a fraction of their grade. It's not like English class.

▶ Keeping in mind that this lesson focuses on writing about alternative energy in a physics class, jot down your thoughts on the following questions:

1. What are the good points about the lesson?

2. What are the weak points about the lesson?

3. What, if anything, would you change about the lesson?

RATIONALE

Writing is a powerful way of learning and questioning across content areas. Once the sole province of English classrooms, writing is now seen as an important bridge between students' prior knowledge and ideas expressed in science, social studies, mathematics, and other content area texts. You need to be well informed about the writing process and ways to ensure students can use writing effectively in a variety of subjects. This chapter introduces you to contemporary thinking about the writing process and shows you how to use writing successfully to help students learn and reflect on concepts in your classroom.

LEARNING OBJECTIVES

■ Understand the distinction between composing and transcribing.

■ Be familiar with various teaching strategies that help students use writing to learn and writing to inform.

■ Be able to use various approaches to evaluate student's writing.

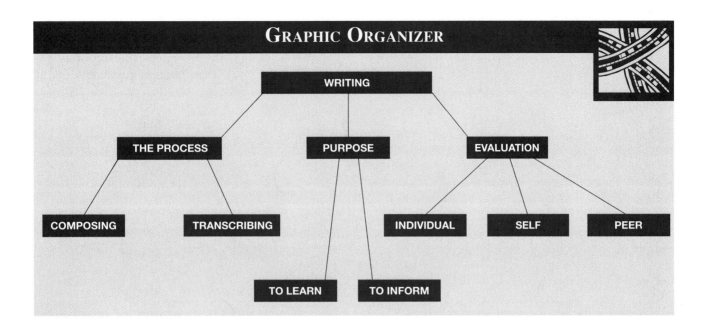

GRAPHIC ORGANIZER

WRITING

- THE PROCESS
  - COMPOSING
  - TRANSCRIBING
- PURPOSE
  - TO LEARN
  - TO INFORM
- EVALUATION
  - INDIVIDUAL
  - SELF
  - PEER

The Writing Process

Real writing, the forms of writing most of us use in our daily lives, consists of writing to schedule, rank, plan, map, inquire, record, recall, organize, evaluate, and report. We use writing to share our ideas with others. We use writing as a means of reflection. Research on the reading-writing relationship demonstrates that writing engages readers in critical reflection on issues that arise in content classes (Tierney & Shanahan, 1991).

Calkins (1994, p. 17) has this to say about writing: "Teaching writing is a matter of faith. We demonstrate that faith when we listen well, when we refer to our students as writers, when we expect them to love writing and to pour heart and soul into it."

Writing is a craft, and like any craft, our writing progresses, sometimes haltingly and in small increments, through many stages. We may let ideas incubate for a time, simply tossing scraps of hastily written notes in a folder, collecting articles, and throwing them in the pile. Eventually, we are ready to organize this disorganized collection into categories having a tentative structure. The structure may be a narrative or one of the expository patterns introduced earlier in the text. Writing a draft, revising as we go, and sharing our draft with others eventually lead to a finished piece of writing we can feel good about. Students need to see some of their writing evolve in this fashion. Other writing may be more exploratory, much like a diary that is not intended for public reading but may contribute to learning in your classroom. Thus, some writing that you engage students in will be designated to help inform others about a topic; other writing activities will assist their learning. There should be room for both forms of writing in content classrooms.

Before exploring specific strategies that help students use writing to learn and to inform, we want to define and consider two important aspects of the writing process, composing and transcribing.

Composing and Transcribing

Composing is the ongoing process of generating and shaping ideas before writing and as the actual writing unfolds. Composing involves thinking about ideas, weighing them, and putting them in some kind of order. Brainstorming, creating, clustering, and categorizing are some of the processes students use in composing. Out of these prereading musings come new ways of looking at topics in content classrooms. Stafford (1986, p. 25) said, "A writer is not so much someone who has something to say as he is someone who has found a process that will bring about new things he would not have thought of if he had not started to say them."

As a student gets started composing at a word processor or simply begins writing on a piece of paper, transcribing facilitates or inhibits the development of a finished product. *Transcribing* is a term that describes the mechanics of writing, including spelling, punctuation, capitalization, handwriting, formatting, and neatness. During the early draft stages of writing, when composing dominates a student's thoughts, placing too much emphasis on the conventions of transcribing may interfere with the development of ideas. Certainly when students are engaged in reflective journal writing, which they do primarily for their own purposes, transcribing should be less of a concern than when they are preparing a final draft of a paper for a larger audience. As we look at the practice of journal writing in content classrooms, remember that composing issues are at the forefront. Personal journal writing is one of the best ways for students to explore ideas without feeling pressed to produce perfect spelling and grammar. In addition, it is a powerful way for you to carry on a dialogue about the class with individual students. Journal writing is the first writing to learn strategy we will consider.

 ## Writing to Learn

In many content classrooms, students feel that the authority for their learning resides exclusively with the teacher. Yet in classes where students write often, as much as four and five times a week, they feel like they are in the driver's seat (Hansen, 1987). Writing becomes a powerful vehicle for guiding their learning—a filter through which they can sift and examine concepts and see how these sometimes obscure notions may connect with their lives. Writing-to-learn activities initiate students to various methods for using writing to explore and integrate ideas arising from a content area.

Journal Writing

Observational studies of classrooms reveal far too little sustained writing of a personal nature (Fulwiler, 1986). Yet in our day-to-day world, we see teachers, business people, scientists, and artists frequently jotting down random ideas or notes in a journal for their own purposes. When ideas wing briefly into short-term memory, a journal is an ideal place to pin them down for later consideration. In social studies, a student's journal may consider how the Bill of Rights might relate to students' rights in a high school environment. In science, a journal entry might wonder about gene splicing and its impact on future generations. In art, a journal comment may state how a student interprets a surrealistic painting. Or, a journal entry may have no higher purpose than to state, "I stayed up late last night. Today I'm having a lot of trouble concentrating on your lecture about the Roman Empire." In this way, *journal writing* can communicate a student's feelings and emotions, and provide you with some sense of how your lessons are progressing for individual students on various days. In our crowded classrooms, journals can serve the important need to communicate attitudes and interests beyond the typical rapid fire charge through endless facts and concepts (Martin, 1992).

As you begin to use journal writing in your own subject area, consider the following principles (Bean, 1994):

1. Journal writing should become a regular part of your teaching. Students need to write in their journals on a daily basis.

During the first five minutes of class, journals can be an ideal way to enter a topic or recap a previous

day's lesson. For example, in a social studies classroom, on the first day of a unit students worked through an anticipation-reaction guide activity on the Bill of Rights. One of the statements read: Students should have the right to select the classes they take. At the beginning of the next day's class, the teacher gives students an opportunity to comment further in their journals on this idea. Jeff writes:

> *I think it's a good idea. But only if we pick our class schedule every other week. That way, at least some of the time we have to take classes that are good for us, even though we may not like them. Like math. Math would be okay every other week. But I know this isn't going to happen. We have to do whatever the government tells us to do. It's depressing.*

Jeff was undoubtedly reluctant to express these opinions in the large class discussion the previous day. But in the privacy of his journal, he is free to explore divergent proposals. Journals can be used to explore content area concepts from a personal perspective, so it is important for students to have opportunities to pick what they want to write about. Therefore, you may want to alternate days devoted to some commentary on previous or upcoming lessons with days devoted to reflections on general topics students choose individually. The next principle suggests how you can demonstrate the range of topics students may wish to explore in their journals.

2. You should model journal writing by keeping your own journal and sharing entries aloud with students.

Just as sustained silent reading works best when you join in by reading a novel of your choice, journal writing takes on real importance in students' eyes when you also participate. For example, your entries may range from commentaries on how a unit is progressing to entries that chronicle your efforts to reduce your 10 kilometer running time.

3. You should look at students' journals and respond to their thoughts.

We recognize that it is unrealistic to expect a teacher to collect endless stacks of journals every day and respond to them. Rather, collect journals randomly so that you see every student's journal a few times in the course of a semester. In order to keep some parts of the journal completely private, you may have students use a looseleaf notebook with dividers labeled public and private (Fulwiler, 1986). In this way you can at least respond to those sections marked public while not inhibiting opportunities for private comment. How much time should students spend each day writing in their journals?

4. Allot five to ten minutes for journal writing.

These four principles should not imply that journals be used in a rigid, formulaic fashion that may become stultifying over time. Rather, we recommend that you make them a flexible and creative regular part of your teaching repertoire. You can even use journals as a way to interrupt a lecture, lab, or activity in order to let students reflect on what they understand at that intermediate phase of a lesson. Using journals will do much to foster students' enthusiasm and personal investment in the content you are trying to teach.

Dialogue journals, where you maintain an ongoing written dialogue with your students, provide a unique window on their concept understanding, confusion, concerns, and complaints (Bean & Zulich, 1989). In terms of concept understanding, this is a private place where students can express confusion without fear of embarrassment. The dialogue journal offers you a second chance, a chance to reteach information that may not have been understood during the first attempt. In addition, dialogue journals open the door to fluency for second language learners (Holmes & Moulton, 1997). Students find that dialogue journals are non-threatening because of their uncorrected, ungraded format. Since they are written in a conversational style, dialogue journals reduce the stress of clinging to a dictionary and worrying constantly about translating to the native language. Rather, students can experiment as they would in a free writing activity. Finally, dialogue journals offer students a sense that they do have a voice in how the class progresses. Thus, you might alter your teaching based on this written feedback from students (Shuy, 1988).

Other forms of journal writing allow students to respond to their reading in creative ways. For example, students can write a letter to the author posing questions about a novel or text (Ollmann, 1996). Students can take the part of a character in a novel and write a journal entry based on their reactions to a powerful episode. Journal entries can be made on e-mail and sent to students in a far off classroom for their dialogue responses. The possibilities are endless and, increasingly, involve electronic media (Jody & Saccardi, 1996).

ACTIVITY

Think about the most challenging group of students you have taught. Write a journal entry describing your feelings now as you think back on the impact your teaching may or may not have had on these students. Exchange your entry with a colleague in class. Discuss the teaching experience you wrote about and your views on journal writing in a content classroom.

Possible Sentences

Possible Sentences is another writing-to-learn strategy that helps students use technical vocabulary and related concepts in your content area. This strategy places students in an active role in which they predict an author's use of language in a text and evaluate their written predictions against the actual text passage (Moore & Moore, 1992). Possible Sentences engages students in higher order reasoning to identify examples in the text that support their prereading sentences or to revise their sentences after considering the text version. This exercise gives students a vested interest in reading the text to check their prereading possible sentence predictions. A Possible Sentences lesson has four steps.

Step One. List on the board or overhead key terms from a chapter or reading selection. The words should be well defined by the context and pronounced several times for the students. For example:

Target Words

pigment
albinism
enzymes
melanin
suntan
albino

Passage

Albinism*

The absence of pigmentation in the skin, hair, and eyes in albinos is the result of a deficiency in the manufacture of pigment (melanin) by the body. Albinism is a metabolic disorder resulting from the absence or inactivity of a specific enzyme. Enzymes are complex compounds which act as catalytic agents or mediators of chemical changes in living forms. This enzyme is involved in the formation of melanin. The condition is not restricted to humans and it has been found in many animals: snakes, salamanders, gorillas, rats, mice, Easter bunnies, and even ravens, to name a few.

Human albinos are characterized by white translucent skin and white hair. Because of the lack of pigment in the iris, the eyes are red due to blood vessels. There is no way to overcome albinism. The necessary information to produce the right enzyme has not been inherited and will never be acquired. The specific enzyme or the melanin pigment would have to be injected continuously into each and every pigment cell of the skin, scalp, and eyes in order to produce a normally pigmented individual.

Albinos need continuous protection from sunlight since they burn very easily. Their skin cannot develop a suntan since tans are nothing more than the accumulation of melanin as a response to an increase in the ultraviolet radiation of sunlight. They are also more susceptible to skin diseases and tend to have poor vision. They are otherwise perfectly normal people.

*Brum, G. D., Castro, P., & Quinn, R. D. *Biology and Man.* Dubuque, IA: Kendall/Hunt, 1978, p. 57.

Step Two. Individual students select any two of the words and dictate or *write a sentence* using them. The teacher writes the sentences on the board exactly as dictated, whether the information in them is accurate or not. For instance:

Possible Sentences

    a.   Suntans come from having a lot of enzymes in your skin.

    b.   A albino is a person who has no melanin.

    c.   An albino can never get a suntan.

    d.   Albinism is the missing of pigment in the skin.

Step Three. After an arbitrary number of sentences have been generated, the students search through the passage to *verify the sentences* on the board. A game twist can be added to this by having teams that are supposed to generate as many sentences as possible with unique pairs of the words listed. In this example there are 15 different possible pairs of words that can be used. Once each team generates its sentences, the opposing teams challenge (with books closed, of course) the accuracy of each set of individual sentences. Points can be given for each accurate sentence. Penalty points can be deducted for inaccurate challenges.

Step Four. The possible sentences are corrected on the board and students are given an opportunity to enter them into their notebooks. For instance:

Revised Possible Sentences

    a.   Suntans come from having a lot of melanin in your skin.

    b.   An albino is a person who has no melanin.

    c.   An albino can never get a suntan.

    d.   Albinism is the absence of pigment in the skin.

Possible Sentences will tease out any misconceptions students have about a topic. Writing sentences is generally a nonthreatening activity, even for second language learners. We have found that students enjoy Possible Sentences. They enthusiastically pursue text reading to verify their predictions. Additionally, research by Stahl and Kapinus (1991) verified the effectiveness of the strategy.

Probable Passages

Probable Passages (Wood, 1984), a writing strategy that is similar to Possible Sentences, involves larger, paragraph length sections of a text. Although Probable Passages was developed for use with predictable story patterns, it works equally well with many of the expository text patterns introduced earlier in the text. Probable Passages is especially appropriate for those text patterns that branch into cause-effect, compare-contrast, and problem-solving structures. As in the Possible Sentences strategy, Probable Passages capitalizes on prediction and verification of student-authored text passages that are compared with the original text.

The following steps should be followed in developing a Probable Passages lesson.

Step One. Carefully analyze the text selection for the most significant concepts and identify vocabulary that may need special emphasis. If the text has a clear pattern of organization (e.g., problem-solution), categorize the vocabulary under these text structure labels. Present the words you have identified on the board or overhead projector. For example, the Probable Passages lesson that follows accompanies a problem-solution reading selection from a health class on hypothermia.

Problem	Solution
hypothermia	moving muscles
body temperature	protection
shivering	heater
numbness	eating
hallucinations	stamina

Step Two. Tell students about the text structure categories that you have used to label the key words. If students are not already familiar with the text structure of the passage, you can introduce this concept through a cartoon or other concrete visual.

Step Three. Students receive a copy of an incomplete text selection. Only the problem portion of the selection is provided with blanks for those words listed under this category (i.e., hypothermia, body temperature, shivering). The second part of the text frame should give students an opening sentence that foreshadows the second half of the text passage, in this case, the solution part. The following incomplete text frame demonstrates this step.

Hypothermia

_____ is a drop in the normal _____ _____ below 98.6 degrees. Anyone exposed to very cold temperatures for too long can experience this condition. Your body burns up its food resources, resulting in a loss of heat. It is a particularly dangerous problem for surfers and skiers during the winter months.

Although the symptoms of hypothermia include _____ and _____ of the extremities, these symptoms may not be heeded because people lapse into _____ . High up on a mountain or far out in the surf, hypothermia can lead to a loss of strength and coordination, endangering the life of a skier or surfer.

Hypothermia can be avoided through a common-sense approach to sports like surfing in cold water and skiing. *(Now use the words from the "problem" side of the list to write the rest of this probable passage the way you think an author might.)*

Step Four. Before students attempt to write their probable passage by filling in the words from the problem column in the passage, and then writing the solution section, go over each word, discussing definitions as needed. Then *ask students to construct a probable passage.* Here is one a student wrote.

Hypothermia

(Hypothermia) is a drop in the normal *(body temperature)* below 98.6 degrees. Anyone exposed to very cold temperatures for too long can experience this condition. Your body burns up its food resources, resulting in a loss of heat. It is a particularly dangerous problem for surfers and skiers during the winter months.

Although the symptoms of hypothermia include *(shivering)* and *(numbness)* of the extremities, these symptoms may not be heeded because people lapse into *(hallucinations)*. High up on a mountain or far out in the surf, hypothermia can lead to a loss of strength and coordination, endangering the life of a skier or surfer.

Hypothermia can be avoided through a common sense approach to sports like surfing in cold water and skiing. *The clothes you wear surfing and skiing should give protection from the elements. If you surf, wear a wetsuit. If you ski, wear a parka and ski pants. Moving your muscles by flexing your arms and legs on the chair lift keeps up your stamina. If these steps don't work out and you do get hypothermia, warm up in the lodge next to a heater or by a fire at the beach. Eating and drinking warm foods will help. Better yet, stay inside and be a couch potato when it's cold outside!*

Step Five. Have students read the original selection so they can evaluate how close their probable passage came to the original passage. Notice that this student's composition included all of the words from the solution side of the list. Moreover, the passage addresses the reader directly, referring to "you." The original passage contained a few more details but it is actually not as vibrant as this student's creation. After they have had a chance to compare their passage with the original, you may want to have students exchange their probable passages. Here is the solution half of the original text.

Hypothermia

Hypothermia can be avoided through a common-sense approach to sports like surfing in cold water and skiing. Keeping in good physical shape helps increase *stamina* and wards off the effects of the cold. Wearing adequate *protection* from the elements in the form of a good three to five millimeter wetsuit and boots for surfing or gore-tex fabrics for high mountain skiing keeps out the cold. *Moving muscles* vigorously generates heat as well.

If a surfer or skier does experience hypothermia, the best solution is to warm up as soon as possible. Hot non-alcoholic beverages and a car *heater* help. *Eating* to build up the store of caloric energy in the body also helps. But the best approach is to take preventative steps before this condition develops.

Step Six. Once they have had a chance to compare their probable passage to the original text, students *should edit their passage to include any missing or contradictory information.*

A Probable Passage lesson helps students anchor concepts within a pattern of organization that fosters comprehension and recall. Writing about concepts from their own perspective is an opportunity students experience far too rarely.

Cubing

In order to explore a topic from various dimensions, consider using cubing (Tompkins, 1990). The concrete visual of a cube with its six sides serves as a starting point to consider the multiple dimensions of topics in nutrition, science, social studies, mathematics, and other content areas. To introduce cubing, start with a familiar topic and then treat more complex topics once students have a good grasp of how cubing works.

Cubing involves the following steps.

Step One. Introduce the topic on the board (e.g., ice cream.).

Step Two. Have students in small groups examine the topic from the following six sides of the cube:

- *Describe it* (including its colors, shapes, and sizes, if applicable)
- *Compare it* (what is it similar to or different from?)
- *Associate it* (what does it make you think of?)
- *Analyze it* (tell how it is made or what it is composed of)
- *Apply it* (what can you do with it? How is it used?)
- *Argue for or against it* (take a stand and list reasons for supporting it)

The following cubes show one student's response to the ice cream cubing assignment:

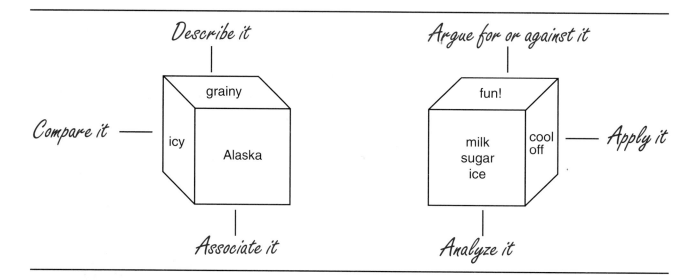

This particular student *described* ice cream as grainy. She *compared* ice cream with an icy she might buy at a convenience store, and she *associated* ice cream with Alaska because it is cold and snowy. In the second half of the cube, she listed the ingredients as milk (it's actually cream or butter fat), sugar, and ice in the *analyze it* box. In the *apply it* box she said that it helps us cool off, and she naturally *argued for* ice cream because it is fun. In comparing her cube with other students, she revised the ingredients and left the other boxes the same.

Students should spend only five to ten minutes on each side of the cube. Once they have a good grasp of the process using familiar topics like the ice cream example, you can introduce more difficult content area topics such as solar cars in science, the Bill of Rights

in history, and authors in English. Initially, students should begin by using the six sides of the cube to compose descriptive paragraphs. Cubing can then form the basis for longer writing assignments including persuasive essays, letters to the editor, and extended reports treated later in this chapter.

Writing Roulette

The next writing-to-learn strategy we are going to explore is *Writing Roulette*. This strategy was originally created to help students become more fluent in writing by having them write about anything at all for a specific period of time (Shuman, 1979). A kitchen timer would be set for five minutes or so, and when it went off, students would pass their writing on to a peer who continues developing the passage for another five minutes or so. Writing Roulette helped students overcome worries about perfect grammar and spelling and moved them into a composing mode.

Bean (1992b) modified the original Writing Roulette strategy for use in content learning. First, instead of writing whatever comes to mind, students are told to use a simple three part story structure for the activity so that three different students write each distinct part of the story. Second, they review content material within the framework of the story by selecting key vocabulary words from their expository reading and including these words in each section they write. The process of conducting a Writing Roulette session is as follows.

Step One. Provide a simple structure for the story, consisting of three major elements or divisions.

    a.   A setting and characters
    b.   A problem or goal for the main character
    c.   A resolution

Step Two. Advise students that each section of the story must use at least two words from the lesson or unit they have been studying. These words should be underlined in the story. You can have students review their vocabulary collections, or you can simply supply a list of technical terminology from which they can choose six words.

Step Three. Set a specific time limit for the first story section (e.g., five minutes for the setting). You can use a kitchen timer for this.

Step Four. When time is up, have students exchange papers or collect and shuffle them so that a second author writes the problem or goal section. Advise students to read the paper they receive and continue the story. Set a time limit for this writing as well.

Step Five. Exchange papers one last time so a third author can provide a resolution for the story. Then, have students return the story to the original author and share aloud those stories that are particularly interesting or that use content vocabulary in creative ways.

Writing Roulette is a good way to have students review important vocabulary and concepts before an essay exam or quiz. It is best introduced after students have used other strategies such as graphic organizers and semantic mapping so that they have a good understanding of content vocabulary. The example that follows is a Writing Roulette story developed by three preservice content teachers. The words are taken from the glossary of our text.

Student 1

Gertrude and Susie were on their way home from school. "Gertrude," said Susie, "that *antic-*

ipation guide we use in class was really great."

"Yeh," replied Gertrude. "And didn't you just love the *graphic organizers?* I can't wait to get home and call all our friends and let them know about our class."

Gertrude and Susie continue down the street, chatting happily.

Student 2

The big history test was rapidly approaching. Gertrude reread her graphic organizer and called Susie on the phone to discuss *study strategies.* She felt her *comprehension* had suffered because she did all of her reading in front of the television. She had never missed an episode of "Dance Fever" since the show's inception. Susie tried to help Gertrude fill in the blank spaces their teacher had left in the graphic organizer. They stayed on the phone for three hours in anticipation of the big *test.*

Student 3

The next day, Gertrude entered the classroom to face the test. She whispered to Susie, "I hope he gives us an *anticipation guide* to help us with this test."

The teacher came around and placed a cloze test on each student's desk. Gertrude took a look at it and almost died. Every other word has been deleted. Gertrude whispered to Susie, "Do you have any idea how to do this test?"

Susie said, "Sure, use your knowledge of *morphemic analysis* to *slice* the *response mode,* which will require you to have fewer pieces of information. Then the *scope of information* search will be halved."

Gertrude gave Susie a blank stare. Susie said, "guess!"

Gertrude knew she would fail, but, fortunately for her, the teacher pulled down the overhead screen, knocking down the wall clock, and a large plastic potted fern onto his big toe. Class was immediately terminated, and Gertrude went whistling out of the classroom, knowing she had escaped a fate worse than death.

Students find Writing Roulette a pleasurable and creative approach to reviewing technical vocabulary and concepts. Since it takes a full period to conduct a Writing Roulette session, you should plan to allot this time just to the activity. Once students have completed their stories, they enjoy exchanging and reading each other's creations in the small group setting. Writing Roulette capitalizes on a familiar narrative structure to review concepts presented in expository material.

The ReWrite Strategy

ReWrite is a music strategy that combines concept learning and the creation of musical verses within a comprehensive pre-reading and post-reading lesson framework (Bean, 1997). Music has the power to enhance abstract reasoning. Musical performance typically occurs in high interest cooperative settings with clear, performance-based outcomes (Miller & Coen, 1994). Song writing can be used to teach concepts in biology, mathematics, history, art, and other content areas.

You do not need to be an accomplished musician to use the ReWrite song writing strategy that follows. Using instrumental music as a foundation for a song your students write or having a music teacher create an instrumental background piece works quite well. Karaoke, the sing-along activity that is popular all over the country, has spawned an endless array of tapes and videotapes of music that can be used for this activity. Or, a teacher can use alternate forms of music like rap and hip hop which require minimal or no musical accompaniment. The lyrics are the important ingredient in the ReWrite song writing strategy.

Day One

Step One. As in any lesson planning, you need to do a careful task analysis of concepts and strategies needed for the reading assignment. In the example that follows, students were engaged in a science unit on entomology, or the study of insects. The insect students read about in this lesson was the crab spider, a prevalent garden pest on the Big Island of Hawaii since its arrival in 1985 (Nishida & Tenorio, 1993; Tenbruggencate, 1990).

To start this ReWrite lesson, concepts that most students would have about crab spiders were incorporated in a blues song. Thus, the song contained commonsense nonscientific knowledge about crab spiders that most students living on the Big Island might know from working around their gardens. The song follows with guitar chords included.

Crab Spiders
(Key of E; Blues Shuffle)

E
Crab spiders hang their webs all over the place
I go outside to work and they just get tangled in my face
    A
Well I hit them with my rake and they stick to my hand
E
Crawling up my arm like Sherman tanks in sand

B7   A   E
I finally decided what I'm gonna do,
collect all my crab spiders and take em to school
(repeat)
Well I'll let them go when my teacher isn't lookin and they'll cause
So much trouble she'll send us outside while she's searchin
      A   E
For those crab spiders, crab spiders what a waste
B7   A   E
They just lie in wait to get tangled in my face

BRIDGE

E
I spray em with Raid, chlorox too but all that does is make my plants look sick and blue
A
Crab spiders, crab spiders how I hate you guys,
   E
you just exist to drive me wild
B7   A
Until I find a way to get rid of this strange insect
E
Maybe I'll just treat my crab spiders with more respect!

The first verse portrayed the pesky quality of these ubiquitous creatures and the next two verses implied the humor of taking them to school and letting them loose in class as a distraction for the teacher. Finally, common approaches to exterminating crab spiders are recounted. The song ends with the author ready to give up trying to fight the crab spider invasion in the yard and just be nice to these pesky, tank-like insects.

Step Two. Students have a copy of the song and follow along while it is played and sung by the teacher. Or, you can have a musician friend perform it and tape the performance. In this example the information in song form was designed to activate students' prior knowledge before they responded to anticipation guide statements based on a science news article about crab spiders.

Sept Three. Following the introductory song activity, students gathered in small groups to consider and complete the five item anticipation guide on crab spiders that included some factual and critical opinion items. You can use ReWrite without any guide material but, in this instance, we wanted to focus students' discussion on some of the remarkable features of the crab spider. The anticipation guide they completed follows.

Anticipation-Reaction Guide

Crab Spiders

Directions: Before reading, consider each statement with a partner. Write *yes* if you agree and *no* if you disagree. Write your reasons below each statement. After reading the text, go back and review each statement.

You   Author

____   ____   1. Crab spiders are harmless.

____   ____   2. A crab spider's web is more deadly than other spider webs.

____   ____   3. We have had crab spiders on our island for many years.

____   ____   4. A crab spider's egg sac can contain more than 100 eggs.

____   ____   5. Fear of spiders is silly.

Most students viewed the crab spider as harmful based on their experiences. They reported receiving bites that swelled up and talked about very painful bites inflicted on their younger siblings who happened to accidentally bump against one of the crab spider's thick webs. They were less sure about statements two through four and very certain number five simply ignored the facts. Fear of spiders was, in their opinion, quite justified.

Day Two

Step Four. Following a pre-reading discussion of the statements, students were assigned reading of the crab spider article in class. They then engaged in a post-reading discussion of the anticipation guide statements. After reading the article they generally agreed with items two, three, and four from the guide. The more open-ended items, particularly the fear of spiders is silly statement, produced few changes in their initial opinions about crab spiders. Indeed, when they discovered that crab spiders were called "the land equivalent of drift net fleets at sea" and their thick, intricate community of webs termed "walls of death" for flying insects, they were impressed. Students used this text-based information to defend their general fear of all spiders (Tenbruggencate, p. E3).

Step Five. Students stay in their groups and write a new crab spider song by creating verses that reflects their new knowledge. In our example, each group shared their verse with the other groups by reading it aloud.

Day Three

Step Six. Students' verses were assembled and typed at home before the next class. Copies were then made

of the students' song and Crab Spider Blues was performed at the start of the next class with each group singing their respective verses. This performance served as a review of text information and set the stage for subsequent insect study. The ReWrite version produced by students follows.

CRAB SPIDER BLUES

Crab spiders work in teams hanging walls of death
Between bushes and trees, under eaves, across a doorway or in trees
Big mama in the middle and daddy goofin off on the side
They wait for prey and take their breath away

Thelacantha bevispina down the back of my shirt
They are difficult to remove and darn they hurt
Their bite may swell up like a sting from a bee
Why do these things always happen to me?

The mothers like to lay about a hundred eggs
And when they pop out they like to bite my legs
There's no killin these bugs at all
Smash um when they're big, squash um when they're small

If you're wondering when the crab spider arrived
They've been around since 1985
The Big Island was cursed because they were the first
The answer to how they came is never the same

Students genuinely enjoy this activity, and the ReWrite song becomes a memorable way to learn and critique content area concepts.

The last writing-to-learn strategy we are going to consider is the Guided Writing Procedure. The GWP guides students through prereading and postreading stages of a lesson.

The Guided Writing Procedure

The *Guided Writing Procedure* (GWP) gives students practice in developing a coherent written account of a topic they are studying in the text (Bean, 1994; Searfoss, Smith, & Bean, 1981; Smith & Bean, 1980). The GWP helps students examine their prior knowledge of a topic. They can then modify their previous knowledge based on the text reading. In contrast to the strategies we have introduced up to this point, the GWP entails editing writing for both content and form. The GWP is designed to achieve the following teaching objectives:

1. To activate and sample students' prior knowledge of a topic before they do any text reading.

2. To sample and evaluate students' written expression in a content area.
3. To improve students' written expression through guided instruction.
4. To facilitate the synthesis and retention of content area material.

Research designed to gauge the impact of the GWP on students' content learning and writing shows that using the GWP significantly improves the quality of the writing that students produce. They are more adept at integrating information from text and prior knowledge, and these students produce writing that is carefully edited and readable (Konopak, Martin, & Martin, 1987).

The GWP usually spans three days of content instruction and involves the following steps.

Day One

Step One. Write the topic heading you are introducing on the board and have *students brainstorm words or phrases* that come to mind when they think about this topic. For example, social studies students who were about to read a chapter describing conditions during the Depression of 1929 generated six ideas based on their prior knowledge of this topic.

Step Two. Record students' ideas verbatim on the board or overhead. Engage students in a discussion of their ideas, and ask them to explain how they are related to the topic being considered. Students produced the following list for the causes of the Depression of 1929.

no jobs	stocks crash
no money	everything is cheap
poverty	bad investments

Step Three. Guide students in constructing an outline, graphic organizer, or semantic map of these ideas with appropriate category labels. For example:

Causes and Effects of the Depression

   I. Causes
      a. bad investments
      b. stocks crash

  II. Effects
      a. no jobs
      b. no money
      c. poverty
      d. everything is cheap

Step Four. Tell students to individually write a short paragraph or two as a first draft, with the outline as a guide to content and organization. You should tell them to direct this draft to a specific audience. A reasonable audience for this information is another class member or a classmate who is absent for this lesson.

Step Five. Collect students' first drafts and rapidly analyze the paragraphs, using the GWP checklist that follows. You should not make any marks on students' papers. The first draft that follows was written by a student based on the six ideas generated in the brainstorming on the Depression.

Causes and Effects of the Depression

The awful Depression of 1929 was caused by the stock market crash. People made bad investments and lost all their money. Some people bought too much stock on credit. They went to far into det.

When the stock market crashed people lost a lot of money. There wasn't money to pay people for work. People without jobs sunk into poverty. Everything was dirt cheap. You could probably go to a movie for a dime!

This student constructed a first draft that has a clear topic sentence and good organization. At this prereading stage, students had only limited knowledge of the causes and effects of the Depression, so the draft is understandably brief. He made some fairly common spelling errors that the teacher simply pointed out in the mechanics section of the GWP checklist. We are now ready for day two.

Day Two

Step Six. Return students' drafts and checklists. Have students make necessary edits and polish their first drafts, based on the guidelines you offered on the checklist. You can circulate among students to provide extra help. You can also use this time for individual conferences with students experiencing real difficulty with the writing process. For example, second language learners generally benefit from extra, one-on-one discussion of their writing efforts. You may want to display some sample drafts on the overhead and model the process of editing for organization of ideas, style, and mechanics.

Step Seven. Have students turn in their second draft and the original GWP checklist they used to guide their editing. You can then record any comments, particularly praise, on the bottom of the original checklist.

Step Eight. Assign text reading, explaining to students that the purpose of this reading is to locate additional information, especially supporting details and examples, that they can include in a final draft of their writing.

Day Three

Step Nine. Now that they have acquired additional knowledge about the topic (in this case, the Depression), *engage students in a group discussion to revise the original outline to include this text*

GWP CHECKLIST

(✔ = okay; O = needs revision; ? = can't tell)

Criteria

Organization of Ideas

Clear topic ✔

Supporting details/examples O

Logical flow ✔

Comments: *Good organization of ideas. The text will give you details and examples.*

Style
Shows variety in

Word choice ✔

Sentence length O

Comments: *Short sentences need to be balanced by some that are longer.*

Mechanics

Complete sentences ✔

Capitalization ✔

Punctuation ✔

Spelling O

Comments: *too far (vs. to); debt (vs. det); sank (vs. sunk)*

---

information. Any misconceptions can be cleared up as well. Here, the text that students read added little to their basic understanding of the causes of the Depression. However, it did expand on the effects of the Depression on workers in the cities and on farmers. Thus, their new outline contained a blend of their original ideas about the Depression and the new information discussed in the text.

Step Ten. Students should then revise and expand their compositions, based on new information from the text. You may want to have them include lecture and discussion information if the text is limited in its coverage of the topic. Students can work in pairs or small groups while you come around to help them link text and prior knowledge concepts. Then have students turn in these final drafts for a grade or give a quiz on this informa-tion. These compositions can be used as a lead-in to a unit (in this case, on the New Deal). They can also become part of the guide material you use with future classes, creating a very real audience for students' efforts. The student who wrote the original draft on the Depression produced the following final version.

Causes and Effects of the Depression

The awful Depression of 1929 was caused by bad investments in the stock market. People took great risks with money, stringing themselves out in debt by buying too much stock on credit. The banks also made bad investments and many had to close after the stock market crashed. The Depression that started with the stock market crash of 1929 was a business downturn that, different from the ones before it, lasted for 10 years!

The effects of the Depression were many. Because people lost so much money, they stopped buying goods. The factories had to close and by 1932, 13 million people, or one in four, were out of work. Young people hopped trains to seek work in other towns. Homeless people lived on the edge of the big cities in tiny shacks called Hoovervilles, after President Hoover. Even the farms suffered. Farmers grew too much corn, which they couldn't sell. Since they couldn't sell the corn, they couldn't pay for their tractors and other equipment. They lost their farms, and droughts made things even worse. The Dust Bowl in the early 1930s wiped out even more farmers. People sank into poverty. Everything was dirt cheap. You could probably go to a movie for a dime, but I would rather live now!

This student's final version now contains supporting details from the text. Furthermore, he includes his own views about living during that era.

The GWP is an in-depth exploration of a text reading assignment. Since it is time consuming, you should plan on using it as a lead-in to a unit so that students approach their reading with some power over the text. For example, in the Depression outline stage, students begin to see the text as a cause-effect organizational pattern, which helped them read fluently and selectively for key ideas and details to revise their original GWP compositions.

Causes and Effects of the Depression
I. Causes
   a.   bad investments by people and banks
   b.   the stock market crash
   c.   business downturn for 10 years
II. Effects
   a.   people stopped buying goods
   b.   factories closed
   c.   by 1932, 13 million jobless workers (one of every four)
   d.   young people hopped trains to find work
   e.   homeless people lived on the outskirts of town in shacks called "Hoovervilles," after President Hoover
   f.   farmers had too much surplus corn, which they could not sell
   g.   farmers lost their farms—droughts also led to the Dust Bowl in the early 1930s
   h.   poverty was common

 ## Writing to Inform

Writing for an audience of peers, especially to argue a particular point of view, can help students become analytical readers. The strategies considered next emphasize both analytical reading and writing.

Autobiographies

When students are asked to write an autobiography of their unique literacy histories from the earliest memories they have up to the present, this activity provides a powerful window on their experiences and feelings about reading (Bean & Readence, 1995). A *reading autobiography* charting experiences at early, middle, and later stages of reading can be shaped to focus on reading in science, mathematics and so on. Autobiographies should be shared in class in small groups and dicscussed. In the activity that follows, we designed this autobiography format for English. You can also modify the format to focus the autobiography on your content area and further reduce the scope of writing to encompass a particular period like middle or high school.

Biographies

Once students have written an autobiography, the transition to reading and writing *biographies* about an important figure in science, physical education, mathematics, history, music, or art is fairly easy. Daisy (1997) suggested that trade book biographies offer a powerful way to enrich textbook concepts in a fashion that has human interest. In addition, women and persons of color are featured in biographies in greater depth than their contributions might display in a content area textbook that surveys many topics (Daisy, 1997). The following steps will help you get started using biographies in your content area.

Step One. Work with your librarian to ensure there is a good collection of biographies for your content area that encompasses women and persons of color.

Step Two. Have students self select a biography to read and write about in some creative format. Daisy (1997) offers a wide array of possible project options including:

1. Write about how the world in the biography you read is different from your world.

2. Write a journal or e-mail message from the perspective of the book character.

3. Write a movie review of the story in the book.

Reading Autobiography

Beginning with your earliest memories of reading or being read to, retrace your experiences as a reader up to and including the present time. As you think about these experiences, making notes, try to include as much of the following information as possible:

1. The kinds of books you read or that were read to you at particular ages. If you can't remember specific titles and authors, describe the plots, characters, themes, or content you can recall.

2. Your reading or lack of reading when you first became an independent reader.

3. What you read or what was read to you both at school and at home during your elementary school years. (Don't be embarrassed if no one read to you or if you didn't read. Just write about the lack of reading in your life.)

4. Facts and feelings about what you read as you moved through the grades up to and including senior high and beyond.

5. Your present reading habits and preferences (or lack thereof).

6. The people (family members, teachers, friends, and others) who either turned you off or turned you on to reading and why.

7. Places where you acquired or now acquire books.

8. The feelings and sensations you associate with reading.

After you have taken notes on your experiences as a reader, write a short autobiographical sketch (3 pages maximum) on your reading experiences based on the eight guideline questions above. Put your development into chronological order so that your autobiography shows the stages you have gone through as a reader. In the final section, review your personal history as a reader and discuss how your own experiences might influence you as a content area teacher interested in helping students cope with unfriendly textbooks and interested in developing in your students, a desire to read for enjoyment.

As you write your reading autobiography, be candid and honest. If you like, use an informal writing style as though you were writing in your journal. During our next class meeting, I will ask you to share these experiences with a small group.

---

4. Write and act out a historical, you-are-there scene, dressed as the character.

5. Write a biopoem.

The following template is useful in helping students structure their biopoems (Diamond & Moore, 1995).

Line 1. First name
Line 2. Four traits that describe the character
Line 3. Relative of
Line 4. Lover of (3 things or people)
Line 5. Who feels (3 items)
Line 6. Who needs (3 things)
Line 7. Who fears (3 things)
Line 8. Who gives (3 things)
Line 9. Who would like to see (3 items)
Line 10. Resident of
Line 11. Last name

Step Three. Have students share their biography project with a small group or the whole class.

For example, sixth grader Kristen read a biography about a famous show dog Duke and wrote a biopoem about her dog, Lady Kathryn, in her middle school language arts class. Duke was Lady Kathryn's father.

Biopoem

Lady
A smart, loving, and sweet dog
Relative of Duke, a dog show champion
Lover of chewys, people, and attention
Who needs her family, chewy, and soft pillows

Who fears loud noises, new places, and new people
Who gives kisses, cute smiles, and playful attitudes
Who would like to see a huge treat, a huge stuffed animal and other small puppies
Resident of Nevada
Kathryn

Thus, *biopoems* can take many forms and be created on virtually any topic across the content areas. In science, students can write about the heart, various animals, plants, and so on. They are particularly applicable to biographies but very versatile as a creative way of writing to inform.

Biographies in music range from classical pianists to Jimi Hendrix and The Rolling Stones. With the help of your librarian, you should be able to locate biographies relevant to many content fields including physical education, agriculture, art, music, history, science, mathematics, vocational education and so on. Searching for and selecting a biography to read and write about forms a great foundation for research paper writing. Use your imagination to create additional project options that involve writing to inform.

Research Papers

At its worst, a research paper assignment may amount to no more than students engaged in the busywork of copying facts laboriously cataloged for a teacher who knows this information in the first place. In this instance, the paper is put off as long as possible and hurriedly thrown together the night before it is due. The teacher then pays an inordinate amount of attention to the form of the paper, poison pen in hand to circle in red any grammar and spelling errors.

At its best, a research paper is the culmination of a student's efforts to become an expert in some subtopic of a field so this knowledge can be shared with an audience of peers (Calkins, 1994). This may range from developing an insider's knowledge of sharks in science to an understanding of how parapsychologists explore phenomena such as poltergeist in a psychology class. You can probably recall writing papers of this sort a few times during your years in school. But notice we said "a few times." Opportunities to become actively involved in pursuing a topic of genuine personal interest are all too rare.

In this section we want to outline some general steps to consider as you assign research papers in your content classroom.

Step One. Selecting and narrowing a topic is often a difficult task for teachers and students alike. Davey (1987) recommends having students form cooperative research groups for this stage of the process. A research team of two to five students with a recorder

can brainstorm subtopics within the general area you suggest. For example, if the topic was earthquakes, students might narrow this to a list consisting of famous earthquakes, California earthquakes, science of earthquakes, and so on.

Step Two. Once the topic has been chosen, *the research team can then meet to plan how they are going to tackle the topic.* They can brainstorm possible questions for their topic and place them on notecards. For example, if the topic were the science of earthquakes, possible questions might include: What causes earthquakes? Can scientists predict when they will occur? Where do they occur most often? Davey (1987) recommends that all questions be considered at this brainstorming stage. Once all possible questions have been elicited, they should be categorized and transformed into statements that will guide the research and notetaking stage.

Step Three. The research team should identify potential sources of information, including encyclopedias, textbooks, films, and experts who may be interviewed. If your school has access to computer data-bases that contain up-to-date encyclopedias, these may also be a good place to locate information.

Once each research team has identified their resources for the paper, they should develop a time line that delineates specific dates when they will finish each task. Thus, they need a date for completing the collection of information in the form of notes, another date for a paper outline, one for the first draft, and a date for the second draft. The search for information can be divided among team members so that a portion of the team reads and annotates encyclopedia information while another dyad interviews an expert on earthquakes.

Step Four. Once information has been collected, *students should regroup in their teams to categorize and consider the ideas they have.* This is a good time to transform the headings that guided the information search into a tentative outline. The Science of Earthquakes outline might look like this.

I. Earthquake
   A. Definition
II. Cause of earthquakes
   A. Early myths
   B. Modern tectonic theory
III. Where they occur the most
   A. Pacific belt
   B. Mediterranean belt
IV. Effect of earthquakes
   A. Landslides
   B. Tsunamis
V. How they are studied
   A. Seismographs
   B. Earthquake waves

Once the outline is prepared, students can begin writing their individual reports. Be sure they realize that the outline is merely a tentative guide—it may be altered as the writing progresses and new insights develop.

Step Five. The first draft of the paper can now be written. Once the first draft is completed, students should exchange papers and use the writing guide checklist that accompanied the Guided Writing Procedure to peer-edit the papers.

Step Six. Based on suggested edits by their peers as well as yourself, students can now complete the second and final draft. Naturally, this process takes time. Students need adequate class time to meet in their groups, and they need enough time to allow for two drafts of the paper. Davey (1987) recommends providing student groups with a form where they can list team members, the topic, categories to be explored, resources, and the timeline proposed. The teacher then reviews this material for each group and signs-off to indicate topic approval. Students may also need a checklist, particularly for the group recorder, that indicates the various stages of the process (e.g., brainstorming, researching, organizing, and writing), along with the sub-steps for each procedure (e.g., for brainstorming: generate questions, categorize the questions and write them as statements; identify sources; and set timelines). This will help focus the group effort on the various steps in the process.

In addition to carefully describing the parameters of a writing assignment as extensive as a research paper, you may want to share with students some model papers that were completed in a previous class. More importantly, papers written by former students can become important sources of information for the present class, giving students a functional audience for their writing aside from the usual teacher as examiner-audience. At their best, research papers should be memorable experiences for students that result in in-depth knowledge and appreciation of subtopics that might otherwise go unnoticed in a frenetic effort to cover too much content in too short a time.

I-Search Papers

The I-Search paper is an alternative to the more traditional research paper (Macrorie, 1988). Students investigate a topic of their choosing by interviewing experts, visiting places, and telling the story of their search. In the more traditional research paper there is a tendency for students to report on a topic by reading and distilling the works of others. The I-Search paper consists of the following steps (Macrorie, 1988):

Step One. Choosing a topic. Students should select topics of personal interest. For example, Jennifer, a middle school student, had been a regular visitor to the zoo for years. She was mystified by the Pandas and her I-Search paper investigated how they were cared for in the city zoo. Another student, Fabio, wanted to find out more about how guitars are made. His I-Search paper took him on a journey to a local luthier.

Step Two. Carry-out the search. Share the topic with the class and see if anyone has some ideas about where to find an expert to interview. For example, Jennifer's interest in Panda's put her in contact with the head veterinarian at the city zoo. Fabio's search sent him to a luthier. Before contacting and interviewing the veterinarian and luthier, these students did some background reading on their respective topics. Based on this background reading, they created some interview questions on their respective topics. For example, Jennifer asked the veterinarian at the zoo, "Why are Pandas on the endangered species list?" Fabio asked, "How much does a handmade koa guitar cost to build?"

Step Three. Conduct the interview. Using a tape recorder to retain the information they needed for the I-Search paper, Jennifer and Fabio visited and interviewed the experts they located. They got recommendations for further reading into the topic from these experts. For example, when Fabio interviewed a luthier, the guitar maker said "read *The Guitar Handbook* (Denyer, 1982)."

Step Four. Writing the paper. Use the I-Search experience as a way of telling the story of how the paper evolved. Anything important in the search process should be included and the format can follow the four categories of information listed below:

(a) *What the student knew or did not know when the topic was selected.* For example, Jennifer did not know that there are only about 1000 Pandas living in the mountains in China. The Pandas depend heavily on the food source of their bamboo forests which are vulnerable to logging and a natural life and death cycle.

(b) *Why the student decided to write on this topic.* In Jennifer's case, she worked as a volunteer at the zoo. She had a long-standing interest in biology and in becoming a veterinarian specializing in the care of large, endangered zoo animals. Fabio played an old koa guitar that once belonged to his grandfather, and he was interested in how it was made. He dreamed about someday making his own guitar.

(c) *The search should be described.* Fabio's paper described his visit to luthier Bob Gleason of Pegasus Guitars. Fabio commented on the old industrial warehouse where the luthier worked and how neat everything was. Fabio spent two afternoons at the guitar maker's workshop and borrowed the book entitled, *The Guitar Handbook,* to further research his paper.

(d) *What the student learned.* Jennifer included information on the Panda's diet in the zoo (i.e., bamboo, apples, carrots, sweet potatoes, pans of slurpy ice, and mixtures of milk, eggs, and ground vegetables), sleep habits (i.e., 12 to 14 hours-per-day), and reproduction. In addition, she learned that in China, breeding programs are used to raise Pandas in captivity to be released into the wild.

Finally, the I-Search paper should conclude with a list of sources, experts, and key people involved in supplying ideas and insights for the paper (Macrorie, 1988).

The I-Search paper goes well with cooperative learning. For example, rather than using individual I-Search topics, a small group or team of students can collaborate to investigate a topic about which they share a common interest. The I-Search paper is also a good alternative to the traditional research paper for multicultural topics, second language learners, and at-risk students because of its experiential nature (Alejandro, 1989).

Imaginative Writing to Inform Assignments

Discussing text reading and writing an in-depth research report are mainstays of content learning. But it is equally important to provide a variety of writing opportunities, especially opportunities for imaginative writing. In this section we offer some imaginative writing assignments that lend themselves to a variety of content areas. You can undoubtedly think of other possibilities.

Students can project themselves into the lives of people in historical contexts or animals in various habitats by writing a diary entry from a unique perspective (Hansen, 1987). For example, have social studies students write a diary entry as if they were hobos riding the rail during the Depression. In the area of ecology, they could write a diary entry from the perspective of a whale or dolphin passing through an ocean channel near one of our polluted city harbors.

Similarly, have students write a "Who Am I?" piece in which they portray topics such as "I am your heart, I am your lungs, I am President Roosevelt, I am a camera," and so on. This exercise can require researching on a topic in detail to transform what might otherwise be dull expository prose into a lively, personal account (Hansen, 1987).

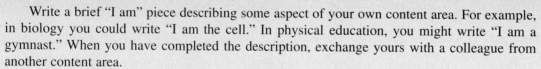

ACTIVITY

Write a brief "I am" piece describing some aspect of your own content area. For example, in biology you could write "I am the cell." In physical education, you might write "I am a gymnast." When you have completed the description, exchange yours with a colleague from another content area.

Imaginative writing expands students' sense of audience and encourages creativity. Smith (1986) offers a number of suggestions for imaginative writing that informs the reader. In business education, students can write real letters to a newspaper column or the Small Business Association, asking for advice about their business interests. They can write a business plan for a small business they wish to start, such as yard cleaning or car detailing. Some students may want to interview a small business owner and create an oral history of the trials and tribulations of business ownership.

In social studies, students can write about a historical event from the perspective of a person experiencing it. For example, what was it like to be a woman on a ranch during cattle drives, isolated from other women, responsible for a family and livestock? Students can write fictional accounts about historical

events, transforming expository prose into a more lively narrative form. In mathematics, students can create a story using math symbols in place of some words. In science, defending an unpopular theory, such as the notion that there is such a thing as earthquake weather, and directing this defense to a newspaper or a peer audience requires both research and imagination. In foreign language classes, acting in the role of a visiting student writing a diary entry about the first day in the United States can illuminate cultural diversity.

In music, drama, and art, writing a critical review of a concert or interviewing an artist for the newspaper helps broaden the audience for student writing. Finally, in health and physical education, keeping a sports diary that chronicles jogging or swimming progress and diet strategies demonstrates the day-to-day usefulness of writing to inform.

Responding to Writing

As students develop research papers and lengthy pieces of writing in your content area, your skill at responding to their writing becomes crucial (Moore, 1992). You may remember having a paper returned from a teacher covered with red marks attesting to your ability to produce sentences that were "awk" (i.e., awkward), and phrases that were, in the teacher's eyes, "frags" (i.e., fragments) (Stanford, 1979). When students receive a barrage of negative criticism for their writing efforts, they come to associate writing with frustration, depression, self-doubt, and avoidance. Furthermore, they may come to view revision as a process that involves merely making surface level changes similar to proofreading rather than a process that entails deeper structural and organizational changes (Fitzgerald, 1987). In contrast, we believe that students need to be able to take risks in portraying their ideas in writing without simultaneously balancing total attention to the mechanics of grammar and spelling, except in the revision stage of the second draft. You should avoid riddling a student's paper with red marks that focus on mechanical errors and consider alternate means of responding to students' writing. This is especially important in working with second language learners who may be very intimidated by writing in English.

Valuing students' writing should be at the top of your list when you conference with students (Hansen, 1996). Finding value in the content of their writing, treating students as writers, and encouraging growth through comparisons of early and later writing make a difference (Hansen, 1996). Indeed, Hansen (p.188) defined evaluation as "the act of finding value in a piece of writing" and we agree. Hanson also recommended that teachers display their own attempts at writing in content areas and act as co-learners in the writing process. Autobiographies, journals, research papers, and imaginative writing all offer opportunities to participate with your students as writers. In our research in secondary classrooms, we freewrite with students on various topics related to American literature.

Beaven (1977) recommended various ways to respond to students' writing that avoid the pitfalls of the poison red pen approach. First, taping comments you have, referring to particular parts of a student's paper, provides a more positive approach than marking every error. Second, beginning any comments about a student's paper with some positive praise alleviates anxiety and opens the door for revision. Third, writing marginal questions that probe areas of the paper that need revision directs the student to take responsibility for this process. Fourth, using an analytical checklist like the GWP checklist provides a means of guiding revision without marking up a student's paper. Fifth, individual conferences in combination with the checklist can be more productive than merely returning a paper with marginal comments. Finally, helping students use effective self-evaluation to revise their writing based on a series of generic questions will also lessen your paper load and encourage independence.

We want to discuss three of these six response schemes in detail. Individual conferences, self-evaluation, and peer evaluation deserve attention.

Individual Conferences

An individual conference is a conversation between a teacher and student for the purpose of evaluating and pointing out areas for revision of a draft of a paper (Newkirk, 1986). These conferences can be organized with a sign-up sheet on a first-come, first-served basis, or you can circulate about the room meeting with students as needed. The conversations you have with students should be purposeful, resulting in specific ideas for revision of a draft. Having a series of generic questions in mind to guide the individual conference will help the student participate actively in these sessions rather than passively by hoping you will do the revising. The following questions are recommended (Newkirk, 1986, p. 121):

1. What do you like best about this draft?

2. What do you like least?

3. What gave you the most trouble in writing this?

4. What kind of reaction do you want your readers to have—amusement, anger, increased understanding?

5. What surprised you when you wrote this? What came out differently than you expected?

6. What is the most important thing you learned about your topic in writing this?

These questions, in combination with the Writing Guide Checklist, should place the emphasis on the student's ideas, but there is always a tendency in teaching for the teacher to do most of the talking. Listening carefully and holding back your natural desire to grab the paper and revise in a way you think appropriate gives a student responsibility for this important process.

Ideally, students need to learn effective means of self-evaluation. The individual conferences you conduct using a series of generic questions can form the basis for effective self-evaluation.

Self-Evaluation

The Writing Guide Checklist introduced with the Guided Writing Procedure can serve as a guide for self-evaluation. Similarly, a series of questions like the following may also focus the writer on areas needing revision (Bean, 1994).

1. What makes you happy about this writing?

2. Do you excite your reader with a good beginning?

3. Is there a clear topic sentence?

4. Do you back up your ideas with details and examples?

5. Do you use a variety of words to express your ideas?

6. Are your sentences different lengths?

7. Do you use complete sentences?

8. Did you check your writing for correct capitalization, punctuation, and spelling?

Although checklists and questions can help students detect areas needing revision, a writer's distinct style is more difficult to define. Writing that expresses each student's individual interest in his or her own unique style is often a pleasure to read. However, many of the expository texts students read seem to have had the author's voice edited out of them. If these are the only models of writing students read in a content area, their own writing may have this same bland quality. In addition to texts, students need to read tradebooks in science, social studies, mathematics, and business that demonstrate the author's enthusiasm for a topic and unique voice.

In addition to self-evaluation, peer evaluation can play an important role in the revision process. If you have ever tried to evaluate your own writing objectively, you know how hard this process can be. You know what you meant to say, even if the actual version you produced on paper is incoherent. A peer reader will quickly find these problem areas.

Peer Evaluation

Teams of two students can become skilled at evaluating each other's writing when they have some practice and clear guidelines for the process. We have found that students can comfortably practice peer editing by starting with some writing samples from a lower grade. They can apply the Writing Guide Checklist to these samples without feeling self-conscious about critiquing a classmate's writing. Once they are skilled at responding to these papers, they can then exchange papers with a peer and collaborate to polish their first drafts.

The Writing Guide Checklist offers a good general series of composing and transcribing considerations for any content area writing. However, students should begin a peer editing session by first complimenting their partner on some aspect of the paper. The following general comments help students grasp this important first step (Moore, Moore, Cunningham, & Cunningham, 1986, p. 125): (1) "I thought the most interesting part of your paper was . . .," (2) "You gave the most complete information about . . ."

Moore et al. (1986) also suggested that students phrase any negative comments as questions. For example, "Can you tell me more about . . ." The approach avoids engendering any defensive feelings as a peer helps in the revision process.

In peer editing, merely finding problems in a paper is not enough. Unlike the red pen "awks" and "frags" we all remember trying to decipher and resolve, a peer reader should offer some solutions to the problems that have been identified. For example, the reader can suggest alternative organizational structures, revised sentences, correct spellings, and format changes. With the use of word processing among student writers, these changes should not be overwhelming.

Individual conferences, self-evaluation, and peer evaluation all help content teachers manage the paper load, the biggest single obstacle to writing assignments in many content classrooms.

The fact that you can probably remember those content area papers you have written over the years where *you* became the class expert on some topic, whether it was sharks or the stock market, attests to the power of writing as a mode of learning and reflection. It is worth the trouble. It takes real effort to guide students through various drafts for longer papers and real restraint to resist overcorrecting writing that is intended only for the writer's eyes as a bridge to learning.

Calkins (1994) says this about writing, and we agree:

> We write to communicate, plan, petition, remember, announce, list imagine . . . but above all, we write to hold our lives in our hands and to make something of them. There is no plot line in the bewildering complexity of our lives but that which we make for ourselves. Writing allows us to turn the chaos into something beautiful, to frame selected moments, to uncover and celebrate the organizing patterns of our existence. (p. 8)

SUMMARY

In this chapter we briefly discussed the writing process and its relationship to reading with an emphasis on the distinction between composing, where the writer places attention on ideas, and transcribing activities, including editing for appropriate grammar and spelling. Two major forms of writing in the content areas were considered: (a) writing to learn and (b) writing to inform. We examined seven writing-to-learn strategies: (1) journal writing; (2) possible sentences; (3) probable passages; (4) cubing; (5) writing roulette; (6) ReWrite; and (7) the guided writing procedure. In the writing-to-inform section, we explored six topic areas: (1) autobiography; (2) biographies; (3) biopoems: (4) research papers; (5) I-Search papers; and, (6) imaginative writing to inform. Finally, we discussed responding to students' writing with an emphasis on three approaches: (1) individual conferences; (2) self-evaluation; and (3) peer evaluation.

Now go back to the writing vignette at the beginning of the chapter. React again to the lesson as you did before. Compare your answers with those you made before you read the chapter.

MINI PROJECT

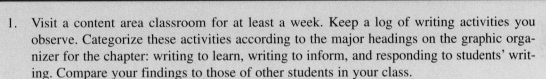

1. Visit a content area classroom for at least a week. Keep a log of writing activities you observe. Categorize these activities according to the major headings on the graphic organizer for the chapter: writing to learn, writing to inform, and responding to students' writing. Compare your findings to those of other students in your class.

2. Examine the writing activities recommended in a major student text in your content area. Using the headings from this chapter, determine what types of writing are being emphasized. Compare your findings to those of colleagues in class.

3. Using the text chapter on the CD-ROM entitled, "What causes weather patterns?," select one of the writing-to-learn strategies in Chapter Eleven. Conduct a lesson with a small group of students or your peers. Write a description and evaluation of this lesson and share it with colleagues in class.

4. Select one of the writing-to-inform activities and conduct a lesson with students in your content area. Respond to students' writing using the writing guide checklist, and conduct at least one individual conference or peer editing session, using the guidelines in this chapter. Write a description of your experience and share it with colleagues.

GROUP PROJECTS

In the context of content area literacy, explain the following analogy:

reading: writing

AS

reading to learn: writing to learn.

Compare and contrast the processes of composing and transcribing.

In your own content area list five examples of how you could encourage imaginative writing behaviors. Then explain why imaginative writing is important.

T W E L V E

STUDYING

SETTING

Sam Valuta's 10th grade world history class. Mr. Valuta and his students just completed a unit on the Baltic nations and their efforts to achieve independence. A unit test is scheduled for the next class meeting, and Mr. Valuta is suggesting ways to study for this essay test.

THE LESSON

Mr. Valuta reviews material on the Baltic Nations of Latvia, Estonia, and Lithuania covered in this unit. He engages students in a discussion of the three nations' cultural and linguistic differences and problems of banding together politically in the Council of Baltic States and economically in a Baltic common market to develop a unified front in negotiations with Moscow. Mr. Valuta then highlights the general area of essay test questions he plans to ask and he tells students about various study strategies they might use in preparing for the essay test. These strategies come from his own relatively recent experiences in college as a history major faced with countless blue book essay exams.

T: "I know you are worried about taking an essay test on this material. But if you study hard you'll do fine. I want to tell you about some study strategies you can use. They work for me and they should work for you too."

S: Students are listening more than usual and ready to take notes.

T: "You all know how to outline, so you might simply take the section of the text on the Baltic States and outline this information. Just writing it out, even copying it from the book should help you memorize it."

S: "We do that anyway. Sometimes it works okay, sometimes it doesn't. What else can we do Mr. Valuta? Personally, I'm really worried about this test. Is it one big question or smaller ones?"

T: "I can't really tell you the exact question but I can tell you that the difficulty of getting three very different groups of people like the Latvians, Estonians, and Lithuanians together for a common cause is an important part of what you need to know. As for other study strategies, I mostly rely on the outline and memorize approach myself but you could try something like this. Take each subheading in the section of the text on the Baltic Nations and turn it into a question. Then see if you can answer the question based on your memory for reading this section. If you can successfully get most of the information then you'll probably do fine on the essay test."

S: "But we haven't practiced doing this at all. We've just been reading, taking notes on your lectures, talking about the book, and watching films. How do we know what to expect in an essay test?"

T: "That's the whole idea—you don't. It wouldn't be a test if you already had the question and practiced writing an essay. This way, it will be a true test of your memory and if you do well you can feel really good about the study strategy you used."

The bell rings and students file out talking among themselves. They express high anxiety and a sense of powerlessness in the face of this impending essay exam.

▶ Keeping in mind that this lesson was designed to help students prepare for an essay exam on the Baltic Nations, jot down your thoughts on the following questions:

1. What are the good points about the lesson?

2. What are the weak points about the lesson?

3. What, if anything, would you change about the lesson?

RATIONALE

As teachers, the fruit of your labors will be *learning,* which can be defined as "transfer of information from short-term memory to long-term memory" (Gall, Gall, Jacobsen, & Bullock, 1990, p. 18). Hopefully, what your students learn will have much to do with math, English, or the sciences, and little to do with accuracy in hurling paper projectiles—although both entail learning. To put it in different words, any experience-based modification of schemata involves learning, whether or not one would consider the modification beneficial.

In a much narrower sense, learning can be defined in terms of the acquisition of specific information in content areas, and the preceding chapters of this text have dealt primarily with the means by which this acquisition process can be facilitated. One focus of the present chapter is on study strategies that help students retain and retrieve information.

Everyone has had the experience of walking into an examination, such as the SAT or GRE, only to find the answers to certain questions elusive due to memory failure. For example, the solution to a simple geometry problem may require knowing the formula for finding the circumference of a circle. (Let's see, is that πr^2, $2 \pi r$, or $2 \pi r^2$?) A failure to extract the necessary information from memory may result because: (1) you never bothered to learn the formula in the first place; (2) you learned it at one time but have for some reason failed to retain the formula in your memory; or (3) you did learn the formula and it is still locked in your memory, but you are unable to retrieve or recall the formula. In any event, the net effect is the same, a wrong answer on the test. Clearly, the ability to retain and recall information is as important as the ability to learn it in the first place. For this reason, study strategies are the business of every content teacher. Unfortunatley, recent research has indicated that both preservice and inservice teachers seem to lack the knowledge of study strategies and do not value them (Jackson & Cunningham, 1994).

A second reason for teaching study strategies in content area classes is to develop in students those habits that encourage and assist independent learning. To the extent that students learn to study effectively on their own, they will be capable of continued reading and learning in the absence of explicit external guidance (Memory & Moore, 1992).

Study strategies (the traditional study skills curriculum) have included aspects of instruction as diverse as notetaking, map reading, uses of the card catalog, and speed reading (Christen & Searfoss, 1992). It has been the hodgepodge of the reading profession and the dumping ground for miscellaneous skills that everyone wants their students to know but no one wants to teach. The purpose of this chapter is not to cover all bases. Rather, we want to introduce some carefully selected independent study strategies and instructional procedures that will help students retain and recall information directly related to reading assignments.

LEARNING OBJECTIVES

- Justify the time required to guide students toward effective study strategies in your content area.

- Understand the general learning principles that underlie the study strategies described in this chapter.

- Guide students in developing study strategies that improve retention and recall of material from your content area.

GRAPHIC ORGANIZER

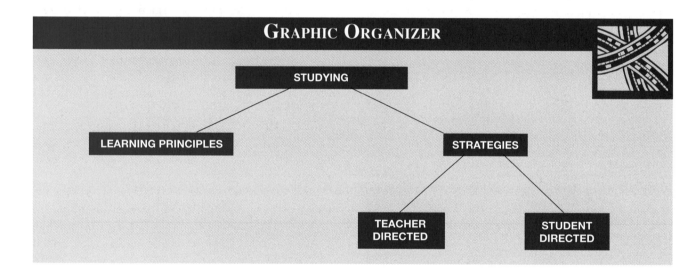

Principles of Effective Studying

If I were compelled to sum up in a single word all that is embraced in the expression 'a good memory,' I should use the word attention. Indeed, I would define education, moral and intellectual, as attention (Aiken, 1896, p. 74).

Attention

Read through the following passage one time, and be prepared to answer a single question:

An *empty* hotel elevator stops and one person enters. The elevator goes up two floors and six people get on; up three more floors and three people get on. The elevator goes down one floor and seven people get off; down one more floor and one person gets off. The elevator then shoots up ten floors and two people get on. Now, without looking back, how many times did the elevator stop?

The answer is six; you probably got it wrong. Why? The second word in this old joke is a distractor. The fact that the elevator is empty has no bearing on the answer to the question. However, the reader, not knowing the question in advance, guesses or assumes that keeping track of numbers of people is the pertinent task. The real rub lies in the fact that tallying the number of elevator stops is much easier than calculating how many people get on and off.

The principle in this is that comprehension and learning/memory are not at all the same thing. It is quite possible to read with good comprehension and at the same time fail to retain the information. In most instances, the individual's active attention is a powerful factor in placing information in a durable memory store. It is a matter of common sense and common experience. Everyone remembers Miss Frock (the fourth grade teacher) who said, "If you don't pay attention, you won't remember anything."

There is, however, another aspect of attention which has less to do with willingness or appropriateness of attention than capacity to attend. Generally, human beings are capable of attending consciously to only one task at a time (Gall, Gall, Jacobsen, & Bullock, 1990). For instance, it is quite impossible to attend to two conversations at precisely the same time, although it is possible to quickly switch attention back and forth between conversations or other tasks which require conscious attention. This principle of *capacity limitation* for attention will be a critical consideration in discussion of specific study strategies later in the chapter.

Goal Orientation

One of the most serious and frequent impediments to learning is the counterproductive study goal. Students often read a textbook assignment for the sake of completing it, i.e., to be able to tell the teacher, without fibbing, that they have in fact read the assignment. When the student's attention is focused on getting through X number of pages rather than on comprehending and retaining information, the result is almost certain to be inferior comprehension and retention. Students who fail to read the last two paragraphs of a chapter because the teacher accidentally designated reading pages 79–93 instead of 79–94 demonstrate a counterproductive study goal. They meet the letter of the assignment but not its spirit. Constructive purpose, given by the teacher and embraced by the students, is essential to effective study.

Organization

Pronounce each digit in the following number one time, and then try to recall the number from memory:

1248163264128

Difficult, wasn't it? Now, try again.

1 2 4 8 16 32 64 128

The second time should have been much easier. If you sensed the geometric progression, you should have been able to reproduce the original number sequence with minimal strain on memory. It is much easier to remember one number (in this case, 1) and one rule (in this case, digits are produced by doubling the preceding number) than it is to recall what appears to be a random series of digits. This is *organization,* the arrangement of parts of a whole in such a manner that the parts are related to each other. The analogy to study strategies is obvious; whenever information can be organized into meaningful patterns, retention and retrieval of information will be facilitated.

A second type of mental organization is *chunking.* Bits of information are said to be chunked when they are transformed into one large bit of information. For example, the letters *h c r a o* can be transformed into the word, roach. The advantage in chunking is that a larger bit of information, e.g., roach, requires no more memory than a smaller bit of information, e.g., *c,* (Miller, 1956). Because it permits the storage of large amounts of information without placing a corresponding strain on memory, chunking is an efficient means of organizing information.

A third type of mental organization is *mnemonics,* association devices for triggering recall. Perhaps the most familiar mnemonic device is the *acronym.* The process of acronymy is one in which words are formed by combining the initial letters or segments of a series of words. AWOL (absent without leave), VIP (very important person), and radar (radio detecting and ranging) are common examples of acronyms. Tying a string around your finger, remembering how to spell "piece" with the phrase "piece of pie," or improving recall of names by distorting them (e.g., "Baldwin" becomes "bald one") represent other types of mnemonic devices.

ACTIVITY

Directions: Develop a set of at least 10 specific mnemonic devices that could be used to assist in the recall of specific information in your content area. Include acronyms but do not limit your devices to them.

Rehearsal

The acquisition, retention, and recall of information are all assisted by rehearsal or practice. *Rehearsal* is a natural strategy that people use to keep information in memory. In the case of short-term memory, information is repeated over and over until the immediate need for information desists. For instance, it is normal to look up a telephone number, rehearse it rapidly during the act of dialing, and then forget the number as soon as the dialing has been completed.

In the case of long-term memory, recall of information is improved most through *distributed* practice, in which rehearsals are separated by some break. For example, the retention and recall of specific facts and historical trends derived from a social studies lecture will be better with frequent, spaced, and brief periods of study (rehearsal) than with a single massive study session.

Time On Task

While it is almost certainly true that the organization of practice affects retention and recall (e.g., distributed versus massed practice), it is equally true of the raw amount of time spent practicing. In fact, it has been argued that some strategies or teaching techniques appear to improve learning primarily because they result in students spending more time on learning tasks, and not because the techniques are better than others (Carver, 1987; Dyer, Riley, & Yekovich, 1979). For example, which of the following strategies would result in the best recall: (1) reading and then outlining a textbook chapter; or (2) reading and then answering teacher-prepared questions over the content? To some degree, the answer would be dependent upon the amount of time each technique caused students to study.

Depth of Processing

Most college graduates are capable of solving an algebra problem such as (a):

$$a. \quad x - 14 = 23$$

On the other hand most college graduates probably could not solve an equation like (b), in spite of the fact that they were undoubtedly forced in high school to work problems at this level of difficulty:

$$b. \quad y = \frac{x^3 \times 5x^2 + 6x}{x + 3}$$

One justification for introducing difficult material is that it helps to guarantee the long-term retention of basic principles and processes. In other words, it is possible that people retain the ability to solve problem (a), not because it is easy but because they were made to expend great mental energies solving problems like (b). This is the principle of *depth of processing,* which asserts that there is a greater likelihood of long-term retention and recall when: (1) the mental activity demands a deeper level of thinking, (2) more schemata are committed to the task, and (3) the degree of semantic analysis is high (Anderson & Armbruster, 1984). The depth of processing principle also explains why a new vocabulary word and its definition will be remembered longer and with greater accuracy by most people if the word is introduced with such elements as context, morphemic analysis, and an etymology. You guarantee better memory for the word and its fundamental meaning by forcing a deeper, more expansive mental processing of the word and its associations.

Encoding Specificity

In addition to the effective study principles of attention, goal orientation, organization, and rehearsal, another principle plays an often overlooked role in the effectiveness of a student's study effort. The principle of *encoding specificity* refers to the way in which a student encodes or studies text information and the degree to which this encoding process matches subsequent recall tasks (Gall, Gall, Jacobsen, & Bullock, 1990). For example, if a student studies information in biology on cell structure and function using a graphic organizer with the expectation that this information will be tested on a simple matching test, and is then required to write an essay explaining cell structure and function, the likelihood of success is low. Why? The original cell structure and function information was encoded in a fashion that does not match the more involved organizational task of writing an essay. It would be far better to give students guidance and practice in essay writing about the topic rather than having them study in a way that would likely impede their success on the essay test. On the other hand, if you want to keep grade inflation under control, simply violate the principle of encoding specificity on a regular basis by developing tests that in no way match students' study strategies!

Specific Strategies

Strategy implies intent. A strategy is not an accident but is rather the planned means to an end. In general, it is best to plan study strategies that have the following characteristics:

1. They help students focus attention on important information.

2. They provide students with meaningful study goals.

3. They help students organize information.

4. They cause students to practice.

5. They encourage deep processing of information.

The study strategies that follow are plans that teachers and students can implement cooperatively to further the acquisition, retention, and recall of information.

Listening and Taking Notes

Notetaking during lectures and discussions is one of the most common events in the classroom, yet there is considerable confusion over the purposes and best methods of taking notes. In fact, there are many note-taking systems but none of them have empirical documentation (Heinrichs & LaBranche, 1986).

Notetaking has two presumed functions, external storage and encoding. The *external storage* (the notes themselves) of information serves as a substitute for memory and gives students an opportunity to review material that might otherwise have been forgotten. The *encoding* function presumably improves the comprehension and retention of information by forcing the notetaker to transform lecture material into personally meaningful language (depth of processing principle). The difference between external storage and encoding is often described as a contrast between taking and having notes. The validity of the encoding function is based on the assumption that during the course of a lecture students will be able to mentally transform what they are hearing. Pauk (1979) rejects this assumption on the grounds that fast presentation rates during lectures preclude the reflective thought necessary for such encoding. In fact, it is quite possible that taking any kind of notes is detrimental to learning if the material is presented too quickly. The consensus is that the external storage function in notetaking is more important than the encoding function (Spires & Stone, 1989).

In addition to the question of notetaking purposes, there is also disagreement regarding the best procedures for notetaking. For instance, it is customary for students to take notes in *parallel,* i.e., to be writing and listening at the same time. However, research (Aiken, Thomas, & Shennum, 1975) suggests that *spaced* notetaking improves recall of lecture material. A spaced presentation is one in which the lecture is broken into segments, followed by intervals of silence several minutes long. Students listen during each lecture segment and then make notes at the interval which follows. Why this should be an effective notetaking procedure is explained in part by the limits of human attention. If people can concentrate on only one task at a time, why should we expect students to write and lis-

ten effectively at the same time? Most notetakers probably switch back and forth; i.e., they listen for a few seconds and then hear, perhaps, but do not listen during those seconds in which individual notes are recorded. The result for many notetakers is incomplete lecture information that has been received in bits and pieces. In contrast, a spaced notetaking procedure permits students to focus their complete attention on listening to the teacher and on encoding lecture information into meaningful notes.

The following statements, based on research, summarize what is presently hypothesized about notetaking (McAndrew, 1983; Spires & Stone, 1989):

1. The external storage of notes is more important than the act of taking notes (encoding).

2. Parallel notetaking may interfere with the reception of forthcoming lecture information, especially when students do not engage in self-monitoring of their comprehension.

3. Teachers should use a spaced lecture format.

4. The rate at which notes are delivered appears to affect the value of notes.

5. The value of notes is much reduced if the notes are not used for practice.

6. Teachers should place important information on the blackboard to cue notetaking.

7. Teachers should use handouts to supplement notetaking.

Teacher Strategies. It is easy to assume that the quality of student notes is nothing more than a function of students' intelligence and other attributes. However, the lecture situation is a meeting of minds, and the organization and presentation format of the lecture can affect the quality of the notes radically. Here is a list of suggestions that will make notetaking easier and more efficient for students in your lectures and class presentations.

1. Do not lecture if students are expected to write down and remember everything you say. Instead, type the material and hand it out. Lectures are more interesting if they include elements of discussion.

2. Lectures typically follow the same organizational patterns found in texts (Lopate, 1987), e.g., cause/effect and comparison/contrast. Point these patterns out to students while you are lecturing, and tell them about how you have organized your notes. For example, if you have three points to make under each of two headings, let students know so that they can make appropriate room in their notes.

3. Notetaking should not be a game in which the student has to guess about what is important. It is absurd to assume that novices in chemistry or political science should, without guidance, instantly sort essential ideas from trivial details. Write important information on the board, or just tell students when to take notes and when not to.

4. Speak slowly.

5. Use a spaced notetaking procedure. Allow students to listen to your lecture for ten minutes or so. Then give them time to write and ask you questions. This will prevent the students from having to write and listen at the same time (capacity limitation problem).

6. Give students a few minutes at the end of class to revise and/or supplement their notes, and make them do it!

7. Give students distributed practice with their notes. Encourage them to review their notes on a nightly basis or in class. You can give students frequent quizzes over lecture material, allowing them to review their notes before the quiz or even allowing an open-notebook quiz. Another review possibility is to have students create questions strictly from their notes for a class review. In general, anything you can do to get the students to modify and refer back to their notes will boost their recall and retention.

8. Have open-note, but closed-book, quizzes to give students an idea of the quality of their notes. Students who take the time to revise notes and to review them will perform better; this in turn will encourage others to revise and review.

Student Strategies. We believe that it is a good idea for students to learn to take good notes, and we define good notes as any notes, however disorganized, sloppy, or idiosyncratic, that will serve as a successful warehouse for lecture information. We know of no one best notetaking procedure for all people of all ages in all subject areas. Therefore, we recommend considerable latitude in individual notetaking systems.

The notetaking procedure we recommend for students is the *Verbatim Split Page Procedure.* VSPP is a blend of various notetaking systems and is comprised of recording, organizing, and studying from notes.

1. *Recording Notes.* Begin teaching VSPP by having students divide their notebook paper so that 40 percent of each page lies to the left and 60 percent to the right. Instruct students to take notes only on the lefthand side during lectures. All notes should be verbatim and clipped. The idea is to expend minimum amounts of mental energy on writing in order that full attention can be focused on listening to the lecture.

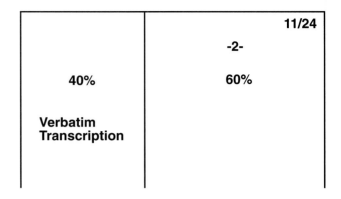

2. *Organizing Notes.* Nearly everyone has had the experience of taking abundant notes for a class, only to find those notes either unreadable or bizarre when it came time to study for the final exam. Abbreviated words, telegraphic sentences, and hasty scribbles may seem quite lucid to the notetaker at the time they are written; however, as the context in which the idiosyncratic shorthand was produced fades, notes of this sort rapidly lose meaning and integrity. For this reason, it is necessary to reorganize notes during significant pauses within the lecture or immediately following the lecture.

The right side of the notebook paper is used for reorganizing and expanding upon the scribbles to the left. Students should be encouraged to:

1. Place lecture information in an outline format;

2. Interpret notes and then encode them in their own words;

3. Expand notes to include lecture information that the student didn't have time to note; and

4. Write out whole words, phrases, and sentences so that notes will be clear in the future. (See Figure 1.)

It is sometimes recommended that students take notes in an outline format. This is an extremely difficult task for two reasons. First, deciding which ideas are superordinate and which are subordinate requires attention that notetakers can't spare as they play the role of listener. Secondly, lectures are hardly ever organized and presented in ways which immediately

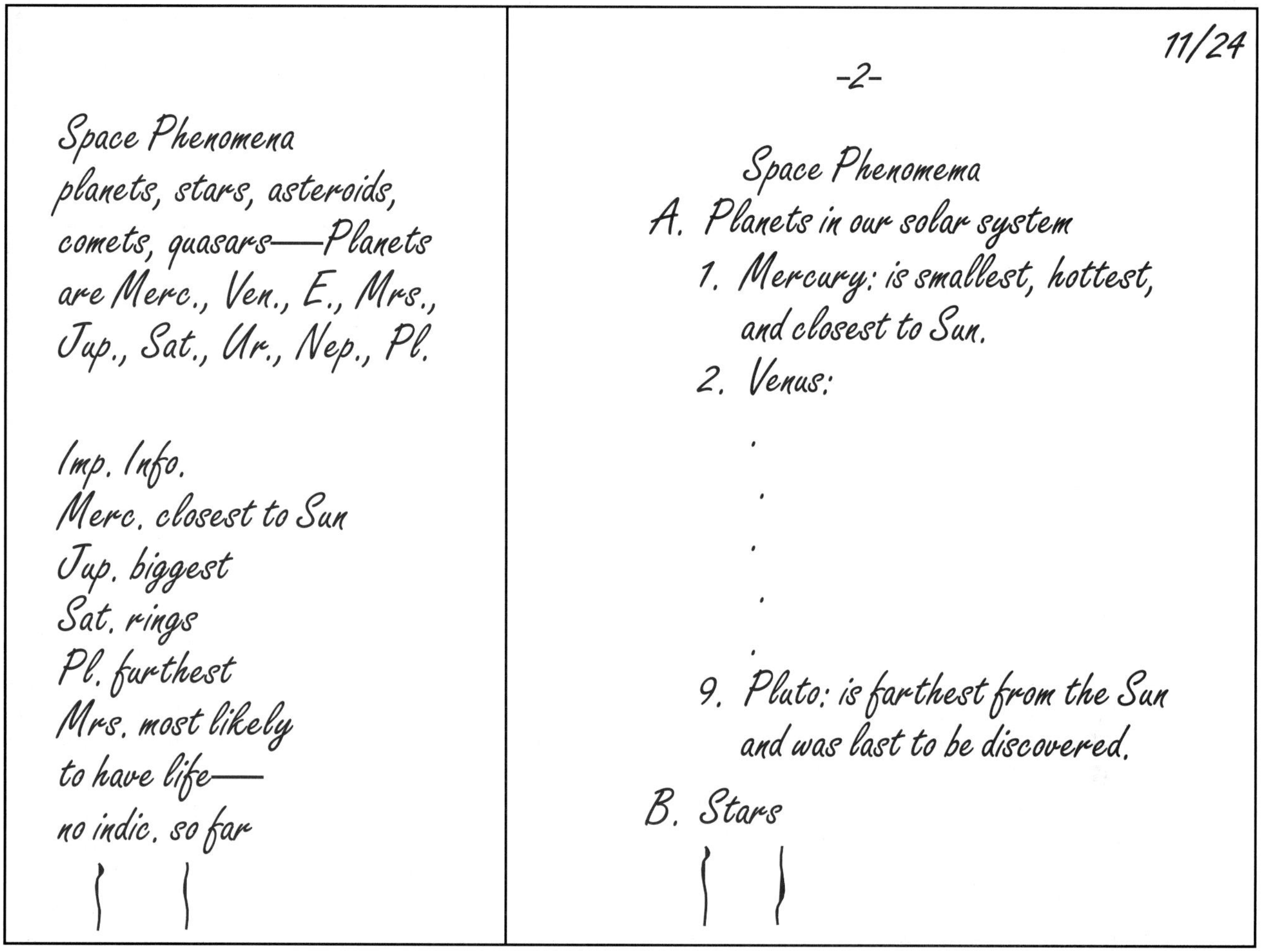

Space Phenomena
planets, stars, asteroids, comets, quasars—Planets are Merc., Ven., E., Mrs., Jup., Sat., Ur., Nep., Pl.

Imp. Info.
Merc. closest to Sun
Jup. biggest
Sat. rings
Pl. furthest
Mrs. most likely to have life—
no indic. so far

-2-

Space Phenomema
A. Planets in our solar system
   1. Mercury: is smallest, hottest, and closest to Sun.
   2. Venus:
   .
   .
   .
   .
   .
   9. Pluto: is farthest from the Sun and was last to be discovered.
B. Stars

Figure 1. Organizing Notes

lend themselves to outline notetaking. In Figure 1 it is clear that the lecture on space phenomena began with an overview of superordinate concepts and then later presented subordinate bits of information. In reality, most lectures and other teacher presentations are punctuated frequently with digressions and slices of knowledge that are improperly layered within the lecture. With the help of limited verbatim notes, students should be able to rethink and reorganize the lecture material AFTER the lecture is over and when the entire presentation is fresh in their minds.

In addition to the split-page notetaking structure, teaching students to consciously self-monitor their notetaking before a lecture begins, and after the lecture ends, can improve their notetaking performance (Spires & Stone, 1989). Based on teacher modeling of the following self-questioning routine, students should begin and end lecture notetaking with the following questions:

Before the lecture begins:

1. What is my purpose for listening to this lecture?

2. Am I interested in this topic and, if not, how will I increase interest and concentration? (e.g., through an argumentative stance where I disagree with the author's point of view)

After the lecture ends:

1. Did I achieve my purpose?

2. Did I maintain concentration and deal with comprehension failures?

Adding a comprehension monitoring dimension to the split-page procedure increases students' active processing and prepares them for the more advanced lecture and notetaking tasks they will encounter in college.

Metacognition

Broadly defined, *metacognition* refers to awareness of one's own mental processes, that is, knowing how you know what to do. It entails an effort to manage one's own thoughts through conscious planning. People who have good metacognitive skills understand their own

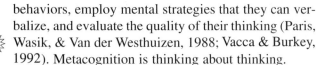

behaviors, employ mental strategies that they can verbalize, and evaluate the quality of their thinking (Paris, Wasik, & Van der Westhuizen, 1988; Vacca & Burkey, 1992). Metacognition is thinking about thinking.

Most children do not have good metacognitive skills. The most common response children give when asked why they have done something is: "I don't know." Sometimes they hide behind the "I don't know" when they do not wish to respond to parents, teachers, or other authority figures. For example:

Dad to teenage
Daughter: "I told you to be home at 12 last night. Why did you come home at 3 A.M.?"

Teenage Daughter
to Dad: "I don't know."

Of course, the real thought of the teenage daughter is: "Jimmy and I were too busy kissing to pay attention to your stupid rule." On the other hand, young people frequently do not understand or even attempt to monitor their own thought processes, and this is often true in the area of reading comprehension. Too many students rove mindlessly through a textbook assignment without any clearly defined purposes or conscious strategies for learning. Current research in the area of metacognition indicates that students who have good metacognitive skills are better comprehenders (Wade & Reynolds, 1989). Therefore, helping your students to develop their metacognitive awareness is fundamental to study strategies.

Teacher Strategies. One approach to developing metacognition in students is the *think-aloud* technique (Nist & Kirby, 1986; Randall, Fairbanks, & Kennedy, 1986). The think-aloud technique is a teacher-modeling strategy in which the teacher reads aloud from a text and verbalizes whatever comes to mind in an effort to show students how to reason during reading. The teacher's verbalized thoughts may include questions, predictions, paraphrases, evaluative statements, and even text-irrelevant comments. Here are the steps in the strategy:

1. Select a passage between 100 and 300 words long in your subject area. The passage should be fairly difficult so that your reasoning is actually useful to the students. If the passage is too easy the students will not see the value of what you are doing.

2. Prepare your comments for the think-aloud based on your experiences. Because the material will not really be difficult for you, you need to plan an idealized set of think-aloud

responses. You will be acting the part of a student with good metacognitive skills.

3. Explain to the students exactly what you are doing, e.g., "I am going to show you how I think when I read."

4. Read the passage to the class and insert your planned think-alouds as you go.

5. When you are finished, give students a chance to ask you questions about how you think or about the think-aloud procedure itself.

6. Have students practice thinking aloud with smaller segments of the text.

The paragraph below exemplifies a think-aloud for a biology text. The teacher's questions and statements are indicated by superscripts within the paragraph and referenced below the paragraph.

Amniocentesis[1] is a technique used by fetologists[2] when the parents are known or suspected to carry one of several types of genetic disease or when the woman is over age 40.[3] Older women are more likely to have a fetus with Down's syndrome.[4] The diseases specifically tested for are caused by having an extra or missing chromosome, a chromosome which has been broken,[5] or a metabolic disease such as phenylketonuria.[6] A hypodermic needle is inserted through the abdomen of the pregnant woman[7] and into the amnion.[8] A small amount of amniotic fluid, containing fetal cells,[9] is drawn into the syringe. These cells are then cultured (grown) for a period of time; when enough culture cells are available, they can be tested for many metabolic defects. Cells can also be specially stained and prepared so that the chromosomes can be seen under a microscope.[10] (Brum, 1978, p. 105).

1. Looks like this is the topic. I better remember this word.

2. What's this? Someone who studies feet?

3. I didn't know people that old could have babies.

4. OK, I know about that. A boy in our church has it.

5. How do you lose a chromosome or get it broken? Could it happen to me if I play football or get in an accident? How will I know?

6. I wonder what nerd made up this word.

7. Ouch!

8. Better ask the teacher what this is.

9. I get it now. Fetal refers to fetus, an unborn baby. That explains what a fetologist is, an unborn baby doctor.

10. Sounds cool; I'd like to see it.

Student Strategies. Most of the strategies in this text will improve metacognitive skills to some extent. For instance, Loxterman, Beck, and McKeown (1994) found that when middle grades students used a think-aloud strategy they improved their comprehension, particularly with more friendly text. Nevertheless, students need a guiding mental strategy for studying. *PLAE* (Simpson & Nist, 1984; Nist, Simpson, Olejnik, & Mealey, 1991) is an acronym that stands for *P*replan, *L*ist, *A*ctivate, *E*valuate.

> Preplan: Plan how to study. This may entail asking questions such as: "Should I summarize, take notes, or reread?" "What kind of a test is the instructor going to give?" "Do I want to study by myself or in a small group?"
>
> List: The answers to such questions should result in planned behaviors rather than thoughtless or

reflexive ones. The planned behaviors should be written down. For example: "I will read this chapter twice." "I will ask my teacher whether the test will be essay or multiple-choice." "I will ask Marty and Beth if they want to study with me tomorrow."

> Activate: This is a monitoring behavior. Basically the student needs to regularly ask, "Am I following my plan?"
>
> Evaluate: Students assess whether or not the plan has worked. For example: "Was it worth studying with Marty and Beth?" "Would I do it again?"

PLAE is deceptively simple, so much so that you may be tempted to dismiss it as superfluous. Yet we believe that a strategy as simple as this is fundamental and not at all too obvious to bother with as you are teaching. How many times have you gotten to school or the office only to discover that you had forgotten your lunch, house keys, wallet, purse, term paper, or other important item? If the average American adult simply stopped at the front door before leaving and asked, "Do I have everything I need to take with me?" it would probably save millions in gasoline and aspirin.

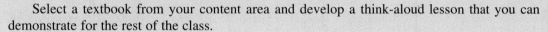

ACTIVITY

Select a textbook from your content area and develop a think-aloud lesson that you can demonstrate for the rest of the class.

Reading Daily Assignments

One of the content teacher's ever-present problems is how to get students to comprehend better and retain more information from textbook reading assignments (Henk & Helfeldt, 1992). How does the teacher convert the passive page-watcher into a reader who is actively engaged in reconstructing and evaluating the author's thoughts?

Unfortunately, the best method of responding while reading, writing in the text, is not an option for most students because the books belong to the school. Underlining main ideas, starring important terms, asking and answering questions, and making evaluative comments in the margins combine to make a highly personal and convenient response mode during reading. In the absence of this option, however, it is necessary to consider alternative study strategies.

Teacher Strategies. Avoid giving assignments such as, "OK, read pages 24–43 for Monday." Assignments

like this make the completion of page 43 the objective of the assignment. A much better assignment would be "OK, read pages 27–43. When you are finished you should be able to answer these questions . . ." or "As you are reading, write down at least 10 words, facts, procedures, or explanations you didn't understand." By the time you have finished detailing the reading assignment, your students should be able to answer the following questions:

1. What is this reading assignment about?

2. Why am I reading this?

3. What should I know when I have finished?

In fact, students have a right to this information and should be encouraged to ask for it whenever they find themselves facing purposeless reading assignments.

Student Strategies. The two strategies we recommend for daily reading assignments are FLIP and Student-Generated Questions.

FLIP, *F*riendliness, *L*anguage, *I*nterest, and *P*rior knowledge (Schumm & Mangrum, 1991), is a text-book previewing procedure designed to teach students how to evaluate the difficulty of daily reading assignments and allocate study time in a realistic manner. The strategy is highly personal and intentionally subjective because students need to learn how to manage reading and study assignments in ways which are consistent with their own abilities, interests, and schedules. The FLIP chart on page 215 can be used when students are initially learning textbook reading assignments. The steps are described below and correspond to categories on the FLIP chart.

1. Students record the reading assignment on the top of the FLIP chart.

2. Students skim the reading assignment and make a value judgement for each of the four FLIP categories: Friendliness, Language, Interest, and Prior knowledge. In the case of vocabulary, students read three paragraphs at random to check the level of unfamiliar vocabulary. Each of the four categories is given a rating from 1 to 5 with 1 being the most negative and 5 being the most positive.

3. Based on the FLIP category ratings, students make an overall assessment of how comfortable the reading level is for them.

4. Students identify their purpose for reading, estimate how fast they should attempt to read, and then budget their reading time by dividing the assignment into as many chunks as they feel are necessary.

The FLIP procedure requires considerable metacognition on the part of students, and learning to make decisions about their own reading behaviors may be difficult for many of them at first. For this reason it is recommended that teachers select an assignment and model FLIP with a think-aloud and the help of an overhead projector. Students can complete the FLIP chart as part of a group activity in which the students fill in the chart as the teacher completes each step of the think-aloud.

Schumm and Mangrum note that the purpose of FLIP is not to have students fill out and turn in forms. Instead they view FLIP as a set of metacognitive training wheels which helps students become aware of factors that influence their reading comprehension. Sooner or later students should learn to make FLIP decisions automatically and without the need for a chart.

In addition to the comprehension techniques presented in Chapters 9 and 10, we recommend using *student-generated questions* when they read. Questions can be used for purposes of in-class review or they may

be questions that the student truly does not know the answer to. We highly recommend using the ReQuest procedure (Chapter 10) to teach students how to ask questions at different levels: text explicit (reading the lines), text implicit (reading between the lines), and experience-based (reading beyond the lines). Be patient; some students will have a very difficult time formulating questions that involve inferences (text implicit). There are three basic strategies to give students for deriving questions from reading assignments:

1. *Personal Review.* Students should ask questions in order to eliminate confusions left over from their reading assignment. Each question should have a page number along with it so that you and the class can refer directly to the source of the confusion. In many cases, students with the greatest comprehension problems will be the least likely to volunteer questions. Praise these reluctant students for asking questions, even if the questions seem superfluous or oblique.

2. *Class Review.* Assign students to write a set number of questions based on a reading assignment. You might, for example, assign them to create three text explicit questions, two experience-based questions, and one text implicit question. During the following class you can have students take turns asking and answering questions, or you might create teams for a question-and-answer showdown. In any case give lots of praise for good questions, especially if they are text implicit.

3. *Stump the Teacher.* Students will enjoy creating questions to test you. Again, try to get them to generate legitimate questions at a variety of levels by modeling for them the kinds of questions you might ask one of your college professors. Students may at first be inclined to ask trivial, text explicit questions, e.g., "How many words are on page 144?" However, with guidance from you the students should begin to ask the kinds of questions that will stimulate class discussions.

Graphic Comprehension

Graphic comprehension, or *graphic literacy,* refers to the ability to interpret charts, maps, graphs, and other visual presentations that are commonly used to supplement the prose of textbooks, nonfiction trade books, and newspapers. These visual representations of concepts in nonverbal or semiverbal form tend to be difficult for students, yet are ignored as specific instructional objectives in basals and other school texts (Fry, 1981).

FLIP Chart *

Title of Assignment_____

Number of pages _____

General directions: Rate each of the four FLIP categories on a 1–5 scale (5 = high). Then determine your purpose for reading and appropriate reading rate, and budget your reading/study time.

F = Friendliness: How friendly is my assignment?

Directions: Examine your assignment to see if it includes the friendly elements listed below.

Friendly text features

Table of contents	Index	Glossary
Chapter introductions	Headings	Subheadings
Margin notes	Study questions	Chapter summary
Key terms highlighted	Graphs	Charts
Pictures	Signal words	Lists of key facts

1 - - - - - - - - - - - - - - 2 - - - - - - - - - - - - - - - - - - - 3 - - - - - - - - - - - - - - - - - - - 4 - - - - - - - - - - - - - - - - - 5

No friendly   Some friendly   Many friendly
text features   text features   text features

Friendliness rating _____

L = Language: How difficult is the language in my reading assignment?

Directions: Skim the chapter quickly to determine the number of new terms. Read 3 random paragraphs to get a feel for the vocabulary level and number of long, complicated sentences.

1 - - - - - - - - - - - - - - 2 - - - - - - - - - - - - - - - - - - - 3 - - - - - - - - - - - - - - - - - - - 4 - - - - - - - - - - - - - - - - - 5

Many new words;   Some new words;   No new words; clear
complicated   somewhat complicated   sentences
sentences   sentences

Language rating _____

I = Interest: How interesting is my reading assignment?

Directions: Read the title, introduction, heading/subheadings, and summary. Examine the pictures and graphics included.

1 - - - - - - - - - - - - - - 2 - - - - - - - - - - - - - - - - - - - 3 - - - - - - - - - - - - - - - - - - - 4 - - - - - - - - - - - - - - - - - 5

Boring   Somewhat   Very
        interesting   interesting

Interest rating _____

P = Prior knowledge: What do I already know about the material covered in my reading assignment?

Directions: Think about the title, introduction, headings/subheadings, and summary.

1 - - - - - - - - - - - - - - 2 - - - - - - - - - - - - - - - - - - - 3 - - - - - - - - - - - - - - - - - - - 4 - - - - - - - - - - - - - - - - - 5

Mostly new   Some new   Mostly familiar
information   infomation   information

Prior knowledge rating _____
FLIP Rating Total _____

Overall, this reading assignment appears to be at:
☐ a comfortable reading level for me
☐ a somewhat comfortable reading level for me
☐ an uncomfortable reading level for me

My purpose for reading is (circle one):
  A. personal pleasure
  B. to prepare for class discussions
  C. to answer written questions for class assignment or for homework
  D. to prepare for a test
  E. other: _____
  _____

My reading rate should be (circle one):
  A. slow - allowing time for rereading if necessary
  B. medium - careful and analytical
  C. fast - steady, skipping sections that are about information I already know

Active reading time
Chunk #1, pages_____-_____, estimated time: _____ min.
Chunk #2, pages_____-_____, estimated time: _____ min.
Chunk #3, pages_____-_____, estimated time: _____ min.
Chunk #4, pages_____-_____, estimated time: _____ min.

Total estimate time: _____ min.

* Figure from FLIP: A framework for content area reading. Jeanne Shay Schumm and Charles T. Mangrum II, *Journal of Reading,* 35(2), 120-124. October 1991. Reprinted with permission of Jeanne Shay Schumm and the International Reading Association.

Teacher Strategies. Do not assume that your students will understand even simple pie graphs. If the purposes and designs of graphs have never been explained to them, many students will automatically skip graphs, an unfortunate behavior, since graphs are designed to improve comprehension—not create interference.

As a prereading activity, you should introduce graphs as you would new and important vocabulary. Have students open their texts to the graphs. Then explain the purposes of the graphs to them and demonstrate correct procedures for their interpretations, e.g., how to plot points on a complex quantitative graph. We also recommend that you try the *Graphic Information Lesson* (Reinking, 1986). The GIL has three stages:

1. In the *introductory stage* the teacher shows the students a graph and explains the mechanics of its use. Then the teacher asks text explicit, text implicit, and experience-based questions that are designed to enlighten the students as to the relationship between the graph and the rest of the text. Students can also learn to judge whether the graph is supplemental, redundant, or complementary to the text.

2. In the *synthesizing stage* the teacher presents teacher-made *pseudographics,* graphs that are related to current text material but which may or may not be accurate or believable. The students have to be able to relate the new graph to what they have learned from the text in order to judge its validity. They must also document their decision with a page number from the text.

3. In the *application stage* students are asked to: a) develop their own pseudographs to accompany the text, or b) critique the author's use of graphic aids. (Examples of pseudographs follow.)

Test Preparation

Evaluation tends to be an anxiety-producing situation for teachers or students. Anxiety can be reduced and learning maximized if teachers prepare students for specific examinations and if students learn how to study for and take tests intelligently.

Teacher Strategies. Middle and secondary students typically fear examinations and mistrust teachers' motivations. Many students develop a neurosis over tests because they have stereotyped teachers as a group of ogres who try to trick them with unfair questions or who purposely do not reveal what material a test will cover so that they can have the pleasure of

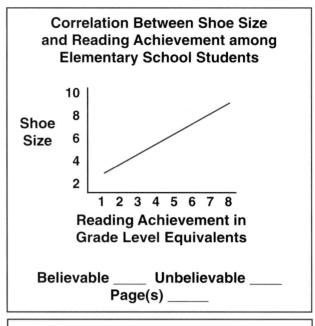

Correlation Between Shoe Size and Reading Achievement among Elementary School Students

Shoe Size

Reading Achievement in Grade Level Equivalents

Believable _____ Unbelievable _____
Page(s) _____

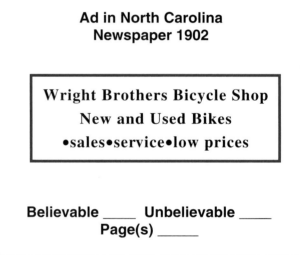

Ad in North Carolina Newspaper 1902

**Wright Brothers Bicycle Shop
New and Used Bikes
•sales•service•low prices**

Believable _____ Unbelievable _____
Page(s) _____

Examples of Pseudographs

doling out bad grades. To prove to your students that you are not a test-ogre we suggest that you: a) give students precise information about what material an exam will cover, and b) give students ungraded practice in taking the kinds of tests they will later have to negotiate for grades. We recommend the *Fake Pop Quiz* (FPQ).

The FPQ is a quiz which is designed to reinforce rather than test recently introduced information. The purpose of the quiz format is to stimulate interest. Students are considerably more alert following, "Get your pencils ready; it's time for a fake pop quiz," than they are after hearing, "Get your pencils ready; it's time to do some review exercises." Tests are really a lot of fun once the anxiety over being externally evaluated has been neutralized. In addition, students appreciate test simulations because they know that the teacher is trying to prepare them for the true evaluation that inevitably follows.

FPQ's can be brief interludes in daily lessons (placed on the blackboard) or comprehensive reviews prepared on dittos. In either case, the quiz should be preceded by general directions, either verbal or written, along the lines of the following:

> Today we are having a fake pop quiz on earth science vocabulary. Obviously, the score you get on this quiz won't affect your grade in the course, but it will give you some practice and an idea of how well prepared you are for a real test. When everyone has finished the quiz, you will score your own and get two points for each correct answer. Good luck! (The FPQ may be open- or closed-book depending upon the teacher's objectives and the nature of the exercises.)

Once students have finished the quiz, specific questions can serve as guides to classroom discussion. The FPQ offers a golden opportunity to focus on text implicit and experience-based kinds of questions.

Student Strategies. Students can acquire confidence in their own test-taking abilities if they learn how to prepare for exams and how to cope with them logically. The following information can help your students meet these objectives.

Test-taking skills refer to long-term study strategies as well as to strategies that students can use while taking exams, often referred to as testwiseness. You should be doing frequent reviews of text material, class notes, and other assigned materials. Remember, lots of short study sessions are better than a few giant cramming sessions. Students can be given the following advice for preparing for content area exams:

When you hear about the test.

1. Find out as much as you can about the test itself.

2. Find out exactly when the test will be given.

3. Ask your teachers to discuss the kinds of questions that will be on the test, e.g., multiple choice, true-false, or essay.

4. If your teachers give essay tests, ask them what they look for in a good essay answer.

5. Ask your teachers to give you examples of test items and good test answers. Many will be willing to do this, but almost none will do it if you don't ask.

6. Try to guess which questions your teacher will ask.

The night before the test.

1. A light study session should be enough. Do not cram!

2. Make sure you have pencils, pens, paper, a watch, a calculator (if permissible), and any other materials you may need for the exam.

3. Get a good night's sleep.

The day of the test.

1. Eat a good breakfast.

2. Tell yourself that you will do well on the exam.

3. Make sure you have all the materials you need for the exam.

4. Do not cram right before the test. That is the worst thing you can do. Cramming can cause students to forget important information. Cramming also causes needless test anxiety.

Testwiseness refers to a series of principles that can be applied to exams independently of subject area knowledge. To be testwise is to be able to (1) exploit the flaws in teacher-made exams, and (2) apply logic, common sense, and good organization in test-taking situations. Testwiseness by itself will not guarantee good grades in grade school or college. There is no substitute for studying hard and being knowledgeable. However, testwiseness skills can help students to do a better job on classroom tests.

The present discussion will be limited to the most common types of exams: multiple choice, true/false, and essay.

Multiple Choice Tests. Students probably take more multiple choice tests than any other kind. The most usual variety of multiple choice item consists of a stem and several options. For example:

World War II ended in   (Stem)

1. 1960
2 1944   (Options)
3. 1945
4. 1955

The following strategies will help students to be testwise on multiple choice tests.

1. Read all directions carefully. It is not unusual for students to get poor grades on exams simply because they fail to read and follow directions.

2. Budget your time so that you are certain to finish the test. Students sometimes spend too much time on one part of the test and then fail to finish another. Nothing hurts a test grade worse than leaving items blank.

3. Do not waste time on items which are very difficult. Come back to them at the end of the exam.

4. Assume that each item has a correct answer and that you are smart enough to figure it out one way or another.

5. Always guess if you don't know the answer. Never leave a multiple choice question blank.

6. If the right answer is not obvious to you right away, try to eliminate obvious wrong or silly answers and then guess from among those that remain. For example,

The speed of sound is

   A. 3700 feet per second
   B. 1087 feet per second
   C. 0
   D. 186 miles per second

You should be able to eliminate answer C right away. That would give you a 1/3 chance of guessing right instead of 1/4 chance.

7. Whenever two of the options are identical, both answers must be wrong. For example,

The universal donor is

   A. O –
   B. H_2O
   C. AB
   D. water

8. Whenever two of the options are opposites, one of them is always wrong and the other is often, but not always, right. For example,

A proton is a

   A. positively charged particle
   B. free atom
   C. negatively charged particle
   D. displaced neutron

9. Be aware that the answer to a question may appear in the stem of another question. For example, the answer to item *I* can be found in the stem of item II.

I. A z-score is a

   A. percentile equivalent
   B. concept in criterion referenced testing
   C. measure of standard error
   D. standardized score

II. Standardized scores such as z-scores and t-scores are based on

   A. standard deviations
   B. stanines
   C. chi squares
   D. grade equivalents

10. Be alert for alternatives that do not match the stem grammatically. Teachers sometimes make this mistake. For example,

The smallest unit of sound capable of making a meaning distinction in language is a

   A. morpheme
   B. allophone
   C. phoneme
   D. tagmeme

11. When alternatives seem equally good, select the one that is longest and seems to hold the most information. For example,

In the United States, inferior intellectual development is most often caused by

   A. poor nutrition
   B. divorce
   C. the combined effects of heritability and environmental deprivation
   D. television

12. When all else fails, select an option which is not the first choice or the last. For example,

The probability of rolling a 12 with two dice is

   A. 3 in 12
   B. 1 in 12
   C. 1 in 36
   D. 2 in 19

True-False Tests. True-false questions are actually statements that students must decide are true or untrue. Major examinations are seldom composed entirely of true-false questions. However, many teachers like to include a section of these on their tests. True-false tests are feared by many students, who believe that teachers are trying to trick them into a lower grade. In reality most teachers are just interested in finding out how much the students know. Here are some testwise principles for true-false tests.

1. Read all directions carefully.

2. Budget your time so that you are certain to finish the test.

3. Always guess if you don't know the answer. Never leave a true-false question blank.

4. If any part of the statement is false, the correct answer for the item is "false." For example, the following item is false because the second part of the statement is false.

The United States entered World War II after the Japanese attacked San Francisco.

5. Be alert for the words "never" and "always." These absolutes often indicate a wrong answer. For example, item *A* is false because it does occasionally rain in the desert. On the other hand, item *B* is true because the word "never" is qualified.

    A. It never rains in the Sahara Desert.
    B. It almost never rains in the Sahara Desert.

ACTIVITY

Identify a course outside your area of expertise. Ask the instructor if you can take one of his or her multiple choice exams to practice your test-taking strategies.

6. Long statements are somewhat more likely to be true than short statements. For example, *A* is true and *B* is false.

    A. In the poem *Ozymandias* Shelley uses irony to make a statement about the mortality of man.
    B. Ozymandias was a monk.

7. Assume that the teacher is asking straightforward questions. In other words, do not turn an obviously true statement into a false one by creating wild possible exceptions in your mind. For example, item *A* is true in spite of the fact that *B, C,* and *D* are, if you have a strong imagination, contradictions to the statement.

    A. Shoes are an important part of the business person's physical appearance.
    B. Business people don't wear horse shoes.
    C. Brake shoes are not part of the business person's appearance.
    D. If your pants are too long and cover your shoes, then the shoes won't make any difference.

Essay Tests. Essay tests are among the most difficult exams because they require recall of information, good writing skills, and good organization. Here are some testwise principles for essay tests, followed by an essay test preparation strategy.

1. Read all directions carefully. Essay tests often use in their directions key words that you must clearly understand. Here are some of the key words and their meanings:

Key Word	Meaning
enumerate	to name one at a time
illustrate	to explain with examples
trace	to tell the history or development of something from the earliest to the most recent time
compare	to point out similarities and differences
contrast	to point out differences
summarize	to give a brief version of the most important points
evaluate	to judge the merit of
justify	to give reasons for
critique	to summarize and evaluate

Two answers (A and B) are given below for the same essay question. Answer B is a better answer because the writer followed directions and compared (noted similarities and differences) the topics under discussion.

Directions: Compare saccadic and pursuit eye movements.

Answer A: There are two basic kinds of eye movements: saccadic and pursuit. Saccadic movements are used when you go from object to object when the objects are at rest. Pursuit movements follow a moving target. During the act of reading saccadic movements allow the reader to stop on a line of print and pick up information. The word saccade means little jerk.

Answer B: There are two basic kinds of eye movements: saccadic and pursuit. They are the same in the sense that both of them are used to locate visual information. However, they are physically different. Saccadic movements are jumps while the pursuit movement is smooth. Another difference is that saccadic movements let the eyes go from one still object to another while pursuit movement follows a moving target.

2. Budget your time so that you are certain to finish the test. Check to see how much each essay question is worth. Spend the most time on the questions that are worth the most points.

3. Always give some kind of an answer, even if you don't understand the question.

4. Unless the directions say otherwise, never give a minimal answer. Teachers will expect you to elaborate and to give full explanations on an essay. For the essay question below, responses *A*, *B*, and *C* technically answer the question, but only *C* meets the spirit of the essay exam by giving an explanation.

Questions: Do you believe that American troops should fight in foreign wars?
Answer A: No.
Answer B: No. I don't think that Americans should fight in foreign wars.
Answer C: No. I think war is immoral. We should not fight unless we are attacked. Besides, when we sent troops to other countries it makes us look like fascist-capitalistic dogs.

5. Use the technical language of the course when writing an essay. Remember, the teacher wants to find out how much you know. And that includes your knowledge of the appropriate vocabulary. Compare answers *A* and *B* for the essay question below. *B* is a better answer because it uses more technical language.

Question: Summarize the process of conception and the initial stage of prenatal development.
Answer A: The male cell goes up to the egg and digs its way inside. Once this happens the genetic material from the man and the woman mix to form the genetic pattern for the baby.

After this happens the cell begins to split up again and again as the fertilized egg works its way down to the uterus where it will attach itself to the woman's body.

Answer B: The male sperm cell digs its way into the ovum and the egg is fertilized. Once this happens the chromosomes from the sperm cell and the chromosomes from the ovum mix to form the genetic pattern for the baby. After this happens the fertilized ovum begins to reproduce itself through a process called mitosis. As this process continues, the fertilized egg, now called a zygote, works its way down the fallopian tube to the uterus where it will attach itself to the wall of the uterus.

6. Pay attention to capitalization, punctuation, spelling, grammar, and neatness. Proof for these things as you reread your answers. Remember, the grading of essays is largely subjective. A careless presentation of your answer can only reduce your grade.

PORPE: An Essay Writing Strategy

In addition to general student strategies for essay preparation, Simpson (1992) developed and validated a powerful integrated study strategy under the acronym PORPE (Simpson, Stahl, & Hayes, 1989). PORPE stands for: (a) predict; (b) organize; (c) rehearse; (d) practice; and, (e) evaluate. This five-step strategy involves students in the following sequence of activities:

1. *Predicting* potential essay questions,

2. *Organizing* key ideas using their own words,

3. *Rehearsing* the key ideas,

4. *Practicing* the recall of the key ideas in a self assigned writing task that requires analytical thinking, and

5. *Evaluating* the completeness, accuracy, and appropriateness of the essay in terms of the self predicted essay question.

Unlike many sink or swim essay exam experiences students have, PORPE does not assume that students readily grasp the preparatory and analytical steps involved in writing a strong essay question response. Rather, PORPE offers a step-by-step process to guide students' independent studying for an essay test. Each of the five steps is elaborated in the following section along with a student-predicted essay question from physical education and a student's response.

Step One: Predict. Once students have finished a reading assignment in a unit or lesson where an essay test will be given, have them create potential essay questions, particularly those eliciting higher order thinking through analysis, comparison, and critique. Simpson cautions that you should not assume students grasp the language of essay questions. Rather, she recommends conducting a short session on the language of essay questions including such common requests as explain, criticize, compare, and contrast. In addition, she recommends teacher modeling of the question prediction step. Following this teacher-directed assistance, ask students to create their own predicted essay questions and share these in small groups.

Step Two: Organize. In preparation for responding to the predicted essay question, students should outline, map, or use a graphic organizer to organize the information they plan to use in their written response. Initial teacher modeling and small group sharing of outlines or graphic organizers is also helpful in this step.

Step Three: Rehearse. The idea in this step is to develop a long-term memory for the information in the outline or graphic organizer that needs to be easily retrieved at the time of essay question response. Simpson recommends self-testing by reciting the overall organizational structure of the outline or graphic organizer and writing it out from memory.

Step Four: Practice. This is a key step as students are asked to write the answer to their predicted essay question from recall. However, prior to actually writing, they should sketch the outline or graphic organizer of their rehearsed response to guide the structure and content of their essay.

Step Five: Evaluate. An important final step involves having students evaluate their practice essay answers. You may wish to provide students with a checklist that reiterates the criteria for a good essay response. Simpson recommends including a checklist like the one that follows:

		Below Average	Average	Above Average
1.	The writer answered the question directly.	1	2	3
2.	There was an introductory sentence which restated the essay question or took a position on the question.	1	2	3
3.	The essay was organized with major points or ideas that were made obvious to the reader.	1	2	3
4.	The essay had relevant details or examples to prove and clarify each point.	1	2	3
5.	The writer used transitions to cue the reader.	1	2	3
6.	The writer had knowledge of the content and made sense.	1	2	3

In the example that follows, Ardis, a student in physical education carried out the various steps of PORPE to answer her predicted essay question in preparation for a test. The test was based on the topic, Prosocial Skills for Human Movement, and the teacher indicated that there would be a series of short essay questions.

Step One: Predict. Ardis predicted that the teacher would ask her to: Explain how games reflect culture, based on a subheading in the text chapter on Multicultural Considerations in Physical Education.

Step Two: Organize. Next, Ardis developed a graphic organizer (page 222) showing how games reflect culture based on the information in this section of the text.

Step Three: Rehearse. Ardis then studied, recited, and tested herself on her memory for these key ideas in preparation for writing an essay response.

Step Four: Practice. In this most difficult step, Ardis composes a practice answer to her essay question by first sketching the graphic organizer she created as a guide in writing her response.

Ardis' Practice Essay

Games reflect culture because they represent the values of a cultural group. For example, cooperation and teamwork

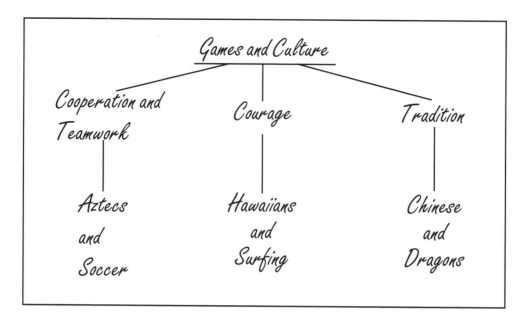

<table>
<tr><td></td><td></td><td>Games and Culture</td><td></td></tr>
<tr><td>Cooperation and Teamwork</td><td>Courage</td><td></td><td>Tradition</td></tr>
<tr><td>Aztecs and Soccer</td><td>Hawaiians and Surfing</td><td></td><td>Chinese and Dragons</td></tr>
</table>

are highly valued by Native American Indians. The game of soccer we play in P. E. that needs careful teamwork was played by the ancient Aztecs in Mexico. Another example is the Hawaiian value of courage or "koa." The ancient Hawaiian royalty fearlessly surfed large waves on heavy koa boards. They tried to ride with a smooth casual style that is now a crucial skill in modern longboarding. And the Chinese value tradition. Their New Year's celebration maintain the ancient traditions by featuring the dragon which symbolizes prosperity, authority, and royalty. Each of these games, soccer, surfing, and the folk dance of the Chinese dragon, display the cultural values of their respective cultural groups.

Step Five: Evaluate. Applying the checklist to Ardis' essay response, she has clearly written a very coherent and carefully planned answer.

		Below Average	Average	Above Average
1.	The writer answered the question directly.	1	2	③
2.	There was an introductory sentence which restated the essay question or took a position on the question.	1	2	③
3.	The essay was organized with major points or ideas that were made obvious to the reader.	1	②	3
4.	The essay had relevant details or examples to prove and clarify each point.	1	2	③
5.	The writer used transitions to cue the reader.	1	②	3
6.	The writer had knowledge of the content and made sense.	1	2	③

It is not surprising that Ardis' essay meets each of these criteria. She applied the steps involved in PORPE and was fully prepared for the essay question. Indeed, research by Simpson, Stahl, and Hayes (1989) aimed at validating PORPE showed that students using this strategy significantly outpaced students using a more traditional read and answer chapter questions approach. Although PORPE takes time to use with students, it develops a studying approach that will serve students well as they advance into more difficult text material in college. Moreover, the movement away from multiple-choice assessment and the increasing interest in essay questions that tap critical thinking make PORPE an ideal strategy to share with your students. Its acronym is admittedly odd, sounding a lot like "porpoise." But it could be worse—how about SHARK!

SUMMARY

In this chapter we have provided a rationale for introducing study strategies in content area classrooms. Time on task, distributed practice, organization, attention, and depth of processing have been described in terms of how they affect retention and recall of information. Strategies that exploit these principles of learning have been introduced: VSPP, think-aloud, FLIP, PLAE, GIL, FPQ, and PORPE. In addition, the chapter has presented basic information on graphic literacy and test-taking skills, including the student-oriented PORPE.

Now go back to the study vignette at the beginning of the chapter. Reacting to the lesson as you did before. Compare your responses with those you made before you read the chapter.

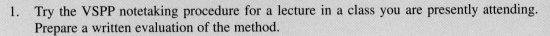

MINI PROJECT

1. Try the VSPP notetaking procedure for a lecture in a class you are presently attending. Prepare a written evaluation of the method.

2. Interview a small group of college students to determine the test-taking strategies they use. List the different strategies they report and then provide a written evaluation indicating the quality of their metacognitive skills in test-taking.

GROUP PROJECTS

- Draw an "unbelievable" pseudograph suitable for your content area. Describe the pseudograph and explain how you might use it with a class of students.

- Compare the following key words, which frequently appear in essay questions: illustrate, contrast, and justify.

- Evaluate the metaphor, metacognitive training wheels, as it pertains to FLIP.

- Explain the relationship between the principle of encoding specificity and students' need to understand the precise nature of the exams they will have to take.

GLOSSARY

Accommodation: the process of adjusting one's existing cognitive structure to accept new information.

Accretion: the accumulation of facts within existing schemata.

Acronym: a word that is formed by combining the initial letters or segments of a series of words.

Aiming Toward Content: teaching which focuses on content acquisition with no consideration for how to acquire that information.

Analogical Guide: a form of study guide in which students use familiar concepts to learn and retain new information.

Anecdotal Records: notes teachers use to record students' behaviors as they interact with text.

Anticipation Guide: a prereading strategy that activates students' ideas about a topic by asking them to react to a series of guide statements related to that topic.

Assimilation: the process whereby new information is simply added to one's existing cognitive structure.

Attitudes: those feelings that cause a reader to approach or avoid a reading situation.

Biographies: Reading and writing about an important figure in any content area.

Biopoem: A creative poetry framework for writing about virtually any major figure or topic in the content areas.

Bottom-Up Processing: reading that progresses from the surface features of print with little regard for comprehension.

Bound Morpheme: a meaningful language unit that occurs only as an attachment to words or other morphemes, e.g., tele-.

Capacity Limitation: refers to the theory that human beings are capable of attending consciously to only one task at a time.

Cause-Effect: a pattern of text organization linking reasons with results.

CD-ROM: computer hardware which reads data from a laser disk and is capable of storing large amounts of data.

Censorship: the indirect supervision of morality by regulating films, books, magazines, music, and other information to which people may have access.

Chunking: a type of mental organization in which related bits of information are processed as a single unit.

Clues and Questions: vocabulary review procedure that centers on student-generated questions and answers.

Cognitive Structure: the interrelated network of our experiences, organized in memory through a system of categories.

Comparison-Contrast: a pattern or text organization that demonstrates likenesses and differences between things or ideas.

Composing: the process of generating and shaping ideas before writing begins and as the actual writing unfolds.

Connotation: subtle shades of meaning that define a word; there can also be specific grammatical and semantic conditions that delimit a word's appropriate usage.

Content Area Literacy: the level of reading and writing still necessary to read, comprehend, and react to appropriate instructional materials in a given content area.

Content Reading Inventory: a teacher-made and text-based test designed to assess students' ability to effectively read and learn from the text.

Context Clues: a decoding technique that consists of utilizing surrounding words and their meaning to identify unfamiliar words.

Contextual: refers to the connotative meaning of words in context.

Contextual Redefinition: a vocabulary strategy in which the teacher places new vocabulary in self-defining or high utility contexts.

Cooperative Learning: an equal partnership in which paired students study together with a mutual goal of mastering academic information.

Criterion: a relative standard, or score, that implies adequate achievement without reference to the performance of others.

Criterion-referenced test: a test of specific content, measuring individual performances without comparison to the entire group.

Cubing: writing strategy which allow students to consider the multiple dimensions of topics; students examine topics by describing, comparing, associating, analyzing, applying, and arguing.

Culture: a collection of values, beliefs, and standards which influences how students think, feel, and behave in various social settings.

Debriefing: feedback by students in the form of self-reports, introspection, and hindsights.

Decoding: any process whereby a coded message is converted back into thought.

Definitional: refers to the denotative meaning of words

Denotation: the broad meanings of words.

Depth of Processing: a memory principle that asserts that the likelihood of long-term retention and recall is greater when a mental activity involves close semantic analysis and cognitive attention.

Developmental Bilingual Education: similar to transitional bilingual education without a specified phase-out of the native language.

Diagnostic Test: a test employed to determine specific skill strengths and weaknesses of students.

Dialogue Journals: journals in which the teacher maintains an ongoing written dialogue with students.

Directed Reading-Thinking Activity: a self-questioning process that encourages students to predict oncoming information in text and sets purposes for reading that are personally interesting.

Distributed Practice: rehearsals separated by breaks.

Diversity: the varied student characteristics of language, culture, and learning differences.

Encoding: any process whereby thought or meaning is converted into a code.

Encoding Specificity: the way in which a student studies text information and the degree to which this process matches subsequent recall tasks.

English as a Second Language: structured lessons in English while maintaining facility in the native language.

Etymology: study of the history of words and their origins.

Experience-Based: thinking that requires drawing an inference that is not derivable from the text, but rather from one's existing schemata, i.e., reading beyond the lines.

Expressive Vocabulary: words that a person can use properly when speaking or writing.

Extension Activities: pencil and paper exercises designed to reinforce and expand the schemata of newly acquired content area vocabulary.

External Reference: any source of information outside the passage being read.

External Storage: in notetaking, a written substitute for memory.

Fake Pop Quiz: a quiz designed to reinforce, rather than test, recently introduced information.

Feature Analysis: an instructional strategy in which sets of new concepts or vocabulary are defined and discriminated by identifying the unique characteristics of each member of the set.

Field Notes: assessment information collected purposefully and recorded systematically over time.

FLIP: friendliness, language, interest, prior knowledge; a technique for helping students preview a reading assignment.

Formal Tests: standardized, norm-referenced tests used to monitor student progress.

Free Morpheme: a morpheme that can stand by itself, e.g., boy.

Free Response and Opinion-Proof: students read and note in writing points of agreement or dispute for later class discussion.

General Vocabulary: words that are not specifically associated with any one teaching area and are assimilated into existing schemata.

Glossary: an alphabetized list of technical words and their definitions used in a textbook or other work.

Graphic Information Lesson: strategy designed to teach students how to interpret graphs.

Graphic Literacy: ability to interpret graphs and other visual presentations in text.

Graphic Organizer: a visual aid that defines hierarchical relationships among concepts and that lends itself to the teaching of technical vocabulary.

Group Test: a test administered in a group situation.

Guided Listening Procedure: a comprehension strategy employed on a listening level; the purpose is to enhance recall and organization of text information as well as to promote student self-inquiry.

Guided Reading Procedure: an integrated lesson approach designed to insure that students understand and remember key information from their text.

Guided Writing Procedure: an integrated lesson approach that serves as an alternative to the guided reading procedure by capitalizing on writing as a means to commit information to long-term memory.

Hypermedia: hypertext with sounds and pictures.

Hypertext: large and easily programmed linked visual and text databases.

Immersion Bilingual Education: all instruction is in the second language.

Index: an alphabetized list of important terms and topics and the page numbers on which they occur in the text.

Individualization: incorporating the gamut of grouping procedures—whole group, small group, and individual—within the confines of a well-developed instructional plan utilizing the textbook and with the teacher acting as facilitator of learning.

Individual Test: a test that may be administered on only an individual basis.

Informal Conversations: an informal means of getting students to talk about what they are learning as well as how they are learning.

Informal Tests: teacher-made or published tests that employ a criterion to monitor student progress.

Information Index: a device used to structure the information search by keying students into the location of important concepts.

Inquiry-Charts: strategy for nurturing critical reading in content classrooms by having students examine multiple sources of information and charting their findings.

Integrated Thematic Units: teams of teachers from various subject areas collaborate to create units and lessons with a central theme.

Interests: what students like to read about.

Internet: a highly complex, interlinked system of computers forming a worldwide communication network.

I-Search Paper: an alternative to the traditional research paper such that students investigate topics of their choosing by interviewing experts, visiting places, and telling the story of their search in a written report.

Journal Writing: writing to explore ideas freely without worrying unduly about mechanics.

Knowledge Base: professional literature on research and best practices in teacher education.

Knowledge Rating: strategy for establishing what students already know about a topic by having them rate how well they know the vocabulary words.

K-W-L: a three-step integrated strategy designed to encourage active reading of expository text; K = what we know before reading, W = what we want to find out during reading, L = what we learned after reading.

Learning: a change that occurs in an organism at a particular time as a function of experience.

Learning Centers: organized classroom centers designed to facilitate the acquisition of new information or to reinforce it.

Learning Disabilities: a significant discrepancy between a student's intellectual potential for learning and current achievement scores, as well as processing difficulties with print and production difficulties with writing.

Lesson Planning: teacher planning that includes learning objectives, set induction, content outline, activities, lesson closure, resources and materials, evaluation, and student assignments.

Levels of Text Understanding: the differing levels of thinking involved in reading text material; e.g. text explicit, text implicit, experience-based.

Library Power: strategies designed to expand the reading horizons of children by introducing them to the wealth of books in the school library.

Listen-Read-Discuss: an integrated strategy involving students in a guided lecture, independent reading, and summary discussion to ensure in-depth comprehension.

Listening Guide: used to guide listening to an oral presentation; a skeletal outline of the important concepts arranged in the order and relationship in which they occur to aid students as they listen and fill in the appropriate information.

Literacy: the ability and willingness to use reading and writing to construct meaning from printed text based on the particular social context.

Literate: being able to read and write.

Literature Response Journals: journals where students reflect and write their thoughts so they can share their views with the teacher, peers, or parents.

Long-Term Memory: an organized store of information based on a person's cumulative experiences.

Macrostructure: the author's pattern of organization which binds together its complex system of paragraphs.

Mainstreaming: placing students with physical and learning disabilities in regular classrooms to provide the least restrictive learning environment.

Metacognition: awareness of one's own mental processes.

Metadiscourse: text intrusions in which the author talks directly to the reader about the information in the text.

Microstructure: the author's ideas and supporting details at the sentence level.

Miscues: observed responses to printed text that do not conform exactly to the print and may preserve (e.g. auto for car) or disrupt meaning (e.g. cat for car).

Mnemonic: a strategy for remembering one thing by associating it with something else.

Modeling: a report by an individual of the mental operations involved in their comprehension process to illustrate its logical steps to others.

Morpheme: the smallest unit of language that has an associated meaning.

Morphemic Analysis: the analysis of affixes and roots to decode unknown words.

Multicultural Literature: literature by and about people who represent groups often on the fringes of the socio-political mainstream.

Multiple Text Inquiry Discussion: Students read across various sources to synthesize and discuss a topic.

Naturalistic Assessment: assessment based upon observing and interacting with students as they respond to the naturally occurring activities of the classroom.

Norms: a set of scores against which the test performance of others may be compared.

Objectives: the specific learning expectations a teacher plans for a lesson including students' performance, products, learning conditions, and criteria for successful performance.

Observation: teachers' attempts at making judgments about students during instruction.

Observation Guide: structured guide used to record teachers' observations of students.

Options Guide: a form of study guide in which students predict, discuss, and evaluate options available to key political and historical figures.

Organization: the arrangements of parts of a whole in such a manner that the parts are related to each other.

Parallel Notetaking: listening and taking notes at the same time.

Passive Failure: a term describing students who are resigned to fail and believe they do not have the ability to succeed in their learning.

Percentile rank: the position of a score in relation to the entire group of scores,

Phony Document: A critical reading strategy where students read, research, and authenticate information in a letter or other document.

PLAE: guidance strategy for studying which consists of preplanning, listing, activating, and evaluating.

Planning Pyramid: a planning guide that helps a teacher organize lesson and unit concepts according to students' diverse abilities and interests.

Polar Opposites: a teaching strategy using contrasting words to critique a reading selection.

Portfolios: systematic collections of students' work in the classroom used for ongoing diagnosis of their abilities.

Possible Sentences: a vocabulary teaching strategy in which students use new vocabulary to create sentences for verification when reading.

Prediction Guide: a means of assessing students' prior knowledge about a topic through a series of fact-based statements that students determine are true or false before reading.

Presenting Content and Processes Concurrently: teaching that provides direct instruction in the processes necessary to acquire content as well as in what content is to be acquired.

Presenting Isolated Skills: teaching that consists of the direct teaching of skills with no consideration for content.

Prior Knowledge: an individual's background experience.

Probable Passages: a writing strategy in which students predict and create paragraph-length sections of a text.

Problem-Solution: a pattern of text organization exemplified by an interaction of a problem and a potential answer to that problem.

Pseudographics: student- or teacher-made graphs that may not be an accurate representation of text material.

Qualitative Factors of Readability: non-measurable variables of text selection that include prior knowledge, text organization, and interest, among others.

Quantitative Factors of Readability: language variables of word length and sentence length as counted and measured in readability estimates.

Raygor Readability Estimate: a readability formula based on word and sentence length; noted for ease of administration and reduced potential for error.

Reaction Guide: a postreading strategy used to stimulate review of a selection by asking students to react to a series of guide statements related to the selection.

Readability Formulas: mathematically derived indices of text difficulty based on an analysis of linguistic variables, the two most common being word length and sentence length.

Readers Theatre: Students read aloud in a dramatic fashion to present key text concepts.

Readiness Principle: refers to the mental state in which an individual is prepared to derive maximum meaning from a learning situation with a minimum of frustration.

Reading Autobiography: A personalized account of early, middle, and recent reading experiences.

Receptive Vocabulary: words that can be read and comprehended in print or heard and understood in spoken context.

Rehearsal: the repeating of information for the purpose of retaining the information in memory.

Reliability: the degree to which a test gives consistent results when administered repeatedly.

ReQuest: a reciprocal questioning procedure that helps students adopt an active, questioning approach to text reading.

Response Bias: writing down what one believes an examiner wants rather than what the examinee really believes.

Response Mode: the type of response required by students' assigned questions, e.g., recall vs. recognition.

Restructuring: a major modification of existing schemata.

ReWrite: A music strategy involving the writing of musiczl verses about content area concepts.

Schemata: a category system of the mind containing information about the surrounding environment; the plural of schema.

Schema Theory: describes the process by which we add to (assimilate) or adjust (accommodate) our existing cognitive structure in the face of new or discordant information.

Scope of Information Search: the number of concepts for which students are held responsible in a given reading assignment.

Self-Concept: how one views oneself.

Semantic Map: a diagram that groups related concepts.

Short-Term Memory: the "working memory:" which holds incoming information temporarily until a decision is made to include this information in long-term memory.

Signal Words: the key words that cue a particular pattern of text organization.

Simple Listing: a pattern of text organization characterized by a listing of items or ideas without regard to order.

Slicing: simplifying the complexity of learning tasks by reexamining those that are required and recasting them to ease the demands placed on students.

Sociolinguistics: the study of language in a cultural context.

Spaced Notetaking: taking notes during intervals of silence between segments of a lecture.

Standard deviation: a measure of dispersion or variability of a group of scores.

Standard Error of Measurement: the variation, or built-in error, in standardized test scores.

Standardized scores: General term for describing a variety of transformed rqw scores that can be compared across other individuals.

Standardized Test: a formal test instrument utilizing norms as a basis for student comparison of achievement.

Stanines: standardized score with a mean of five and a standard deviation of two.

Strategy: the planned means to an end.

Student-Generated Questions: questions students derive on their own from their reading assignments.

Student Interviews: a more formal means of getting students to talk about what they are learning as well as how they are learning.

Study Guide: a strategy that focuses students' attention on the major ideas of a selection at three levels of comprehension.

Study Strategies: the specific strategies that focus on locating, retaining, and recalling information.

Surveying the Text: a prereading strategy that involves some form of preliminary look at a reading selection before more intensive reading is undertaken.

Survey Test: usually a standardized test that measures global areas of achievement, such as vocabulary or comprehension.

Sustained Silent Reading: a systematic program that establishes regular reading times for students to practice their reading skills on pleasurable and self-selected content-related materials.

Talking Drawings: a lesson prereading and postreading strategy that helps students visualize their knowledge of a topic.

Technical Vocabulary: words uniquely related to particular academic disciplines; the words are accommodated by modifying old schemata or creating new schemata.

Test Ceiling: the upper limit placed on an individual's performance at a particular grade level on a standardized test.

Test Floor: the lower limit placed on an individual's performance at a particular grade level on a standardized test.

Testwiseness: a series of principles that can be applied to exams independently of subject area knowledge.

Textbook Adaptations: study guides, graphic organizers, and other guide material a teacher provides to aid student learning of the content material.

Text Explicit: thinking that requires only getting facts as literally stated by an author, i.e., reading the lines.

Text Implicit: thinking that requires an inference from the text to derive an answer to a question, i.e., reading between the lines.

Text Preview: a teacher-devised introductory passage that provides a detailed framework for comprehending a reading selection.

Text Structure: the various organizational patterns writers and readers use to encode and decode thoughts.

Thematic Unit: a series of lessons developed around a theme such as "environmental beautification."

Think-Aloud: teacher modeling strategy whereby one's thoughts about how a text is comprehended are verbalized for students.

Time Order: a pattern of text organization exemplifying a sequential relationship between ideas or events over the passage of time.

TOAST: strategy for independently studying vocabulary using the acronym derived from the procedural steps—test, organize, anchor, say, and test.

Top-Down Processing: selectively applying one's conceptual knowledge to the comprehension of content area ideas.

Transcribing: refers to the mechanics of writing including spelling, punctuation, capitalization, handwriting, formatting, and neatness.

Transitional Bilingual Education: content area instruction in a native language while a student receives second language instruction for a three year period with the native language slowly phased out.

Tuning: a gradual modification of existing schemata.

Two-Way Bilingual Education: both native English and non-native English speakers learn each other's language while they do the bulk of their content learning in the strong, native language.

Unit Blueprint: a unit planning structure that includes the unit topic, goals and objectives, content outline, learning activities resources and materials, and evaluation plan.

Unit of Instruction: a related series of lessons lasting from 1 to 6 weeks.

Unit Plan: a plan of instruction in which students explore and respond to a selected topic through their interaction with a variety of integrated activities designed to enhance their knowledge and attitude.

Validity: the degree of accuracy with which a test measures what it is intended to measure.

Verbal and Visual Word Association Strategy: a mnemonic strategy in which students associate a word they are trying to learn with personal examples or a concrete drawing.

Verbatim Split Page Procedure: a comprehensive method of taking notes during lectures.

Vocabulary: a corpus of many thousands of words and their associated meanings.

Vocabulary Self-Collection Strategy: a vocabulary acquisition technique designed to teach students how to select the most important vocabulary from reading assignments.

Word: a pattern of auditory or visual symbols that represent schemata, or concepts.

Word Analogies: exercises requiring students to draw inferences and expose subtle word associations.

Word Associations: a technique designed to measure students' knowledge about a topic through association.

Word Map: a visual representation of a definition.

Writing Roulette: a strategy in which students create a simple story containing some of the technical vocabulary they are learning.

Young Adult Literature: selections of interest to readers ages 12 to 20.

BIBLIOGRAPHY

Chapter 1

Recommended Readings

Bean, T. W., & Readence, J. E. (1995). A comparative study of content area literacy students' attitudes toward reading through autobiography analysis. In K. A. Hinchman, D. J. Leu, & C. K. Kinzer (Eds.), *Perspectives on literacy research and practice*. Forty-fourth yearbook of the National Reading Conference (pp. 325–333). Chicago: National Reading Conference.

    A study which uses teachers' autobiographies as a means to examine their attitudes toward reading.

Bean, T. W., & Readence, J. E. (1995). Content area reading: Current state of the art. In J. Flood, D. Lapp, & N. Farnan (Eds.), *Content area reading and learning: Instructional strategies* (2nd ed.). Boston: Allyn & Bacon.

    Discusses the current status of content area reading and the issues surrounding it and describes how this approach assists in the development of a literate society.

Come Romine, B. G., McKenna, M. C., & Robinson, R. D. (1996). Reading coursework requirements for middle and high school content area teachers: A U.S. survey. *Journal of Adolescent & Adult Literacy, 40,* 194–198.

    Presents the results of a survey examining licensure requirements in reading in the U.S., making the point that a required course for teachers in content literacy is a positive step in helping students learn with text.

Moore, D. W. (1996). Contexts for literacy in secondary schools. In D. J. Leu, C. K. Kinzer, & K. A. Hinchman (Eds.), *Literacies for the 21st century: Research and practice*. Forty-fifth yearbook of the National Reading Conference (pp. 15–46). Chicago: National Reading Conference.

    Discusses recent research focusing on secondary school teachers' and students' experiences during classroom literacy events.

Readence, J. E., Kile, R. S., & Mallette, M. H. (1997). Secondary teachers' beliefs about literacy: Emerging voices. In D. E. Alvermann, K. A. Hinchman, D. W. Moore, S. F. Phelps, & D. R. Waff (Eds.), *Reconceptualizing the literacies in adolescents' lives*. Mahwah, NJ: Erlbaum.

    Emphasizes the importance of teachers' personal beliefs about literacy in framing their knowledge about teaching and in impacting how they teach.

Rose, M. (1989). *Lives on the boundary: The struggles and achievements of America's underprepared*. New York: Free Press.

    A personal account of literacy and culture, focusing on those who have trouble reading and writing in the schools.

References

Applebee, A. (1992). Stability and change in the high school canon. *English Journal,* 81, 27–32.

Armbruster, B. B., Anderson, T. H., Armstrong, J. O., Wise, M. A., Janisch, C., & Meyer, L. A. (1991). Reading and questioning in content area lessons. *JRB: A Journal of Literacy,* 23, 35–59.

Bean, T. W., & Readence, J. E. (1995). Content area reading: Current state of the art. In J. Flood, D. Lapp, & N. Farnan (Eds.), *Content area reading and learning: Instructional strategies* (2nd ed.). Boston: Allyn & Bacon.

Carey-Webb, A. (1993). Racism and *Huckleberry Finn:* Censorship, dialogue, and change. *English Journal, 82,* 22–34.

Gersten, R., & Woodward, J. (1994). The language-minority student and special education: Issues, trends, and paradoxes. *Exceptional Children, 60,* 310–322.

Goodlad, J. I. (1984). *A place called school*. New York: McGraw-Hill.

Hinchman, K. (1985). Reading and the plans of secondary teachers: A qualitative study. In J. A. Niles & R. V. Lalik (Eds.), *Issues in literacy: A research perspective* (pp. 251–256). Thirty-fourth Yearbook of the National Reading Conference. Rochester, NY: National Reading Conference.

International Reading Association and National Council of Teachers of English. (1996). *Standards for the English language arts*. Newark, DE and Urbana, IL: Authors.

Johnson, D. W., Maruyama, G., Johnson, R., Nelson, D., & Skon, L. (1981). Effects of cooperative, competitive and individualistic goal structures on achievement: A meta-analysis. *Psychological Bulletin, 89,* 47–62.

Kaestle, C. F. (1991). *Literacy in the United States*. New Haven: Yale University Press.

Macedo, D. P. (1993). Literacy for stupidification: The pedagogy of big lies. *Harvard Educational Review, 63,* 183–206.

Moore, D. W., & Readence, J. E. (1992). Approaches to content area reading instruction. In E. K. Dishner,

T. W. Bean, J. E. Readence, & D. W. Moore (Eds.), *Reading in the content areas: Improving classroom instruction* (3rd ed., pp. 52–57). Dubuque, IA: Kendall/Hunt Publishing Company.

O'Brien, D. G., & Stewart, R. A. (1992). Resistance to content area reading instruction: Dimensions and solutions. In E. K. Dishner, T. W. Bean, J. E. Readence, & D. W. Moore (Eds.), *Reading in the content areas: Improving classroom instruction* (3rd ed., pp. 30–40). Dubuque, IA: Kendall/Hunt.

O'Brien, D. G., Stewart, R. A., & Moje, E. B. (1995). Why content literacy is difficult to infuse into the secondary school: Complexities of curriculum, pedagogy, and school culture. *Reading Research Quarterly, 30,* 442–463.

Postman, N. (1979). *Teaching as conserving activity.* New York: Delacorte Press.

Rose, M. (1989). *Lives on the boundary: The struggles and achievements of America's underprepared.* New York: Free Press.

Sartre, J. (1948). *The emotions: Outline of a theory.* New York: Book Sales.

Schallert, D. L., & Kleiman, G. M. (1979, June). *Some reasons why teachers are easier to understand than textbooks* (Reading Educ. Rep. No. 9). Urbana: University of Illinois, Center for the Study of Reading.

Searfoss, L. W., & Maddox, E. J. (1992). Student rights, teacher rights in content area instructional programs. In E. K. Dishner, T. W. Bean, J. E. Readence, & D. W. Moore (Eds.), *Reading in the content areas: Improving classroom instruction* (3rd ed., pp. 41–51). Dubuque, IA: Kendall/Hunt.

Singer, H. (1979). Research: Slogans and attitudes. *Journal of Reading, 22,* 756–757.

Tierney, R. J., & Shanahan, T. (1991). Research on the reading-writing relationship: Interactions. transactions, and outcomes. In R. Barr, M. L. Kamil, P. Mosenthal, & P. D. Pearson (Eds.) *Handbook of reading research: Volume II* (pp. 246–280). New York: Longman.

Wood, K. (1992). Effective content area instructional practices in middle and secondary level classrooms. In E. K. Dishner, T. W. Bean, J. E. Readence, & D. W. Moore (Eds.), *Reading in the content areas: Improving classroom instruction* (3rd ed., pp. 58–70). Dubuque, IA: Kendall/Hunt.

Wood, K. D. (1987). Fostering cooperative learning in middle and secondary level classrooms. *Journal of Reading, 41,* 10–18.

Chapter 2

Recommended Readings

Levy, S. (1994). *Insanely great: The life and times of Macintosh, the computer that changed everything.* New York: Viking.

A clever history of the Macintosh computer.

Postman, N. (1992). *Technology: The surrender of culture to technology.* New York: Alfred Knopf.

An analysis of the role technology plays in defining contemporary culture—everything from religion and art to politics.

Provenzo, E. F., Jr. (1991). *Video kids: Making sense of Nintendo.* Cambridge: Harvard University Press.

Examines social issues related to video game culture. For example, does playing violent video games make children more violent in real life?

References

Bosco, J. (1989). The organization of schools and the use of computers to improve schooling. *Peabody Journal of Education, 64,* 111–29.

Cook, D. L. (1962). The automization of Socrates. *Theory Into Practice, 1,* 9–19.

Cuban, L. (1986). *Teachers and machines. The classroom use of technology since 1920.* New York: Teachers College Press.

Goldstein, L., & Liu, N. (1994). An integrated approach to the design of an immersion program. *TESOL Quarterly, 28,* 705–725.

Heide, A., & Stilborne, L. (1996). *The teacher's complete and easy guide to the Internet.* Toronto: Trifolium Books.

Levy, S. (1990, June 14). Brave new world. *Rolling Stone.*

Milk, R. D. (1990). Preparing ESL and bilingual teachers for changing roles: Immersion for teachers of LEP students. *TESOL Quarterly, 24,* 407–426.

Papert, S. (1980). *Mindstorms.* New York: Basic Books.

Piaget, J. (1976). *To understand is to invent.* New York: Penguin Books.

Provenzo, E. F., Jr. (1991). *Video kids. Making sense of Nintendo.* Cambridge: Harvard University Press.

Ryder, R. J., & Graves, M. F. (1996). Using the Internet to enhance students' reading, writing, and information-gathering skills. *Journal of Adolescent & Adult Literacy, 40,* 244–254.

Chapter 3

Recommended Readings

Alvermann, D. E., Hinchman, K. A., Moore, D. W., Phelps, S. F., & Waff, D. (Eds.), *Reconceptualizing the literacies in adolescents' lives.* Mahwah, NJ: Erlbaum.

This book places adolescents' voices at the forefront of improving content area classrooms in middle and secondary grades. Their recommendations are made in an effort to reform and reshape classrooms that often silence adolescents' sense of involvement in their learning.

Bean, T. W. (1999). Reading in the content areas. In M. L. Kamil, P. B. Mosenthal, P. D. Pearson, & R. Barr

(Eds.), *Handbook of reading research: Volume III*. Mahwah, NJ: Erlbaum.

> This chapter plots historical trends and future directions in research devoted to content area classrooms. Recent studies from a sociocultural perspective extend earlier work on content learning strategies.

Jackson, F. R. (1994). Seven strategies to support a culturally responsive pedagogy. *Journal of Reading, 37*, 298–303.

> The author argues for classrooms that are bicultural and capitalize on students' language, heritage, and diversity. Seven specific strategies to make your classroom an attractive place for the diverse student body you serve are illustrated.

Ladson-Billings, G. (1994). *The dreamkeepers: Successful teachers of African-American children*. San Francisco, CA: Jossey-Bass.

> The author profiles eight outstanding teachers and their classrooms in a community where many children would be viewed at-risk in literacy and content learning. The book provides a powerful model for tapping students' cultural knowledge in learning new content area concepts.

Nieto, S. (1996). *Affirming diversity: The sociopolitical context of multicultural education* (2nd ed.). New York: Longman.

> The case studies that illustrate many of the author's points about cultural and linguistic diversity in our classroom argue for needed reforms in content area literacy instruction. Nieto brings a wealth of personal experience to the topic as well as specific strategies to address the needs of our increasingly diverse student body.

Rose, M. (1995). *Possible lives: The promise of public education in America*. New York: Houghton Mifflin.

> The author takes the reader into classrooms spanning the United States. Teacher and student voices provide a very different perspective on content learning than alarmist reports that typify our perceptions of the state of public education. Mike Rose is a superb writer, and this book reads like a novel.

Salend, S. J. (1994). *Effective mainstreaming: Creating inclusive classrooms* (2nd ed.). New York: Macmillan.

> Individual chapters discuss approaches to mainstreaming in the core subjects of mathematics, science, and social studies. Introductory chapters offer a comprehensive view of recent advances in mainstreaming.

Schifini, A. (1994). Language, literacy, and content instruction: Strategies for teachers. In K. Spangenberg-Urbschat & R. Pritchard (Eds.), *Kids come in all languages: Reading instruction for ESL students* (pp. 158–179). Newark, DE: International Reading Association.

> This chapter contains concrete examples of strategies aimed at assisting second language learners in grasping content area concepts in English language textbooks.

References

Alvermann, D. E., O'Brien, D. G., & Dillon, D. R. (1990). What teachers do when they say they're having discussions of content area reading assignments: A qualitative analysis. *Reading Research Quarterly, 25*, 296–322.

Alvermann, D. E., Dillon, D. R., & O'Brien, D. G. (1987). *Using discussion to promote reading comprehension*. Newark, DE: International Reading Association.

Alvermann, D. E., Smith, L. C., & Readence, J. E. (1985). Prior knowledge activation and the comprehension of compatible and incompatible text. *Reading Research Quarterly, 20*, 420–436.

Asher, S. R. (1980). Topic interest and children's reading comprehension. In R. J. Spiro, B. C. Bruce, & W. F. Brewer (Eds.), *Theoretical issues in reading comprehension* (pp. 525–534). Hillsdale, NJ: Erlbaum.

Asher, S. R., Hymel, S., & Wigfield, A. (1978). Influence of topic interest on childrens' reading comprehension. *Journal of Reading Behavior, 10*, 35–47.

Au, K. H. (1993). *Literacy instruction in multicultural settings*. Fort Worth, TX: Harcourt Brace.

Baldwin, R. S., Peleg-Bruckner, Z., & McClintock, A. (1985). Effects of topic interest on childrens' reading comprehension. *Reading Research Quarterly, 20*, 497–504.

Bean, T. W. (1994). Writing across the curriculum. In L. W. Searfoss & J. E. Readence, *Helping children learn to read* (3rd ed., pp. 326–361). Boston: Allyn & Bacon.

Bean, T. W. (1998). Teacher literacy histories and adolescent voices: Changing content area classrooms. In D. E. Alvermann, K. A. Hinchman, D. W. Moore, S. F. Phelps, & D. Waff (Eds.), *Reconceptualizing the literacies in adolescents' lives*. Mahwah, NJ: Erlbaum.

Bean, T. W., Valerio, P. C., Money Senior, H., & White, F. (1997, December). *Secondary English students' engagement in reading and interpreting a multicultural young adult novel*. Paper presented at the National Reading Conference, Scottsdale, AZ.

Bean, T. W., Cowan, S., & Searles, D. (1990). Text-based analogies. *Reading Psychology, 11*, 323–334.

Bean, T. W., Singer, H., & Cowan, W. (1985). Analogical study guides: Improving comprehension in science. *Journal of Reading, 29*, 246–250.

Belloni, L. F., & Jongsma, E. A. (1978). The effects of interest on reading comprehension of low achieving students. *Journal of Reading, 22*, 106–109.

Bennett, C. I. (1990). *Comprehensive multicultural education*. Boston: Allyn & Bacon.

Bergknut, L. L. (1997). Stink eye. In A. Von Alemann & M. Kunz (Eds.), *Kanilehua* (pp. 32–33). Hilo: University of Hawaii at Hilo/Hawaii Community College Board of Student Publications.

Bloome, D. (1987). Reading as a social process in a middle school classroom. In D. Bloome (Ed.), *Literacy and schooling* (pp. 123–149). Norwood, NJ: Ablex.

Brainerd, C. J. (1983). Working-memory systems and cognitive development. In C. J. Brainerd (Ed.), *Recent advances in cognitive development theory* (pp. 167–236). New York: Springer-Verlag.

Chinn, C. A., & Brewer, W. F. (1993). The role of anomalous data in knowledge acquisition: A theoretical framework and implications for science instruction. *Review of Educational Research, 63,* 1–49.

Craik, F. I., & Lockhart, R. S. (1972). Levels of processing: A framework for memory research. *Journal of Verbal Learning and Verbal Behavior, 11,* 671–684.

Duffy, T. M., & Jonassen, D. H. (1992). Constructivism: New implications for instructional technology. In T. M. Duffy & D. H. Jonassen (Eds.), *Constructivism and the technology of instruction* (pp. 1–16). Hillsdale, NJ: Erlbaum.

Fleischman, P. (1990). *Saturnalia.* New York: Harper/Collins.

Good, T. L., & Brophy, J. E. (1997). *Looking in classrooms* (4th ed.). New York: Longman.

Goodlad, J. I. (1984). *A place called school.* New York: McGraw-Hill.

Grabe, W. (1991). Current development in second language research. *TESOL Quarterly, 25,* 375–406.

Green, J., & Bloome. D. (1983). Ethnography and reading: Issues, approaches, criteria, and findings. In J. A. Niles & L. A. Harris (Eds.), *Searches for meaning in reading/language processing and instruction.* Thirty-second Yearbook of the National Reading Conference (pp. 6–30). Rochester, NY: National Reading Conference.

Guthrie, J. T., & Greaney, V. (1991). Literacy acts. In R. Barr, M. L. Kamil, P. Mosenthal, & P. D. Pearson (Eds.), *Handbook of reading research: Volume II* (pp. 68–96). New York: Longman.

Halford, G. S. (1993). *Children's understanding: The development of mental models.* Hillsdale, NJ: Erlbaum.

Hall, E. T. (1959). *The silent language.* New York: Doubleday.

Hamilton, S. F. (1983). Socialization for learning: Insights from ecological research in classrooms. *The Reading Teacher, 37,* 150–156.

Hernandez, I. B. (1992). *Heartbeat drumbeat.* Houston, TX: Arte Publico Press.

Hudelson, S. (1994). Working with second language learners. In L. W. Searfoss & J. E. Readence, *Helping children learn to read* (3rd ed., pp. 362–391). Boston: Allyn & Bacon.

Hynd, C. R., Qian, G., Ridgeway, V. G., & Pickle, M. (1991). Promoting conceptual change with science texts and discussion. *Journal of Reading, 34,* 596–601.

Kasper, L. F. (1994). Improved reading performance for ESL students through academic course pairing. *Journal of Reading, 37,* 376–384.

Kinney, G. (1993). *W. K. Kellogg transcultural education grant.* Hilo: Department of Baccalaureate Nursing, University of Hawaii at Hilo.

Krashen, S. D., & Terrell, T. D. (1983). *The natural approach: Language acquisition in the classroom.* Hayward, CA: Alemany Press.

Ladson-Billings, G. (1995). But that's just good teaching! The case for culturally relevant pedagogy. *Theory Into Practice, 34,* 159–165.

Laird, D. M., & Jossen, C. (1983). *Wili Wai Kula and the three mongooses.* Honolulu, HI: Barbaby Books.

Meyer, B. J. F., & Rice, G. E. (1984). The structure of text. In P. D. Pearson (Ed.), *Handbook of reading research* (pp. 319–351). New York: Longman.

Miller, G. A. (1956). The magical number seven plus or minus two: Some limits on our capacity for processing information. *Psychological Review, 63,* 81–96

Miyawaki, T. (1960). *Happy origami.* Hiroshima, Japan: Biken-Sha.

Nieto, S. (1996). *Affirming diversity: The sociopolitical context of multicultural education* (2nd ed.). New York: Longman.

Norman, D. A. (1976). *Memory and attention.* New York: John Wiley and Sons.

Ogbu, J. U. (1992). Adaptation to minority status and impact on school success. *Theory Into Practice, 31,* 287–295.

Pearson, P. D., & Fielding, L. (1991). Comprehension instruction. In R. Barr, M. L. Kamil, P. Mosenthal, & P. D. Pearson (Eds.), *Handbook of reading research: Volume II* (pp. 815–860). New York: Longman.

Perez, S. A. (1982). Visual imagery instruction to improve reading comprehension. In C. Carter (Ed.), *Non-native and nonstandard dialect students* (pp. 69–71). Urbana, IL: National Council of Teachers of English.

Purcell-Gates, V. (1995). *Other peoples' words: The cycle of low literacy.* Cambridge, MA: Harvard University Press.

Rumelhart, D. E., & Norman, D. A. (1981). Analogical processes in learning. In J. R. Anderson (Ed.), *Cognitive skills and their acquisition* (pp. 335–359). Hillsdale, NJ: Erlbaum.

Salend, S. J. (1994). *Effective mainstreaming: Creating inclusive classrooms* (2nd ed.). New York: Macmillan.

Schifini, A. (1994). Language, literacy, and content instruction: Strategies for teachers. In K. Spangenberg-Urbschat & R. Pritchard (Eds.), *Kids come in all languages: Reading instruction for ESL students* (pp. 158–179). Newark, DE: International Reading Association.

Schraw, G., & Dennison, R. S. (1994). The effect of reader purpose on interest and recall. *Journal of Reading Behavior, 26,* 1–18.

Searfoss, L. W., Bean, T. W., & Gelfer, J. I. (1998). *Developing literacy naturally.* Dubuque, IA: Kendall/Hunt.

Searfoss, L. W., & Readence, J. E. (1994). *Helping children learn to read* (3rd ed.). Englewood Cliffs, NJ: Prentice-Hall.

Spiro, R. J., Feltovich, P. J., Coulson, R. L., & Anderson, D. (1989). Multiple analogies of complex concepts; Antidotes for analogy-induced misconception in advanced knowledge acquisition. In S. Vosniadou & A. Ortony (Eds.), *Similarity and analogical reasoning* (pp. 498–531). Cambridge, MA: Cambridge University Press.

Tierney, R. J., & Pearson, P. D. (1992a). Learning to learn from text: A framework for improving classroom practice. In E. K. Dishner, T. W. Bean, J. E. Readence, & D. W. Moore (Eds.), *Reading in the content areas: Improving classroom instruction* (3rd ed., pp. 87–103). Dubuque, IA: Kendall/Hunt.

Tierney, R. J., & Pearson, P. D. (1992b). A revisionist perspective on "learning to learn from text: A framework for improving classroom practice." In E. K. Dishner, T. W. Bean, J. E. Readence, & D. W. Moore (Eds.), *Reading in the content areas: Improving classroom instruction* (3rd ed., pp. 82–86). Dubuque, IA: Kendall/Hunt.

Tierney, R. J., & Shanahan, T. (1991). Research on the reading-writing relationship: Interactions, transactions, and outcomes. In R. Barr, M. L. Kamil, P. Mosenthal, & P. D. Pearson (Eds.), *Handbook of reading research: Volume I*I (pp. 246–280). New York: Longman.

Tompkins, G. E. (1990). *Teaching writing: Balancing process and product.* Columbus, OH: Merrill.

Van Dijk, T. A., & Kintsch, W. (1983). *Strategies of discourse comprehension.* New York: Academic Press.

Vaughn, S., Schumm, J. S., Klinger, J., & Saumell, L. (1995). Students' views of instructional practices: Implications for inclusion. *Learning Disability Quarterly, 18,* 236–248.

Vosniadou, S., & Brewer, W. F. (1987). Theories of knowledge restructuring in development. *Review of Educational Research, 57,* 51–67.

Warner, L. S. (1993). *From slave to abolitionist: The life of William Wells Brown.* New York: Dial Books.

Weaver, C. A., & Kintsch, W. (1991). Expository text. In R. Barr, M. L. Kamil, P. Mosenthal, & P. D. Pearson (Eds.), *Handbook of reading research: Volume II* (pp. 230–245). New York: Longman.

Wigfield, A., & Asher, S. R. (1984). Social and motivational influences on reading. In P. D. Pearson (Ed.), *Handbook of reading research* (pp. 423–452). New York: Longman.

Chapter 4

Recommended Readings

Klare, G. R. (1984). Readability. In P. D. Pearson (Ed.), *Handbook of reading research* (pp. 681–744). New York: Longman.

> Provides a comprehensive discussion and review of the literature on readability and readability formulas.

Leonard, W. H., & Penick, J. E. (1993). What's important in selecting a biology textbook? *The American Biology Teacher, 55*(1), 14–19.

> Provides a checklist for biology textbook selection, indicating that the concerns discussed in this chapter are also concerns in the subject matter disciplines.

Loxterman, J. A., Beck, I. L., & McKeown, M. G. (1994). The effects of thinking aloud during reading on students' comprehension of more or less coherent text. *Reading Research Quarterly, 29,* 352–367.

> Study which showed that more friendly text, and more friendly text using think alouds, enhanced the comprehension of sixth grade readers.

Simmons, J. S. (Ed.). (1994). *Censorship: A threat to reading, learning, thinking.* Newark, DE: International Reading Association.

> This book provides a number of approaches for teachers dealing with censorship.

Singer, H. (1992). Friendly texts: Description and criteria. In E. K. Dishner, T. W. Bean, J. E. Readence, & D. W. Moore (Eds.), *Reading in the content areas: Improving classroom instruction* (3rd ed., pp. 155–170). Dubuque, IA: Kendall/Hunt Publishing Company.

> Describes text features that enhance or inhibit comprehension and provides an accompanying text evaluation checklist.

Zakaluk, B. L., & Samuels, S. J. (Eds.) (1988). *Readability: Its past, present, and future.* Newark, DE: International Reading Association.

> A series of readings on the role of readability in research and practice from its early years to predictions about its future.

References

Anyon, J. (1979). Ideology and United States history books. *Harvard Education Review, 49,* 361–386.

Baldwin, R. S., & Kaufman, R. K. (1979). A concurrent validity study of the Raygor readability graph. *Journal of Reading, 23,* 148–153.

Bean, T. W., Singer, H., Cowen, S., & Searles, D. (1987, December). *Acquiring concepts from biology text: A study of text-based learning aids and reader-based strategies.* Paper presented at the annual meeting of the National Reading Conference, St. Petersburg, FL.

Davison, A., & Kantor, R. N. (1982). On the failure of readability formulas to define readable texts: A case study from adaptations. *Reading Research Quarterly, 17,* 187–209.

Donelson, K. (1975). Censorship: Some issues and problems. *Theory Into Practice, 14,* 186–194.

Donelson, K. (1990). "You can't have that book in my school library": Books under attack in the *Newsletter on Intellectual Freedom,* 1952–1989. *The High School Journal, 74,* 1–7.

Fitzgerald, F. (1977). *American revised: The history of school books in the 20th century.* Boston: Little, Brown.

Freebody, P., & Anderson, R. C. (1983). Effects of vocabulary difficulty, text cohesion, and schema availability on reading comprehension. *Reading Research Quarterly, 18,* 277–305.

Harrington-Lueker, D. (1991). Book battles. *The American School Board Journal, 178,* 18–21, 37.

Klare, G. R. (1984). Readability. In P. D. Pearson (Ed.), *Handbook of reading research* (pp. 681–744). New York: Longman.

Kretschmer, J. C. (1984). Computerizing and comparing the Rix readability index. *Journal of Reading, 27,* 490–499.

Leonard, W. H., & Penick, J. E. (1993). What's important in selecting a biology textbook? *The American Biology Teacher, 55*(1), 14–19.

Palmatier, R. A., & Strader, S. S. (1977). Teacher performance in assessment of comparative reading difficulty of content materials. In P. D. Pearson (Ed.), *Reading: Theory, research, and practice* (pp. 60–62). Twenty-sixth yearbook of the National Reading Conference. Clemson, SC: National Reading Conference.

Pearson, P. D. (1974–1975). The effects of grammatical complexity on children's comprehension, recall, and conception of certain semantic relations. *Reading Research Quarterly, 10,* 155–192.

Pearson, P. D., & Fielding, L. (1991). Comprehension instruction. In R. Barr, M. L. Kamil, P. B. Mosenthal, & P. D. Pearson (Eds.), *Handbook of reading research: Volume II* (pp. 815–860). New York: Longman.

Postman, N. (1970). The politics of reading. *Harvard Educational Review, 40,* 244–252.

Raygor, A. L. (1977). The Raygor readability estimate: A quick and easy way to determine difficulty. In P. D. Pearson (Ed.), *Reading: Theory, research, and practice* (pp. 259–263). Twenty-sixth yearbook of the National Reading Conference. Clemson, SC: National Reading Conference.

Redway, J. W., & Hinman, R. (1916). *Natural school geography.* New York: American Book Company.

Singer, H. (1992). Friendly texts: Description and criteria. In E. K. Dishner, T. W. Bean, J. E. Readence, & D. W. Moore (Eds.), *Reading in the content areas: Improving classroom instruction* (3rd ed., pp. 155–170). Dubuque, IA: Kendall/Hunt Publishing Company.

The Miami Herald. (1991, July 27). NY to rewrite textbooks, tell more about minorities. Miami, FL: *The Miami Herald,* 6a.

———. (1982, April 17). Huck Finn is no racist. Miami, FL: *The Miami Herald.*

Zahorik, J. A. (1991). Teaching style and textbooks. *Teaching and Teacher Education, 7,* 185–196.

Chapter 5

Recommended Readings

Farr, R. (1992). Putting it all together: Solving the reading assessment puzzle. *The Reading Teacher, 46,* 26–37.

    An analysis of the state of the art of reading assessment.

Gillespie, C. S., Ford, K. L., Gillespie, R. D., & Leavell, A. G. (1996). Portfolio assessment: Some questions, some answers, some recommendations. *Journal of Adolescent & Adult Reading, 39,* 480–491.

    Review of research on portfolio assessment and use at the secondary level.

Henk, W. A. (1993). New directions in reading assessment. *Reading and Writing Quarterly: Overcoming Learning Difficulties, 9,* 103–120.

    A discussion of how our current view of the reading process has affected assessment trends.

Hubbard, R. S., & Power, B. M. (1993). *The art of classroom inquiry: Handbook for teacher-researchers.* Portsmouth, NH: Heinemann.

    Discusses various ways for teachers to collect data in classrooms, with numerous examples of field notes, anecdotal records, etc.

Moje, E. B., Brozo, W. G., & Haas, J. Portfolios in a high school classroom: Challenges to change. *Reading Research and Instruction, 33,* 275–292.

    Research study of portfolio implementation in a French classroom, with suggestions for their usage delineated.

Tierney, R. J., Readence, J. E., & Dishner, E. K. (1995). *Reading strategies and practices: A compendium* (4th ed.). Boston: Allyn & Bacon.

    Unit 14 of this text presents detailed descriptions of various assessment procedures.

Valencia, S. W., Hiebert, E. H., & Afflerbach, P.P. (1994). *Authentic reading assessment: Practices and possibilities.* Newark, DE: International Reading Association.

    A discussion of the role of naturalistic assessment in reading and learning.

References

Blachowicz, C. L. Z. (1991). Vocabulary instruction in content classes for special needs learners: Why and how? *Reading, Writing, and Learning Disabilities, 7,* 297–308.

Fry, E. B. (1972). *Reading instruction for classroom and clinic.* New York: McGraw-Hill.

Gillespie, C. S., Ford, K. L., Gillespie, R. D., & Leavell, A. G. (1996). Portfolio assessment: Some questions, some answers, some recommendations. *Journal of Adolescent & Adult Reading, 39,* 480–491.

Moje, E. B., Brozo, W. G., & Haas, J. Portfolios in a high school classroom: Challenges to change. *Reading Research and Instruction, 33,* 275–292.

Moore, D. W. (1986). A case for naturalistic assessment of reading comprehension. In E. K. Dishner, T. W. Bean, J. E. Readence, & D. W. Moore (Eds.), *Reading in the content areas: Improving classroom instruction* (2nd ed., pp. 159–170). Dubuque, IA: Kendall/Hunt.

Nichols, J. N. (1983). Using prediction to increase content area interest and understanding. *Journal of Reading, 27,* 225–228.

Rakes, Thomas A., & Smith, L. J. (1992). Assessing reading skills in the content areas. In E. K. Dishner, T. W. Bean, J. E. Readence, & D. W. Moore (Eds.), *Reading in the content areas: Improving classroom instruction* (3rd ed., pp. 399–413). Dubuque, IA: Kendall/Hunt.

Readence, J. E., & Martin, M. A. (1988). Comprehension assessment: Alternatives to standardized tests. In S. M. Glazer, L. W. Searfoss, & L. M. Gentile (Eds.), *Reexamining reading/writing diagnosis: New trends in procedures for classrooms and clinics* (pp. 67–80). Newark, DE: International Reading Association.

Readence, J. E., & Moore, D. W. (1992). Why questions? A historical perspective on standardized reading comprehension tests. In E. K. Dishner, T. W. Bean, J. E. Readence, & D. W. Moore (Eds.), *Reading in the content areas: Improving classroom instruction* (3rd ed., pp. 390–398). Dubuque, IA: Kendall/Hunt.

Sternberg, R. J. (1991). Are we reading too much into reading comprehension tests? *Journal of Reading, 34,* 540–545.

Tierney, R. J., Carter, M. A., & Desai, L. E. (1991). *Portfolio assessment in the reading-writing classroom.* Norwood, MA: Christopher-Gordon.

Valencia, S. W., Hiebert, E. H., & Afflerbach, P. P. (1994). *Authentic reading assessment: Practices and possibilities.* Newark, DE: International Reading Association.

Webster, B. (1984, December 12). Science sheds light on bats. *The Register,* Santa Ana, CA.

Zakaluk, B. L., Samuels, S. J., & Taylor, B. M. (1986). A simple technique for estimating prior knowledge: Word association. *Journal of Reading, 30,* 56–60.

Chapter 6

Recommended Readings

Heide, A., & Stilborne, L. (1996). *The teacher's complete and easy guide to the Internet.* Toronto, Ontario, Canada: Trifolium Books.

> This book contains basic information on using the Internet in lesson design as well as numerous website listings for teachers.

Kagan, S. (1992). *Cooperative learning.* San Juan Capistrano, CA: Kagan Cooperative Learning.

> This book includes an extensive array of cooperative small group approaches applicable to many content area classes. Strategies such as think-pair-share and jigsaw are described with a number of examples from various content areas.

Leu, D. J., & Leu, D. D. (1997). *Teaching with the Internet: Lessons from the classroom.* Norwood, MA: Christopher-Gordon.

> A teacher-friendly guidebook on integrating Internet experiences and classroom lessons.

Moore, K. D., & Quinn, C. (1994). *Secondary instructional methods.* Dubuque, IA: WCB Brown & Benchmark.

> This text includes detailed information on unit and lesson planning with example materials.

Salend, S. J. (1994). *Effective mainstreaming: Creating inclusive classrooms* (2nd ed.). New York: Macmillan.

> Chapters in the second half of this text describe specific strategies for accommodating individual differences in lesson planning across various content areas.

Sizer, T. R. (1992). *Horace's school: Redesigning the American high school.* New York: Houghton Mifflin.

> This book includes a number of examples of integrated, thematic teaching and culminating projects, exhibitions, and other real life means of displaying knowledge that go well beyond the narrow confines of traditional teach, assign, assess classroom approaches.

References

Armstrong, D. G., & Savage, T. V. (1994). *Secondary education: An introduction* (3rd ed.). New York: Macmillan.

Bean, T. W. (1998). Teacher literacy histories and adolescent voices: Changing content area classrooms. In D. E. Alvermann, K. A. Hinchman, D. W. Moore, S. F. Phelps, & D. Waff (Eds.), *Reconceptualizing the literacies in adolescents' lives.* Mahwah, NJ: Lawrence Erlbaum.

Britzman, D. P. (1991). *Practice makes practice: A critical study of learning to teach.* Albany: State University of New York Press.

Earle, R. A., & Sanders, P. L. (1986). Individualizing reading assignments. In E. K. Dishner, T. W. Bean, J. E. Readence, & D. W. Moore (Eds.), *Reading in the content areas: Improving classroom instruction* (2nd ed., pp. 310–314). Dubuque, IA: Kendall/Hunt.

Freedman, S. G. (1990). *Small victories: The real world of a teacher, her students, & their high school.* New York: Harper & Row.

George, J. C. (1989). *Shark beneath the reef.* New York: Harper/Collins.

Grimmett, P. R., Erickson, G. L., MacKinnon, A. M., & Riecken, T. J. (1990). Reflective practice in teacher education. In R. T. Clift, W. R. Houston, & M. C. Pugach (Eds.), *Encouraging reflective practice in education* (pp. 20–38). New York: Teachers College.

Hinchman, K. A. How teachers use the textbook: Lessons from three secondary school classrooms (1992). In E. K. Dishner, T. W. Bean, J. E. Readence, & D. W. Moore (Eds.), *Reading in the content areas: Improving classroom instruction* (3rd ed., pp. 282–293). Dubuque, IA: Kendall/Hunt.

Howorth, P. C. (1991). *Sharks.* Las Vegas, NV: KC Publications.

Hunt, L. C., Jr., & Sheldon, W. D. (1950). Characteristics of the reading of a group of ninth-grade pupils. *School Review, 58,* 348–353.

Johnston, P. H., & Winograd, P. N. (1985). Passive failure in reading. *Journal of Reading Behavior, 17,* 279–301.

Kagan, S. (1992). *Cooperative learning.* San Juan Capistrano, CA: Kagan Cooperative Learning.

Lemonick, M. D. (1997, August 11). Under attack! *Time,* pp. 59–64.

Mader, S. (1990). *Biology.* Dubuque, IA: William C. Brown.

McConnell, S. (1993). Talking drawings: A strategy for assisting learners. *Journal of Reading, 36,* 260–269.

McDonald, J., & Czerniak, C. (1994). Developing interdisciplinary units: Strategies and examples. *School Science and Mathematics, 94,* 5–10.

McGovern, A. (1978). *Shark lady: True adventures of Eugenie Clark.* New York: Four Winds Press.

Millies, G. S. P. (1992). The relationship between a teacher's life and teaching. In W. H. Schubert & W. C. Ayers (Eds.), *Teacher lore: Learning from our own experience* (pp. 25–42). New York: Longman.

Moore, K. D., & Quinn, C. (1994). *Secondary instructional methods.* Dubuque, IA: WCB Brown & Benchmark.

Pearson, P. D., & Johnson, D. D. (1978). *Teaching reading comprehension.* New York: Holt, Rinehart, and Winston.

Prince, E. F., & Collier, G. M. (1993). *Basic horsemanship: English and western.* New York: Doubleday.

Readence, J. E., Dishner, E. K. Adapting instruction in content classrooms to meet individual student needs. In E. K. Dishner, T. W. Bean, J. E. Readence, & D. W. Moore (Eds.), *Reading in the content areas: Improving classroom instruction* (3rd ed., pp. 434–441). Dubuque, IA: Kendall/Hunt.

Reinking, D., Mealey, D., & Ridgeway, V. G. (1993). Developing preservice teachers' conditional knowledge of content area reading strategies. *Journal of Reading, 36,* 458–469.

Salend, S. J. (1994). *Effective mainstreaming: Creating inclusive classrooms* (2nd ed.). New York: Macmillan.

Sizer, T. R. (1992). *Horace's school: Redesigning the American high school.* New York: Houghton Mifflin.

Sperry, A. (1963). *Call it courage.* New York: Scholastic.

Suzumoto, A. (1991). *Sharks Hawaii.* Honolulu, HI: Bishop Museum Press.

Taylor, L. (1993). *Sharks of Hawaii: Their biology and cultural significance.* Honolulu: University of Hawaii Press.

Tierney, R. J., Readence, J. E., & Dishner, E. K. (1995). *Reading strategies and practices: A compendium* (4th ed.). Boston: Allyn & Bacon.

Vaughn, S., Schumm, J. S., Johnson, F., & Dougherty, T. (1991, April). *What do students think when teachers make adaptations?* Paper presented at the annual meeting of the American Educational Research Association, Chicago.

Wood, K. D. (1992). Fostering cooperative learning in middle and secondary classrooms. In E. K. Dishner, T. W. Bean, J. E. Readence, & D. W. Moore (Eds.), *Reading in the content areas: Improving classroom instruction* (3rd ed., pp. 424–434). Dubuque, IA: Kendall/Hunt.

Chapter 7

Recommended Readings

Alexander, J. E., & Cobb, J. (1992). Assessing attitudes in middle and secondary schools and community colleges. *Journal of Reading, 36,* 146–149.

> Contains a good listing of additional attitude measures including those specific to the fields of English, social studies, and science.

Bean, T. W., Kile, R. S., & Readence, J. E. (1996). Using trade books to encourage critical thinking about citizenship in high school social studies. *Social Education, 60,* 227–230.

> Using David Klass's award winning novel, *California Blue* (1994), this article demonstrates how to use a variety of content area literacy strategies (e.g., Polar Opposites) to engage students in a vibrant discussion of the main character's decision-making.

Cramer, E. H., & Castle, M. (1994). *Fostering a love of reading: The affective domain in reading education.* Newark, DE: International Reading Association.

> This collection of readings explores attitude assessment and an array of promising strategies for developing a lifelong interest in voluntary reading.

Cullinan, B. E. (1993). *Fact and fiction: Literature across the curriculum.* Newark, DE: International Reading Association.

> This edited volume includes chapters on using literature in mathematics, science, history, and a chapter on multicultural literature.

Guthrie, J. T., & Wigfield, A. (1997). *Reading engagement: Motivating readers through integrated instruction.* Newark, DE: International Reading Association.

> An excellent collection of readings devoted to fostering literacy engagement in fiction and nonfiction material.

Harris, V. J. (1993). *Teaching multicultural literature in grades K–8.* Norwood, MA: Christopher-Gordon.

> Defines multicultural literature and argues for careful selection of books that accurately portray diverse groups. This is an edited volume with chapters encompassing African-American, Asian-Pacific, Puerto Rican, Mexican-American, and Caribbean literature as well as a good listing of sources for multicultural literature.

McMahon, S. I., & Raphael, T. E. (1997). *The book club connection.* New York: Teachers College Press.

> This edited book of readings offers detailed descriptions of classroom book clubs in action. This is essential reading to fully explore all the possibilities that book clubs offer.

Monseau, V. R. (1996). *Responding to young adult literature.* Portsmouth, NH: Heinemann.

> This American Library Association series book describes a variety of reader response modes and formats for exploring young adult literature.

Monseau, V. R., & Salvner, G. M. (1992). *Reading their world: The young adult novel in the classroom.* Portsmouth, NH: Boynton/Cook.

> This edited volume includes information on young adult multicultural literature and a Chapter on using the young adult novel across the curriculum.

Nilsen, A. P., & Donelson, K. L. (1993). *Literature for today's young adults* (4th ed.). New York: HarperCollins.

> This major text features extensive annotations of books and a compilation of the authors' selections for best young adult literature spanning the years 1967 to 1992.

Schon, I. (1994). Recommended books in English about Latinos. *Journal of Reading, 37,* 446—447.

> The author annotates biographies of well-known Latinos and historical selections.

Trelease, J. (1989). *The new read-aloud handbook.* New York: Penguin.

> This is one of the best books on reading aloud to others. A listing of books that lend themselves to reading aloud is included.

References

Achebe, C. (1958). *Things fall apart.* Portsmouth, NH: Heinemann.

Alexander, J. E., & Cobb, J. (1992). Assessing attitudes in middle and secondary schools and community colleges. *Journal of Reading, 36,* 146–149.

Anaya, R. (1972). *Bless me Ultima.* San Francisco, CA: Tonatiuh Press.

Aoki, E. M. (1993). Turning the page: Asian-Pacific American children's literature. In V. J. Harris (Ed.), *Teaching multicultural literature in grades K–8* (pp. 109–135). Norwood, MA: Christopher-Gordon.

Applebee, A. N. (1989). *A study of book length works taught in high school English classes.* Report Series 1.2, Albany: Center for the Learning and Teaching of Literature, State University of New York.

Aranha, J. (1985). Sustained silent reading goes East. *The Reading Teacher, 29,* 214–217.

Au, K. H. (1993). *Literacy instruction in multicultural settings.* Fort Worth, TX: Harcourt Brace Jovanovich.

Baldwin, R. S., Johnson, D., & Peer, G. G. (1980). *Bookmatch.* Tulsa, OK: Educational Development Corporation.

Baldwin, R. S., & Leavell, A. G. (1992). When was the last time you read a textbook just for kicks? In E. K. Dishner, T. W. Bean, J. E. Readence, & D. W. Moore (Eds.), *Reading in the content areas: Improving classroom instruction* (3rd ed., pp. 105–111). Dubuque, IA: Kendall/Hunt.

Beach, R. W., & Marshall, J. D. (1991). *Teaching literature in the secondary school.* New York: Harcourt Brace Jovanovich.

Bean, T. W. (1993, December). *A constructivist view of preservice teachers' attitudes toward reading through case study analysis of autobiographies.* Paper presented at the National Reading Conference, Charleston, SC.

Bean, T. W., Valerio, P. C., Money Senior, H., & White, F. (1997, December). *Secondary English students' engagement in reading and interpreting a multicultural young adult novel.* Paper presented at the National Reading Conference, Scottsdale, AZ.

Bean, T. W., Kile, R. S., & Readence, J. E. (1996). Using trade books to encourage critical thinking about citizenship in high school social studies. *Social Education, 60,* 227–230.

Bishop, R. S. (1993). Multicultural literature for children: Making informed choices. In V. J. Harris (Ed.), *Teaching multicultural literature in grades K–8* (pp. 37–53). Norwood, MA: Christopher-Gordon.

Brozo, W. G., Valerio, P. C., & Salazar, M. M. (1996). A walk through Gracie's garden: Literacy and cultural explorations in a Mexican-American junior high school. *Journal of Adolescent & Adult Literacy, 40,* 2–8.

Bryant, B. (1992). *The saddle club: Show horse.* New York: Bantam Skylark.

Cothern, N. B., & Collins, M. D. (1992). An exploration: Attitude acquisition and reading instruction. *Reading Research and Instruction, 31,* 84–97.

Cramer, E. H., & Castle, M. (1994). *Fostering a love of reading: The affective domain in reading education.* Newark, DE: International Reading Association.

Crew, L. (1989). *Children of the river.* New York: Dell.

Deci, E. L. (1992). The relation of interest to the motivation of behavior: A self-determination theory perspective. In K. A. Renninger, S. Hidi, & A. Krapp (Eds.), *The role of interest in learning and development* (pp. 43–70). Hillsdale, NJ: Erlbaum.

Fleischman, P. (1990). *Saturnalia.* New York: HarperCollins.

Fuhler, C. J. (1994). Response journals: Just one more time with feeling. *Journal of Reading, 37,* 400–405.

George, J. C. (1989). *Shark beneath the reef.* New York: HarperCollins.

Gerlach, J. M. (1992). The young adult novel across the curriculum. In V. R. Monseau & G. M. Salvner (Eds.), *Reading their world: The young adult novel in the classroom* (pp. 113–131). Portsmouth, NH: Boynton/Cook.

Godina, H. (1996). The canonical debate-implementing multicultural literature and perspectives. *Journal of Adolescent & Adult Literacy, 39,* 544–545.

Guthrie, J. T., & Wigfield, A. (1997). Reading engagement: A rationale for theory and learning. In J. T. Guthrie & A. Wigfield (Eds.), *Reading engagement: Motivating readers through integrated instruction* (pp. 1–12). Newark, DE: International Reading Association.

Guthrie, J. T., & Greaney, V. (1991). Literacy acts. In R. Barr, M. L. Kamil, P. Mosenthal, & P. D. Pearson (Eds.), *Handbook of reading research: Volume II* (pp. 68–96). New York: Longman.

Guzzetti, B. J., Kowalinski, B. J., & McGowan, T. (1992). Using a literature-based approach to teaching social studies. *Journal of Reading, 36,* 114–121.

Hawthorne, N. (1850). *The scarlet letter.* Boston, MA: Ticknor, Reed, and Fields.

Highfield, K., & Folkert, J. (1997). Book club: The content-area connection. In S. I. McMahon & T. E. Raphael (Eds.), *The book club connection* (pp. 286–298). New York: Teachers College Press.

Hinton, S. E. (1967). *The outsiders.* New York: Viking.

Hobbs, W. (1988). *Changes in latitudes.* New York: Avon.

Houston, J. W., & Houston, J. D. (1973). *Farewell to Manzanar.* New York: Bantam.

Kincaid, J. (1988). *A small place.* New York: Penguin.

Klass, D. (1994). *California blue.* New York: Scholastic.

Knowles, J. (1960). *A separate peace.* New York: Macmillan.

Langer, J. (1989). *The process of understanding literature.* Report Series 2.1. Albany: Center for the Learning and Teaching of Literature, State University of New York.

Leung, C. B. (1993, December). *Bicultural perspectives and reader response: Four young readers respond to Jean Fritz's Homesick.* Paper presented at the National Reading Conference, Charleston, SC.

Levstik, L. S. (1993). Making the past come to life. In B. E. Cullinan (Ed.), *Fact and fiction: Literature across the curriculum* (pp. 5–13). Newark, DE: International Reading Association.

Lyons M. E. (1992). *Letter from a slave girl: The story of Harriet Jacobs.* New York: Charles Scribner's Sons.

Manna, A. L., & Misheff, S. (1987). What teachers say about their own reading development. *Journal of Reading, 31,* 160–168.

McConnell, S. (1993). Talking drawings: A strategy for assisting learners. *Journal of Reading, 36,* 260–269.

McCracken, R. A. (1971). Initiating sustained silent reading. *Journal of Reading, 14,* 521–524.

McKenna, M. C., Kear, D. J., & Ellsworth, R. A. (1995). Children's attitudes toward reading: A national survey. *Reading Research Quarterly, 30,* 934–956.

McMahon, S. I., & Raphael, T. E. (1997). *The book club connection.* New York: Teachers College Press.

Miller, D. E. (1993). The literature project: Using literature to improve the self-concept of at-risk adolescent females. *Journal of Reading, 36,* 442–446.

Monseau, V. R. (1996). *Responding to young adult literature.* Portsmouth, NH: Heinemann.

Myers, W. D. (1988). *Fallen angels.* New York: Scholastic.

Nieto, S. (1996). *Affirming diversity: The sociopolitical context of multicultural education* (2nd ed.). New York: Longman.

Nilsen, A. P., & Donelson, K. L. (1993). *Literature for today's young adults* (4th ed.). New York: HarperCollins.

Palmer, R. G., & Stewart, R. A. (1997). Nonfiction trade books in content area instruction: Realities and potential. *Journal of Adolescent & Adult Literacy, 40,* 630–641.

Rosenblatt, L. M. (1978). *The reader, the text, the poem.* Carbondale, IL: Southern Illinois University Press.

Salinger, J. D. (1951). *The catcher in the rye.* Boston, MA: Little, Brown.

Savage, J. F. (1994). *Teaching reading using literature.* Dubuque, IA: WCB Brown & Benchmark.

Schiefele, U. (1992). Topic interest and levels of text comprehension. In K. A. Renninger, S. Hidi, & A. Krapp (Eds.), *The role of interest in learning and development* (pp. 151–182). Hillsdale, NJ: Erlbaum.

Soto, G. (1992). *Pacific crossing.* New York: Harcourt Brace Jovanovich.

Stover, L. T., & Tway, E. (1992). Cultural diversity and the young adult novel. In V. R. Monseau & G. M. Salvner (Eds.), *Reading their world: The young adult novel in the classroom* (pp. 132–153). Portsmouth, NH: Boynton/Cook.

Taylor, M. D. (1976). *Roll of thunder, hear my cry.* New York: Trumpet Club.

Van Amerongen, J. (1987, January 12). *The neighborhood.* New York: Cowles Syndicate.

Vogel, M., & Zancanella, D. (1991). The story world of adolescents in and out of the classroom. *English Journal, 80,* 54–60.

Voight, C. (1991). *The Vandemark mummy.* New York: Fawcett.

Walker, A. (1983). *The color purple.* New York: Harcourt, Brace, Jovanovich.

Warner, L. S. (1976). *From slave to abolitionist: The life of William Wells Brown.* New York: Dial.

Winkler, K. J. (1994, January 12). An African writer at a crossroads. *The Chronicle of Higher Education,* A-9.

Wolfe, E. (1990). *Lonely heart.* New York: Angel Entertainment.

Young, T. A., & Vardell, S. (1993). Weaving readers' theatre and nonfiction into the curriculum. *The Reading Teacher, 46,* 396–406.

Chapter 8

Recommended Readings

Beck, I., & McKeown, M. (1991). Conditions of vocabulary acquisition. In R. Barr, M. L. Kamil, P. B. Mosenthal, & P. D. Pearson (Eds.), *Handbook of reading research: Volume II* (pp. 789-814). New York: Longman.

A review of the literature discussing the issues underlying vocabulary learning and the sources of that learning.

Ernst, M. S., & Thurber, J. (1960). *In a word.* Great Neck, NY: Channel Press.

An interesting collection of words with colorful etymologies. Humorous cartoons by Thurber accompany many of the entries.

Shu, H., Anderson, R. C., & Zhang, H. (1995). Incidental learning of word meanings while reading: A Chinese and American cross-cultural study. *Reading Research Quarterly, 30,* 76–95.

Research study which found that the incidental acquisition of word meanings while reading narrative material is a cross-cultural universal in written language development.

Tierney, R. J., Readence, J. E., & Dishner, E. K. (1995). *Reading strategies and practices: A compendium* (4th ed.). Boston: Allyn & Bacon.

Unit 8 contains a variety of meaning vocabulary strategies with appropriate examples.

Watts, S. M. (1995). Vocabulary instruction during reading lessons in six classrooms. *Journal of Reading Behavior, 27,* 399–424.

Study which revealed that effective vocabulary instruction, as characterized in the research literature, was rarely seen in fifth and sixth grade classrooms.

References

Beck, I., & McKeown, M. (1991). Conditions of vocabulary acquisition. In R. Barr, M. L. Kamil, P. B. Mosenthal, & P. D. Pearson (Eds.), *Handbook of reading research: Volume II* (pp. 789–814). New York: Longman.

Berger, M. (1981). *Disastrous volcanoes.* New York: Franklin Watts.

Cunningham, P. M. Big words carry big content. (1992a). In E. K. Dishner, T. W. Bean, J. E. Readence, & D. W. Moore (Eds.), *Reading in the content areas: Improving classroom instruction* (3rd ed., pp. 202–210). Dubuque, IA: Kendall/Hunt.

Cunningham, P. M. Content area vocabulary: Building and connecting meaning. (1992b). In E. K. Dishner, T. W. Bean, J. E. Readence, & D. W. Moore (Eds.), *Reading in the content areas: Improving classroom instruction* (3rd ed., pp. 182–189). Dubuque, IA: Kendall/Hunt.

Dana, C., & Rodriguez, M. (1992). TOAST: A system to study vocabulary. *Reading Research and Instruction, 31*(4), 78–84.

Dunston, P. (1992). A critique of graphic organizer research. *Reading Research and Instruction, 31*(2), 57–65.

Eeds, M., & Cockrum, W. A. (1985). Teaching word meanings by expanding schemata vs. dictionary work vs. reading in context. *Journal of Reading, 28,* 492–497.

Funk, C. E. (1950). *Thereby hangs a tale: Stories of curious word origins.* New York: Harper & Brothers.

Haggard, M. R. (1992). Integrated content and long-term vocabulary learning with the vocabulary self-collection strategy. In E. K. Dishner, T. W. Bean, J. E. Readence, & D. W. Moore (Eds.), *Reading in the content areas: Improving classroom instruction* (3rd ed., pp. 190–196). Dubuque, IA: Kendall/Hunt.

Heimlich, J. E., & Pittelman, S. D. (1986). *Semantic mapping: Classroom applications.* Newark, DE: International Reading Association.

Jenkins, J. R., Matlock, B., & Slocum, T. A. (1989). Two approaches to vocabulary instruction: The teaching of individual word meanings and practice in deriving word meaning from context. *Reading Research Quarterly, 24,* 215–235.

Konopak, B. C., & Mealey, D. L. Vocabulary learning in the content areas. (1992). In E. K. Dishner, T. W. Bean, J. E. Readence, & D. W. Moore (Eds.), *Reading in the content areas: Improving classroom instruction* (3rd ed., pp. 174–182). Dubuque, IA: Kendall/Hunt.

Maurer, D. W. (1955). Whiz mob. *Publication of the American Dialect Society*, No. 24.

Memory, D. M. Guiding students to independent decoding in content area classes. (1992). In E. K. Dishner, T. W. Bean, J. E. Readence, & D. W. Moore (Eds.), *Reading in the content areas: Improving classroom instruction* (3rd ed., pp. 210–218). Dubuque, IA: Kendall/Hunt.

Moore, D. W., & Readence, J. E. (1984). A quantitative and qualitative review of graphic organizer research. *Journal of Educational Research, 78,* 11–17.

Pittelman, S. D., Heimlich, J. E., Berglund, R. L., & French, M. P. (1991). *Semantic feature analysis: Classroom applications.* Newark, DE: International Reading Association.

Rapp-Haggard Ruddell, M. Integrated content and long-term vocabulary learning with the vocabulary self-collection strategy. (1992). In E. K. Dishner, T. W. Bean, J. E. Readence, & D. W. Moore (Eds.), *Reading in the content areas: Improving classroom instruction* (3rd ed., pp. 190–196). Dubuque, IA: Kendall/Hunt.

Schatz, E. K., & Baldwin, R. S. (1986). Context clues are unreliable predictors of word meanings. *Reading Research Quarterly, 21,* 439–453.

Schwartz, R. M. (1988). Learning to learn vocabulary in content area textbooks. *Journal of Reading, 32,* 108–118.

Shu, H., Anderson, R. C., & Zhang, H. (1995). Incidental learning of word meanings while reading: A Chinese and American cross-cultural study. *Reading Research Quarterly, 30,* 76–95.

Tierney, R. J., Readence, J. E., & Dishner, E. K. (1995). *Reading strategies and practices: A compendium* (4th ed.). Boston: Allyn & Bacon.

White, T. G., Power, M. A., & White, S. (1989). Morphological analysis: Implications for teaching and understanding vocabulary growth. *Reading Research Quarterly, 24,* 283–304.

Chapter 9

Recommended Readings

Armbruster, B. B., Anderson, T. H., & Ostertag, J. (1989). Teaching text structure to improve reading and writing. *The Reading Teacher, 43,* 130–137.

Presents research-based information on using text structure visual frameworks to help students organize and summarize ideas in a text. The article provides detailed information on structuring effective lessons that move students toward thinking like writers.

Dole, J. A., Duffy, G. G., Roehler, L. R., & Pearson, P. D. (1991). Moving from the old to the new: Research on reading comprehension instruction. *Review of Educational Research, 61,* 239–264.

Reviews the research on comprehension and offers recommendations for instruction.

Fitzgerald, J. (1990). *Reading comprehension instruction 1783-1987: A review of trends and research.* Newark, DE: International Reading Association.

Presents analysis of reading comprehension instruction charting the substantial progress teachers and researchers have made since early efforts to guide students' text comprehension.

Irwin, J. W. (1991). *Teaching reading comprehension processes* (2nd ed.). Englewood Cliffs, NJ: Prentice-Hall.

A text presenting various strategies for teaching comprehension.

McIntosh, M. E., & Draper, R. J. (1995). Applying the question-answer relationship strategy in mathematics. *Journal of Adolescent & Adult Literacy, 39,* 120–131.

Demonstrates the application of the levels of comprehension construct to the mathematics classroom.

Moorman, G. B., & Blanton, W. E. (1990). The Information Text Reading Activity (ITRA): Engaging students in meaningful learning. *Journal of Reading, 34,* 174–183.

Presents a valuable prereading and postreading instructional framework and related matrix that shows each stage of a lesson in the ITRA and corresponding teaching strategies.

Pearson, P. D., & Fielding, L. (1991). Comprehension instruction. In R. Barr, M. L. Kamil, P. B. Mosenthal, & P. D. Pearson (Eds.), *Handbook of reading research: Volume II* (pp. 815–860). New York: Longman.

The authors provide an extensive review of comprehension research that supports many of the strategies highlighted in the present Chapter aimed at helping students grasp text structure, use visual representations of information, and engage in cooperative discussion of text ideas.

Randall, S. N. (1996). Information charts: A strategy for organizing student research. *Journal of Adolescent & Adult Literacy, 39,* 536–542.

Provides a discussion of the use of I-Charts for independent student research.

Tierney, R. J., Readence, J. E., & Dishner, E. K. (1995). *Reading strategies and practices: A compendium* (4th ed.). Boston: Allyn & Bacon.

Units 5, 7, and 9 describe numerous comprehension strategies.

References

Armbruster, B. B., Anderson, T. H., Armstrong, J. O., Wise, M. A., Janisch, C., & Meyer, L. (1991). Reading and questioning in content area lessons. *Journal of Reading Behavior, 23,* 35–59.

Armbruster, B. B., Anderson, T. H., & Ostertag, J. (1989). Teaching text structure to improve reading and writing. *The Reading Teacher, 43*, 130–137.

Bean, T. W. (1985). Classroom questioning strategies: Directions for applied research. In A. C. Graesser & J. B. Black (Eds.), *The psychology of questions* (pp. 335–358). Hillsdale, NJ: Erlbaum.

Bean, T. W., & Pardi, R. (1979). A field-test of a guided reading strategy. *Journal of Reading, 23*, 144–147.

Bean, T. W., Sorter, J., Singer, H., & Frazee, C. (1986). Teaching students how to make predictions about events in history with a graphic organizer plus options guide. *Journal of Reading, 29*, 739–745.

Blanton, W. E., Wood, K. D., & Moorman, G. B. (1990). The role of purpose in reading instruction. *The Reading Teacher, 43*, 486–493.

Cunningham, J. W. A taxonomy of questions for content reading. (1992). In E. K. Dishner, T. W. Bean, J. E. Readence, & D. W. Moore (Eds.), *Reading in the content areas: Improving classroom instruction* (3rd ed., pp. 220–226). Dubuque, IA: Kendall/Hunt.

Dole, J. A., Valencia, S. W., Greer, E. A., & Waldrop, J. L. (1991). Effects of two types of prereading instruction on the comprehension of narrative and expository text. *Reading Research Quarterly, 26*, 142–159.

Durkin, D. (1978–1979). What classroom observations reveal about reading comprehension instruction. *Reading Research Quarterly, 14*, 481–533.

Gillespie, C. (1990). Questions about student-generated questions. *Journal of Reading, 34*, 250–257.

Goodlad, J. I. (1983). A study of schooling: Some findings and hypotheses. *Phi Delta Kappan, 64*, 465–470.

Gordon, C. J. (1990). Contexts for expository text structure use. *Reading Research and Instruction, 29*, 55–72.

Hoffman, J. V. (1992). Critical reading/thinking across the curriculum: Using I-charts to support learning. *Language Arts, 69*, 121–127.

Manzo, A. V. (1975). Guided reading procedure. *Journal of Reading, 18*, 287–291.

Manzo, A. V., & Casale, U. P. (1985). Listen-read-discuss: A content heuristic. *Journal of Reading, 28*, 732–734.

McGee, L. M., & Richgels, D. J. (1992). Attending to text structure: A comprehension strategy. In E. K. Dishner, T. W. Bean, J. E. Readence, & D. W. Moore (Eds.), *Reading in the content areas: Improving classroom instruction* (3rd ed., pp. 234–247). Dubuque, IA: Kendall/Hunt.

Meyer, B. J. F., Brandt, D., & Bluth, G. J. (1980). Use of top-level structure in text: Key for reading comprehension of ninth-grade students. *Reading Research Quarterly, 16*, 72–103.

Meyer, B. J. F., & Freedle, R. O. (1984). Effects of discourse type on recall. *American Educational Research Journal, 21*, 121–143.

Niles, O. S., & Memory, D. (1977). Teacher's edition. *Reading tactics.* Glenview, IL: Scott Foresman.

Ogle, D. (1992). KWL in action: Secondary teachers find applications that work. In E. K. Dishner, T. W. Bean, J. E. Readence, & D. W. Moore (Eds.), *Content area reading: Improving classroom instruction* (3rd ed., pp. 270–282). Dubuque, IA: Kendall/Hunt.

Pearson, P. D., & Johnson, D. D. (1978). *Teaching reading comprehension.* New York: Holt, Rinehart and Winston.

Pearson, P. D., & Fielding, L. (1991). Comprehension instruction. In R. Barr, M. L. Kamil, P. B. Mosenthal, & P. D. Pearson (Eds.), *Handbook of reading research: Volume II* (pp. 815–860). New York: Longman.

Raphael, T. E. (1984). Teaching learners about sources of information for answering comprehension questions. *Journal of Reading, 27*, 303–311.

Randall, S. N. (1996). Information charts: A strategy for organizing student research. *Journal of Adolescent & Adult Literacy, 39*, 536–542.

Rumelhart, D. E. (1975). Notes on a schema for stories. In D. G. Bobrow & A. M. Collins (Eds.), *Representation and understanding: Studies in cognitive science.* New York: Academic Press.

Sippola, A.E. (1995). K-W-L-S. *The Reading Teacher, 48*, 542-543.

Stahl, S. A., Hare, V. C., Sinatra, R., & Gregory, J. F. (1991). Defining the role of prior knowledge and vocabulary in reading comprehension: The retiring of number 41. *Journal of Reading Behavior, 23*, 487–508.

Taylor, B. M., & Samuels, S. J. (1983). Children's use of text structure in the recall of expository material. *American Educational Research Journal, 20*, 517–528.

Tierney, R. J., Soter, A., O'Flahavan, J. F., & McGinley, W. (1989). The effects of reading and writing upon thinking critically. *Reading Research Quarterly, 24*, 134–173.

Vacca, R. T. (1973). A means of building comprehension of social studies content. In H. L. Herber & R. L. Barron (Eds.), *Research in reading in the content areas: Second year report* (pp. 75–83). Syracuse, NY: Syracuse University Reading and Language Arts Center.

Wittrock, M. C. (1985). Teaching learners generative strategies for enhancing reading comprehension. *Theory Into Practice, 24*, 123–126.

Chapter 10

Recommended Readings

Alvermann, D. E. (1991). The discussion web: A graphic aid for learning across the curriculum. *The Reading Teacher, 45*, 92–99.

   Combines a graphic aid with discussion to enhance comprehension.

Alvermann, D. E., & Moore, D. W. (1991). Secondary school reading. In R. Barr, M. L. Kamil, P. B. Mosenthal, & P. D. Pearson (Eds.), *Handbook of reading research: Volume II* (pp. 951–983). New York: Longman.

   The authors point out those strategies that are supported by research and argue that too little prereading instruction is offered students. They emphasize the use of reading guides and self-questioning strategies like DRTA to move students toward independent learning from text.

Beck, I. L., McKeown, M. G., Hamilton, R. C., & Kucan, L. (1997). *Questioning the author: An approach for enhancing student engagement with text.* Newark, DE: International Reading Association.

   This book provides a number of classroom examples and guidelines based on research into planning and orchestrating questioning and discussion.

Gambrell, L. B., & Almasi, J. F. (1996). *Lively discussions! Fostering engaged reading.* Newark, DE: International Reading Association.

   This edited book contains a wealth of information and classroom examples of how to guide and assess discussions.

Moore, D. W., Readence, J. E., & Rickelman, R. J. (1988). *Prereading activities for content area reading and learning* (2nd ed.). Newark, DE: International Reading Association.

   A succinct and readable explanation of comprehension strategies.

Pearson, P. D., & Fielding, L. (1991). Comprehension instruction. In R. Barr, M. L. Kamil, P. B. Mosenthal, & P. D. Pearson (Eds.), *Handbook of reading research: Volume II* (pp. 815–860). New York: Longman.

   The authors provide an extensive review of comprehension research that supports many of the strategies highlighted in the present chapter aimed at helping students grasp text structure, use visual representations of information, and engage in cooperative discussion of text ideas.

Santa, C. M., & Alvermann, D. E. (1991). *Science learning: Processes and applications.* Newark, DE: International Reading Association.

   An edited collection of papers that encompasses analyses of science textbook characteristic and practical classroom strategies designed to improve students' learning in science.

Tierney, R. J., Readence, J. E., & Dishner, E. K. (1995) *Reading strategies and practices: A compendium* (4th ed.). Boston: Allyn & Bacon.

   Contains a wealth of practical teaching strategies with appropriate cautions and comments to the reader on their use in classrooms.

References

Alvermann, D. E., Dillon, D. R., & O'Brien, D. G. (1987). *Using discussion to promote reading comprehension.* Newark, DE: International Reading Association.

Alvermann, D. E., O'Brien, D. G., & Dillon, D. R. (1990). What teachers do when they say they're having discussions of content area reading assignments: A qualitative analysis. *Reading Research Quarterly, 25*, 296–322.

Armstrong, D. P., Patberg, J., & Dewitz, P. (1988). Reading guides-helping students understand. *Journal of Reading, 31*, 532–541.

Barron, R. F. (1979). Research for the classroom teacher: Recent developments on the structured overview as an advance organizer. In H. L. Herber & J. D. Riley (Eds.), *Research in reading in the content areas: The fourth report* (pp. 171–173). Syracuse, NY: Syracuse University Reading and Language Arts Center.

Bean, T. W. (1992a). Combining text previews and three level study guides to develop critical reading in history. In E. K. Dishner, T. W. Bean, J. E. Readence, & D. W. Moore (Eds.), *Reading in the content areas: Improving classroom instruction* (3rd ed., pp. 264–269). Dubuque, IA: Kendall/Hunt.

Bean, T. W. (1997). Preservice teachers' selection and use of content area literacy strategies. *Journal of Educational Research, 90*, 154–163.

Bean, T. W., & Bishop, A. L. (1992). Polar opposites: A strategy for guiding students' critical reading and discussion. In E. K. Dishner, T. W. Bean, J. E. Readence, & D. W. Moore (Eds.), *Reading in the content areas: Improving classroom instruction* (3rd ed., pp. 247–254). Dubuque, IA: Kendall/Hunt.

Bean, T. W., Searles, D., Singer, H., & Cowan, S. (1990). Learning concepts from biology text through pictorial analogies and an analogical study guide. *Journal of Educational Research, 83*, 233–237.

Bean, T. W., Singer, H., & Cowan, S. (1985). Analogical study guides: Improving comprehension in science. *Journal of Reading, 29*, 246–250.

Bean, T. W., Singer, H., Sorter, J., & Frazee, C. (1986). The effect of metacognitive instruction in outlining and graphic organizer construction on students' comprehension in a tenth-grade world history class. *Journal of Reading Behavior, 18*, 153–169.

Conley, M. W. (1987). Grouping. In D. E. Alvermann, D. W. Moore, & M. W. Conley (Eds.), *Research within reach: Secondary school reading* (pp. 130–140). Newark, DE: International Reading Association.

Duffelmeyer, F. A., & Baum, D. D. (1992). The extended anticipation guide revisited. *Journal of Reading, 35,* 654–656.

Durkin, D. (1978–1979). What classroom observations reveal about reading comprehension instruction. *Reading Research Quarterly, 14,* 481–533.

Ericson, B., Hubler, M., Bean, T. W., Smith, C. C., & McKenzie, J. V. (1987). Increasing critical reading in junior high classrooms. *Journal of Reading, 30,* 430–439.

Facione, P. (1984). Toward a theory of critical thinking. *Liberal Education, 30,* 253–261.

Graves, M. F., Cooke, C. L., & LaBerge, M. L. (1983). The effects of previewing difficult short stories on low ability junior high school students' comprehension, recall, and attitudes. *Reading Research Quarterly, 18,* 262–276.

Hartman, D. K., & Allison, J. (1996). Promoting inquiry-oriented discussions using multiple texts. In L. B. Gambrell & J. F. Almasi (Eds.), *Lively discussions! Fostering engaged reading* (pp. 106–133). Newark, DE: International Reading Association.

Hawthorne, N. (1986). *The scarlet letter.* New York: Penguin.

Head, M. H., & Readence, J. E. (1992). Anticipation guides: Using prediction to promote learning from text. In E. K. Dishner, T. W. Bean, J. E. Readence, & D. W. Moore (Eds.), *Reading in the content areas: Improving classroom instruction* (3rd ed., pp. 227–233). Dubuque, IA: Kendall/Hunt.

Jimenez, R. T. (1997). The strategic reading abilities and potential of five low-literacy Latina/o readers in middle school. *Reading Research Quarterly, 32,* 224–243.

Kleeman, C. (1983). Polar opposites guide for world geography. In T. W. Bean (Ed.), *Reading and learning from text course of study.* Anaheim, CA: Anaheim Union High School District.

Laffey, J. L., & Steele, J. L. (1979). Tell no teacher . . . In H. L. Herber & J. D. Riley (Eds.), *Research in reading in the content areas: The fourth report* (pp. 177–185). Syracuse, NY: Syracuse University Reading and Language Arts Center.

Larson, C. O., & Dansereau, D. F. (1986). Cooperative learning in dyads. *Journal of Reading, 29,* 516–520.

Manzo, A. V. (1969). The request procedure. *Journal of Reading, 13,* 123–126.

McCormick, S. (1989). Effects of previews on more skilled and less skilled readers' comprehension of expository text. *Journal of Reading Behavior, 21,* 219–234.

Merkley, D. J. (1997). Modified anticipation guide. *The Reading Teacher, 50,* 365–368.

Miller, A. (1976). *The crucible.* New York: Penguin.

Raphael, T. E.(1986). Teaching question answer relationships, revisited. *The Reading Teacher, 39,* 516–522.

Rayl, D. (1983). Physical fitness film anticipation guide. In T. W. Bean (Ed.), *Reading and learning from text course of study.* Anaheim, CA: Anaheim Union High School District.

Schwartz, M., & O'Connor, J. R. (1975). *New exploring a changing world.* New York: Globe Book.

Short, D. J. (1994). Expanding middle school horizons: Integrating language, culture, and social studies. *TESOL Quarterly, 28,* 581–608.

This article provides a number of strategies for working with second language students in the classroom.

Stauffer, R. (1969). *Directing reading maturity as a cognitive process.* New York: Harper & Row.

Stevens, R. J., Madden, N. A., Slavin, R. E., & Farnish, A. M. (1987). Cooperative integrated reading and composition: Two field experiments. *Reading Research Quarterly, 22,* 433–454.

Stockton, F. R. (1884). *The lady or the tiger and other stories.* New York: Charles Scribner and Sons.

Tan, A. (1991). *The kitchen god's wife.* New York: Ballantine.

Vacca, R. T. (1977). An investigation of a functional reading strategy in seventh grade social studies. In H. L. Herber & R. T. Vacca (Eds.), *Research in reading in the content areas: The third report* (pp. 116–131). Syracuse, NY: Syracuse University Reading and Language Arts Center.

Vanderhoof, B., Miller E., Clegg, L. B., & Patterson, J. (1992). Real or fake? The phony document as a teaching strategy. *Social Education, 56,* 169–171.

Wood, K. D. (1987). Fostering cooperative learning in middle and secondary classrooms. *Journal of Reading, 31,* 10-18.

Wood, K. D., Lapp, D., & Flood, J. (1992). *Guiding readers through text: A review of study guides.* Newark, DE: International Reading Association.

Chapter 11

Recommended Readings

Calkins, L. M. (1994). *The art of teaching writing* (2nd ed.). Portsmouth, NH: Heinemann.

This is a powerful book that chronicles the author's many years of helping students and teachers to appreciate the subtleties of teaching writing.

Daisy, P. (1997). Promoting literacy in secondary content area classrooms with biography projects. *Journal of Adolescent & Adult Literacy, 40,* 270–278.

The author offers useful insights on biography projects along with resources for locating books that center on women and underrepresented groups in history and other content areas. Includes a lengthy list of reader response projects for sharing biographies.

Heide, A., & Stilborne, L. (1996). *The teacher's complete and easy guide to the Internet.* Toronto, Ontario, Canada: Trifolium Books. Available: http://www.pubcouncil.ca/trifolium.

> In their listing of web site resources, the authors include the following web sites for high school student writers: Inkspot (http://www.interlog.com/~ohi/inkspot/young.html) and Writes of Passage (http://www.writes.org/index.htm). Their book includes additional websites helpful to young writers.

Ollman, H. E. (1996). Creating higher level thinking with reading response. *Journal of Adolescent & Adult Literacy, 39,* 576–581.

> Provides seven creative reading response formats and strategies you can use in various content areas.

Tierney, R. J., Carter, M. A., & Desai, L. E. (1991). *Portfolio assessment in the reading-writing classroom.* Norwood, MA: Christopher-Gordon Publishers.

> Provides a comprehensive introduction and detailed demonstration of how to start and sustain the use of portfolios as an assessment tool that goes well beyond standardized assessments of writing.

Tompkins, G. E. (1990). *Teaching writing: Balancing process and product.* Columbus, OH: Merrill.

> This book features a wealth of writing strategies, a detailed discussion of the writing process, and a section on writing across the curriculum.

References

Alejandro, A. (1989). Cars: A culturally integrated "I-Search" module. *English Journal, 78,* 41–44.

Bean, T. W. (1992b). Combining writing fluency and vocabulary development through writing roulette. In E. K. Dishner, T. W. Bean, J. E. Readence, & D. W. Moore (Eds.), *Reading in the content areas: Improving classroom instruction* (3rd ed., pp. 319–323). Dubuque, IA: Kendall/Hunt.

Bean, T. W. (1994). Writing across the curriculum. In L. W. Searfoss & J. E. Readence, *Helping children learn to read* (3rd ed.). Boston: Allyn and Bacon.

Bean, T. W. (1997, May). ReWrite: A music strategy for exploring content area concepts. *Reading Online.* Online journal of the International Reading Association. Available: http://www.readingonline.org

Bean, T. W., & Readence, J. E. (1995). A comparative study of content area literacy students' attitudes toward reading through autobiography analysis. In K. A. Hinchman, D. J. Leu, & C. K. Kinzer (Eds.), *Perspectives on literacy research and practice* (pp. 325–333). Forty-fourth Yearbook of the National Reading Conference. Chicago, IL: National Reading Conference.

Bean, T. W., & Zulich, J. (1989). Using dialogue journals to foster reflective practice with preservice content-area teachers. *Teacher Education Quarterly, 16,* 33–40.

Beaven, M. H. (1977). Individualized goal setting, self-evaluation, and peer evaluation. In C. R. Cooper & L. Odell (Eds.), *Evaluating writing: Describing, measuring, judging* (pp. 135–156). Urbana, IL: National Council of Teachers of English.

Calkins, L. M. (1994). *The art of teaching writing* (2nd ed.). Portsmouth, NH: Heinemann.

Daisy, P. (1997). Promoting literacy in secondary content area classrooms with biography projects. *Journal of Adolescent & Adult Literacy, 40,* 270–278.

Davey, B. (1987). Team for success: Guided practice in study skills through cooperative research reports. *Journal of Reading, 31,* 701–705.

Denyer, R. (1982). *The guitar handbook.* New York: Knopf.

Diamond, B. J., & Moore, M. A. (1995). *Multicultural literacy: Mirroring the reality of the classroom.* White Plains, NY: Longman.

Fitzgerald, J. (1987). Research on revision in writing. *Review of Educational Research, 57,* 481–506.

Fulwiler, T. (1986). Journals across the disciplines. In E. K. Dishner, T. W. Bean, J. E. Readence, & D. W. Moore (Eds.), *Reading in the content areas: Improving classroom instruction* (2nd ed., pp. 360–366). Dubuque, IA: Kendall/Hunt.

Hansen, J. (1996). Evaluation: The center of writing instruction. *The Reading Teacher, 50,* 188–195.

Hansen, J. (1987). *When writers read.* Portsmouth, NH: Heinemann.

Holmes, V. L., & Moulton, M. R. (1997). Dialogue journals as an ESL learning strategy. *Journal of Adolescent & Adult Literacy, 40,* 616–621.

Jody, M., & Saccardi, M. (1996) *Computer conversations: Readers and books online.* Urbana, IL: National Council of Teachers of English.

Konopak, B. C., Martin, S. H., & Martin, M. A. (1987). An integrated communication arts approach for enhancing students' learning in the content areas. *Reading Research and Instruction, 26,* 275–289.

Macrorie, K. (1988). *The I-search paper.* Portsmouth, NH: Heinemann.

Martin, S. H. Using journals to promote learning across the curriculum. (1992). In E. K. Dishner, T. W. Bean, J. E. Readence, & D. W. Moore (Eds.), *Reading in the content areas: Improving classroom instruction* (3rd ed., pp. 311–318). Dubuque, IA: Kendall/Hunt.

Miller, A., & Coen, D. (1994). The case for music in the schools. *Phi Delta Kappan, 75,* 459–461.

Moore, S. A. Revising writing in the content areas: A revision. (1992). In E. K. Dishner, T. W. Bean, J. E. Readence, & D. W. Moore (Eds.), *Reading in the content areas: Improving classroom instruction* (3rd ed., pp. 303–310). Dubuque, IA: Kendall/Hunt.

Moore, D. W., & Moore, S. A. (1992). Possible sentences: An update. In E. K. Dishner, T. W. Bean, J. E. Readence, & D. W. Moore (Eds.), *Reading in the content areas: Improving classroom instruction* (3rd ed., pp. 196–202). Dubuque, IA: Kendall/Hunt.

Moore, D. W., Moore, S. A., Cunningham, P. M., & Cunningham, J. W. (1986). *Developing readers and writers in the content areas.* White Plains, NY: Longman.

Newkirk, T. (1986). Time for questions: Responding to writing. In T. Newkirk (Ed.), *To compose* (pp. 121–124). Portsmouth, NH: Heinemann.

Nishida, G. A., & Tenorio, J. M. (1993). *What bit me? Identifying Hawaii's stinging and biting insects and their kin.* Honolulu: University of Hawaii Press.

Ollman, H. E. (1996). Creating higher level thinking with reading response. *Journal of Adolescent & Adult Literacy, 39,* 576–581.

Searfoss, L. W., Smith, C. C., & Bean, T. W. (1981). An integrated language strategy for second language learners. *TESOL Quarterly, 15,* 383–389.

Shuman, R. B. (1979). Writing roulette: Taking a chance on not grading. In G. Stanford (Ed.), *How to handle the paper load* (pp. 3–5). Urbana, IL: National Council of Teachers of English.

Shuy, R. W. (1988). Discourse level language functions: Complaining. In J. Staton, R. W. Shuy, J. K. Peyton, & L. Reed (Eds.), *Dialogue journal communication: Classroom, linguistic, social and cognitive views* (pp. 143–161). Norwood, NJ: Ablex.

Smith, C. C., & Bean, T. W. (1980). The guided writing procedure: Integrating content teaching and writing improvement. *Reading World, 19,* 290–294.

Smith, T. R. (1986). *Handbook for planning an effective writing program: Kindergarten through grade twelve* (4th ed.). Sacramento, CA: California State Department of Education.

Stafford, W. (1986). A way of writing. In T. Newkirk (Ed.), *To compose* (pp. 25–27). Portsmouth, NH: Heinemann.

Stahl, S. A., & Kapinus, B. A. (1991). Predicting word meanings to teach content area vocabulary. *The Reading Teacher, 45,* 36–43.

Stanford, B. (Ed.). (1979). *How to handle the paper load.* Urbana, IL: National Council of Teachers of English.

Tenbruggencate, J. (1990). Crab spider becoming a pest. *The Sunday Star-Bulletin & Advertiser.* December 30th. Honolulu, HI: Gannett Pacific Corp.

Tierney, R. J., & Shanahan, T. (1991). Research on the reading-writing relationship: Interactions, transactions, and outcomes. In R. Barr, M. L. Kamil, P. Mosenthal, & P. D. Pearson (Eds.), *Handbook of reading research: Volume II* (pp. 246–280). New York: Longman.

Tompkins, G. E. (1990). *Teaching writing: Balancing process and product.* Columbus, OH: Merrill.

Wood, K. D. (1984). Probable passages: A writing strategy. *The Reading Teacher, 37,* 496–499.

Chapter 12

Recommended Readings

Flippo, R. F., & Caverly, D. C. (1991). *Teaching reading and study strategies at the college level.* Newark, DE: International Reading Association.

This collection of papers provides a good theoretical foundation and discussion of the various teacher-directed and student-directed teaching strategies aimed at developing independent learners. Although the title indicates a college level target population, the book offers valuable information on strategies often used at the secondary level to give students a strong college preparatory experience.

Gall, M. D., Gall, J. P., Jacobsen, D. R., & Bullock, T. L. (1990). *Tools for learning: A guide to teaching study skills.* Alexandria, VA: Association for Supervision and Curriculum Development.

This publication contains a review of theory and research underpinning study strategy instruction along with sections on notetaking, test taking, and self-management.

Jackson, F. R., & Cunningham, J. W. (1994). Investigating secondary content teachers' and preservice teachers' conceptions of study strategy instruction. *Reading Research and Instruction, 34,* 111–135.

Research which indicated a lack of knowledge and valuing of study strategies by teachers as well as a confusion of what effective study strategy instruction involved, particularly with preservice teachers.

Paris, S. G., Wasik, B. A., & Van der Westhuizen, G. (1988). Meta-metacognition: A review of research on metacognition and reading. In J. E. Readence & R. S. Baldwin (Eds.), *Dialogues in literacy research* (pp. 143–166). Thirty-seventh Yearbook of the National Reading Conference, Chicago, IL: National Reading Conference.

A methodical, comprehensive, and readable review of the literature of metacognition.

Paris, S. G., Wasik, B. A., & Turner, J. C. (1991). The development of strategic readers. In R. Barr, M. L. Kamil, P. B. Mosenthal, & P. D. Pearson (Eds.), *Handbook of reading research: Volume II* (pp. 609–640). New York: Longman.

Provides a contemporary discussion of metacognitive research and those parental, peer, teacher, and classroom climate factors that encourage or discourage the development of skilled independent readers.

Rakes, G. C., Rakes, T. A., & Smith, L. J. (1995). Using visuals to enhance secondary students' reading comprehension of expository text. *Journal of Adolescent & Adult Literacy, 39,* 46–54.

A discussion of strategies for students to use to enhance their understanding of graphic aids.

References

Aiken, C. (1896). *Methods of mind training.* New York: Harper.

Aiken, E. G., Thomas, G. S., & Shennum, W. A. (1975). Memory for a lecture: Effects of notes, lecture rates, and informational density. *Journal of Educational Psychology, 67,* 439–444.

Anderson, T. H., & Armbruster, B. B. (1984). Studying. In P. D. Pearson (Ed.), *Handbook of reading research* (pp. 657–679). New York: Longman.

Brum, G. D. (1978). *Biology and man.* Dubuque, IA: Kendall/Hunt.

Carver, R. P. (1987). Should reading comprehension skills be taught? In J. E. Readence & R. S. Baldwin (Eds.), *Research in literacy: Merging perspectives* (pp. 115–126). Thirty-sixth Yearbook of the National Reading Conference. Rochester, NY: National Reading Conference.

Christen, W. L., & Searfoss, L. W. (1992). Placing learning and study strategies in the classroom. In E. K. Dishner, T. W. Bean, J. E. Readence, & D. W. Moore (Eds.), *Reading in the content areas: Improving classroom instruction* (3rd ed., pp. 378–386). Dubuque, IA: Kendall/Hunt.

Dyer, J. W., Riley, J., & Yekovich, R. R. (1979). An analysis of three study skills: Notetaking, summarizing and rereading. *Journal of Educational Research, 73,* 3–7.

Fry, E. (1981). Graphical literacy. *Journal of Reading, 24,* 383–390.

Gall, M. D., Gall, J. P., Jacobsen, D. R., & Bullock, T. L. (1990). *Tools for learning. A guide to teaching study skills.* Alexandria, VA: Association for Supervision and Curriculum Development.

Heinrichs, A. S., & LaBranche, S. P. (1986). Content analysis of 47 college learning skill textbooks. *Reading Research and Instruction, 25,* 277–287.

Henk, W. A., & Helfeldt, J. P. (1992). Helping readers with procedural text in the content areas and beyond. In E. K. Dishner, T. W. Bean, J. E. Readence, & D. W. Moore (Eds.), *Reading in the content areas: Improving classroom instruction* (3rd ed., pp. 348–364). Dubuque, IA: Kendall/Hunt.

Jackson, F. R., & Cunningham, J. W. (1994). Investigating secondary content teachers' and preservice teachers' conceptions of study strategy instruction. *Reading Research and Instruction, 34,* 111–135.

Lopate, K. (1987). *The organization of college lectures in selected introductory level courses.* Unpublished doctoral dissertation, University of Miami, Coral Gables, FL.

Loxterman, J. A., Beck, I. L., & McKeown, M. G. (1994). The effects of thinking aloud during reading on students' comprehension of more or less coherent text. *Reading Research Quarterly, 29,* 352–367.

McAndrew, D. A. (1983). Underlining and notetaking: Some suggestions from research. *Journal of Reading, 27,* 103–108.

Memory, D. M., & Moore, D. W. Three time-honored approaches to study: An update. (1992). In E. K. Dishner, T. W. Bean, J. E. Readence, & D. W. Moore (Eds.), *Reading in the content areas: Improving classroom instruction* (3rd ed., pp. 326–339). Dubuque, IA: Kendall/Hunt.

Miller, G. A. (1956). The magical number seven plus or minus two: Some limits on our capacity for processing information. *Psychological Review, 63,* 81–97.

Nist, S. L., & Kirby, K. (1986). Teaching comprehension and study strategies through modeling and thinking aloud. *Reading Research and Instruction, 25,* 254–264.

Nist, S. L., Simpson, M. L., Olejnik, S., & Mealey (1991). The relationship between self-selected study processes and test performance. *American Educational Research Journal, 28,* 849–874.

Paris, S. G., Wasik, B. A., & Van der Westhuizen, G. (1988). Meta-metacognition: A review of research on metacognition and reading. In J. E. Readence & R. S. Baldwin (Eds.), *Dialogues in literacy research* (pp. 143–166). Thirty-seventh Yearbook of the National Reading Conference. Chicago, IL: National Reading Conference.

Pauk, W. (1979). Notetaking: More bad advice exploded. *Reading World, 18,* 300–303.

Randall, A., Fairbanks, M. M., & Kennedy, M. L. (1986). Using think-aloud protocols diagnostically with college readers. *Reading Research and Instruction, 25,* 240–253.

Reinking, D. (1986). Integrating graphic aids into content area instruction: The graphic information lesson. *Journal of Reading, 30,* 146–151.

Schumm, J. S., & Mangrum, C. T. (1991). FLIP: A framework for content area reading. *Journal of Reading, 35,* 120–124.

Simpson, M. L. (1986). PORPE: A writing strategy for studying and learning in the content areas. *Journal of Reading, 29,* 407–414.

Simpson, M. L. (1992). PORPE: A study strategy for learning in the content areas. In E. K. Dishner, T. W. Bean, J. E. Readence, & D. W. Moore (Eds.), *Reading in the content areas: Improving classroom instruction* (pp. 340–348). Dubuque, IA: Kendall/Hunt.

Simpson, M. L., & Nist, S. L. (1984). PLAE: A model for planning successful independent learning. *Journal of Reading, 28,* 218–223.

Simpson, M. L., Stahl, N. A., & Hayes, C. G. (1989). PORPE: A research validation. *Journal of Reading, 33,* 22–29.

Spires, H. A., & Stone, P. D. (1989). The directed note-taking activity: A self-questioning approach. *Journal of Reading, 33,* 36–39.

Vacca, R. T., & Burkey, L. (1992). Metacognition and comprehension: Showing students how to learn from text. In E. K. Dishner, T. W. Bean, J. E. Readence, & D. W. Moore (Eds.), *Reading in the content areas: Improving classroom instruction* (3rd ed., pp. 255–263). Dubuque, IA: Kendall/Hunt.

Wade, S. E., & Reynolds, R. E. (1989). Developing metacognitive awareness. *Journal of Reading, 33,* 6–14.

INDEX

F

Fake Pop Quiz (FPQ), 216
Fallacy of grade-level reporting, and standardized testing, 65-66
Fallen Angels (Myers), 112, 113
Farewell to Manzanar (Houston and Houston), 112
Feature analysis, 131-32
Field notes, 71
Finding My Voice (Lee), 114
First Sightings (Loughery), 113
FLIP chart, 215
FLIP procedure, 214
Formal tests, 63
Freedom and justice, book list for, 112
From Slave to Abolitionist (Warner), 23, 112
Fry graph, 48

G

Geography, book list, 113
Glossary, defined, 121
Glossary of terms, 225-30
Goal orientation, and studying, 207
Graphic comprehension, and studying, 214-16
Graphic Information Lesson (Reinking), 216
Graphic organizer, defined, 125
Graphic organizers, and post-reading, 180-81
Grolier Electronic Encyclopedia, 17
Groups, types of study, 95
Guessing, and standardized testing, 65
Guided reading procedure (GRP), 154-56
Guided writing procedure (GWP), 193-96
Guides, and reading strategies, 168-75
analogical, 173-75
options, 170-73
study, 168-70

H

Hawaiian cultural values, 30
Heartbeat Drumbeat (Hernandez), 28, 114
History, book list, 113-14
Huckleberry Finn, The Adventures of (Twain), 7
Hypermedia, 17

I

I-search papers, 199-200
Ideographic symbol, 29
If Your Name Was Changed at Ellis Island (Levine), 17
Imaginative writing to inform, 200
Immersion bilingual education, 25
Index, defined, 121
Individualization, 95
Informal tests, 64
Information, organization of, 147-48
Information index, 97
Information search, scope of, 97
Innappropriate norms, and standardized testing, 64
Inquiry charts, 150-53
Instruction groups, 95
Interest, and standardized testing, 65

Interest inventories, 105
International Reading Association, 112
Internet, 18
Interviews, 71-72
informal conversations, 72
student, 72

J

Jaunita Fights the School Board (Velasquez), 114
Journal of Adolescent & Adult Literacy, 112
Journal writing, 186-87

K

Kitchen God's Wife, The (Tan), 112, 181
Knowledge base, defined, 6-7
K-W-L lesson framework, 149-53

L

Language
and classroom social context, 38-39
and reading-writing relationship, 37-38
of students, 37
of text, 36-37
Les Miserables (Hugo), 142
Lesson design, and culture, 27-28
Lesson planning, 80-98
developing units, 83-86
feedback, 82
learning activities, 87-92
modeling content reading process, 82
and thematic units, 92-97
Libraries, and literature, 111-12
Linguistic factors, in text comprehension, 31
Listen-read-discuss strategies, 153-54
and guided reading procedure, 154-56
Listening, and studying, 209
Listening guides, 96
Literacy, defined, 4
Literature, 99-115
assessment of attitudes, 102-6
book clubs, 111
interest inventories, 105
libraries, 111-12
multicultural, 107-8
readers theater, 111
reading aloud to students, 109
reading attitude survey, 103
response journals, 110
response strategies, 110-11
sustained silent reading, 109-10
trade books, 108-14
young adult, 106-8

M

Macrostructure, 36
Magazines for Kids and Teens (Stoll), 113
Mainstreaming, defined, 30
Malcolm X (Meyers), 17
Mathematica (Wolfram), 17
Mean, 63
Memory, 25
characteristics of, 34-36
long-term, 35-36
short-term, 34-35
Metacognition, and studying, 211-13
Metadiscourse, 51

Mnemonics, 207
Morpheme, defined, 119
Motivation, 34
Multiculturalism, and literature, 107-8
Multiple text inquiry, 181
Music, book list, 114

N

National Council for the Accreditation of Teacher Education (NCATE), 6-7
National Council of Teachers of English (NCTE), 7, 112
Naturalistic assessment, defined, 70
Norms, 63, 64
Note taking, and studying, 209-11
Notes
organizing, 211
recording, 210

O

Observation, 70
Observation guide, 71
Options guides, 170-73
Organization, and studying, 207
Outlining, 92
"Ozymandias" (Shelley), 219

P

Passage, length of reading, 96
Passive failure, defined, 94
Peer evaluation, 202
Percentile rank, 63-64
Phony document strategy, 178-79
Physical education, book list, 114
Piaget, Jean, 18, 32
Plain City (Hamilton), 114
Planning. *See* Lesson planning
Planning, and individuality, 94-96
Polar opposites, and post-reading, 179-80
PORPE, and studying, 220-23
Portfolios, 72-73
Positional sensing equipment, 17
Possible sentences, 187-88
Post-reading strategies, 175-81
discussion groups, 176-77
graphic organizers, 180-81
multiple text inquiry, 181
phony document strategy, 178-79
polar opposites, 179-80
reaction guides, 177-78
Postreading phase, 96
Prediction guides, 74-75
Prereading, 159-67
anticipation guide, 159-61
directed reading-thinking activity, 166-67
ReQuest strategy, 164-66
text previews, 161-64
Prereading phase, 95
Prior knowledge
and comprehension, 144
in memory, 31-32
and reader interest, 33-34
and standardized testing, 65
Prior knowledge, assessing, 73-75
knowledge rating, 73-74
prediction guide, 74-75
word association, 74
Probable passages, 188-89
Pronouns, 50

R

Raw score, 63
Raygor Readability Estimate, 48-49, 57, 58
Reaction guides, 177-78
Readability
   Fry graph, 48
   measurement, 48
   quantitative factors, 48
   Raygor Readability Estimate, 48-49
   and student-centered factors, 51
   of textbooks, 47-49
Readability formulas, 50
Reader interest, and prior knowledge, 33-34
Readers theater, 111
Reading aloud to students, 109
Reading attitude survey, 103
Reading daily assignments, 213-14
Reading phase, 95
Reading process, 23-41
   and culture, 25-31
   and diversity, 25-31
   and language, 25-31
   and text comprehension, 31-39
Reading strategies, 167-75
   analogical guides, 173-75
   options guides, 170-73
   study guides, 168-70
Reading-writing relationship, 37-38
Rehearsal, and studying, 208
Reliability, and standardized testing, 64
ReQuest strategy, 164-66
Research groups, 95
Research papers, 198-99
Response journals, and literature, 110
Response strategies, and literature, 110-11
Restructuring, 32
Rewrite strategy, 192-93
Roll of Thunder, Hear My Cry (Taylor), 112, 113
Rosetta Stone (CD-ROM program), 41, 263

S

Saturnalia (Fleischman), 28, 112, 113
Scarlet Letter, The (Hawthorne), 181
Schema theory, 32
Science, book list, 114
Second language, 18, 25-27
Self-evaluation, 202
Semantic mapping, 130
Shadow Brothers, The (Cannon), 114
Shakespeare, sonnets of, 28
Shark Beneath the Reef (George), 114
Sharks, 84-90
Sharks Hawaii (Suzumoto), 88
Sherman Anti-Trust Act, 36
Signal words, 148
Slam! (Myers), 114
Slicing, defined, 96
Small group learning, 9
Social context, of classroom, 38-39
Social studies, book list, 114
Sociolinguistics, defined, 38
Standard deviation, 63
Standard error of measurement, 65
Standardized testing, 64-66
   and comprehension skills, 65
   extraneous factors, 65
   fallacy of grade-level reporting, 65-66
   and guessing, 65

inappropriate norms, 64
   and interest, 65
   and prior knowledge, 65
   and reliability, 64
   standard error of measurement, 65
   test floors and ceilings, 65
   timed testing, 65
   and validity, 64
Standardized tests, 63
Standards for the English Language Arts, 7
Stanine, 63
"Stink Eye" (Bergknut), 26
Student strategies
   and metacognition, 213
   and studying, 210
   and test preparation, 217
Study guides, 168-70
Studying, principles of, 206-8
   attention, 206-7
   depth of processing, 208
   encoding specificity, 208
   goal orientation, 207
   organization, 207
   rehearsal, 208
   time on task, 208
Studying strategies, 208-23
   daily assignments, 213-14
   graphic comprehension, 214-16
   listening, 209
   metacognition, 211-13
   note taking, 209-11
   PORPE, 220-23
   test preparation, 216-20
Super Mario Brothers, 19
Survey tests, 64
Sustained silent reading (SSR), 109-10

T

Talking Drawings (McConnell), 87
Teacher strategies
   and metacognition, 212-13
   and studying, 209-10
   and test preparation, 216-17
Teacher-student interaction patterns, 39
Teachers and Machines (Cuban), 16
Technology, and text, 9
Test floors and ceilings, and standardized testing, 65
Test preparation, and studying, 216-20
Tests. *See also* Assessment
   essay, 219-20
   multiple choice, 217-18
   true-false, 218-19
Testwiseness, defined, 217
Text(s)
   defined, 181
   and guidance, 8
   and language, 36-37
   and social context, 7
   and teachers' roles, 6
Text comprehension, 31-39
   cognitive factors in, 31-39
   and concept learning, 32-33
   linguistic factors in, 36-39
   and motivation, 34
   and prior knowledge in memory, 31-32
   and reader interest, 33-34
Text evaluation checklist, 52
Text implicit comprehension, 145-46
Text organization, patterns of, 149
Text previews, 161-64
Text structure, 25, 148-49
   cause/effect, 148

comparison/contrast, 148
   explicating, 148-49
   problem/solution, 148
   signal words, 148
   time order, 148
Textbook aids, and vocabulary, 121
Textbook(s)
   adaptations for disabilities, 31
   defined, 42
Textbook(s), evaluation of, 42-59
   checklist, 52
   guidelines, 51-53
   political characteristics, 43-47
   qualitative factors in, 49-51
   readability, 47-49
Textbook(s), integration of, 7-9
   concurrent processes, 7, 8
   guidance, 8
   isolated skills, 8
   language processes, 8
   small group learning, 9
   and technology, 9
Textbook(s), introduction of, 53-57
   previewing, 54-57
Textbook(s), political characteristics of, 43-47
   adoption policies, 46-47
   and censorship, 45-46
   and minorities, 43-44
Thematic unit, defined, 92
Thereby Hangs a Tale (Funk), 128
Time on task, and studying, 208
Timed testing, and standardized testing, 65
TOAST, 135
Trade book sources, and literature, 112-14
Trade books, and literature, 108-14
Transcribing, 185-86
Transitional bilingual education, 25
Tuning, defined, 32

U

Understanding, and comprehension, 144-45
Unit of instruction, defined, 81
Units
   developing, 83-86
   outlining, 84-86

V

Validity, and standardized testing, 64
Vandemark Mummy, The (Voight), 112
Verbatim Split Page Procedure (VSPP), 210
Virtual reality, 17
Vocabulary difficulty, 50
Vocabulary Self-Collection Strategy (VSS), 134
Vocabulary, 116-41
   in context, 121
   decoding, 119, 122-23
   defined, 119
   and effective instruction, 123-24
   extension activities, 136-40
   external references and, 121-22
   independent strategies, 133-36
   morphemic analysis, 119-20
   teacher-directed strategies, 124-33
   and textbooks, 122-23
   words as a concept, 118

HOW TO USE THE *CONTENT AREA LITERACY* DIGITAL SUPPLEMENT CD-ROM

The CD-ROM accompanying this textbook contains a full novel (*The Call of the Wild*), short stories, complete chapters from middle and high school subject area textbooks, and dozens of articles on literacy. In all, more than 500 pages of original source material and information on topics such as comprehension strategies, assessment, and multicultural education can be found. The CD-ROM will provide you with a variety of practical applications of literacy theory as well as help you to become proficient with the Adobe Acrobat™ Reader 3.0, a sophisticated search engine with thousands of research applications. To the best of our knowledge *Content Area Literacy: An Integrated Approach* is the first textbook in teacher education to provide every student with a CD-ROM that supplements the curriculum of the text.

Some of the articles on the CD-ROM are from *Theory Into Practice* (*TIP*), published by the College of Education at The Ohio State University. *TIP* is a distinguished journal with articles and reviews on a broad range of topics and issues in education. Each issue of *TIP* is organized around a theme that features scholarly discussions of current and future concerns and ideas in education. In 1997, *TIP* created a major breakthrough in educational technology by becoming the first periodical to have all of its past volumes (12,000 pages) digitized and placed on a single, searchable CD-ROM called *Theory Into Practice—Digital* (*TIP-D*). More information about *TIP* and *TIP-D* is available on the CD-ROM.

The CD-ROM is a dual platform product, which means that you can install it on a MacIntosh™ or a PC. In either case your computer must have 8 MB of RAM and 20 MB of available hard drive space. Make sure you follow the installation procedure designed for your computer.

Windows™ 95 Installation

Install from your CD-ROM drive.
Double-click on "My Computer".
Double-click on your CD-ROM drive.
Double-click "Winsetup" folder.
Double-click "Rdr_srch".
Double-click "32 bit".
Double-click "Setup".
Follow directions on the screen.

To activate the program you must restart your computer. Remember to keep the CD in the CD-ROM drive because only the Acrobat™ Reader has been installed on the hard drive. Access the database as follows:

Open your CD-ROM drive.
Double-click Mainmenu OR Mainmenu.pdf.

Windows™ 3.1 Installation

Install from your CD-ROM drive.
Open "File Manager".
Double-click "Winsetup".
Double-click "Rdr_srch".
Double-click "16 bit".
Double-click "set-up.exe" and follow the directions on the screen.

To activate the program you must restart your computer. Remember to keep the CD in the CD-ROM drive because only the Acrobat™ Reader has been installed on the hard drive. Access the database as follows:

Select your CD-ROM drive.
Double-click Mainmenu OR Mainmenu.pdf.

MacIntosh™ Installation

Install from your CD-ROM drive.
Open MAC folder.
Double-click "Readers_S".
Double-click "Reader".
Double-click "Install_O" and follow the directions on the screen.

To activate the program you must restart your computer. Remember to keep the CD in the CD-ROM drive because only the Acrobat™ Reader has been installed on the hard drive. Access the database as follows:

Open MacIntosh™ HD (Do not attempt to open the database from the CD-ROM drive.)
Double-click "Acrobat™ 3.0 icon".
Double-click "Acrobat™ Reader 3.0 icon".
File.............Open.
Click "Desktop".
Double-click Mainmenu OR Mainmenu.pdf.

For MacIntosh users, if you encounter difficulty opening the CD after you have installed successfully, follow these instructions:

From the Apple logo open "Control Panel".
Open "General Controls".
Set document to "Folder that is set by the application".
Restart your computer.

How to Go from the Book to the CD-ROM

You can find information on the CD-ROM by using the Table of Contents on the CD or by using the Acrobat Reader search engine. The first way is the fastest if you only want to get to one of the articles, stories, or practice chapters referenced in the text and highlighted in blue, with the CD icon CD in the margin. Just follow these directions:

1. Start from the CD Main Menu, which is what you should be looking at right now if you've followed the installation procedures above.

2. Click on the box around the heading "TABLE OF CONTENTS".

3. Use the page down key or the scroll down arrow to move through the Table of Contents until you come to *The Telltale Heart* by Edgar Allan Poe.

4. Click on the red navigational link around *The Telltale Heart* to jump to the story.

5. Click on the navigational link on the title page of the story to return to the Table of Contents.

6. Use the page up key or scroll up arrow to get back to the beginning of the Table of Contents.

7. Click on the blue navigational link on the Table of Contents to get back to the Main Menu.

The rest of the information in Appendix A will show you how to navigate the CD-ROM, how to use the search engine, and how to **magnify the print on your computer screen to make it more readable.**

Search Preferences

The first thing to do now is set the preferences for your computer so that you will get the best possible resolution on your monitor as well as the most efficient search performances. There are several default values in the Adobe Acrobat™ Reader 3.0 that you should change. The following adjustments will insure that search results are complete and that they will be available to you in chronological order. You can make these changes from any location in the database, and we recommend you do so immediately.

From the Main Menu click on the yellow navigation link around "Table of Contents." Now click on *File*, move the cursor to *Preferences*, and click on *General*. The General Preferences box should now be on the screen. If the option *Smooth Text and Monochrome Images* is off, click it on. Click *OK*.

Click on *File*, move the cursor to *Preferences*, and click on *Search*. The Acrobat Search Preferences box should now be on the screen. In the Results section of the box, click on the options button for *Sort By*. Select *Title*.

Introducing the Acrobat™ Reader 3.0 Toolbar

If you are already familiar with the Acrobat™ Reader or consider yourself a database veteran, the brief toolbar descriptions below may be all you need to get started navigating and searching the database. Otherwise, we suggest you work through the navigation and search tutorials that follow this introduction. We should also mention that the toolbar contains a number of icons for operations which are nonfunctional in this particular database, and they will be referred to only briefly.

 Displays only the text page and eliminates thumbnails, miniature views of document pages which are displayed in the overview on the left side of the screen.

 Displays both the text page and bookmarks. However, in this database, there is no provision for bookmarks.

 Displays both the text page and thumbnails, miniature views of document pages which are displayed in the overview area on the left side of the screen. Clicking on a thumbnail will cause that page to appear in the main viewing area.

 Selects the hand (cursor). When you have finished using the zoom-in tool, this icon will return you to the standard hand cursor.

 Selects the zoom-in tool. The zoom-in looks like a little magnifying glass. Successive clicking allows you to magnify any portion of the text up to 800%.

Selects the text selection tool. However, in this database, there are no editing functions so the icon is of no use.

 Displays the first page of each document file (e.g., article).

 Displays the previous page.

 Displays the next page.

 Displays the last page of each document file (e.g., article).

 Goes to the previous view. The *previous* and *next view* icons allow the user to move back and forth along the trail of decisions.

 Returns to the next view.

 Sets the size of the page on the screen to a standard referred to as 100%. There are many ways to alter the size of a page: the zoom-in tool, the next two icons on the toolbar, and the magnification bar at the bottom of the screen.

 Sets the size of the page so that the entire page fits in the window.

 Sets the page to the maximum width that will fit in the window.

 Displays the Find dialog box. Searches using the Find command are limited to a single document (e.g., one article) and are non indexed searches, which are slow compared with indexed searches. Only the first instance of the search target is identified. Repeated searches using the **Find Again** function are necessary to locate successive instances of the target word or phrase. However, all symbols and combinations of symbols are acceptable search targets.

 Displays the Search dialog box. The Search command is a set of powerful tools that permit a variety of fast, full-text, indexed searches of the entire database. The Search command options and some creativity on your part will allow you to expand or narrow a search. The **Match Case** option finds targets that match upper and lower case specifications (e.g., *Hunting* vs *hunting*). The **Proximity** option finds the pair of words that are physically close to each other in each document file (e.g., a search entered as *language and instruction* will result in finding the single context in each of the articles and literary works where the words *language* and *instruction* are closest together). The **Word Stemming** option finds all words in the database that have the same linguistic root (e.g., *teach, teacher, teaching*). The **Sounds Like** option finds targets which are similar in spelling to the word or phrase entered in the search box (e.g., a search for *pedigogical* will result in finding instances of *pedagogical*). The **Thesaurus** option finds words with similar meanings (e.g., targeting the word *ugly* will result in the identification of *offensive, evil, sick,* etc.). You can also conduct **Boolean** searches. Search time is dependent upon the amount of RAM in your computer and the complexity of the search request. A phrase search takes longer than a word search, and high frequency words such as *the* and *in* increase search time.

Displays search results. Clicking *View* will take you to the first instance of the target word or phrase in the highlighted article, story, chapter, or activity. Items containing hits will be presented in chronological order if you have followed the instructions on page 256. (For other options see "Setting Preference Parameters" on page 260.) Highlighting and selecting a Table of Contents will take you to the first chronological instance of the target in the Table of Contents. This is a search option that limits the search to authors and titles. You can safely ignore the **Info** option in the Search Results box.

 Displays the previous one in the sequence of hits in the database following a search.

 Displays the next one in the sequence of hits in the database following a search.

Navigational Tutorial

From the Main Menu click on the yellow box encasing the option Table of Contents (TOC). This will take you to a listing of the CD-ROM contents.

Click on the red box surrounding *The Call of the Wild*. You should arrive at the title page of the book. Now click on the scroll down arrow in the lower right corner of your screen until you get to the very top of the next page. In the upper left hand corner of the page you will see a red navigational box. Click on this box to return to the title page. To return to the TOC, click on the red box in the upper left corner of the title page.

Now return to the title page of *The Call of the Wild*. On the lower left side of the screen is a box with a little magnifying glass and a percentage inside it. (Let's call it "MG%".) Move the cursor hand to MG% and hold down the left mouse button. You will see a set of vertical options appear. While keeping the mouse button down, move the cursor to Fit Visible and then release the button. This is the setting that provides maximum magnification while still allowing the page to fit the screen horizontally. Play with the other settings in the MG% box to see what happens.

Return to the TOC and click on the "Stress" chapter listed under Chapter 6 in the TOC. To the immediate left of the MG% box is another box that tells you what page you are on. It should say "Page 1 of 20." Click on the page box. Then type 8 in the Go To Page box and click *OK*. Scroll down or use the Page Down key until you come to the cartoon at the bottom of the page. This should put you on page 8 of the PDF (Portable Document File) and page 205 of the original text. The distinction is important when it comes to printing out an article because you will need to specify document page numbers rather than the original page numbers in the article or story.

Go to the toolbar and click on the zoom icon, 5th from the left (magnifying glass with a + in it). Now use the zoom icon to target some of the less readable writing in the cartoon and click. Retarget and click again. And again. To return the page to normal viewing size, use MG% and set to Fit Visible. To return the hand cursor, click on the toolbar hand icon.

At this point you may be wondering why the print is so small on the screen. To begin with, your monitor has fewer than 100 dots per square inch (dpi) with which to make symbols while most printers use 300 dpi. Also, some journals use very small print. The sentence you are currently reading is in 12 point Times New Roman font and uses fewer than 100 characters per line. Some of the printing in journal articles is in 8 point font and has over 200 characters per line. The larger the print in the original, the clearer and larger it will be on your computer screen.

To jump to the first page of a document file—in this case "Stress"—click the 7th icon from the left on the toolbar. This should put you on the title page.

Now jump to the last page of "Stress" by clicking the 10th icon from the left on the toolbar. You should be on PDF page 20 (see page box in lower left of screen.)

Toolbar icons 8 and 9 allow you to move through the document file one page at a time. Note that these icons take you to the top of each page and that the screen can't hold a full vertical page of text without reducing the print size to the point of illegibility. You can move a line at a time using the scroll arrows on the extreme right of the screen. On most computers the page up and page down buttons will allow you to move through the database one screen at a time.

Toolbar icons 11 and 12 allow you to move back and forth along the trail of your decision making. Play with these two icons and you will readily see what they do.

Search Tutorial

Learning to conduct fast and efficient searches requires both practice and some heuristic problem solving skills. The structure of the database and the flexibility of the Adobe search engine lend themselves to creative applications that go far beyond the fundamentals described below. Do not be afraid to play with the options. Remember that you are working in a **R**ead **O**nly **M**emory environment, so you can't accidentally save something onto the CD-ROM that will ruin it.

Click on the search icon (binoculars with page). The box that appears should say "Adobe Acrobat Search" at the top. If it doesn't, you probably clicked the wrong binoculars. Try again.

The Search Box has three options to the right and five on the bottom. All of the options on the bottom should be neutral. If any of the accompanying little white boxes has a check in it, click it off. The cursor should be blinking in the text box; if it isn't, click on *clear* and the cursor will appear. Indexes are preinstalled so you shouldn't need this option.

Type *reading* into the text box and click on *search* or just hit the enter key. The Search Results box will appear listing in chronological order all issues in which the work *reading* appears. Double click on *Call of the Wild* to go to the first instance of *reading* in that book.

Successive clicking on the last icon of the toolbar will take you forward in the chain of target hits (every instance of *reading*) throughout the database—if you are so inclined. Click through a few pages. The next to the last icon on the right will move you back through the chain of instances of *reading*.

Click on the Results Icon. The first document listed in the Search Results box is aTable of Contents. Double clicking on aTable of Contents will take you to the first instance of *reading* in the Table of Contents. Successive clicking on the last icon in the toolbar will allow you to find all of the articles that have the word *reading* in the title.

Go back to the Search Box (binoculars plus page) and enter the term *Hunting*. Click on the **Match Case** option and then click *Search*. This option will result in finding only those instances of the target that have the same pattern of upper and lower case letters. Without the Match Case option the computer will find all instances of *hunting* regardless of capitalization.

You can conduct **Boolean** searches using the words *and, or,* and *not,* which have mathematical rather than the usual verbal meanings. For example, open the search box and type in the words *reading and writing.* The computer will find all instances of either word in any article, chapter, or story in which both words happen to occur. If you want to find the exact phrase *reading and writing,* you must put quote marks around the expression (e.g., "reading and writing") to tell the computer that *and* is a word and not a Boolean operator. Also note that & (ampersand), (comma), and ! (exclamation point followed by a space) may be used instead of *and, or,* and *not,* respectively, as Boolean operators. Generally, avoid symbols and punctuation marks when conducting searches.

Return to the Search Box and search again for *reading and writing,* but this time click on the **Proximity Search** option. The computer will identify the instance of the words *reading* and *writing* that occur closest to each other in each article or story.

Return to the Search Box. Click off **Proximity;** click on the **Word Stemming** option; click *clear;* and enter *electric* in the text box. The computer will highlight words that have that stem, e.g., *electric, electrical, electricity.*

Return to the Search Box. Click off **Word Stemming;** click on the **Thesaurus** option; and enter the word *terror.* A search will result in *fear, horror,* and other words with similar denotations being highlighted.

The **Sounds Like** option allows you to search for targets when spelling is in doubt. For example, searching for *pedigogy* will result in finding *pedagogy* if the Sounds Like option is used. However, the **Wild Card** search is usually superior because it results in fewer false positives.

Wild Card searches permit you to use the symbols * and ? to represent indeterminate letters and symbols where the ? represents a single element and the * represents as many as will fit a given parameter. For example, searching for *fi?* will allow you to find the words *fin, fit,* and *fix;* searching for *fi??* will result in finding words such as *find, fire,* and *fits;* entering the term *n*r* will result in finding *never, number,* and *numerator.* These options work well when you aren't quite sure how to spell an author's name. For instance, if you weren't sure how to spell Emmanouel, you could just enter wild card characters in place of the letters you were doubtful of (e.g., E*an*l) to find references to the author of *Personal Fitness.*

Finally, these search functions can be combined in various ways (e.g., **Boolean** plus **Wild Card** plus **Match Case**). And some functions are mutually exclusive, for example, **Proximity** and **Thesaurus** can't be used at the same time. In time you will develop a unique set of strategies to meet your particular research needs.

Printing from the Database

To print, go to the menu bar and select *File.* Then click *Print.* Keep the following in mind:

1. The default in the print menu is set to print out entire PDF documents. You will need to change the button to *Current Page* or specify which pages you want to print unless you want to print out an entire chapter.

2. Remember that "pages" refers to PDF (document) pages and NOT to original text pages. Be sure to use PDF page numbers whenever you are printing from the database.

3. The more powerful your printer the faster it will spool and print. If the buffer is very small, it may not work at all. Computers with Pentium processors seem to work well with almost any ink jet or laser printer.

How to Use the Acrobat™ Reader Help Files

The Help option in Acrobat™ Reader is not correlated with your actions or location in the database. For instance, if you have accessed the Search Dialog (binoculars plus page), clicking on *Help* will not give you direct assistance in searching. The Help option actually provides a set of user's guides, some of which are relevant to working in the current database and some of which are not. From the Help option menu the following selections provide useful information and you should look through them when you have a chance.

> Reader Online Guide
> > Using Acrobat Reader   (General Information)
> > Viewing PDF Documents   (Navigation & Printing)
> > Plug-In Help . . . Using Acrobat Search   (Detailed Search Instructions)

Inside the Help files, clicking on the targets in the upper right hand corner of each page will return you through the hierarchy of menus in the help file you selected. To exit the Help option altogether, click on *File* and then *Close*.

Setting Preference Parameters

Because the Acrobat™ Reader 3.0 has been installed on your hard drive, it is possible to make a variety of permanent adjustments in the way the Reader operates. In most cases you will want to retain the original settings. However, if you do make changes, we urge you to keep a record of them so that you can return to the original settings should they interfere with navigating or searching the database. To access Preference Parameters, click *File* and then *Preferences*. Within the preferences menu there are two relevant categories: General and Search. If you click on *General* you will see the option Default Page Layout at the top right. If you click on the option button to the right of it and set the parameter to *Continuous,* it will allow you to scroll through pages so that you can see the bottom of one page and the top of the next. One disadvantage to continuous page layout is that it disables the Fit Visible option; another is that it may cause your computer to freeze all navigation and search functions, in which case you will have to click *File* and then *Exit* in order to recover.

From the Preferences menu click *Search,* which should give you the Acrobat Search Preferences dialog box. In the Results section click the *Sort By* button. Selecting *Title* will cause search results to be presented in chronological order. Selecting *Score* will cause search results to be presented according to the number and density of hits in the various documents. The other Sort By options are unlikely to be productive. The Show Top ____ Documents option allows you to control the number of documents (issues) that will be presented in the Search Results box following a search of the database.

Caveat on Error

In the process of digitizing the articles and stories, errors in the originals have been allowed to remain for the sake of historical accuracy, and new errors have been introduced inadvertently. These new errors will be reduced over time as successive editions of the *Digital Supplement* are published.

Trouble-Shooting

Make sure all your equipment is turned on and functioning properly and read the relevant directions in this user's guide.

> Problem: You can't access the database at all.
>
> Solution(s):   Make sure the CD-ROM is in the CD-ROM drive. Only the Acrobat™ Reader 3.0 has been installed on your hard drive because the database takes up over 600 megabytes.
>
> Problem: Your Acrobat™ Reader toolbar is different from the one described in this user's guide.
>
> Solution(s):   You probably have an older version of the Reader and elected not to install Reader 3.0 during the installation process. Reinstall the CD-ROM and do choose to install Reader 3.0 this time.

Problem: Print quality is poor.

Solution(s): If you have a Print Quality option in the Print dialog box, make sure the setting is at about 300 dpi. A lower dpi setting will degrade print quality.

If you are using a dot matrix printer, expect poor quality printing. You really need an ink jet or laser printer.

Make sure your printer is on, on line, and functioning properly.

Problem: Printing from the database is slow or doesn't work at all.

Solution(s): If you have a Print Quality option in the Print dialog box, make sure the setting is at about 300 dpi. A higher dpi setting will slow down printing without improving quality.

Equipment makes a big difference. A Pentium with 16 Megs of RAM and a good laser printer will print a page in one or two seconds. By contrast, a 486 processor with only 8 Megs of RAM and an inexpensive ink jet printer may take 60 seconds to print a page of text and several minutes to print a page with pictures or graphics. It is even possible that the combined power of the computer and printer is so low that you can't print at all.

Make sure your printer is on, on line, and functioning properly.

Check *Print Setup* under *File* to make sure that the printer identified in the setup is identical to the one attached to your computer.

Problem: The wrong pages are printing out.

Solution(s): Use the PDF page numbers in the lower left corner of the screen and NOT the original text page numbers to print out specific pages or articles.

There are three Print Range options in the Print dialog box: the entire document, the current page (PCs only), and specified pages. Unfortunately, the default is set to print the entire document and you must manually set the print range unless you want to print out an entire article or chapter.

Problem: After a search, highlighted words are distorted.

Solution(s): Click *File,* then click *Preferences* and *General.* Try different combinations of on/off for the following preferences:

_____ Smooth Text and Monochrome Images
_____ Use Calibrated Color for Display

Problem: The Search option is grayed out in the Adobe Acrobat Search dialog box.

Solution(s): The Khun Indx has been lost and needs to be reinstalled.

Click *Indexes* in the Search dialog box.
Click *Add.*
Double click *KHUNINDX. PDX.*
Click *OK.*

Problem:	Search time is slow
Solution(s):	Search time is determined almost entirely by the resources of your computer, although some search parameters take longer than others. The clock speed of your processor, amount of RAM, and configuration of your CD-ROM drive are the principal determinants of access time. If you are working with the minimum 8 Megs of RAM, you might want to consider upgrading your system to 16 Megs of RAM. It should make a big difference.
Problem:	You can't edit the database.
Solution(s):	The *Digital Supplement* was specifically designed so that it could not be edited, and attempts to do so are a violation of copyright.
Problem:	All navigation and search functions are frozen.
Solution(s):	Click *File* and *Exit.* Then close out of all CD-ROM applications and reenter the database.
	If that doesn't work, shut down the computer and restart it after waiting a minute.
	As a last resort, delete Acrobat™ Reader from your hard drive and reinstall the *Digital Supplement.*
Problem:	You've changed some of the Acrobat™ Reader Preferences, and everything is a mess.
Solution(s):	Deleting Acrobat™ Reader from your hard drive and reinstalling the *Digital Supplement* will reset all of the preferences.

The award-winning program designed by teachers & students to make it faster and easier than ever before to learn a new language.

QUICK START

Macintosh

Insert the CD-ROM into your drive. Double-click on the CD-ROM icon. Double-click the MacSetup folder. Open The Rosetta Stone 2.2.4 folder. Launch the program by double-clicking The Rosetta Stone icon.

Windows 3.1

Start Windows. Insert the CD-ROM into your drive. In the Program Manager, select "Run..." from the File menu. Type "d:\winsetup\rosetta\setup" and press Enter. Follow the directions on the screen. The program is now installed and can be launched from its Program Group.

Windows 95

Insert the CD-ROM into your drive. Click on the "Start" button on the Windows task bar. Select "Run..." from the menu. Type "d:\winsetup\rosetta\setup" and press Enter. Follow the directions on the screen. The program is now installed and can be launched from its Program Group.

Once the application is running, double-click on one of the chapters in the list (start with chapter 01-01).

 The Main Menu will appear. Click on the button in the lower left corner. When the five choices come up, click on Run Mode 1. You will hear a spoken phrase and see written text. Click on the picture that you think matches the phrase. If you choose the correct picture, the program will give you the next prompt.

 If you want to hear the phrase again, click on the Speaker button in the upper left corner.

 To look up answers, click on the Book icon beside the Runner icon. This puts you in one of the Browser modes. Click on the Speaker button of any picture that you want to learn about. To get back into Run Mode 1, click on the Runner icon beside the Book icon.

 To leave either mode, click on the Bail-Out button.

MAIN MENU

 Runner (1-5) allows you to select Run Modes one through five. Each of these five Run Modes prompts you with a voice and/or written text and asks you to choose from four pictures.

 Runner (6-10) allows you to select Run Modes six through ten. Each of these five Run Modes prompts you with a single picture and asks you to choose from four spoken and/or written texts.

 Runner (11-12) allows you to select Run Modes eleven and twelve. These two Run Modes present voice & written text only.

 Tutorial has three variations that will guide you by employing a combination of Run Modes. You will be re-tested on questions you have missed. One of the tutorials will challenge you with random screens.

 Dictation allows you to work on your writing skills. In Dictation when you click on a Speaker button, you hear a spoken phrase. Use the keyboard to type the corresponding text.

 Browsers let you page through chapters and see and hear the information before you go to one of the Run Modes. You can also switch to a Browser Mode at any time from within a Run Mode. Click and hold on the microphone icon to record your voice, then release it to hear what you said. To hear your voice again, click on the Speaker button on the Control Panel; to hear the native speaker, click on a Speaker button at the center of the screen.

 The Setup Screen allows you to select yes/no sounds and icons, adjust volume and change special Test, Delay and Timer options. Entering the Setup Screen from the Main Menu, gives you access to all Setup functions.

 The Bail Out button is used throughout the program to mean "Take me back to the previous function." From the Main Menu, it will return you to the Chapter Selection Screen.

SYSTEM REQUIREMENTS

Mac OS:

68040 CPU or better

Mac OS 7.0 or later

512x384x265 color display

2x CD-ROM drive

8MB RAM (16MB Power PC)

Voice-recording feature requires a microphone.

Windows:

486DX processor or better

Windows 3.1, 95, or NT 4.0

640x480x256 color display

2x CD-ROM drive

8MB RAM (16MB for Win 95, 32 MB for NT)

4 MB free hard drive space

Windows compatible sound card

Voice-recording feature requires a microphone.

Fairfield Language Technologies
165 South Main Street, Harrisonburg VA 22801 USA
(800) 788-0822 • (540) 432-6166 • Fax (540) 432-0953 • e-mail: info@trstone.com